THE
WTO
AFTER
SEATTLE

EDITED BY
JEFFREY J. SCHOTT

THE
WTO
AFTER
SEATTLE

INSTITUTE FOR INTERNATIONAL ECONOMICS
Washington, DC
July 2000

Jeffrey J. Schott, senior fellow, was a senior associate at the Carnegie Endowment for International Peace (1982–83) and an international economist at the US Treasury (1974–82). He is the author, coauthor, or editor of numerous books on the trading system, including *Launching New Global Trade Talks: An Action Agenda* (1998), *Restarting Fast Track* (1998), *The World Trading System: Challenges Ahead* (1996), *The Uruguay Round: An Assessment* (1994), *Western Hemisphere Economic Integration* (1994), *NAFTA: An Assessment* (rev. ed. 1993), *North American Free Trade: Issues and Recommendations* (1992), *Completing the Uruguay Round: A Results-Oriented Approach to the GATT Trade Negotiations* (1990), *Free Trade Areas and U.S. Trade Policy* (1989), *The Canada–United States Free Trade Agreement: The Global Impact* (1988), *Auction Quotas and United States Trade Policy* (1987), and *Trading for Growth: The Next Round of Trade Negotiations* (1985).

INSTITUTE FOR INTERNATIONAL ECONOMICS
11 Dupont Circle, NW
Washington, DC 20036-1207
(202) 328-9000   FAX: (202) 328-5432
http://www.iie.com

C. Fred Bergsten, *Director*
Brigitte Coulton, *Director of Publications and Web Development*
Brett Kitchen, *Marketing Director*

Typesetting by Sandra F. Watts
Printing by Kirby Lithographic Company, Inc.

Printed in the United States of America
02 01 00   5 4 3 2

Library of Congress Cataloging-in-Publication Data

The WTO after Seattle / Jeffrey J. Schott, editor.
    p. cm.
1. World Trade Organization.   2. International trade.   3. Foreign trade regulation.   4. World Trade Organization—Developing countries.   I. Schott, Jeffrey J., 1949-
HF1385.W778   2000
382'.92
                                00-039668

ISBN 0-88132-290-3

Dedicated to the memory of

Julius L. Katz,

a man of great substance and integrity,

a good friend, and a distinguished public servant

who made important contributions to all of the major

US trade agreements of the past forty years.

Contents

Preface

The Seattle Host Organization, which sponsored the Third Ministerial Meeting of the World Trade Organization (WTO) in November-December 1999, asked the Institute to organize a full-day conference during that same week on the issues surrounding a new round of multilateral trade negotiations that the Ministerial itself would be discussing. Our conference, which aimed to provide an overview of the WTO agenda and addressed a wide range of the issues being considered for it, was one of six major private-sector meetings that took place to promote public debate and understanding of global trade topics. It was held on 30 November 1999, as violent demonstrations blocked adjacent streets, and turned out to be one of the few sessions that day to proceed without significant disruption (though one of our speakers, former WTO Director General Renato Ruggiero, was unable to get to our hotel and at times we had a captive audience because of security lock-downs).

We designed the Seattle conference to provide a strategic overview of the key issues confronting governments preparing for a new WTO Round, the diverse concerns and priorities of member countries, and the institutional reforms needed to make the WTO work better and strengthen public support for the trade body. The program covered many of the topics debated during a similar conference that we held in Washington in late October but devoted more time to national perspectives and new issues to take advantage of the rich mix of people—both proponents and critics of the WTO—that came to Seattle. Speakers included former officials and trade experts from both developed and developing countries as well as the heads of the International Labor Organization, the UN Conference on Trade and Development, and (in absentia) the former director general of the WTO itself. The several hundred participants represented a diverse array of people from government, business, labor, academia, and other nongovernmental organizations.

The "Seattle Round" was not to be. The launch of any new round of multilateral trade negotiations was indeed postponed indefinitely. The street protesters claimed victory but, in large measure, the Ministerial collapsed because of fractious disputes among member countries. The main problems were inside rather than outside the conference hall. The damage to the WTO was largely self-inflicted.

The problems exposed during the Seattle meetings thus deserve careful analysis and a thoughtful response. We had initially planned to immediately publish the papers and comments from our Seattle and Washington conferences but instead asked the authors to revise their analyses in light of the outcome at Seattle. The resulting volume, *The WTO after Seattle*, is the first comprehensive effort to look forward from that event and recommend what the WTO needs to do to address the challenges to world trade policy in an increasingly globalized economy. The Institute has also launched a series of *Globalization Balance Sheet* projects on specific aspects of the backlash against globalization, which will be released over the next year or so, but we hope this volume will promote a more informed debate on the WTO itself and how it can contribute to the betterment of its member countries.

The Institute for International Economics is a private nonprofit institution for the study and discussion of international economic policy. Its purpose is to analyze important issues in that area and develop and communicate practical new approaches for dealing with them. The Institute is completely nonpartisan.

The Institute is funded largely by philanthropic foundations. Major institutional grants are now being received from the William M. Keck, Jr. Foundation and the Starr Foundation. A number of other foundations and private corporations contribute to the highly diversified financial resources of the Institute. About 26 percent of the Institute's resources in our latest fiscal year were provided by contributors outside the United States, including about 11 percent from Japan.

The Board of Directors bears overall responsibility for the Institute and gives general guidance and approval to its research program—including the identification of topics that are likely to become important over the medium run (one to three years), and which should be addressed by the Institute. The Director, working closely with the staff and outside Advisory Committee, is responsible for the development of particular projects and makes the final decision to publish an individual study.

The Institute hopes that its studies and other activities will contribute to building a stronger foundation for international economic policy around the world. We invite readers of these publications to let us know how they think we can best accomplish this objective.

C. Fred Bergsten
Director
July 2000

Foreword

Reflections from Seattle

Renato Ruggiero

The very success of the WTO is why it is such a strong—and prominent—institution today. It is this success that explains why so many people—representing such a great variety of objectives and needs—came to Seattle to present their beliefs. But the success of the WTO also points to the need to look beyond the trading system for answers when addressing the challenges of a new round.

It is a new world—very different from the world that launched the Uruguay Round just a decade and a half ago. The Cold War is over. Even more significant is the rise of the developing world as a major power in the international economy as a result of the shift to freer markets and open trade—an event that could rank with the industrial revolution in historical significance. All this is taking place against the backdrop of globalization—the linking together of countries at different levels of development by technology, information, and ideas, as well as by economics. The presence in Seattle of thousands of people from all over the world signaled a new reality, still very much incomplete and unbalanced, that is taking shape. Each of these events alone would have widened the frontiers of the trading system and tested its ability to adapt. Together they represent a fundamental challenge to the way this system works and a dramatic expansion of the role the WTO is being asked to play.

How is the WTO to make decisions and set priorities on the basis of consensus among 130-plus members, including trade powers such as Brazil, India, South Africa, and soon China, not to mention the United States

Renato Ruggiero served as director-general of the World Trade Organization from 1995 to 1999.

and the European Union? How can it hope to cope with new issues such as investment or competition policy while avoiding institutional over-stretch? How is it to manage the interface with nontrade issues such as health policy, the environment, labor standards, and human rights? And how will it avoid a "democratic deficit"—the concern that the trading system is out of touch with the very people it was designed to serve?

For almost 50 years, the trade policy debate was essentially about free trade versus protectionism. Although this is obviously still important, the WTO now finds itself at the center of a new and much more complex debate about how to manage global economic interdependence. Why is the WTO in this position? In part it is the victim of its own success. The WTO was created in 1995 to be a pillar of this globalizing world. Our goal was an ambitious one—to build a universal trading system bringing all economies under one institutional roof and one set of rules while preserving special and differential treatment for developing countries.

In the first five years of its existence, the WTO moved substantially toward these ambitions. We now have 135 members, four-fifths of which are developing or transition economies. China seems poised to join, and an additional 29 candidates are waiting in line, including Russia, Saudi Arabia, and Vietnam. We have brought some of the most advanced sectors of the world economy into the system, with sweeping agreements in information technologies, telecommunications, and financial services —underlining the reality that multilateralism, rather than regionalism, offers the most viable framework for globalized trade. Our efforts to integrate the least-developed countries has achieved strong support, and we have begun important dialogue with nongovernmental organizations. Most important, we have established a binding dispute settlement mechanism, which is not only used by a growing number of countries—large and small—but is respected by them as well.

The WTO's role among international institutions has grown significantly, and its increased political significance was underlined by the presence of world leaders at the GATT's 50th anniversary celebration in May 1998. Again, without such a success story in the first years of its life, there would not have been thousands of people in the streets of Seattle.

For as the WTO becomes more important to the world economy, it also becomes a growing focal point for public hopes and concerns: How should the world protect endangered species and promote sustainable development? Should trade be linked to labor standards and human rights? Can we preserve cultural identities in an age of borderless communications? Can we have an open world economy without a stable financial system? And what about eradicating poverty, reducing inequalities, and promoting the rights of women? These and many other issues are a world away from "traditional" trade concerns such as tariffs or quotas. And yet all find themselves part, directly or indirectly, of the new trade agenda. All appear interlinked to our publics—to be many facets of a single issue. All will be expressed more loudly and insistently in an age when the images of ethnic cleansing, starving children, or burning rain forests come into our homes every night via television. People will demand answers, and rightly so.

My point is not that the WTO as an institution has responsibility for answering all of these questions. We cannot—and should not—ask the WTO to also become a development agency, an environmental policeman, or a watchdog for labor and human rights. This organization cannot be allowed to gradually drift away from its trade vocation. It would serve neither the WTO nor any other cause if it were to pretend it could offer solutions to every nontrade issue.

But equally clearly, the WTO cannot operate in isolation from the concerns of the world in which it exists. Deeper integration means that trade and commercial exchanges do not take place in a vacuum. More than ever before, trade and the rules of the trading system intersect with a broad array of other policies and issues—from investment and competition policy to environmental, developmental, health, and labor standards. We have to improve the relationship between all these issues and the trade system so as to respond to the desire for a coherent and balanced consideration of different policies and objectives. Our ability to advance trade, build a stronger system, and move forward in a new round will hinge on our ability to make simultaneous progress on these issues. How do we do this? First, we must move toward a more collective leadership—one that reflects the reality of a multipolar world, and especially the emergence of developing-country powers. This does not mean that the G-7/G-8 is suddenly any less important. It means simply that the advanced economies alone are no longer enough to provide international leadership. The new G-22, even if it exists only at the level of finance ministers, is already indicative of the kind of broader international leadership that is needed.

Second, we need to look at the policy challenges we face as pieces of an interconnected puzzle. We can no longer treat trade, finance, the environment, development issues, health, and human rights as separate sectoral issues. Both nationally and internationally, we need to give more thought to how we coordinate policy goals, harmonize an expanding web of international agreements, and commit ourselves to agreed common actions. As we enter a new century, we need a new vision of security—human security—that reflects the reality that financial crises or environmental degradation are equally threatening to the global peace and demand an equally collective response.

Third, we need a new forum for the management of these complex issues—one that is truly representative of the new global realities and that brings world leaders together to tackle an expanded policy agenda and the new challenges of globalization. Certainly we need greater cooperation and coherence among the WTO, the International Monetary Fund (IMF), the World Bank, the United Nations, and other international organizations. But there are limits to what can be accomplished horizontally—international bureaucrats talking to other international bureaucrats. If we want real coherence in global policymaking and a comprehensive international agenda, then coordination has to come from the top, and it must be driven by elected leaders.

Fourth, there is a need for a clear mandate from leaders to promote a common global strategy and common global actions. We need a common strategy—among international institutions, national administration, and civil society—for strengthening the international rule of law, eradicating poverty, and reducing worldwide inequalities within a set period. We need a common strategy to achieve a sustainable environment in developing and developed countries alike, and we need a common strategy to eliminate the greatest part of global trade barriers, at least reflecting on a multilateral level what governments have already agreed to in regional arrangements. This strategy must be focused on people and values more than on governments, harnessing interdependence and globalization to address today's challenges. An annual report to the world's leaders should indicate the progress we have made toward achieving these common goals.

Which brings me to my final point: progress in resolving the challenge of the new century will hinge on our ability not just to build a coherent global architecture, but to build a political constituency for globalization, backed by a new vision of internationalism. People associate globalization with free trade, dazzling technologies, and global capital markets. As important as these realities are, they do not capture the full picture. We are linked together by the exchange of ideas, images, and information as well as by the exchange of goods, services, and capital. There is a globalization of our hopes and fears—not just our economies. And it is this human dimension of globalization more than any other that is forcing the international system to change.

In every country and region, the same questions and anxieties are expressed: people want the benefits of global trade and integration, but they fear the effects of globalization on the environment, wage levels, and cultural identities. They recognize the need for greater cooperation and coordination at the international level, but they instinctively resist interference in their domestic affairs. They turn to global organizations to help manage their interdependence, but then they begrudge these same organizations the resources and mandates they need to fulfill their roles. The new polarity of the post-Cold War era is not between left and right, but between those who accept global change and those who resist it.

So at the threshold of a new century, the trading system finds itself at a crossroads. The challenges it faces involve more than the minutiae of technical details or negotiating positions. They involve broader political questions about the kind of international system we want. What are our objectives for the 21st century? And how do we convince a wider public of the value of these goals? The World Bank is advancing its Comprehensive Development Framework. The IMF is examining the financial architecture. The International Labor Organization (ILO) is promoting core labor standards and the United Nations Environment Program (UNEP) is trying to coordinate global environmental policy. Meanwhile, trade ministers struggle to launch a new multilateral trade round. Are these merely parallel tracks—moving forward but never meeting? Or can they be brought together to form pieces of a larger picture—a global vision of the future?

WTO is a rule-based institution whose decision making is based on consensus and whose constituency is 135 countries. Four-fifths of these are developing countries or economies in transition; China and 29 other countries representing over 1.6 billion people are waiting to join. Such an organization cannot be the enemy of the people that stood in the streets of Seattle. The goals of the protesters are right; their target is wrong. A strong multilateral trading system is essential to promote growth and generate the resources needed to meet all their objectives. Without the WTO, we will go back to a world of national barriers, protectionism, economic nationalism, and conflict. History has repeatedly showed where this road can lead.

What we need is not a weaker WTO but a stronger and improved system of global governance of our ever-growing interdependence. This is the strong message that emerged from the conference in Seattle and must be reflected in the next round. In a recent speech, President Bill Clinton called for "globalization with a human face," a phrase that nicely captures the challenges but also the immense potential of our interdependent future. What we sought in Seattle has been called many things: a millennium round, a development round, a services round, a market access round. But if it is to be successful and relevant to the future, it will above all have to be a "round with a human face."

Acknowledgments

Producing an edited volume is easy, as long as one has the support of diligent authors and an experienced production team. Valerie Norville did her usual superb job in editing the manuscript. Brigitte Coulton, Marla Banov, and Kara Davis managed the production process with great efficiency and good humor. Special thanks are due to the Seattle Host Organization, and especially Michael Mullen and Karen Brown, for sponsoring the Institute conference, "The World Trading System: Seattle and Beyond," during the WTO ministerial meetings when many of the papers were originally presented.

Jeffrey J. Schott

OVERVIEW

The WTO after Seattle

JEFFREY J. SCHOTT

The World Trade Organization (WTO) ended the last millennium in disarray. It enters the new one with uncertainty about its mission and its evolving role in international trade relations.

WTO trade ministers convened in Seattle in early December 1999 with the intention of launching the ninth round of multilateral trade negotiations; they left Seattle abruptly without action on the trade agenda after a week marred by rancorous debate and violent street protests. The start of a new trade round has been set back indefinitely.

The collapse of the Seattle ministerial exposed significant differences among member countries concerning what should be on the WTO agenda as well as shortcomings in the manner in which the WTO conducts its business and interacts with other international and nongovernmental organizations (NGOs). In that regard, Seattle demonstrated how much new trade talks are needed to rectify those problems, even though it has further complicated the task of building consensus among the 137 WTO member countries on possible solutions.[1]

Seattle's failure comes at a cost for both developed and developing countries. Trade restrictions protecting inefficient producers have been

Jeffrey J. Schott is a senior fellow at the Institute for International Economics. He benefited from constructive comments from C. Fred Bergsten, Kimberly Ann Elliott, Gary C. Hufbauer, J. David Richardson, T. N. Srinavasan, and Jayashree Watal on previous drafts of this chapter.

1. Georgia became the 137th member of the WTO on 14 June 2000.

given a new lease on life; remedies for the notable flaws in the WTO's dispute settlement procedures, particularly in the area of compliance, have been postponed; special preferences for the least-developed countries have been derailed, at least temporarily; and efforts of WTO critics to block new trade liberalization and to restructure the trading system have been revitalized.

To be sure, stopping the launch of a new round of trade negotiations does not undermine existing WTO rights and obligations, nor block ongoing work in the WTO Council. In that regard, WTO members have already begun to discuss "confidence-building" measures that could be taken to address flaws in WTO procedures and to ensure that all member countries are actively engaged in WTO negotiations. In addition, negotiations on agriculture and services have resumed, as mandated by the Uruguay Round accords in those areas (the so-called built-in agenda). However, those sectoral talks will likely idle in the absence of broader negotiations, and WTO member countries have made little progress toward bridging their differences over the WTO negotiating agenda.

WTO members face a complex challenge in 2000 and beyond: to build consensus on a new agenda for WTO talks that both accommodates the diverse interests of developed and developing countries and broadens public support for the WTO in the major trading nations. The task will not be easy. Short-run political concerns now dominate the trade debate and counsel caution. Long-run benefits from prospective accords are simply too far away to hit the radar screen of elected politicians. Trade officials will need to work hard to overcome political resistance at home and abroad to new trade reforms so that substantive negotiations can proceed.

I cannot do justice in this chapter to the complexities of the economic and political problems facing the WTO. As former WTO Director General Renato Ruggiero notes in the foreword to this volume, their implications stretch well beyond the realm of trade policy. But I can try to offer a few insights on the value of international trade negotiations and the particular importance of proceeding promptly in preparations for the launch of a new WTO Round in 2001. To put these issues in perspective, I turn first to a brief analysis of why the WTO ministerial failed in Seattle. The chapter then addresses why new negotiations are needed, why such talks are important for both the United States and for developing countries,[2] what needs to be included on the negotiating agenda, and what steps need to be taken in 2000 to lay the groundwork for a new round of trade negotiations later next year.

---

2. Among developed countries, I focus on the US interest because of its central role in the trading system. European and Japanese interests and objectives are covered in the chapters by Paemen and Arai, respectively, in this volume.

Why Seattle Soured

The failure of the Seattle ministerial to launch a new round was unique in the history of the postwar global trading system. Never before had countries come together to start a negotiation and failed to do so. Prior rounds were replete with instances of missed deadlines and "time-outs" before talks were completed (for example, the Brussels ministerial in December 1990, which failed to conclude the Uruguay Round), but ministers had never before failed to agree to start talking about trade problems and their possible remedies when they all convened to do so.[3] Never before had the failure involved questions about the legitimacy of the trading system itself.

Why did Seattle fail? To the casual observer watching television or scanning headlines and photos on the newsstand, it appeared that the protesters carried the day. Tens of thousands of people, concerned about environmental protection, human rights, labor standards, and other more parochial concerns demanded that WTO members give greater priority to their causes and restructure trade policies to promote their objectives. Ironically, much of their message got drowned out by the din of the more violent protesters, who usurped the bulk of the media coverage.

Anti-WTO protesters claimed credit for disrupting the Seattle meeting and blocking the launch of a new trade round.[4] The protesters clearly raised a ruckus in Seattle and complicated efforts by WTO delegates to negotiate the terms of reference for a new trade round. Delays due to the protests posed additional problems to negotiators already facing tight time constraints. But these obstacles were not decisive.

Ultimately, the WTO meeting fell victim not to protests *outside* in the streets, but rather to serious substantive disagreements *inside* the convention center among both developed and developing countries over the prospective agenda for new trade talks.[5] The key damage to the WTO was self-inflicted.

The policy differences between WTO members were varied and complex, involving both North-South issues and, more critically, disputes among the major industrial powers. In large measure, the developed countries were reluctant to address their own barriers to trade in goods and

---

3. Although the GATT ministerial in November 1982 rebuffed US proposals for new trade talks, few ministers came to Geneva at that time interested or prepared to engage in new negotiations (Schott 1983).

4. See, for example, the interview with Lori Wallach of Public Citizen in *Foreign Policy*, no. 118 (Spring 2000): 29-55.

5. These differences were exacerbated by residual tensions among member countries over the contentious selection of a new WTO director-general, by ongoing and fractious transatlantic trade disputes, and by the hubris of the American hosts.

services (for example, in agriculture, apparel, and labor services) but demanded that the new talks target protectionism in developing countries. In addition, these countries demanded the faithful implementation of the trade rules (especially regarding intellectual property rights and investment measures) agreed to in the Uruguay Round. For their part, developing countries argued that new concessions should await the fulfillment of trade reforms undertaken by developed countries in the Uruguay Round (especially the phaseout of apparel quotas) as well as compliance with dispute rulings and "best efforts" commitments to encourage technology transfer.

Almost all countries wanted to expand the WTO agenda beyond the issues mandated by the Uruguay Round accords (the "built-in" agenda) but differed markedly on which subjects deserved priority. The United States, for example, pushed for new WTO initiatives on electronic commerce and on trade-related labor and environmental issues, the European Union wanted negotiations on investment and competition policy issues, and Japan argued for reform of antidumping rules. By contrast, developing countries wanted new initiatives to further liberalize tariffs and agricultural restrictions, to constrain the use of antidumping measures against their exports, and to revise the WTO accords on trade-related investment measures (TRIMs) and intellectual property rights (TRIPs) to allow them more time to implement the complex new rules in these areas. In services, developing countries placed priority on removing barriers in sectors where they are competitive, such as labor and maritime services; developed countries favored their own "winners" such as financial, air transport, information, and professional services. "Priorities" of some countries were "nonstarters" for others.

The classic example of this problem involved US efforts to establish a WTO Working Group on Trade and Labor. In the aftermath of the United States' bilateral agreement with China regarding WTO accession, which elicited harsh criticism from US labor leaders, US officials were under great pressure to secure agreement on their proposal to open a WTO forum on this issue.[6] While the US proposal advanced prior to the Seattle meeting was much more modest than earlier US initiatives put forward at the Singapore WTO ministerial in 1996, which were soundly rebuffed by most other WTO members, opposition from developing countries remained intractable. It is hard to conceive of these countries changing course unless the United States responds more favorably to developing countries' priorities in the negotiations.

---

6. Sensitive to labor demands, President Clinton told the *Seattle Post-Intelligencer* just before arriving at the WTO meeting that core labor standards should be a part of WTO agreements and "ultimately I would favor a system in which sanctions would come for violating [such provisions]." Michael Paulson, "Clinton says he will support trade sanctions for worker abuse," *Seattle Post-Intelligencer*, 1 December 1999.

Lest one think that all the problems fell along a North-South divide, it is important to emphasize that one of the biggest hurdles to a successful meeting in Seattle involved substantive differences on numerous issues among "the Quad countries" (the United States, European Union, Japan, and Canada). The United States wanted deep cuts in farm subsidies but opposed efforts to cut peak US industrial tariffs or reform antidumping rules. Europe and Japan resisted agricultural reforms while seeking new talks on investment and competition policy, and Canada and Europe demanded special exemptions for their cultural industries, all of which were opposed by the United States. In short, the Quad countries failed to agree among themselves, which in turn made it difficult for them to lead the process of consensus building among WTO members on launching new trade negotiations.[7]

Unfortunately, the United States, as the leader of the trading system and host of the Seattle ministerial, must assume a good share of the responsibility for these developments. US policy failed to build a consensus either at home or abroad on the importance of new trade negotiations and how they should be structured. In addition, US officials mismanaged the planning and conduct of the negotiating sessions as well as the logistics of the Seattle meeting.[8]

To oversimplify, the problem resulted from two related and inconsistent US objectives: the desire to have a short negotiation, necessitating a limited agenda, and the desire to have concrete results in priority areas for US interests. Illustrative of this strategy was the initial US attempt to secure an "early harvest" of agreements at Seattle to demonstrate that talks could produce concrete results in short order. Its list of "deliverables" included a new pact on information technology products (ITA II), zero tariffs in certain sectors originally discussed in the Asia Pacific Economic Cooperation (APEC) Forum, transparency in government procurement, and an extension of the moratorium on tariffs on electronic commerce. Not surprisingly, this list did not address key concerns of other countries and eventually elicited equally unbalanced demands by developing countries for new trade concessions (including accelerated phaseout of apparel quotas) by the start of the new negotiations. The result: a dialogue of the deaf that inhibited preparations for the Seattle ministerial.

The absence of fast-track authority clearly influenced and constrained US initiatives. To be sure, US negotiators can engage in trade negotiations

---

7. Like the Quad, the members of the Asia Pacific Economic Cooperation (APEC) Forum also failed to work together, as in the past, to secure an agreement in Seattle, contrary to the forthright commitment to that end issued by APEC leaders at Auckland, New Zealand, in September 1999.

8. Incredibly, the host country did not reserve the meeting rooms at the Seattle convention center for a few extra days, which arguably could have produced a compromise text. Instead, the myopic trade officials had to cede the rooms to a convention of optometrists!

without it and have done so in the past (albeit with full confidence that the authority would be forthcoming). After six years of often acrimonious debate and a negative vote by the Congress in 1998, however, the future of fast track is in doubt (Destler 1997; Schott 1998a; Elliott 2000).

The six-year-old impasse over fast track has two important implications for WTO talks. First, it raises questions about the depth of the US political commitment to new trade initiatives. Some countries interpret the impasse over fast track as a sign of political opposition to reform of US trade barriers; others take the argument one step further and suggest that these political constraints signal a desire to renege on past commitments (especially the phaseout of apparel quotas). Second, the lack of fast track has made US negotiators reluctant to pursue talks in areas (such as textiles, antidumping, and competition policy) where changes in current US laws or practices might be required (since those changes might increase opposition to future efforts to renew fast track). As a result, US negotiators opposed proposals regarding other countries' issues of priority concern even as they sought agreement from those countries to the limited US agenda. Naturally, those countries responded in kind: why expose one's own sensitive trade barriers to global talks if the major industrial market seems unlikely to offer concessions in areas of greatest interest to them? Under those circumstances, the task of building an international consensus on a WTO agenda in Seattle became increasingly difficult.

Why a New Round Is Needed

Despite the collapse of the Seattle ministerial, the WTO continues to function, and new talks have been engaged on agriculture and services. The relative calm after the Seattle storm has led some to question whether a new round of trade negotiations is really needed. Instead, they counsel pursuing the built-in agenda, litigating problems through the WTO dispute settlement process, and dealing with emerging issues on an ad hoc basis (e.g., bilateral investment treaties for those issues).

In my view, however, such complacency is not in order. In many respects, the launch of a new WTO Round is even more important now than it was in Seattle, in part to remedy the substantive and institutional problems exposed during the December 1999 meetings.

First, WTO talks would provide a useful buffer against growing protectionist pressures in the United States (and Europe) directed against increased imports from emerging markets.[9] To date, we have not seen significant protectionist legislation in the United States, despite a record

---

9. European antidumping cases against Asian imports have increased sharply.

US merchandise trade deficit of almost \$350 billion in 1999 (equivalent to 3.8 percent of US GDP).[10] When the US economy slows and unemployment increases from its current very low levels, protectionist demands are likely to proliferate.

Second, public support for the WTO and an open international trading system needs to be shored up. In several major trading nations, the WTO is under attack. Public concerns about the effects of globalization (including expanded trade and investment) on domestic production and employment, and on national regulatory policies in areas such as labor and the environment, threaten to undercut support for new WTO initiatives in the United States and other countries. Some groups regard WTO provisions as part of the problem (e.g., rulings against enforcement provisions of US environmental laws); other groups want to refocus WTO obligations so that they help meet other economic and social objectives (e.g., promoting human rights and higher labor standards), even if the WTO is not the primary channel of action. In addition, criticism of the WTO reflects to some extent dissatisfaction with *domestic* programs (or the lack thereof) that seek to provide relief to displaced workers and firms. Governments will face increasing problems in sustaining political support for new trade talks if these issues are not addressed more effectively—both at home and in the WTO.

Third, the implementation of the WTO's Dispute Settlement Understanding (DSU) has exposed a number of problems that need to be fixed to maintain confidence in the enforcement of WTO obligations and, ultimately, the integrity of the WTO itself. Although these problems could be dealt with under regular WTO procedures, attempts over the past two years to resolve them in the course of the WTO's review of the DSU failed. Above all, ambiguities in the compliance provisions of the DSU need to be corrected. Differing interpretations of DSU Articles 21 and 22 have been a source of substantial friction between the United States and the European Union in the banana and beef hormone cases; the recent WTO ruling against the US Foreign Sales Corporation (FSC) program could add substantial fuel to this fire. In addition, procedural reforms are needed to address how panels should use input from experts in highly technical areas when cases so require, as well as to promote the transparency of panel proceedings. Finally, some dispute rulings (e.g., the Fuji-Kodak case regarding competition policy issues) have pointed out important gaps in the trading rules; others have demonstrated the need to clarify specific WTO obligations (for example, the subsidy issues contested in the recent

---

10. The one notable exception has been a failed steel quota bill. However, difficulty in passing the Trade and Development Act of 2000 (combining the Africa and Caribbean Basin trade bills), as well as "permanent normal trade relations" status for China, clearly demonstrated the strong opposition of the textile and steel sectors, among others, to new trade initiatives.

FSC case regarding the tax treatment of certain foreign-source income). New negotiations are needed to strengthen the DSU and remedy problems with existing WTO provisions.

Fourth, WTO members need to correct a few of the WTO's serious birth defects, particularly regarding the management structure of the organization, linkages with other international institutions, and the transparency of WTO operations. If WTO procedures are not seen to be efficient and equitable, and capable of contributing to sustainable economic development, then confidence in the trading system will suffer and countries increasingly will pursue alternative channels for the conduct of trade relations. Such institutional reforms seem mundane, but they touch on national prerogatives and on vested interests in the current system that resist change. Accordingly, consensus on WTO institutional reforms may only be possible in the context of a negotiated package of agreements.

Fifth, the WTO's built-in agenda is not sufficient to produce a successful trade accord and must be supplemented if negotiations are to succeed. Long-standing experience under the General Agreement on Tariffs and Trade (GATT) demonstrates that self-standing negotiations on agriculture never succeed; recent services accords have fared somewhat better (but only when developing countries accepted deals that did not require significant changes in US and European practices).[11] In short, a broader bargain will be needed to allow countries to trade off concessions across sectors and issues and undertake obligations to liberalize long-standing and politically sensitive trade barriers.[12] If the WTO does not undertake a more comprehensive negotiation than that set forth in the built-in agenda, the talks will likely fail and, in so doing, further weaken credibility in the multilateral negotiating process.

To address these problems, WTO members also will have to redress the serious resource constraints that already hamper WTO activities. The Uruguay Round accords greatly expanded the responsibilities of the WTO, but member countries have not provided adequate resources to service new trade negotiations, administer the burgeoning caseload of disputes, conduct trade policy reviews and complex accession negotiations, and collaborate with the World Bank and the International Monetary Fund (IMF) regarding trade reforms of countries in financial crisis. Staffing constraints already limit the scope of cooperative efforts with the IMF and the World Bank to help promote "greater coherence in global

---

11. Since the end of the Uruguay Round, WTO members have concluded accords on basic telecommunications and financial services, and on information technology products. These pacts required few significant changes in existing US practices. By contrast, talks failed on maritime services and on the movement of natural persons, where politically sensitive policies were at issue.

12. In his WTO lecture, Bergsten (1998) argued that prior GATT rounds demonstrated that "large-scale initiatives fare better than modest ones" and thus "big is beautiful."

economic policymaking." Such efforts are particularly needed to help the least-developed countries and countries in transition fully integrate into the world trading system.

Similarly, more than 30 countries, including China, are in the process of acceding to the WTO. Increased membership will further tax the WTO's limited resources and exacerbate management problems.

WTO members need to allocate more funds and perhaps additional authorities to the WTO's director-general and secretariat to better handle these tasks. The 2000 WTO budget is 125.4 million Swiss francs (around $75 million at June 2000 exchange rates) and has not grown much since 1995, despite the enormous increase in demand for services by the secretariat and by panelists and judges in the Dispute Settlement Body. The US share, for example, is 15.7 percent, or about $12 million. Interestingly, the US contribution to the WTO is much smaller than that provided to many other international organizations, including the Organization for Economic Cooperation and Development, or OECD ($55 million), the International Labor Organization ($54 million), and the Organization of American States ($51 million).[13]

Limitations on the WTO budget are penny wise, pound foolish. If member countries expect the WTO to meet a growing range of responsibilities, including increased transparency of operations and consultations with other international and nongovernmental organizations, then the budget will need to be substantially augmented. At a minimum, industrialized countries should immediately double their WTO budget contributions (which would mean an extra $12 million annually for the United States). There is no reason some specialized UN agencies should receive more funds than the world's principal trade forum.

What's in It for the United States?

The United States has been the leader of the postwar global trading system and remains so today. US officials are at the center of efforts to develop an international consensus on the terms of reference for the new WTO negotiations. These efforts are hampered, however, by sharp divisions within and between US political parties regarding the issues and objectives that should be given priority in the WTO talks. As noted above, the six-year-old impasse over fast-track authority reflects these differences and complicates efforts to consolidate political support for US participation in new negotiations. As a result, the United States has not made significant changes in its trade practices since the inception of the WTO,

---

13. All data reflect actual 1997 US budget expenditures.

and it remains reticent to discuss reductions in its remaining trade barriers in the context of prospective WTO agreements.[14]

The United States has broad-based economic and political interests in a successful WTO Round (see C. Fred Bergsten's chapter in this volume). Most of its economic objectives involve liberalizing foreign trade barriers down to US levels, which are generally very low already, and strengthening WTO rules so that foreign trade laws and regulations move up toward US norms. But the United States also has an important political stake in the success of the WTO. As WTO initiatives reinforce market-oriented policies, they also promote democratic reforms and contribute to the integration of developing countries and of countries in transition from former socialist regimes into the rule-based multilateral trading system. These are both key US political objectives.

First, new WTO agreements would help secure greater access to foreign markets for US exports of goods and services. Overall, foreign trade barriers are significantly higher than those protecting the US market; as in the Uruguay Round package, US trading partners would undertake much more extensive liberalization commitments than the United States. In addition, a new WTO Round could help expand US exports of goods and services at a time of record US trade deficits and strengthen the domestic political coalition in support of open trade policies, which has become increasingly fragmented in recent years.[15]

To maintain that coalition, US trade officials need the WTO to succeed in a number of areas. In particular, US trading interests would benefit from the following reforms:

- industrial tariffs: reducing foreign levies down to US levels and/or eliminating tariffs entirely sector by sector (including the eight sectors in APEC's accelerated tariff liberalization proposal and an ITA II);

- agricultural reforms: sharply reducing export and domestic subsidies, clarifying criteria for allowable subsidy exceptions under "blue" and "green box" programs,[16] cutting tariffs, and strengthening disciplines

---

14. To be sure, the US Congress granted unilateral trade preferences for countries in Africa and the Caribbean Basin in May 2000, but the authorizing legislation scaled back significantly the benefits in areas where foreign suppliers are most competitive (e.g., textiles and clothing). Note also that these preferences are not bound in the WTO and thus can be ended without violating WTO obligations.

15. Mann (1999) argues that new trade liberalization could substantially boost US service exports and contribute to a narrowing of the US current-account deficit.

16. The "green box" encompasses programs (e.g., farm extension services and environmental initiatives) that are exempt from subsidy cuts because they are deemed to be "non-trade-distorting." The "blue box" covers direct payments under production-limiting programs that also are exempt from the mandated reductions.

on the administration of tariff-rate quotas (TRQs) and the operation of state trading enterprises;

- services: building on the modest liberalization achieved in the Uruguay Round on a sector-specific basis, with a focus on both infrastructure and financial services, and on new areas such as environmental services, where US firms are world leaders;

- e-commerce: maintaining duty-free treatment of electronic transmissions, and advancing a WTO "work program to ensure technological neutrality in the development of WTO rules, and capacity-building efforts to ensure that developing countries have access to the Internet" (Esserman 1999, 6).

Second, US officials seek more effective compliance with WTO accords and improvements in the WTO system "to make the organization more transparent, responsive, and accessible to citizens" (Esserman 1999). Enforcement of US rights under trade agreements has been a central focus of US trade law for the past 25 years (e.g., section 301 of the Trade Act of 1974) and is integrally tied to US support for a rules-based trading system. Greater transparency in turn promotes compliance with agreed rules, and it facilitates enforcement and dispute settlement procedures. Several WTO initiatives would work toward these goals:

- strengthening the Dispute Settlement Understanding, particularly the compliance provisions,

- improving the transparency of WTO operations, including the publication of documents on a timely basis, increased inputs from interested parties in dispute settlement cases, and better means for "stakeholder organizations" to share their views with WTO delegations,

- promoting transparency in national procurement systems through adoption of WTO core principles in this area.

Third, the United States would like to strengthen WTO rules to help promote the adoption of market-oriented reforms in countries negotiating accession. Strengthening the rights and obligations of the trading system through new WTO accords provides useful guidelines for future policy reform in China and the 30 other countries seeking admission to the world trade club. At the same time, however, WTO members will also need to offer greater technical assistance to support efforts by applicants to adapt their trade regimes to WTO norms and to guide their officials through the accession process.

Fourth, to broaden public support in the United States for overall WTO initiatives, the United States would like to strengthen WTO initiatives dealing with labor and environmental issues. US objectives in these areas are modest compared with earlier proposals but still face strong opposition from developing countries. On labor, the United States would like to establish a forum for discussing trade and labor issues as part of a broader effort to promote compliance with internationally recognized core labor standards. Environmental objectives are less contentious since they build on existing provisions and initiatives in the WTO; in this area, US objectives are to promote environmental reviews of trade pacts as well as reform of specific trade practices (e.g., subsidies) that cause environmental problems.

In sum, the United States has much to gain from a successful package of WTO accords. Of course, the United States will not be able to "free ride" on the WTO Round as it did in the recent services and information technology pacts; it will have to offer concessions if the talks are to succeed.

While the US market is arguably the most open in the world, there are a few notable barriers whose partial liberalization could yield large dividends both in terms of foreign trade concessions and US economic welfare. US negotiators will probably be pressed to accept reforms in three main areas: reductions in peak tariffs (including textiles and clothing), perhaps capped at a level of 15 percent or below; reductions in agricultural protection, including cuts in domestic subsidies and enlargement of TRQs on sugar, citrus, and dairy products; and discrete changes in the implementation of antidumping cases.

What's in It for Developing Countries?

One of the main objectives of trade negotiations over the past two decades has been to integrate developing countries more fully into the world trading system. For most of the GATT era, developing countries were, to a large extent, "free riders" that were not bound tightly to GATT disciplines. The single undertaking of the Uruguay Round substantially changed this imbalance by requiring developing countries to accept all the negotiated agreements, including those containing provisions that would be difficult for many of them to implement in the prescribed period (such as the implementation and enforcement of intellectual property laws and other regulatory policies).

Since the 1980s developing countries have undertaken much more substantial trade reforms (binding many of them in their WTO schedules) than their trading partners in the developed world. Since their trade barriers remain, on average, higher than those in North America, Europe, and Japan, the results of new WTO negotiations will likely also require greater liberalization by the developing countries. From the mercantilist perspective typical of past GATT rounds, one could question the potential value of the new trade pacts, but from a development perspective, these deals have immense importance for developing countries.

Why then is it so important for developing countries to participate actively in new WTO negotiations? The answer is not simple because there is no monolithic position among the large number of developing countries that participate in WTO talks. Developing countries now have widely differing priorities and interests depending on their level of development, on their obligations under regional integration initiatives, and on their dependence on trade in agriculture and commodities, manufacturing, or services. Coalitions among developing countries (such as the Caribbean Regional Negotiating Mechanism and the Group of 15) and between groups of developed and developing countries (e.g., the "Friends of the Round" and the "Cairns Group" of agricultural exporters) now devise common positions that attempt to bridge the gap between developed- and developing-country interests. Recognizing this diversity, let me nonetheless outline what developing countries need from the new talks and a few reasons why they may not ask for it.[17]

First, and most fundamental, developing countries gain from the strengthening of the *rules-based* multilateral trading system. As the weaker partners in the trading system, they benefit the most when the major trading powers play by a common set of rules. In the Uruguay Round, for example, the willingness of the United States and Europe to accept dispute rulings and constrain their unilateral trade actions provided a major benefit for developing countries. The need to ensure compliance with those rulings is, in turn, of critical importance for the integrity of the WTO system and for the developing countries in particular.

Second, WTO negotiations help developing countries undertake and "lock in" reforms needed to advance their development objectives. Ideally, developing countries will implement trade and other reforms unilaterally because it is good for them, but as a practical matter, most countries have difficulty removing the "muscle" of protection (say, the final 10 percent tariff or its regulatory equivalent) without securing support from other sectors of the economy that would gain from negotiated trade reforms in other countries. Simply put, reciprocal trade pacts (in the WTO and among regional partners) are an important part of the political economy of policy reform in developing countries (and in developed countries, too).

Third, WTO accords could help advance agricultural liberalization in the OECD area, especially cuts in subsidies and high tariffs, that would be difficult to achieve outside the context of a large trade bargain. Of course, some developing countries would like to maintain protection for

---

17. For more extensive analysis of developing-country interests in the new WTO Round from different national perspectives, see the chapters by Rubens Ricupero, Jayashree Watal, and A. V. Ganesan in this volume, as well as Krueger (1999) and Srinivasan (1999).

specific products (e.g., Korean rice), and some would like to continue to import subsidized goods that do not compete against local production, but overall they would benefit from increased access to industrial markets for products such as sugar, beef, and fruits and vegetables. In several instances, however, the greatest source of potential growth in developing-country exports would come in areas of greatest import sensitivity in the OECD area.

Fourth, developing countries would gain from cuts in peak tariffs in OECD countries. Reductions in textiles and clothing tariffs are particularly important in light of the imminent demise of quotas in 2005 and the increased competition from China after it accedes to the WTO. Such reductions would also dilute the value of preferences granted suppliers under customs union and free trade agreements. Here again, developing-country demands confront strong protectionist lobbies in the OECD area. Moreover, these demands will likely spur reciprocal requests that developing-country tariffs more generally be either reduced or bound at the current applied rates.

Fifth, developing countries have much to gain from new rules and liberalization in specific service sectors. In many countries, the development of new service sectors and the strengthening of competitiveness in existing industries (e.g., tourism) could open important new growth areas and employment opportunities. For example, the growth of e-commerce could become a viable part of development strategies if countries can improve their infrastructure services, especially telecommunications. Foreign investment in those sectors will be critical; developing countries would thus also gain from WTO investment rules that would reinforce the dramatic opening of their markets that has been achieved over the past decade. In addition, labor services will be an important, albeit contentious, topic for the new round. Given immigration concerns, however, such talks are unlikely to advance unless WTO talks are narrowly focused by type of worker and conditions of employment.

Sixth, developing countries would benefit, like everyone else, from reforms in antidumping rules that constrain the overzealous use of these measures in a growing number of WTO countries. As the Uruguay Round demonstrated, however, reform of the arcane and detailed regulations guiding the administration of national antidumping laws is a complex task that can yield perverse results. Incremental reforms offer better prospects for success; small economies and the least-developed countries would especially benefit from the expansion of the safe harbor provisions (e.g., de minimis thresholds) for developing-country exporters.

The above arguments present a strong case for active participation by developing countries in the new WTO Round. In several areas, however, specific export gains depend on the willingness of developed countries to pare long-entrenched barriers in their least-competitive industries. Many developing countries are skeptical, based upon the experience with OECD countries' implementation of their Uruguay Round commitments and the failure of recent WTO negotiations on maritime services and on the movement of natural persons. With some justification, they question whether key Uruguay Round reforms (e.g., elimination of apparel quotas) that were "back-end loaded" and not scheduled to be fully implemented until 2005 will actually take place. Conversely, other developing countries worry that the liberalization of those barriers will create new competition for their exporters and actually reduce their market share. In addition, some developing countries are less committed to antidumping reform because they are new and extensive users of antidumping measures and have created domestic interests that favor expanding this channel for import relief.

Finally, developing countries will continue to seek special arrangements in WTO accords to accommodate problems related to their development status. The Uruguay Round accords narrowed the scope of "special and differential" (S&D) provisions that previously exempted poorer countries from key GATT obligations. Least-developed countries continue to receive large-scale, permanent exemptions (e.g., from disciplines on subsidies); other developing countries should not be given special treatment. Such provisions tend to distort investment within those economies and deter needed policy reform and industrial adjustment.

Instead, like all other WTO members, developing countries should accept common obligations. But case by case or on a sector- or product-specific basis, they should be afforded *different* transition periods for the full implementation of those obligations (just as developed countries were accorded ten years to phase out their apparel quotas). In other words, "differentiated" treatment should apply only to implementation periods to reflect, for example, the particular needs of small economies. This is especially important in some rule-making areas where developing countries need to develop the administrative or judicial capabilities to implement and enforce new trade disciplines (e.g., TRIPs). The requirements of new trade rules often tax the limited human resources of government agencies. To remedy such problems, WTO members need to work more closely with bilateral and other multilateral institutions to provide appropriate training and support so that developing countries can fully participate and benefit from new trade pacts.

The Negotiating Agenda

Trade ministers failed at Seattle to craft an agenda for new trade talks encompassing the key issues of interest to both developed and developing countries. In part, the task was impeded by concerns of the United States and others that too many subjects on the negotiating table would "overload the circuits" of a new round and prevent progress on the most important issues. Since the results of a new round would be a single undertaking, in which all the accords must be accepted as a package, they feared that the conclusion of the round would be delayed because negotiations in some areas would require many years to be fully resolved. These countries cited the long duration of the Uruguay Round as evidence of how a broad agenda prolongs negotiations, perhaps forgetting that it was the US-EU impasse on agriculture that seized up the talks for years. Once the bilateral deadlock was broken, the rest of the broad-ranging agenda was completed relatively quickly.

In light of the confusion in the Seattle debates, it is important to emphasize some central points about the negotiating agenda. First, agreement on the agenda for a new WTO Round is an agreement on the *problems* that negotiators will try to resolve in new trade talks; it is not a commitment to particular *solutions* to those problems, which may or may not result from the interplay of national interests during the negotiations. To be sure, a broad agenda increases the workload for negotiators and poses a particular burden for those from smaller developing countries. However, the experience of past GATT rounds demonstrates that, in the course of negotiations, the participants sort out priorities among issues on the table and relegate lesser topics to the sidelines. Second, it is not uncommon for issues to be added to the negotiating agenda during the talks. Indeed, two of the issues that received a lot of attention at the end of the Uruguay Round, antidumping and the establishment of the WTO itself, were not mentioned in the Punta del Este declaration that launched those talks.

These factors suggest that the agenda for trade talks needs to be flexible and open-ended. Given the rapid pace of change in international commerce in an era of globalization, new issues invariably will gain prominence during the next round. It is best not to limit the agenda too severely. Once issues are explicitly excluded by the ministerial declaration, they are harder to retrieve in the future (witness trade and labor issues since the Singapore ministerial in December 1996).

What needs to be done to reach agreement on the agenda for a new round? Part of the deal, but only part of it, is encompassed in the WTO's built-in agenda (including agriculture, services, and other issues such as government procurement and subsidies). However, the built-in agenda is not sufficient to produce a successful trade accord, as noted earlier. To take into account the broad range of member-country perspectives, the agenda for new WTO negotiations also will have to address the new issues that pose problems for global commerce in goods and services, as well as the systemic issues that threaten to undercut public support for future WTO initiatives.

In a speech at the GATT's 50th anniversary meeting in Geneva in May 1998, President Clinton suggested that "we must develop an open global trading system that moves as fast as the marketplace."[18] Fortunately, the WTO already meets this standard, since its new institutional framework accommodates continuous negotiations. WTO ministers can start and finish talks on some issues while other subjects remain under debate and new issues are added to the agenda. In this way, countries can conduct a series of seamless trade negotiations, with new talks starting immediately after a package of trade agreements (which I have called a "roundup") is concluded (Schott 1998b).

Roundups would have to encompass in a balanced fashion the objectives of rich and poor alike. Obviously, WTO members will have to avoid blocking or postponing decisions in areas critical to the major trading countries for this process to work. Each roundup would build on the results of the previous accord. Trade ministers can use their regularly scheduled meetings as action-forcing events to put together each package of agreements. Over a decade, the WTO could produce three or four roundups, which cumulatively liberalize significant trade barriers and strengthen member countries' rights and obligations.

To start, new WTO negotiations should pursue several initiatives simultaneously:

- trade liberalization that contributes to economic development and blunts demand for new protection,

- new rule making that establishes rights and obligations in areas inadequately covered by, or not yet subject to, WTO provisions,

- institutional reforms that remedy flaws in the WTO's dispute settlement and management structure, that make WTO operations more transparent, and that allow the WTO to work more closely with other organizations, public and private, to reinforce development programs in WTO member countries.

To be sure, such an approach still requires complicated "horse trading" among a large number of countries. Developed and developing countries will have different interests in each of these areas and place different priorities on liberalization versus rule-making initiatives. But crafting such packages of agreements, I believe, is essential to accommodate trade-offs across sectors and issues, involving both product- or sector-specific liberalization and acceptance of new trade obligations. Without such grand bargains, WTO members will likely fail to dent the strongest trade barriers protecting domestic industries in their key export markets.

---

18. This objective subsequently led US Trade Representative Charlene Barshefsky to call for a three-year deadline for new WTO negotiations to demonstrate that WTO talks can produce results in a timely fashion.

The following sections highlight key substantive issues in each of the three areas noted above that need to be covered in new WTO talks.

Trade Liberalization

Despite the notable progress made in the past eight rounds of GATT negotiations to reduce barriers to trade, important restrictions continue to impede international commerce. The Uruguay Round took hesitant first steps in reducing barriers in agriculture and services as part of a broader effort to rewrite WTO obligations in those areas. Industrial tariffs have been reduced substantially over time, but with key exceptions. Much more needs to be done in each of these areas. At the same time, if progress is to be made on new trade liberalization, countries will also have to review WTO rules regarding trade remedy laws (especially antidumping), which allow them to legally derogate from those reforms under certain conditions.

Agriculture

The Uruguay Round accord provided one of the few commitments in the postwar period to lower farm trade barriers, albeit to a limited extent. That multilateral negotiation succeeded because negotiators could "ante up" a large array of foreign concessions to "pay" for the liberalization of hard-core farm trade barriers. Recall that the Uruguay Round pact on agriculture succeeded only when negotiators linked commitments on intellectual property and textiles to those on agriculture.

WTO members committed in the Uruguay Round to restart negotiations by the year 2000 to promote "progressive reductions" in agricultural supports and protection.[19] Each country has a different idea what this means. As a practical matter, negotiators will resolve definitional issues based on the scope of liberalization that they deem possible. Reducing subsidies or import barriers protecting domestic farmers will require, as it did in the Uruguay Round, significant trade-offs between agriculture, manufacturing, and services reforms.

Not surprisingly, the agenda for agricultural reforms is extensive (see chapter by Timothy Josling). The Uruguay Round barely scratched the surface of trade barriers protecting national markets, and the new negotiations' primary focus will be building on those tentative efforts. Much work remains, in particular, to reduce subsidies, lower tariffs, and liberalize TRQs and other nontariff barriers. In addition, WTO members will

---

19. Talks got off to a bumpy start in March 2000, with the European Union and Japan blocking the appointment of a Brazilian chairman for the negotiating group. Countries agreed, however, to introduce initial negotiating proposals by the end of the year in advance of a stock-taking exercise in March 2001.

have to decide whether to extend the "peace clause," which restrains many farm trade disputes, when it expires at the end of 2003.

Export subsidies remain a problem despite significant cutbacks agreed to in the Uruguay Round; the Cairns Group and the United States have proposed their elimination. To temper such demands, the European Union argues that farm export credits provided by the United States and others also should be included under the existing export subsidy disciplines. Domestic subsidies were also reduced in the last round, but many countries argue that these disciplines are being circumvented via flexible interpretations of "blue box" and "green box" exceptions.[20] Tariffication in the Uruguay Round made some protection more transparent but resulted in many duties in triple digits; indeed, "dirty" tariffication arguably raised some barriers to trade. In addition, in areas where countries made minimum access commitments, improved guidelines are needed to prevent countries from administering TRQs in a manner that further limits access to their markets. Finally, WTO members need to review the growing number of nontariff measures imposed in support of national health and safety regulations to determine whether revisions are needed to the agreement on agriculture, on sanitary and phytosanitary measures, or possibly even a sui generis pact on biotechnology.

In that regard, WTO talks need to address problems related to trade in genetically modified organisms (GMOs). Concerns about the long-term impact on human health and the environment have led several countries to ban or segregate the sale of these products in their markets. The WTO requires that such restrictions be underpinned by sound scientific evidence of potential harm. However, that standard is open to widely varying interpretations.

To date, the scientific case against GMOs is weak, but critics argue that research is incomplete and that governments should be permitted to restrict use of these products on a precautionary basis. However, unbridled acceptance of the "precautionary principle" could open a large loophole for discriminatory trade measures that serve both legitimate and protectionist ends.

Finally, countries need to develop clear, narrow guidelines for granting exceptions to liberalization efforts that are made to promote specific nontrade objectives related to the "multifunctionality" of agriculture. That is, many countries argue that they must sponsor some level of agricultural activity to protect the environment, promote biodiversity, enhance rural economic development, and maintain food security. In so doing, however, WTO rules need to be crafted to guard against the introduction of new nontariff barriers under the guise of broader nontrade objectives.

---

20. For example, some countries argue that US disaster relief programs, which amounted to more than $6 billion in 1998, offset the subsidy cuts undertaken pursuant to the US Freedom to Farm Act.

Services

The Uruguay Round developed a framework of multilateral rights and obligations on trade in services but left much work undone (see chapter by Bernard Hoekman). Recognizing the limitations of their initial effort, WTO members agreed in Article 19 of the General Agreement on Trade in Services (GATS) that new negotiations would be launched by 2000 to put more flesh on the skeletal provisions and commitments previously negotiated. The first session of those new talks took place in Geneva in February 2000.

The services negotiations are one of the most critical components of the WTO agenda. Services are important both as stand-alone products and as critical inputs for the production of a wide range of goods and other services. Improving productivity in service sectors can thus yield extensive growth dividends throughout member economies. To that end, these talks are particularly important for developing countries to help them improve their financial sector and their telecommunications and transportation networks.[21]

New WTO negotiations will focus to a great extent on liberalizing trade in particular sectors, although the agenda also will be cluttered by issues left over from the Uruguay Round (subsidies, safeguards, and government procurement in services). Efforts need to be directed toward building on the very limited liberalization agreed in the basic telecommunications and financial services pacts; broadening reforms to new sectors such as environmental, energy, and entertainment services; and revisiting politically sensitive areas such as maritime and labor services.

What needs to be done? In essence, "liberalization" of services means promoting competition in the marketplace. In many instances, this goal requires regulatory reform and investment promotion.

In many service sectors, negotiators will confront regulatory policies that erect entry barriers to the domestic market. To be sure, some of these policies serve legitimate social and economic objectives (e.g., prudential regulations for the financial sector and certification requirements for professionals). Others, however, mask anticompetitive practices and corrupt administrations that need to be exposed and expunged. In this area, GATS negotiators should consider competition guidelines such as those in the reference paper to the basic telecommunications pact.[22]

---

21. For example, to improve competitiveness of the tourism sector, countries need access to global telecommunications and information services for marketing and reservations and an efficient transportation network to get the people to the market.

22. The reference paper set out six principles that should guide regulatory and institutional reforms to ensure a competitive environment for traded services. The guidelines cover safeguards against abuses by dominant suppliers, interconnection rights, universal service, transparency of licensing criteria, independence of the regulator, and allocation and use of scarce resources (Hufbauer and Wada 1997).

Promoting foreign investment in services is another important channel for enhancing competition (see Sauvé and Wilkie 2000). This goal would be facilitated by the establishment of a general national-treatment obligation in the GATS, replacing the current provision, which affords such treatment only for "scheduled" services.

Unfortunately, negotiations on services will face several critical problems. First, unlike recent talks on basic telecommunications and financial services, developed and developing countries will have different export interests in the various sectors under negotiation. Second and more generally, the positive list approach to scheduling commitments, along with the ability of countries to limit the application of those offers to one of the four modes of supply (cross-border trade, consumption abroad, foreign establishment, and temporary entry of service providers), will continue to constrain the scope and value of liberalization commitments.

Tariffs

Tariffs continue to be a mainstay of the WTO agenda, despite notable success in prior rounds in reducing industrial countries' levies to relatively low average levels. Tariffs imposed by developing countries remain generally high, although the Uruguay Round made significant progress in binding a large share of those duties for the first time. There are problems left over from past GATT efforts that should be addressed in the new WTO round:

- "peak" tariffs on selective products at levels well above the average country tariffs, and the related problem of tariff escalation,

- tariff bindings at rates well above those currently applied that allow governments free reign to raise duties for protectionist purposes without WTO review.

To address these problems, countries traditionally have developed a tariff-cutting formula to implement tariff reductions across the board. In practice, however, such an approach quickly degenerates into a product-by-product negotiation of exceptions to the so-called formula cuts, which is why a problem with peak tariffs and tariff escalation remains. The Uruguay Round experience with "zero-for-zero" sector-specific tariff cuts suffered the same problem, as countries carved out products or entire product categories from the liberalization list. The United States proposed accelerated tariff liberalization (really elimination) in eight sectors but resisted a formula approach to limit the exposure of its high apparel tariffs to new tariff cuts.[23] As a practical matter, however, there is little difference

---

23. The "accelerated tariff liberalization" proposal covered chemicals, forest products, medical equipment and scientific instruments, environmental goods, energy, fish, gems and jewelry, and toys.

between the two approaches since both will necessarily devolve into intensive negotiations over sector- or product-specific exceptions to the general approach.

The second tariff issue involves tariff bindings (i.e., the obligation to apply tariffs on particular products at a rate no greater than the level fixed in national schedules). The Uruguay Round substantially increased the number of bound tariffs, although many developing countries set their bindings at levels well above those currently applied (Schott 1994, 62-64). Those countries have the legal right, which they have exercised at times, to raise their tariffs up to the bound levels to provide added protection for domestic industries. Such "legal" protectionism goes against the grain of WTO disciplines. If countries want to raise tariffs for safeguard reasons, there are ample provisions to do so under the GATT balance of payments and general safeguards clause (Articles XII, XVIII, and XIX). New negotiations should require that tariffs be bound at applied rates.

Antidumping

Trade remedy laws (e.g., safeguards, antidumping, and countervailing measures) provide a safety valve for countries that liberalize their trade barriers. The WTO allows its members to impose temporary import relief (up to four years, with one four-year extension) if imports threaten or cause serious injury to domestic industry, and more lengthy and indefinite protection (subject to five-year reviews) if imports benefit from subsidies or are dumped and cause material injury.

Antidumping is one of the few legal ways for countries to impose protection unilaterally (that is, without WTO preclearance), and it has become the favored import relief measure for a growing number of countries (see chapter by Patrick Messerlin). In the past, antidumping laws were virtually the exclusive domain of the United States, European Community, Canada, Australia, and New Zealand. Since the end of the Uruguay Round, however, new users (primarily developing countries) have accounted for many more cases than the five traditional users. Indeed, over 1993-97, Mexico and Argentina have reported almost as many antidumping actions as the United States. More than two-thirds of antidumping actions during the 1990s were directed against developing countries and countries in transition, illustrating why this is a priority concern for those countries.

The issue of antidumping is a flash point both in US-Japan relations and in US and EU relations with developing countries. The Singapore ministerial in 1996 agreed to examine the "interaction between trade and competition policy, including anticompetitive practices," which many countries defined as encompassing antidumping actions. These countries hoped that US interest in the latter would allow consideration of

constraints on antidumping measures since those actions reduce competition almost by definition (if one assumes that the action is not directed
against predatory practices, as Messerlin convincingly argues in this volume is almost never the case). Instead, the linkage has generated intense
opposition by the United States to new talks in both areas.

Incremental revisions to existing provisions of the Agreement on Antidumping are the most that could be expected from new talks; too many
countries value their recourse to these measures to stem "unfair" import
competition. At a minimum, new negotiations should aim to reduce the
vulnerability of small developing countries to such actions by raising the
de minimis thresholds under which those countries are excluded from
antidumping investigations. Scaling back the existing cumulation rules
would have a similar effect. By comparison, Messerlin proposes more
fundamental reforms that would rationalize WTO rights regarding actions taken primarily to provide temporary import relief (safeguards)
and those taken for procompetitive reasons.

"New" Issues

WTO member countries have put forward a lengthy list of potential new
subjects for negotiations. Several of the new issues actually date back to
the charter for the still-born International Trade Organization of the late
1940s, although they have assumed added importance in a era of globalization. To a very modest extent, almost all are the subject of WTO rules
or ongoing working groups. Many involve activities that go well beyond
the scope and competence of the WTO. For that reason, WTO initiatives
in these areas must be narrowly focused on the trade-related aspects of
each issue and have clearly defined and pragmatic (i.e., achievable) negotiating objectives.

Four topics have been frequently cited as candidates for new WTO
talks: investment, competition policy, the environment, and labor. In addition, electronic commerce has gained attention due to the rapid growth
in international transactions via the internet.

Investment

The Uruguay Round touched only lightly on investment issues in the
Agreement on Trade-Related Investment Measures and in the limited
areas in which countries undertook specific commitments on "commercial presence" (that is, right of establishment) in the GATS. Many
investment issues are not subject to WTO disciplines. Investment incentives and export performance requirements, for example, continue to distort trade and investment flows among WTO member countries. Given
the recent experience in the OECD with negotiations on a Multilateral
Agreement on Investment and the heated opposition that it generated

among nongovernmental organizations, many countries are wary of engaging in broad WTO negotiations in this area (Graham 2000). Instead, they would like to continue the incremental approach to rule making within existing WTO pacts. The WTO has three options for dealing with investment issues, and they are not mutually exclusive.

First, WTO members could promote further progress on breaking down investment barriers by expanding the list of prohibited measures in the TRIMs accord to include, inter alia, joint venture and technology sharing requirements as well as export performance requirements. In his chapter, Theodore H. Moran sets out detailed proposals on what needs to be done and why it would promote economic growth in developing countries.

Second, WTO negotiators could continue to use the GATS talks to expand investment disciplines to a broader range of service activities. Sauvé and Wilkie suggest a number of pragmatic reforms that inter alia would strengthen GATS provisions relating to commercial presence (roughly, establishment rights) and promote greater transparency of investment incentives to service industries (Sauvé and Wilkie 2000, 331-63).

Third, WTO negotiators could craft a new Agreement on Direct Investment that would establish a common framework of rules for goods and services. Ideally, such an accord would provide both most favored nation and national treatment to foreign investors (with exceptions for national security and a few other narrowly defined sectors) as well as disciplines on investment incentives. In so doing, a WTO investment pact would also reinforce the objectives of talks on competition policy, since more open investment regimes promote competition in the domestic market.

Given the importance of foreign direct investment (FDI) for the growth of key sectors in developing economies, these countries should champion the cause of comprehensive investment rules in the WTO (Moran 1998). Most developing countries already recognize the value of FDI in transferring technology and management skills to their economies and have instituted investment reforms that have substantially opened their markets to foreign investors (with a few notable sectoral exceptions). These countries would also benefit from constraints on investment incentives, which they can ill afford to pay when competing with other countries for FDI in new production plants.

Preferably, WTO negotiators would start work immediately on the GATS issues and augment the TRIMs disciplines after the launch of a new round. During the course of the round, one would hope, ongoing discussions in the WTO's working group on trade and investment would then prepare countries to engage in negotiations on a broader investment pact.

Competition Policy

At its core, the WTO is about competition policy writ large. Its aim is to create opportunities for firms to trade and invest in foreign markets, adding a healthy dose of competition for domestic producers. National practices differ, however, in their approach to what constitutes a "healthy" level of competition, and many countries do not have a body of competition law at all. Competition laws and regulations can affect both the entry and distribution of goods and services in a market by encouraging or discouraging market concentration and restrictive business practices. Makers of airplanes and telecommunications equipment already know how such regulatory policies can foreclose export opportunities, but current WTO provisions provide little recourse.

For these and other reasons, competition policy poses complex problems for WTO negotiators. Many countries have difficulty in just crafting internal consensus on trade and competition objectives; forging an international consensus from differing national legal structures and regulatory regimes will be even harder. For that reason, I am sympathetic to the approach proposed by Graham and Richardson (1997), who argue that WTO efforts in this area should be handled in small, incremental steps. The first step should be procedural, with an agreement that competition policy authorities would consult with their counterparts in other WTO countries about practices that impede the access of foreign investors or exporters.

In that regard, the United States and a few other countries have begun to develop bilateral "international competition agreements" (ICAs), which aim to bridge the gap between national regulatory policies. As Graham argues in his chapter, if such accords prove successful, they could provide a stronger foundation for future WTO efforts in this area, including the development of baseline common standards (starting with cartels and mergers) that could be codified in a new pact on trade-related antitrust measures.

Even if this does not come about, the new WTO Round could make progress on competition policy rules in narrowly focused areas. For example, the WTO already has developed regulatory guidelines that establish competition rules for the basic telecommunications sector. As with investment issues, further progress might be possible in specific service sectors building on that precedent.

Environment

Like other "new" areas, trade-related environmental issues already are encompassed in specific provisions of WTO accords and have been under discussion in the WTO since its inception under the auspices of the Committee on Trade and the Environment (CTE). Unfortunately, the CTE has made little progress in defining an agenda for WTO negotiations.

Provisions relating to environmental matters in GATT Article XX, and in the standards and the sanitary and phytosanitary agreements, are ambiguous and have precipitated several high-profile disputes (e.g., the tuna-dolphin and shrimp-sea turtle cases). Rulings in these cases found certain enforcement provisions of environmental laws to be in violation of WTO obligations. Interestingly, the appellate ruling in the sea turtle case confirmed the US right to take action in support of environmental objectives, as long as the measures were implemented in a nondiscriminatory manner.

The WTO cannot become an environmental organization, but the trading rules can be made more environmentally friendly. One way would be to smooth the rough edges of the WTO's strict rules on nondiscrimination, which seem to bar both preferences for traded goods produced in an environmentally friendly fashion and penalties designed to promote compliance with environmental objectives (e.g., protection of endangered species). For example, GATT Article XX exceptions could be expanded to provide "safe harbors" for trade actions consistent with provisions of listed multilateral environmental agreements.[24]

In addition, WTO members should pursue a number of initiatives where trade and environmental interests overlap. First, there should be procedures within the CTE to examine the environmental implications of existing and new WTO accords. Second, countries should negotiate reductions in subsidies that distort trade and generate adverse effects on the environment. For example, agricultural subsidies have promoted overproduction in some regions with adverse effects on soil and water resources. Similar concerns arise in the energy, forestry, and fishery sectors. Third, sector-specific initiatives that promote liberalization of environmental goods and services should be given priority. Finally, WTO talks should revive the generally failed efforts of the CTE to formulate WTO guidelines with respect to eco-labeling and to encourage the transfer of new environmental technologies from the developed to developing countries. In his chapter, Daniel Esty analyzes these problems and suggests how the WTO can contribute to the needed remedies.

Labor

Labor issues are highly contentious among WTO members and also provoke vocal and substantive concern among WTO critics. The 1996 Singapore ministerial clearly rejected WTO negotiations on labor issues, deferred to the International Labor Organization (ILO) regarding the promotion of international labor standards, and noted that the two secretariats would continue their existing (albeit minimal) cooperation. Since that time, developing countries have consistently blocked WTO discussion of labor standards; in fact, the ILO (unlike several other international agencies) has not even been accorded observer status in the WTO.

---

24. However, such exemptions should be strictly defined to minimize distortions to trade.

All countries want their workers to enjoy higher standards of living and cleaner, safer working environments; few tolerate having other countries impose trade sanctions because of their domestic labor policies. To that end, ILO members have agreed on a number of conventions and "principles concerning the fundamental rights which are the subject of those Conventions" and that these "universal rights" should be promoted by all countries. The most recent agreement on labor standards was the June 1999 Convention on the Elimination of the Worst Forms of Child Labor. However, countries differ on what steps should be taken to *implement and enforce* those rights.

As Kimberly Ann Elliott points out in her chapter, ILO delegates have refused to use existing ILO enforcement procedures to promote compliance with ILO conventions, provoking critics in the US labor movement to propose linking ILO standards with WTO enforcement (i.e., trade sanctions). To be sure, current US proposals on trade and labor issues only call for WTO members to establish a working group to "study" a number of employment issues, including exploitative child labor. But US labor unions' demands that such efforts yield recommendations for new and "enforceable" WTO rights have generated fears that such a group in the WTO would be the first step down a "slippery slope" toward new protectionism and thus elicited an immediate veto from most other WTO members. The stridency of the unions' demands, inadvertently reinforced by President Clinton during a press interview en route to Seattle, compounded fears among developing countries that the US initiative was designed to punish rather than to help them promote trade and economic growth. As a result, prospects for including labor issues on the WTO agenda were set back even further.

Given the residue of ill will among WTO members from previous US efforts in this area, it will be difficult to add labor issues to the WTO agenda. Many developing countries remain adamant that the ILO, not the WTO, is the appropriate forum to discuss these matters. In Seattle, however, several countries proposed a compromise that would channel the debate to a consortium of international organizations in which the WTO could play a subsidiary role. Such a result would downplay several labor issues that are clearly linked to WTO provisions (such as the GATT Article XX[e] provisions relating to prison labor and labor practices within export processing zones, or EPZs) as well as enforcement issues. It is unclear whether such a compromise approach could, as a first step, satisfy the demands of the US labor movement for concrete progress on trade-related labor standards.

What should be done in the WTO? First, recognize the obvious. WTO members will not sanction trade retaliation in response to violations of ILO conventions. Removing the threat of such action is a prerequisite to opening discussions on trade-related labor issues in the WTO. But also recognize that US proposals encompass legitimate areas of WTO interest and competence. The WTO should not usurp ILO responsibilities, but it can promote better understanding of potentially trade-distorting labor practices as well as cooperative WTO and ILO initiatives to improve working conditions in their member countries.

Second, to restore trust among member countries, new WTO initiatives in this area need to start with a modest agenda. As I have previously proposed (Schott 1998b), the first steps should be procedural and aim to codify the nascent, informal process evolving between the WTO and ILO. A joint committee of the WTO and ILO secretariats should be commissioned to examine what could be done in the WTO to reinforce national efforts designed to promote better working conditions in all countries (both carrots and sticks).[25] Reports from this committee could then inform future discussions in both organizations.

Third, WTO members should start to work immediately on a narrow labor agenda. As Elliott argues, WTO members should develop a clearer interpretation of the scope of GATT Article XX exceptions (which could cover labor, environment, and health and safety issues). In addition, if broad-based investment talks are launched, as I suggested above, then those talks could usefully deal with the problem of investment incentives resulting from the application of labor standards within EPZs that are different from those generally applied in the country.

Electronic Commerce

The rapid growth in the virtually unregulated domain of electronic commerce should command the attention of WTO negotiators. As Catherine L. Mann and Sarah Cleeland Knight point out in their chapter, the volume of e-commerce is expanding dramatically, although only in countries with efficient telecommunications networks. While e-commerce flows are free of tariffs, the infrastructure of the electronic marketplace—that is, the hardware and the information services that channel these transactions—is subject to a number of trade and investment restrictions. As a result, the cost of internet access is often prohibitive. Simply put, such problems blunt access to the electronic marketplace much more effectively than tariffs, particularly in developing countries.

What should be done? First, a dose of preventive medicine is in order. At the May 1998 WTO Ministerial, member countries agreed not to impose tariffs on electronic commerce for one year. This standstill should be extended so that a work program can be fully developed in both the GATT and GATS contexts that addresses the real and potential distortions to the "production, distribution, marketing, sale or delivery of

---

25. For example, WTO members could consider "green lighting" labor training subsidies (i.e., exempting them from countervailing duties) to facilitate adjustment in relatively labor-intensive industries.

goods and services by electronic means" arising from domestic regulatory policies. As Mann and Knight suggest, the fact that e-commerce issues span both GATT and GATS terrain argues for the establishment of a separate committee on e-commerce under the WTO Council rather than one or several of its subsidiary bodies.

Institutional Reforms

The third leg of the agenda involves institutional reforms of how WTO members work among themselves and interact with other international institutions and NGOs. In particular, WTO reforms are needed to fix the flaws in the WTO's DSU, to make member-country participation in the decision-making (that is, consensus-building) process more representative, and to ensure that the WTO can work more closely with other organizations that promote economic development and international cooperation on labor and environmental issues. Progress in these areas would help rebuild confidence in the rules-based multilateral trading system and allow member countries to work more effectively together, with broader public support, to promote trade and development.

To be sure, not all of the institutional reforms would need to be authorized in new trade accords. Some could be implemented through regular WTO proceedings, particularly those that require budgetary increases for additional staff. Preferably, all of these reforms should be undertaken before the launch of a new trade round or soon thereafter (as I recommend in the final section of this chapter).

Dispute Settlement

The WTO's DSU provides an acid test regarding the commitment of the major trading nations to a rules-based trading system. Unlike the previous GATT system, dispute rulings are binding, and countries are expected to comply, provide compensation, or face multilaterally sanctioned retaliation. As John Jackson notes in his chapter, the DSU has worked remarkably well to date and has been used extensively by both developed and developing countries, but has begun to strain under the weight of a heavy caseload and procedural flaws.

The most glaring problem involves ambiguities in the DSU compliance provisions (Articles 21 and 22), which were highlighted in the fractious US disputes with the European Union on bananas and beef hormones. Panels are authorized to condemn practices but not allowed to rule whether proposed remedies are consistent with WTO obligations; the WTO system breaks down when countries found to be in violation of their obligations undertake changes in their practices that do not redress the problem. Other concerns relate to the high cost of bringing and defending cases before the DSU, which constrains many developing countries' participation; the composition of panels and the types of information that they are allowed to consider; and the distribution of panel rulings. Let me highlight some of the most important reforms needed to address these problems.

First, DSU rules need clear compliance procedures. Panels should not dictate remedies to the offending countries, but neither should they sit by passively if one abuse substitutes for another. Since panelists have detailed information on the issues under dispute, they would be best placed to judge the actions member countries take to bring their practices into conformity with WTO obligations. In essence, what is needed is a preclearance procedure. The country in violation should submit its proposed remedy to the panel that issued the original ruling within a fixed period (say, three months after the panel or appellate ruling). The panel would then issue an advisory opinion on the WTO legality of the proposed action. A negative finding would allow the complainant to seek WTO authorization to retaliate pursuant to DSU Article 22 procedures.

Second, panel procedures need an overhaul from start to finish. The United States and other countries suggest that panel decisions need to be expedited. Shortening the overall time limit for adjudicating a dispute from petition to appellate review, however, would further complicate the task of reaching informed decisions, particularly if the panel is to consider additional briefs from other groups and expert opinions. Rather, more time should be allocated for arguments and panel deliberations. If WTO members eliminated the right to block the establishment of a panel for one month and the short "consultation period" when disputants can comment on the draft final panel report before it is issued, panelists could spend an additional six weeks or so on their analysis without extending the current time limits.[26]

Third, WTO members should prohibit the selection of panelists from Geneva delegations. These officials are not the sole font of wisdom on the trading system, and their participation on panels is impaired because they must work with the disputing countries after the case is finished. Instead, the WTO should establish a permanent roster of nonresident panelists, drawing on academic and legal experts and former officials, who could serve for a fixed term (say, four years).

Fourth, panels should post their rulings on the WTO Web site at the same time that their decision is circulated to the disputing countries. Restricting distribution is a relic of the pre-internet age; all member coun-

---

26. Both practices are holdovers from the old GATT system. The blocking right merely delays the panel process for no reason. Comments on the draft final report were originally meant to fix mistakes and to provide one more attempt at conciliation; the appellate body is now used to review legal issues, and disputants rarely use the consultation period since panel rulings are now binding.

tries have a stake in the proper functioning of the DSU and deserve to review the findings as soon as possible. The document should be posted in its original language; translations into the other official languages should be produced as quickly as possible (subject to budgetary constraints) but should not delay the initial circulation of the decision to the general public.

WTO Decision Making

One of the strengths of the WTO is that decisions are made by consensus. The powerful cannot ignore the weak, but neither can the majority overrule the major trading nations. In general, the consensus rule has not been abused, and votes have rarely been taken.

As Schott and Watal explain in their chapter, the problem in the WTO today is not "consensus rule" but rather the process of "consensus building." The notorious "green room" process, in which decisions are crafted among a small group of countries, no longer adequately represents the expanded WTO membership and, in particular, the large number of developing countries that now have an important stake in world trade. The WTO has outgrown its informal, ad hoc procedures for decision making and needs to establish a steering group that is more efficient and equitable than the procedures that proved so unwieldy in Seattle.

What needs to be done? First, the consensus rule should be reaffirmed; no WTO obligations need be changed. Each member should maintain its right to decide for itself on the agreements and other matters before the WTO; I do not advocate weighted or proportional voting. Second, WTO members should revamp the process by which a small number of countries get together (often in the infamous "green room") to produce draft decisions that can then be "sold" to the broader membership. The process needs to be more efficient in terms of better flow of information to member countries and more equitable in terms of representation.

To that end, WTO members should establish a small steering group (say, 20 representatives) that would be charged with developing consensus on key trade issues before the WTO. Participation should be based on simple, objective criteria that ensure that all regions are adequately represented. At present, many members do not have the staff or sufficient support to participate actively in these meetings. Group representation, on a voluntary basis as proposed by Schott and Watal, could remedy that problem by facilitating information sharing among group members and affording countries the opportunity to participate in a broader range of subjects under negotiation.

Some WTO members, including several developing countries, have balked at such reform because they are currently inside the room and don't want to have their influence diluted by others currently excluded from green room deliberations. But, as demonstrated in Seattle, those countries have even less influence if the process breaks down!

Institutional Linkages

The WTO shares with other international institutions the common goal of raising living standards and promoting sustainable development. However, the WTO has neither the means, expertise, nor mandate to monitor, much less regulate, the diverse array of national programs (such as macroeconomic policy, stewardship of the environment, and labor market reform) that must be coordinated to achieve those goals. Just as national policies need to integrate these diverse issues into a coherent development strategy, the WTO needs to work closely with other international institutions covering these issues to ensure that their respective programs are mutually reinforcing with the trade policies supported by the WTO.

Achieving policy "coherence" among the major international institutions is easier said than done, which perhaps explains why there have been many hortatory declarations on the topic but little concrete action.[27] Bureaucratic politics (both within governments and between organizations) is partly to blame; trade and finance officials, for example, jealously guard their turf against each other. In addition, the structure and mission of the international financial institutions (IFIs) differ from the WTO's, and IFIs can provide money to member countries provided they meet specified conditions. The WTO has a small staff and lacks the financial resources of its Bretton Woods siblings; both inhibit effective policy coordination among the three institutions.

Despite these obstacles, closer ties between the WTO and the IFIs could address some concrete problems. For example, the financial crises in East Asia, Russia, and Latin America during 1997-99 underscored the need for closer cooperation between the WTO and the IFIs to provide trade expertise in the negotiation of reform packages and to ensure that such reforms are sustained over time (via binding in WTO schedules). More broadly, developing countries often find it difficult to implement and enforce new WTO obligations due to inadequate administration or regulatory expertise; many others cannot take advantage of new trade opportunities due to inadequate economic infrastructure. In both cases, more coherent policymaking would allow the World Bank and other development agencies to earmark funds to address these infrastructure needs and to provide training and other technical assistance to government officials so they can meet their WTO commitments.

The WTO also needs to work more closely with the International Labor Organization (ILO) and international environmental organizations and to deepen its dialogue with NGOs in both areas. As a first step, WTO members should grant observer status to the ILO in the trade body. The

---

27. For example, Article III:5 of the agreement establishing the WTO directs the WTO to "cooperate, as appropriate" with the IMF and World Bank to achieve "greater coherence in global economic policymaking."

ILO has untapped potential for dealing with many of the concerns that were raised in Seattle by the United States and others. Since labor issues strike a raw nerve among many WTO members, however, it would be preferable to start addressing trade and labor issues through joint secretariat studies of the linkages and problems (as I suggest above) and through new efforts in the ILO to strengthen the monitoring and enforcement of core labor principles.

Links with environmental organizations are more complicated because of the diversity of institutions that deal with those issues. Nonetheless, WTO staff should be directed to consult regularly with their counterparts in the UN Environmental Program and other organizations and report annually to the CTE on trade-related environmental issues. In addition, the WTO should continue on a regular basis its high-level symposiums on trade and the environment and on trade and development, involving member governments, NGOs, and other international organizations. Promoting dialogue in these areas is an important step in building public support for the WTO.

All these reforms require greater transparency of WTO operations and the willingness of WTO members to draw on information and expertise from outside the trading system. The DSU and decision-making reforms deal with key issues of internal transparency by ensuring that information flows promptly among member governments. Closer linkages to other international institutions would fulfill some of the needs of external transparency by integrating the work of other important groups (including some NGOs) with the WTO work program.[28]

To be sure, this agenda treads lightly on the issue of more direct participation by NGOs in WTO operations. The subject raises important concerns on both sides about democratic values and merits close scrutiny before new initiatives should be considered. However, continued dialogue between the WTO and NGOs is important, which is why I recommend formalizing WTO symposiums on the environment and development. In addition, as I proposed in a letter to the *Financial Times* last September, the WTO should make one of its deputy director generals responsible for new issues and concerns of civil society so there could be a direct channel for communication from NGOs to senior WTO management.

The WTO in 2000

Now that the smoke has cleared from the Seattle ministerial, what can be done to redress the problems facing the trading system and to revive efforts to launch a new round of trade negotiations?

---

28. The tripartite nature of the ILO, for example, means that input from labor representatives as well as officials could be channeled into the WTO process if closer WTO-ILO ties were established.

The first task for the WTO is to rebuild confidence in the organization and in its ability to deal with a diverse array of trade problems. WTO members have already begun to cautiously discuss "confidence-building" measures to address developing countries' concerns about tariff-free treatment for the trade of the least-developed countries, technical assistance, and cooperation in dealing with problems in implementing existing arrangements (particularly on trade-related investment and intellectual property rights). In addition, the WTO has started work on "internal" transparency—that is, making the work of the body more accessible to all its members (as contrasted with "external" transparency, or making WTO operations more accessible to the general public and NGOs).

Unfortunately, these modest steps fall short in addressing the problems of the post-Seattle WTO. Key substantive issues that divided the WTO membership in Seattle remain off the table. Institutional reforms needed to resolve problems with the dispute settlement rules, to make decision making in the WTO more equitable and efficient, and to promote cooperation with other international agencies and NGOs also have been avoided. Proposed trade preferences for the poorest countries limit benefits for key products, and offers of technical assistance fail to match even minimal needs. In short, little has been done to bridge the substantive differences between member countries on the WTO agenda or to broaden public support for the WTO itself and for new negotiations.

Over the near term, prospects for a new trade round are not good. National elections in the United States, Japan, and other key countries will distract attention from global trade talks throughout the year 2000. In Europe, monetary union and enlargement issues, which already presage important economic and institutional reforms, make countries reticent to push new trade liberalization, especially in agriculture. Public support for the WTO in the United States and Europe continues to wane as its efficacy to promote trade reform is questioned by its erstwhile supporters and its legitimacy is questioned by its vocal critics. In short, friends and foes alike have tarnished the WTO's reputation.

Unfortunately, the United States seems unlikely to reassert its leadership role in the trading system, at least until after the election in November 2000. The repercussions of the Seattle meeting, the congressional debate on Chinese accession to the WTO, the absence of fast-track authority, and the presidential campaign make it difficult for US officials to offer to negotiate reductions in US trade barriers. At the same time, however, these factors push the Clinton administration to demand new WTO initiatives on labor and the environment. Crafting a balanced WTO agenda will be difficult given the push-pull of election year politics.

While it will take time and political will to reach agreement on the agenda for the next round of WTO negotiations, the task could be facilitated if governments undertook a number of initiatives that strengthened the institutional structure of the WTO and its capacity to support reforms in developing countries that are needed to strengthen their economic infrastructure. Four broad initiatives should top the WTO agenda for the year 2000: reform of the DSU, reform of the WTO's decision-making process, cooperation with other international organizations to support capacity-building initiatives in developing countries, and commissioning an "eminent persons group" to advise member countries on how to craft an agenda for the next WTO round that is both practical and feasible and that balances the interests of participating countries.

The first task should be to improve the WTO's dispute settlement procedures. Confidence in a rules-based trading system depends in large measure on the willingness of the most powerful trading nations to live by the WTO rules and to comply with rulings of dispute settlement panels. As demonstrated in the bananas and beef hormones cases, the compliance provisions of the WTO's DSU need to be fixed to ensure that countries found in violation of their obligations bring those practices more quickly into conformity with WTO rules. In addition, panels need to be able to draw on outside expertise when warranted by the facts of the case, and panel rulings should be posted immediately on the WTO Web site to ensure full disclosure of the proceedings. These reforms are important to ensure that the WTO system operates equitably and efficiently and thus provides assurance that new rights and obligations developed in prospective trade talks would be faithfully implemented.

Second, WTO decision making needs to be more inclusive and more efficient. Part of the problem in Seattle was that too many countries with a significant stake in the trading system and the new negotiations were excluded from the deliberations on the ministerial declaration. The WTO needs to develop a better system for managing decision making among its large and increasingly active membership, one that is more representative and efficient than the current "green room" process that is aptly criticized for its back room dealings. Schott and Watal (in this volume) provide a detailed proposal on how these goals can be achieved by encouraging countries to form groups that pool resources, distribute information and consult on issues under negotiation, and share representation at the negotiating table.

Third, the WTO needs to strengthen its ties to other international organizations, particularly the International Monetary Fund and the World Bank, to support efforts in developing countries to improve their economic infrastructure and administrative capabilities so that they will be better able to implement economic reforms. Technical assistance is particularly needed in areas such as intellectual property and customs regulation, where WTO obligations have already been undertaken and where countries face problems in fulfilling their Geneva commitments.

Fourth, WTO members should commission a small group of distinguished statesmen and experts in international trade to report to the WTO

Council on initiatives that should be taken to promote world trade and sustainable economic development, reform WTO operations, and strengthen public support for the trading system. One would hope their recommendations would help build consensus among WTO members on the agenda for a new round, much like the GATT Wisemen's Group (Leutwiler et al. 1985) in the run-up to the Uruguay Round and the Group of Three before the Tokyo Round (GATT 1972, 71).[29] I first recommended such a group in 1998, when such a report could have been useful in preparing for the Seattle ministerial (Schott 1998b). More recently, British Prime Minister Tony Blair called for an eminent persons group (EPG) in a speech to the World Economic Forum in Davos, Switzerland, in January 2000 with a more limited mandate "to provide advice on how to improve the WTO's working methods." The idea was also endorsed by Supachai Panitchpakdi, deputy prime minister of Thailand, who cited his experience with the work of the EPG in APEC.[30]

An EPG should be selected, preferably by the WTO director general, and charged with reporting back to the membership by April 2001. Its proposals could then be vetted by WTO countries with the aim of securing agreement on the terms of reference for a new trade round that could be launched at the next ministerial meeting, perhaps in Geneva in September 2001. By that time, the US Congress, it is hoped, will have renewed fast-track authority.[31]

Finally, WTO members might consider a modification of earlier US proposals for concluding a package of agreements by the "kickoff" of a new round that could both spur greater interest and support for the WTO process and create a stronger and more open institutional foundation for conducting new trade talks. Such a package could include the results of several of the institutional initiatives noted above as well as new trade liberalization, which could be implemented immediately at the start of the new trade round. Possible candidates for such advance reform include the extension of the moratorium on tariffs on electronic commerce, the binding of tariff preferences for the least-developed countries, a new "peace clause" for implementation of a narrow range of TRIPs

---

29. The Group of Three was established in January 1971 to prepare proposals on "concrete action that might be taken to deal with the trade problems of developing countries. . . " (*Basic Instruments and Selected Documents*, 71). The group consisted of the chairs of the GATT Contracting Parties, the GATT Council, and the Committee on Trade and Development.

30. Supachai is scheduled to become WTO director-general in September 2002 (see "Fixing the WTO," *Far Eastern Economic Review*, 20 April 2000, 34-35).

31. The first year of the new president's term is probably the most advantageous time to pursue such legislation. A new round could be launched without it, but prospects for a successful conclusion of the talks would diminish substantially if the new president and Congress failed to give the issue high priority in 2001.

and TRIMs obligations, principles on transparency of government procurement practices, and perhaps even an ITA II. Obviously, such a package would have to balance the interests of developed and developing countries. The package presented above is illustrative of what could be done.

Promoting institutional reforms and strengthening linkages with other international organizations would be useful initiatives for the WTO to undertake in 2000. Commissioning an EPG to advise members on substantive issues and WTO reforms could well contribute to consensus building on the WTO agenda. The United States and other WTO countries should pursue these tasks immediately in order to facilitate the launch of new multilateral trade negotiations later next year.

References

Bergsten, C. Fred. 1998. *Fifty Years of the GATT/WTO: Lessons from the Past for Strategies for the Future.* Working Paper 98-3. Washington: Institute for International Economics.

Destler, I. M. 1997. *Renewing Fast-Track Legislation.* POLICY ANALYSES IN INTERNATIONAL ECONOMICS 50. Washington: Institute for International Economics.

Elliott, Kimberly Ann. 2000. (Mis)managing Diversity: Worker Rights and US Trade Policy. *International Negotiation.* Forthcoming.

Esserman, Susan. 1999. American Goals in the Trading System. Testimony before the House Ways and Means Subcommittee on Trade, 5 August.

General Agreement on Tariffs and Trade (GATT). 1972. *Basic Instruments and Selected Documents: 18th Supplement.* Geneva.

Graham, Edward M. 2000. *Fighting the Wrong Enemy: Antiglobal Activists and Multinational Enterprises.* Washington: Institute for International Economics. Forthcoming.

Graham, Edward M., and J. David Richardson, eds. 1997. *Global Competition Policy.* Washington: Institute for International Economics.

Hufbauer, Gary Clyde, and Erika Wada, eds. 1997. *Unfinished Business: Telecommunications after the Uruguay Round.* Washington: Institute for International Economics.

Krueger, Anne O. 1999. *Developing Countries and the Next Round of Multilateral Trade Negotiations.* Policy Research Working Paper 2118. Washington: World Bank, Development Research Group-Trade (May).

Leutwiler, Fritz, et al. 1985. *Trade Policies for a Better Future: Proposals for Action.* Geneva: General Agreement on Tariffs and Trade.

Mann, Catherine L. 1999. *Is the US Trade Deficit Sustainable?* Washington: Institute for International Economics.

Moran, Theodore H. 1998. *Foreign Direct Investment and Development.* Washington: Institute for International Economics.

Sauvé, Pierre, and Christopher Wilkie. 2000. Investment Liberalization in GATS. In Pierre Sauvé and Robert M. Stern, eds., *GATS 2000: New Directions in Services Trade Liberalization.* Washington: Brookings Institution.

Schott, Jeffrey J. 1983. The GATT Ministerial: A Postmortem. *Challenge* (May/June).

Schott, Jeffrey J. 1994. *The Uruguay Round: An Assessment.* Washington: Institute for International Economics.

Schott, Jeffrey J., ed. 1998a. *Restarting Fast Track.* Special Report 11. Washington: Institute for International Economics.

Schott, Jeffrey J., ed. 1998b. *Launching New Global Trade Talks: An Action Agenda*. Special Report 12. Washington: Institute for International Economics.

Schott, Jeffrey J., and Jayashree Watal. 2000. *Decision Making in the WTO*. Institute for International Economics Policy Brief 00-02. Washington: Institute for International Economics.

Srinivasan, T. N. 1999. Developing Countries in the World Trading System: From GATT 1947 to the Third Ministerial Meeting of WTO. Paper prepared for the WTO's High Level Symposium on Trade and Development, Geneva, May (revised draft).

II

INTERESTS AND OBJECTIVES
OF THE MAJOR TRADING NATIONS

2

The United States' Interest in New Global Trade Negotiations

C. FRED BERGSTEN

The United States has compelling economic, foreign policy, and systemic interests in a new round of multilateral liberalizing and rule-making negotiations in the World Trade Organization. All of these interests would be substantially promoted by the early launch and successful conclusion of new WTO talks.

The United States' present political stalemate over trade policy must be overcome if such talks are to be launched and successfully conducted. Even if the stalemate does not halt the nominal launch of new talks, it will block substantive progress. In addition, many of the major countries have ideas about the agenda for a new round that are quite different from those of the United States. These differences must also be overcome. Several modifications in the US negotiating position, which are identified at the end of this chapter, will be necessary to advance US interests by breaking both the domestic and international logjams.

I strongly argue that a wide-ranging new round is in the best interest of the United States. This does not mean, however, that every single American will benefit at every single moment from the results. As with all dynamic economic and social change, further trade liberalization will levy some costs. There will be losers as well as winners.

Policy must address these costs and losers, for economic and humanitarian as well as political reasons. A major set of new projects at the Institute for International Economics is in fact compiling a "globalization balance sheet," which includes in-depth analyses of the adverse impact of trade liberalization on some workers' lifetime earnings and some firms' profits in order to facilitate comparison of the costs and benefits of potential agreements. But it would be folly to ignore the immense benefits

C. Fred Bergsten is director of the Institute for International Economics, Washington.

from further liberalization, and new policies will simply have to be found to directly address the costs thereof.

The Traditional Economic Case

The classic economic case for trade liberalization is clear: improved efficiency in resource utilization. That case holds as much now as in David Ricardo's day and remains at the heart of the rationale for an open trading system.

We also know the contemporary mercantilist case for international trade liberalization from the standpoint of the United States: virtually every other country has much higher barriers than the United States does. American tariffs on industrial products average about 3 percent, and the United States will have virtually no nontariff barriers outside agriculture after its textile quotas are eliminated in 2005 per the Uruguay Round agreement (Hufbauer and Elliott 1994). The world's most rapidly growing markets, in Asia and Latin America, maintain barriers that are three to four times higher. In agriculture, even the other industrial countries maintain protection about five times as great as that of the United States.

Hence truly reciprocal trade liberalization would inherently increase US exports much more than US imports.[1] Indeed, global free trade would be the ideal mercantilist strategy for the United States because it is the only way to completely align others' barriers with its own (Bergsten 1996). These increased exports create jobs of superior quality, with wages that are 13 to 16 percent higher and layoff prospects that are 9 percent lower than the industrial average (Richardson 1996).

Trade Liberalization and Noninflationary Job Creation

There are two relatively new applications of these traditional arguments that make the US case for further liberalization so overwhelming. One argument, discussed in the next section, relates to the role of globalization in ameliorating US trade and current account deficits. The other is the crucial role that globalization has played in the dramatically improved performance of the American economy in the 1990s. Very few economists

---

1. The resulting trade expansion would therefore be most unlikely to depress wages of American workers, even those at lower income levels, whatever one may think of the relationship between wage levels and trade expansion in the past. See the 10-year projections in Cline (1997, appendix A). Moreover, the additional trade expansion would increase the real value of those wages because of the rise in the US standard of living generated by its improved terms of trade.

believed, even as recently as five years ago, that the United States could reduce unemployment below 5½ to 6 percent without triggering inflation. Yet unemployment has been below 5 percent for three years, and near 4 percent for over a year, without any significant pickup in price pressures.

There are two senses in which globalization played a central role in this unprecedented performance. First, lower import prices explain virtually all the decline in inflation between 1996 and 2000. Part of this reduction in inflation is undoubtedly temporary, due to dollar appreciation. But part of it is permanent, due to the competitive pressures generated by the tripling of the role of trade in the economy over the past 30 years. This decline in inflation obviated the need for higher interest rates and tighter monetary policy, which would have ensued in the past. It thus permitted at least one and a half to two additional percentage points of economic growth that would otherwise have been attainable. This increased growth in turn cut unemployment by almost a full percentage point and provided jobs for about a million American citizens who would not have had them without the benefits of globalization.

Second, globalization has played a major role in the sharp pickup in productivity that has sped US growth and that appears to be a permanent feature of the "new economy" landscape. During the last prolonged American economic expansion in the 1960s, many firms and indeed entire industries became complacent and failed to maintain their competitiveness. The result was the prolonged period of American economic difficulty in the 1970s and early 1980s. By contrast, virtually every US company today continues to improve its performance on an almost daily basis—despite 17 years of almost uninterrupted expansion. One key difference from the earlier period is globalization: the firms now realize that they are operating in a fiercely competitive *world* market and must keep moving forward if they are to avoid falling back.

From this perspective, globalization can perhaps be given credit for annual increases of about 0.5 percent in overall American productivity growth over the past five years—about half the standard estimates of the total productivity pickup.[2] This means that globalization contributed 2 to 2½ point-years of growth. This in turn reduced unemployment by about one percentage point, adding about one million jobs on what one would hope is a permanent basis.

Combining these two effects and allowing for some overlap between them, globalization has reduced the unemployment rate in the late 1990s by at least 1.2 percentage points and permitted the creation of at least 1.5 million jobs. Many of these jobs have pulled lower skilled workers, often thought to be unemployable, back into the workforce with major social as well as economic benefits for the nation. Some of

---

2. Econometric analysis shows that fully 40 percent of the increase in US manufacturing productivity can be traced directly to the faster growth rates of plants that export.

these gains are temporary, but a large portion of them likely represent lasting improvements in the US economic situation.

President Clinton has thus been correct in citing trade expansion, along with budget correction and human resources investment, as one of the three central pillars of America's stunning economic success in the 1990s. In assessing the impact of globalization, and thus of future trade liberalization, on the US economy, these job-creating effects of globalization must, of course, be set against any individual job losses and downward wage pressures that have resulted from import increases in particular sectors. But even if job losses caused by adjustment to trade liberalization fall primarily on low-skilled workers, it must be recognized that the aggregate job gains from globalization accrue disproportionately to that same pool of workers.[3]

Further trade liberalization is thus likely to help the US economy improve even further. By contrast, any significant rollback in the openness of the US market could have extremely negative effects on overall economic performance. Such a rollback in fact occurred during the early 1980s, when the Reagan administration, due to both the huge dollar overvaluation that resulted from its own budget deficits and the absence of any liberalizing negotiations until the launch of the Uruguay Round in 1986, applied new import quotas (via "voluntary export restraint agreements") to automobiles, machine tools, and steel and substantially tightened the textile/apparel quotas. The recent near passage by Congress of import quota legislation for steel, along with the continued stalemate over new negotiating authority, is extremely worrisome in light of the strength of the American economy. These developments suggest that protectionist actions could become widespread when the economy slows and unemployment turns upward—in the absence of meaningful new international trade negotiations that restore liberalizing momentum to the trading system. Such negotiations are thus needed to avoid potential losses as well as to generate substantial new gains.

WTO Liberalization and the US Trade Deficit

The second relatively new dimension of the economic case relates to the US trade and current account deficits. These deficits, endemic since the early 1970s, represent the major imbalance in the US economy for the foreseeable future. At virtually any moment, they could trigger a fall of 20 to 30 percent or even more in the exchange rate of the dollar.[4] Such a

---

3. All of these calculations are based on work in progress at the Institute for International Economics by my colleague Adam Posen, who is studying the macroeconomic effects of globalization on the United States.

4. Based on the calculations for "fundamental equilibrium exchange rates" in Wren-Lewis and Driver (1998).

drop could push inflation up by two to three percentage points, raise interest rates by at least as much, and drive down the stock market. These external deficits probably represent the single most serious threat to continued expansion of the economy and to continued full employment.

A comprehensive study of the problem by Catherine L. Mann has uncovered a new element of a constructive long-term solution: a major expansion of US services exports engendered by wide-ranging global liberalization of that sector in new trade talks (Mann 1999). Trade experts are well aware of an economic relationship that has plagued the US external position throughout the postwar period: that US imports grow more rapidly than US exports when the United States and its major trading partners are expanding at similar rates.[5] This relationship, however, applies only to trade in goods. There is in fact some evidence that the relationship is reversed for trade in services—that is, US services exports will grow faster than US services imports in a world of equivalent domestic and foreign growth rates (Wren-Lewis and Driver 1998). Moreover, US services exports are much less import-intensive than US merchandise exports (where every dollar of foreign sales is associated with 60 cents of imports). Hence a **rapid growth in global trade in services could generate a secular narrowing of the US trade and current account deficits.**

The share of services in the economies of the rapidly emerging markets is virtually certain to increase sharply as they mature, as has been the case with all the current high-income countries as they developed. If the developing countries liberalize those sectors, including with respect to foreign investment in services, they will both accelerate their economic growth and enable foreign firms to gain greater access to their expanding markets. The United States has an enormous interest in such an outcome, as it would maximize the opportunities for American producers of services to realize their competitive advantages and provide part of a constructive solution for US trade and current account deficits. Of course, such liberalization will only occur as a result of a global trade negotiation in the WTO, and this is another reason the United States has a major economic interest in such an initiative.

Economists are traditionally skeptical that changes in trade *barriers* can alter trade *balances*, which ultimately derive from macroeconomic forces such as the differences between domestic saving and investment rates. A sharp increase in US services exports, however, would sharply boost the profits of American services firms (which account for more than half of all US corporate profits) and thus raise the national saving rate of the

---

5. Technically, the US income elasticity of demand for imports is (considerably) greater than the foreign income elasticity of demand for US exports. This relationship was originally discovered in Houthakker and Magee (1969) and has been replicated for later periods in numerous subsequent studies.

United States. Over the longer run, the higher value of US exports would also enable the United States to improve its real exchange rate and hence to purchase more foreign products and improve its standard of living. A microeconomic shift of this magnitude could have sizable macroeconomic effects and thus boost the US trade balance as well as the efficiency of global output.[6]

The Foreign Policy Issues

In addition to these economic interests, the United States has a major foreign policy interest in the early launch of a new global trade negotiation. America's trade role has been very uncertain for the last few years, with the absence of negotiating authority since 1994 sharply limiting its ability to galvanize (or even participate in) new negotiations at the global and regional levels.

Largely as a result, the "next generation" free trade initiatives of the post-Uruguay Round era—achievement of "free and open trade and investment" in the Asia Pacific region via the Asia Pacific Economic Cooperation forum (APEC), by 2010 for the industrial countries in the group and by 2020 for the rest, and negotiation of a Free Trade Area of the Americas by 2005—are dead in the water. The failure of US leadership at the WTO ministerial meeting in Seattle in late 1999 dramatized the problem even more clearly.

The need for American trade leadership is compounded by the Senate rejection of the Comprehensive Test Ban Treaty in 1999. Such a blatantly isolationist step by the United States needs to be countered immediately, especially on the trade issue, which is so central to most of the world. A continued failure of American trade leadership, coming on top of the test-ban treaty vote and other foreign policy failures, would have a substantial impact on the image and worldwide credibility of the United States.

The Systemic Issues

Beyond these economic and foreign policy considerations, the United States has systemic interests in the early launch and successful negotiation of a multilateral trade round in the WTO.

First, we know from history that trade policy either moves steadily toward further liberalization or leaves a vacuum that permits backsliding and protectionism to flourish. Events in the United States in the early

---

6. See the data in Mann (1999, especially pp. 88-89).

1980s and again recently, as noted above, add to the empirical evidence for such a dynamic.

This systemic rationale for launching a new negotiation is particularly compelling today because **no meaningful liberalization negotiation is going on anywhere in the world, and the global trading system thus faces a severe risk of sliding backward.** As noted, protectionism in the United States could rise sharply whenever the economy slows and unemployment starts to rise—especially with the trade and current account deficits approaching $400 billion and exceeding 4 percent of GDP. The launch of a new round, with the tangible benefits to American industry and workers that would then become apparent, would significantly improve the prospects for winning congressional approval for new negotiating authority and overcoming the domestic political stalemate that has in turn produced the international stasis.

A second systemic lesson from history is that the new initiative is much more likely to succeed if it is larger rather than smaller. A comprehensive negotiation will engage a much broader array of domestic interests and thus enhance the prospect for political support, whereas the opponents of globalization will oppose virtually any initiative with roughly equivalent force.

The history of US trade policy clearly reveals that large-scale initiatives fare better than modest ones. The political economy is again straightforward: big-picture proposals capture the imagination of top political leaders and thus induce them to provide the leadership needed to win domestic support, provide a foreign policy/national security rationale to amplify the economic case for proceeding, and generate such huge stakes that no political leader is willing to accept blame for failure of the enterprise once it has been launched. "Big is beautiful," therefore, at both the start-up and completion of the process (Bergsten 1998).

The third key systemic issue is the risk of renewed and potentially conflicting regionalism in the face of continued inaction at the multilateral level. All of the major regional initiatives of the 1980s and early 1990s—the Canada-United States Free Trade Agreement, the North American Free Trade Agreement (NAFTA), APEC, Mercosur, and the Free Trade Agreement of the Americas—were motivated at least partly by the faltering of the Uruguay Round. As it turned out, those regional steps prodded the multilateral effort of the General Agreement on Tariffs and Trade back to life, and to ultimate success, so they turned out to be complementary to the multilateral process.

The evolution of that interaction is not so clear on this occasion. We are again witnessing a proliferation of regional liberalization developments: trade agreements between the European Union and the Mediterranean countries, Mexico, and potentially Mercosur; Japan's abandonment of its traditional opposition to preferential deals via its initiatives with Korea, Singapore, and Mexico; bilateral or plurilateral efforts including

Singapore/ASEAN Free Trade Agreement with the Australia-New Zealand Closer Economic Relations Pact, Chile-Korea, and a "Pacific 5" (United States, Australia, Chile, New Zealand, and Singapore); and, for the first time, serious discussions of an East Asian (or at least Northeast Asian) Free Trade Area (Bergsten 2000). All these steps reflect frustration with the slow or nonexistent pace of the multilateral trading system, especially on the part of countries that are eager to liberalize further and faster. They could again spur a restoration of multilateral progress, and that is indeed at least a partial aim of most of them, but they could also accelerate the erosion of the global system if it fails to respond positively.

As the traditional leader of the global trading system and the only country with truly global economic (as well as security) interests, the United States has an enormous stake in reviving the multilateral regime and moving it forward to renewed success and primacy. This systemic concern complements and strongly reinforces the more traditional economic and foreign policy cases discussed above.

Needed: New US Initiatives

In light of these problems in the United States, along with severe economic and political difficulties in some other key countries, the outlook is cloudy. Even if the WTO membership were to agree to "launch" a round, no serious negotiating is likely to take place for some time. An identical situation obtains, for largely the same reasons, with respect to the Free Trade Area of the Americas, which "launched" negotiations in May 1998 but has recorded virtually no results to date. Similar *sitzkriegs* occurred in the Tokyo Round during 1973-77 and the Uruguay Round during 1986-88, but this time the risks of continued inaction are much higher because "fast track" has been rejected twice by the US Congress, not just postponed, and because the rest of the world legitimately questions when any US president will have authority to negotiate.

The United States obviously cannot change the outcome by itself. The European Union in particular but also Japan and the developing countries will have to modify some of their positions to permit a serious effort to begin. They will have to agree to sharply reduce their agricultural subsidies and other protections. They will have to agree to meaningful liberalization of services trade. They will have to accept tighter rules for compliance with WTO dispute settlement decisions. They will have to accept greater transparency for WTO procedures. They will have to agree to work out initiatives on labor standards and environmental issues to enable the United States to break its domestic stalemate.

The United States will also have to make several changes in its stance to break the international logjam:

- endorsement of a "single undertaking" à la Uruguay Round, which is in any event the only way to achieve America's own priority goals of substantially liberalizing world agricultural and services markets (and thereby *strengthening* the domestic coalition for a positive trade policy);

- abandonment of a three-year target for completing the round, which is totally inconsistent with the administration's own goal of major liberalization and out of sync with the *best-case* prospect for obtaining negotiating authority in late 2001 or 2002 (and is undesirable anyway since it is good to keep up the momentum of liberalization once it has started again);

- endorsement of across-the-board "formula cuts" for tariffs, which will greatly facilitate reducing the much higher barriers of most developing countries, rather than trying to protect the few peak tariffs that the United States maintains itself (mainly in apparel and a few farm products, which will have to come down anyway if the overall liberalization package is to be significant);

- inclusion of competition policy on the negotiating agenda, at least in terms of seeking a common framework or principles upon which to proceed to details later, which is at the heart of most current US-Japan "trade disputes" (e.g., Kodak-Fuji) and many US-EU conflicts (e.g., Boeing-McDonnell Douglas);

- inclusion of antidumping policy, where emulation of US practices by a rapidly growing number of major economies will shortly turn the United States into a net target rather than a net user, and where reform is the chief negotiating objective of numerous key countries; and

- inclusion of investment policy, where the United States should and could ally with developing countries (and some industrial countries) to oppose the growing distortions generated by incentive policies and performance requirements.[7]

Conclusion

The United States has strong national interests in launching, and vigorously pursuing, a new multilateral trade negotiation in the WTO. The administration has to do a better job of selling that case, however, and the arguments spelled out above should help. In addition, the administration must modify a number of its positions and make a forceful presentation of such a strengthened approach in the forthcoming international debates.

---

7. As proposed in Moran (1998).

It then needs to follow up domestically with an all-out push to obtain negotiating authority as soon as possible and to present significant *domestic* initiatives both to cushion adjustment to trade dislocation and to help workers prepare themselves to compete in a global economy.

The stakes are enormous. The demonstrated benefits of past liberalization are huge, and the potential benefits to be derived from similar steps in the future are also substantial. Those stakes embrace the paramount economic, foreign policy, and global systemic interests of the United States. The United States must now move decisively in the proposed direction if a new round is to be launched and successfully advanced in the near future.

References

Bergsten, C. Fred. 1996. Globalizing Free Trade. *Foreign Affairs* 75, no. 3 (May/June).

Bergsten, C. Fred. 1998. *Fifty Years of the GATT/WTO: Lessons from the Past for Strategies for the Future.* Working Paper 98-3. Washington: Institute for International Economics.

Bergsten, C. Fred. 2000. *The New Asian Challenge.* Working Paper 00-3. Washington: Institute for International Economics.

Cline, William R. 1997. *Trade and Income Distribution.* Washington: Institute for International Economics.

Houthakker, Hendrik, and Stephen Magee. 1969. Income and Price Elasticities in World Trade. *Review of Economics and Statistics* 51: 111-25.

Hufbauer, Gary Clyde, and Kimberly Ann Elliott. 1994. *Measuring the Costs of Protection in the United States.* Washington: Institute for International Economics.

Mann, Catherine L. 1999. *Is the US Trade Deficit Sustainable?* Washington: Institute for International Economics.

Moran, Theodore H. 1998. *Foreign Direct Investment and Development: The New Policy Agenda for Developing Countries and Economies in Transition.* Washington: Institute for International Economics.

Richardson, J. David. 1996. *Why Exports Matter: More!* Washington: Institute for International Economics.

Wren-Lewis, Simon, and Rebecca L. Driver. 1998. *Real Exchange Rates for the Year 2000.* Washington: Institute for International Economics.

3

The EU Approach to a New Round

HUGO PAEMEN

The European Union has been at the forefront of efforts to launch a new round of multilateral trade negotiations in the World Trade Organization (WTO) in 2000. This initiative has been pursued as an important means to improve the European economy, to foster global economic growth and sustainable development, and to ensure the successful management of globalization.

A comprehensive round would correspond best with the European Union's (EU) widely diversified trade interests. It also offers the best way to take into account the diverse trade interests of the broader WTO membership and thus increases the likelihood that a large number of WTO members would actively participate in the negotiations. The so-called built-in agenda established at the end of the Uruguay Round, mandating new talks on agriculture and services, is not sufficient; additional areas of interest to Europe and other WTO countries will have to be brought into the negotiations in order to facilitate a balanced final package.

To be sure, setting a comprehensive agenda for new trade talks offers no guarantee that negotiations on all the issues will lead to conclusive arrangements. However, it should prevent both the neglect of important specific interests and the frustration of participants that have not had the occasion to introduce their cases.

In brief, the EU approach is a global negotiation without limits. In that respect we Europeans diverge somewhat from the US position. First of all, we think that this sort of negotiation corresponds with our interests and the more diversified structure of our economy. Furthermore, an open, inclusive agenda facilitates progress in negotiations. At the end of the day when you have to make trade-offs, it is easier to do so when

Hugo Paemen is the former European Union Ambassador to the United States.

you have more elements to an acceptable package of agreements than when you have only a few subjects.

Second, a broad-ranging trade round is needed to strengthen the multilateral trading system. The WTO system has been tested by a considerable number of dispute settlement cases. Overall it has worked remarkably well. But important developments have taken place since the conclusion of the Uruguay Round. For example, nobody talked about electronic commerce in the Uruguay Round. More generally, discussion of the impact of globalization was absent. There must be an agenda that corresponds to reality and to people's needs. And the reality is that there is globalization and that people are afraid of it to a certain extent. If these realities are not an integral part of WTO discussions, then the WTO risks becoming irrelevant. For the WTO to remain relevant, its rules must be updated and clarified. New sectors of activity and new sources of difficulty must be considered in new WTO talks and integrated into the trading system. Public concern about issues such as the relationship between the WTO and the protection of the environment or core labor rights are clear examples. So, too, are the increasingly intimate relationships between trade and investment, and the complementary character of trade and competition rules worldwide. From the EU perspective, the logic of the comprehensive approach requires that these issues not be discarded or rejected. Nobody should have the right to veto an item for the agenda. That is why we think that issues not previously included have to be integrated into the WTO discussions.

Third, the WTO has become the reference for international trade. There is not one initiative in international trade that does not revert to the WTO agreement. But in order to remain the reference point for trade and to remain the body of rules that marks how international trade is conducted, the WTO has to be updated. It has to adjust to new developments.

Agriculture

While agriculture issues pose the most difficult political problems for the European Union, Europeans have nonetheless accepted that such reforms should be on the agenda for new trade talks. Europe's commitment to reform of the Common Agricultural Policy (CAP) is evident in several ways.

First of all, Europe began reforming the CAP at the end of the Uruguay Round. It reduced subsidies, narrowing the gap between EU and world market prices.

Second, CAP reform is an essential condition for the proposed enlargement of the Union to countries of Central and Eastern Europe, which have important agricultural sectors. In the context of Agenda 2000, which was set up to guide enlargement of the European Union, there will be additional steps toward CAP reform. For example, at the beginning of this year, the Council of Ministers decided for the first time not to increase the EU budget for agriculture. However, EU enlargement will increase its overall population by 25 percent, agricultural land by 50 percent, and the EU's agricultural population by 100 percent. This budget policy is not tenable without further CAP reform.

Third, the expiration at the end of 2003 of the "peace clause" will have some influence on the way Europe will behave in agriculture during the next round. I don't want to anticipate what is going to be possible or not possible—that is for the negotiators. The European Union continues to stress the "multifunctionality" of the agriculture sector in society, by which they mean that noneconomic considerations play a role in how agricultural policy is worked out. But it is clear that the European Union has accepted the necessity of CAP reform.

Market Access

The European Union favors a substantial swipe at overprotectionist tariffs. Therefore it gives priority to the reduction of tariff peaks. It has proposed a reduction based on a tariff-band approach—defining a low, medium, and high band within which all tariffs would have to fall—in order to simplify the existing tariff schedules. Such an approach could be accompanied by averaged weighted tariff objectives differentiated according to the level of a country's development and could also take into account the sensitivities of certain sectors. In order to meet the concerns of the least-developed countries, the European Union also supports an up-front commitment from all developed countries to implement, no later than the end of the round, duty-free access for essentially all products from least-developed countries.

Services

The European Union has a mandate for comprehensive negotiations to obtain more and better commitments from all WTO members on market access and national treatment. Binding the autonomous levels of liberalization in place since the General Agreement on Trade in Services (GATS) became effective would be a priority, and commitments to further liberalization should be secured. The negotiators have been instructed that the sensitivities of specific sectors have to be taken into account.

Investment

The European Union has long sought a multilateral framework of rules governing international investment, with the objective of securing a stable and predictable climate for investment worldwide. However, the approach in the WTO should be substantially different from the ill-fated negotiations in the Organization for Economic Cooperation and Development (OECD) on the Multilateral Agreement on Investment (MAI).

While Europeans strongly favor discussing investment rules in WTO, we don't necessarily expect that the final objective after three years has to be a full-fledged agreement on investment. We have learned lessons from the MAI experience. Indeed, we were strongly concerned about such talks in the OECD because it seemed irrelevant to discuss global investment rules among a group of countries that represented only industrialized countries. Many of the difficult problems in this area involve relationships between developing and developed countries.

The WTO appears to be the only multilateral forum that can fully take into account the interests of both the developed and developing countries and their positions as home or host countries (or both) to international investors. A framework of multilateral rules for investment has to ensure conditions that are conducive to sustainable development. To this end, such a framework should preserve host countries' ability to regulate the activities of investors in their territories for the achievement of legitimate policy objectives.

Competition Policy

The European Union supports WTO negotiations, as part of a comprehensive round, on a binding framework of multilateral rules on competition. The need for such a framework for the application of competition law to anticompetitive business practices has increased as a result of globalization and the gradual establishment of a single world market for certain products. Such a WTO agreement should include the following: core principles and common rules relating to the adoption of a competition law and its enforcement; common approaches on anticompetitive practices with a significant impact on international trade and investment; provisions for international cooperation (notification, consultation, exchange of nonconfidential information, elements of negative and positive comity, and so on); and dispute settlement procedures to ensure that domestic competition law and enforcement accord with the multilateral provisions.

Environment

In the European concept, trade and environment should play a mutually supportive role in favor of sustainable development. Priority should be attached to clarifying the relationship between WTO rules and trade measures taken pursuant to multilateral environmental agreements, between WTO rules and nonproduct-related "process and product methods" requirements (in particular, the WTO compatibility of ecolabeling schemes), and between multilateral trade rules and core environmental principles, notably the precautionary principle. There should be agreement on multilateral criteria for the scope of action possible under that principle.

Government Procurement

There are many procedural improvements that can be made to the plurilateral accord on government procurement reached in the Uruguay Round. First, WTO rules that promote transparency and nondiscrimination are important because they can also work against fraud, money laundering, and other illicit behavior that is sometimes associated with government procurement. Second, the WTO must not only improve the rules but also expand the coverage of government tenders subject to those disciplines. It will be difficult, for instance, for the European Union to accept new WTO obligations in this area if "Buy American" provisions are exempted. I had a tough time at the end of the Uruguay Round gaining support in Europe for the Government Procurement Agreement without such disciplines, and I wish my successor luck if he has to sell this a second time.

Conclusion

The European Union seeks two broad objectives in new WTO negotiations. First, it seeks a comprehensive and substantial step toward further liberalization of international trade, starting from the built-in agenda agreed upon in the Uruguay Round but with a considerably wider scope. Second, it seeks the strengthening of the multilateral trading system through the integration of rights and obligations in areas that have come to the forefront since the Uruguay Round and that are closely linked to economic globalization.

Europeans hope there will be an agreement on an inclusive agenda. This does not mean that on each and every item there would be agreement at the end of a three-year negotiating period. But if negotiators start by eliminating topics for consideration and if each has the right to say, "I don't want this or that to be discussed," they will only kick off a reductionary process that will not lead to the comprehensive agreement that in the end would be good for everyone.

4

Some Reflections on the Seattle Ministerial: Toward the Relaunching of a New Round

HISAMITSU ARAI

As the saying goes, the road to hell is paved with good intentions. Everybody gathered in Seattle—perhaps with the exception of some diehard vandals—was there with good intentions. We, the Japanese delegation, were determined to launch a new round that would lead the world to a peaceful and prosperous twentieth century. Delegates from the developing world were also eager to see a successful launch of the new round that would guarantee them a fair and equitable share of wealth created by freer trade and investment. I would like to believe that even most demonstrators and protesters were there with a positive (albeit misguided, perhaps) agenda: their own ideals about how the World Trade Organization (WTO) should be managed.

Inside the Seattle Convention Center, despite all the difficulties, the negotiators were making steady progress toward the launch of a new round. In the end, however, miscalculations and tactical errors here and there, put together, snowballed into a massive, negative force that canceled out all the positive developments during the meeting. I will briefly analyze the causes of the failure later in this article.

My Observations at Seattle

In Seattle, I predicted that the WTO ministerial would be either a resounding success or a total failure. The choice was between launching a

Hisamitsu Arai is vice-minister for international affairs for the Japanese Ministry of International Trade and Industry.

comprehensive round or not. Unfortunately, I did not see any prospects for a middle answer. I did not think that we could get even lukewarm support from members for a weak declaration that did little more than confirm the built-in agenda and still be able to call it a success.

Japan, along with the European Union and other members, has consistently advocated adoption of the comprehensive approach to a new round of multilateral trade negotiations. The basic precept behind such an approach is that such negotiations are untenable unless all participating members have a chance to obtain something from the outcome.

What is the comprehensive approach? It encompasses not only market access issues related to trade in goods, agriculture, and services, but trade rules on antidumping, subsidies, technical barriers to trade and other areas, new issues such as investment, and cutting-edge issues involving new technology such as electronic commerce and biotechnology, as well as concerns with respect to civil society.

It is impossible to launch and successfully conclude a new round if participants only pursue specific benefits from specific items in specific sectors without offering any concessions in other sectors or negotiating areas.

Trade negotiating rounds are conducted, by nature, on the basis of give-and-take. One of the reasons the ministers did not have a clear, simple negotiating text for the Seattle Declaration was that so many countries submitted different proposals for the agenda. The comprehensive approach is the only way to address this issue. If the new round could not respond in some way to a substantial portion of these divergent interests, the new round would be doomed to fail. Without a broad agenda, the new round would not have the range of issues on the negotiating table to allow every country both to make concessions and obtain something of benefit.

Some WTO members argued that if we followed the comprehensive approach, the negotiations would become unmanageable and negotiations could not be completed within the projected three-year time frame. But Japan and others were convinced that a new round under the comprehensive approach could indeed be concluded within three years if the participants could find the political will to conduct the negotiations efficiently.

The Uruguay Round took so long partly because the negotiators, in addition to addressing a broad range of substantive issues, had to create an institution to administer the results of the round. This time, that foundation is in place. So why not try to aim for an ambitious agenda? Only by having a broad-based, well-balanced agenda would a new round be able to attract enough support from participants.

Some WTO members suggested that the new round should be a small package centering on the so-called built-in agenda—that is, limited to agriculture and services. This limited approach completely ignored the domestic political problems of the other WTO members. It was unrealistic for any member to believe that other countries would agree to a narrow agenda that would provide all the benefits to that member and would impose all the burdens on other countries.

Moreover, such an approach would jeopardize the built-in agenda itself. When faced with the narrow approach, other members would have no incentive to go forward. Rather than make a series of concessions in areas of concern to a small group of countries, the other countries might well decide that it is better to delay the negotiating timetables, extensively debate the negotiating agenda, and refuse to compromise on the substance.

If the narrow agenda placed certain members in the position of having little or nothing at risk, the other members would have nothing to gain to justify their concessions. Given the frustrations many developing countries felt about the Uruguay Round, these countries would have no incentive to cooperate in new negotiations that offer them nothing.

The comprehensive approach would allow every participant the realistic chance to obtain something of benefit as a result of give-and-take in the negotiations. Every one of the participating governments would have to be able to get some satisfaction from the outcome of the round. Japan tried its best in Seattle to avoid a stalemate. It showed flexibility on the issue of implementation, which is the major concern of many developing countries, and it coordinated positions with a group of countries that favor a comprehensive agenda. It should be noted that many developing countries in Asia and Latin America were in favor of the comprehensive approach.

Finally, let me mention the issue of antidumping, the area in which the views of the United States and the rest of the world, including Japan, were very different. I outlined Japan's position regarding this matter in a 29 November 1999 letter to the editor of the *Financial Times*, which I wrote in response to an opinion by US Commerce Secretary William Daley that the paper had previously printed. My basic message was twofold. First, the United States has increasingly become the target of many antidumping actions by its trading partners. It might not be well known, but according to WTO statistics there have been 64 antidumping cases against products originating in the United States over the past four years, making the United States the second largest target of antidumping investigations in the world, following China.

Second, proponents of the comprehensive approach did not seek to "weaken" US trade laws in the new round. They were only trying to improve the global trade rules that apply to all countries, including the United States. Japan's initiative was comparable to multilateral arms reduction talks: with more discipline over the burgeoning arsenal and application of antidumping measures, all countries would benefit from a more secure and predictable trading system. Concessions made in market access negotiations should not be undercut by abusive antidumping measures. That was the ultimate objective of Japan's initiative in the antidumping area, which many countries supported

Why the Ministerial Failed

Everybody knows what happened in Seattle. There was no single reason for the fiasco. Major participants of the negotiations—particularly the so-called Quadrilateral Group of Japan, the United States, the European Union, and Canada—were not ready to agree on substantive issues such as agriculture, antidumping, investment, and competition, much less issues of trade and environment or labor. Although the differences narrowed considerably during the final days of the negotiations, in the end participants could not formulate a comprehensive package.

In addition to these stumbling blocks on substantive issues, the balance of transparency and efficiency in the conduct of the negotiations was seriously distorted. Many developing countries that were left out of the informal consultation process had serious misgivings about the decision-making mechanism. The result was a serious loss of confidence in the WTO.

All these elements added up to the failure of the ministerial. Negotiators left Seattle frustrated that their good intentions did not result in a new round.

The Way Ahead

I could dwell further on a ministerial postmortem. But the damage is done, and the time for lamenting is over. We must now look beyond Seattle and seriously seek the relaunch of a negotiating round.

The negotiations on the built-in agenda started in February 2000. I welcome this as a positive step. However, I still believe that a comprehensive round is needed in order to have meaningful results out of these negotiations, for the reasons outlined above.

While we explore the way toward a new round, we need to work on a short-term program to restore confidence in the world trading system. Japan fully supports the initiative led by Director General Mike Moore on four priority areas: assistance to least-developed countries through freer access to the developed and developing markets, enhancement of technical cooperation activities toward capacity building for implementation of WTO agreements, a solution to transition problems with some WTO agreements, and improvements in the WTO internal procedures for consultation and decision making, as well as external transparency.

Japan supports the director general's initiative because it believes that the WTO should secure the developing countries' active participation and respond appropriately to their concerns. This will no doubt strengthen the multilateral trading system.

Regarding the first prong of the initiative, Japan believes that developed-country members of the WTO should provide least-developed country members with enhanced market access by extending and implementing tariff-free and quota-free treatment via their respective preferential schemes for essentially all products originating in least-developed countries. While there is a clear need to secure wide participation in this initiative, it is also important to maintain the attractiveness of the package by not excluding a specific sector from the coverage.

Second, a decision could be made to establish a revitalized mechanism within the WTO for capacity building and technical assistance, with a view toward devising "tailor-made" plans that respond to the needs of particular developing countries. This strategy should cover developing countries in general and be based on closer cooperation between the WTO and other international organizations, while emphasizing efficiencies among donors and full participation by recipients. It should also mobilize bilateral, regional, and multilateral assistance programs including the Integrated Framework.

Third, issues relating to implementation will continue to require attention. Particularly in the areas of trade-related investment measures and customs valuation, members should be ready to react sympathetically and flexibly to requests from developing countries for extension of transition periods. Consideration of these requests should be done case by case in accordance with the relevant provision of the WTO agreements. A calendar should be established for the consideration of such requests. Implementation programs and phaseout plans should be an important component of the extensions and could include, where appropriate, an element of technical assistance to facilitate orderly phaseout of WTO-inconsistent measures.

Fourth, a number of measures could be taken to improve the WTO's functioning and to enhance internal and external transparency. While the WTO should continue the practice of decision making by consensus, informal meetings should be broadly representative of the WTO membership at different levels of development and reflect the breadth of substantive views on the issue being discussed. Such meetings should be followed by open meetings in which a report is made on progress achieved and all members are given an opportunity to express their views. The director general has an important role in this respect, and his efforts to involve the broad membership of the WTO should be supported.

Regarding the management of the ministerial conference, the director general should be given more responsibility for drafting a ministerial declaration so as to maintain the efficiency and impartiality of the process. Within the context of a new program for capacity and technical assistance, greater priority should be given to supporting developing-country participation in negotiations, particularly the least developed among them.

A number of steps could be taken with a view toward ensuring external transparency. In view of the experience in Seattle, there is no question that the WTO should expand its outreach activities toward civil society. Most WTO documents could be made publicly accessible at an accelerated pace. Contacts and exchanges of information between the WTO Secretariat and nongovernmental organizations should be encouraged. A more regular organization of symposia and other forms of informal dialogue with civil society are needed on a broader range of WTO issues.

Finally, one other lesson from Seattle is the need for increased cooperation and coordination among major trading partners. Japan has actively engaged in policy dialogues with its quadrilateral partners, as well as other developed and developing countries, toward the relaunching of a new round, and it will continue to do so. The world cannot afford another failure. This time around, we must realize a good result out of good intentions.

5

The World Trading System:
Seattle and Beyond

RUBENS RICUPERO

I feel very much a member of the trade community. As such, it was particularly interesting to be in Seattle, not because of the demonstrations, but because it represented an opportunity to reflect on the deeper meaning of what is taking place. I won't go into such reflections in detail, but I believe it would be a mistake to dismiss the backlash against globalization as just a problem of misinformation or of people who are frustrated and don't know how else to vent their frustrations. I think there is something more. We have to address the protesters' fears and concerns because they have been growing over the last few years. This topic is something of a moving target. A few years ago here in the United States these fears and concerns were centered on the North American Free Trade Agreement (NAFTA), then it was the investment negotiations in the Organization for Economic Cooperation and Development (OECD), and then it was the turn of the World Trade Organization (WTO). Something is definitely going on, and it has to be analyzed.

I see three important events that are more or less related to the subject and that deserve the trade community's attention.

One, of course, was the massive mobilization in Seattle of people against global trade, which took place, paradoxically, in a city that is the hometown of Microsoft—practically the symbol of the globalized economy—and of Boeing. I know that most of those marching were not from Seattle, but it is interesting to reflect on this paradox and on the growing dissatisfaction, here in the heartland of globalization, with the painful aspects of the global economy.

Rubens Ricupero is secretary general of the United Nations Conference on Trade and Development.

The second important event has to do with Microsoft itself—and the recent decision in the antitrust case against it. There are people in the United States who say this particular period of history reminds them of the end of the last century, another era of rapid growth in the American economy. There were many imbalances, many crises. It was the robber baron period, the time when the large corporations were founded. And then the tide began to turn. We had antitrust legislation, Teddy Roosevelt, and the populist movement, all of them culminating in the New Deal. Perhaps this Microsoft decision signals an equally important change: a need to deal with globalization in a better way. Dissatisfaction with globalization is here to stay, but we have to find a way to channel it properly.

The third significant event in my opinion was the breakthrough regarding China's accession to the WTO. Of course, further negotiations are pending, but it is highly significant that the twentieth century ended with the removal of the last major obstacles to China's reintegration not only into the global economy but into the international system as a whole. This is a process that started 30 years ago with the initiatives taken by Nixon and Kissinger and is only now coming to fruition.

While all three of the events I mentioned deal with globalization, the first two are more concerned with the need to find remedies for globalization's ill effects, whereas the third represents an entirely different perspective. Only the third touches directly on a developing country. It is interesting that the backlash against globalization is particularly strong in the industrial world. I am not saying that problems do not exist in the developing world—they do exist and are very serious indeed. But for many developing countries, the priority seems to be to avoid being left out of the growing integration of the world economy. As an African prime minister put it, there is only one thing worse than globalization, and that is to be left outside it—to be even more marginalized by it. That is not to underplay or underestimate the pain of globalization but only to comment on the symbolism of China's movement toward integration into the world economy as the last century drew to a close.

The trade community sometimes labors under the wrong impression that the best path for developing countries is to integrate as rapidly and as fully as possible. This is a mistake, because what counts is not the quantity of integration but the quality. There is such a thing as too much integration of a bad kind.

Take an example from my own country, Brazil. For about 350 years— most of our colonial and monarchical history—Brazilians were fully and perfectly integrated into the world trading system because they exported the totality of their sugar and coffee crops. But this integration was achieved through a perverse mechanism—the Brazilian *latifundia*, or plantation system, and African slavery. So the same forces that integrated Brazil into the world economy disintegrated it domestically. To this day, Brazil's worst problems can be traced back to that bad type of integration.

What the world needs is virtuous integration through trading systems, whereby countries can start with just a few commodities and work their way upward, capturing growing shares of added value, acquiring skills and technologies, and generating jobs with good wages. This is what happened in Japan, Singapore, and the Republic of Korea 100 years ago. Unfortunately, there are very few examples of success in this field, perhaps not more than half a dozen. So how can we make this success more universal, shared by a much larger number of countries? This is the basic problem.

It would be useful at this point, in order to avoid any misunderstanding, to explain where I personally stand, as well as the rest of the staff at the UN Conference on Trade and Development (UNCTAD). First, we believe that developing countries badly need a rules-based multilateral trading system. They probably need it more than other countries because they are weak. Second, we believe that international trade has the potential to become one of the most powerful tools for development, as we have seen in the case of China. Third, we no longer believe, as we did some 25 years ago, that developing countries should set up a parallel, rival trading system—a sort of utopian, alternative trading system. We know very well that there is no alternative to the current one, and we have to try to make the best of it. This does not mean developing countries should passively accept the system as it is, in terms of the decision-making process and particularly in terms of the imbalances that have accumulated over the years.

When I speak of imbalances, I know that some of my friends in the WTO and the leaders of the old General Agreement on Tariffs and Trade (GATT) feel a bit uncomfortable, as if I were suggesting there was some sort of ideological conspiracy against developing countries. But that is not what I am suggesting; I am only speaking of facts. For most of the history of the trading system, the old GATT was more like a club of a very few countries, most of them industrial. Their priority in the early 1960s was the reduction of industrial tariffs, so to some extent it is only natural that areas such as agriculture and textiles and clothing, where those countries were not competitive, were left outside the system. One does not need to be a Marxist or resort to conspiracy theories to understand that. This system was gaining ground during the establishment of the European Common Market, which was built on the basis of a common agricultural policy. That fact also contributed to agriculture's absence from the multilateral trade system negotiations.

Yet despite the underlying official philosophy supporting free trade and free-market theory, this exclusion was not produced through market forces. It was contrary to the market; it turned the market upside down. It came about through massive state intervention, and it practically reversed all the predictions of reputable economists at the turn of the century. Who would have believed 100 years ago that Europe would now be one of the largest agricultural exporters? Belgium and Luxembourg together, for example, are among the top 10 agricultural exporters; Argentina is not. How can one explain that? Is it the market? Can trade theory explain that? Let us admit there is a difference between what we write and what we believe in theoretical terms and what we do in practice.

In Seattle I saw my old friend, former US Trade Representative Carla Hills, and this reminded me of my first interview with her after my appointment as Brazil's ambassador to the United States after my transfer from Geneva, where I had been the chairman of the GATT Contracting Parties. I arrived in Washington in early September 1991 and went to pay my respects to her, imagining that I would be well received because of Brazil's efforts to eliminate its import restrictions. Instead, she gave me a full dressing-down about all Brazil's vices and problems and explained how Brazil was shooting itself in the foot by not recognizing all the marvelous things that could be brought about by the efficient allocation of resources. "Well, Mrs. Hills," I responded, "I have only one question to put to you, and if you can give me a satisfactory answer, I will be very happy. Can you please show me the chapter in David Ricardo or Adam Smith where they explicitly exclude frozen concentrated orange juice from those wonderful things you were telling me about? Because I can't sell my orange juice here." And she laughed and said, "When it comes to orange juice, the problem is not David Ricardo but Representative Sam Gibbons," who chaired the House trade subcommittee and also represented the interests of Florida.

I lost touch with this problem for many years, but recently it came to my attention that orange juice is no longer among Brazil's 10 leading exports to the United States. The tariff in the United States is quite high—about $436 per ton. Even after the Uruguay Round, that rate is coming down extremely slowly. So the Brazilian producers gave up. They decided it was better to join the bandwagon and invest in Florida. And now, despite the fact that Brazil supplies 53 percent of world output in orange juice, the Brazilian crushers are producing more than 30 percent of Florida's orange juice. Even worse, they are considering using Florida as their export base to the European Union because when they export from Brazil they have to present 19 documents to comply with phytosanitary regulations, whereas when they export from Florida they need only one. It is a clear case of import substitution.

I had to contain myself when US Commerce Secretary William Daley addressed those gathered in Seattle, because I have personally suffered from the application of antidumping legislation against Brazilian steel. One of the most glaring examples of violations of the Uruguay Round is the recent agreement signed a few months ago by the Department of Commerce with three of the leading Brazilian steel exporters. It was a so-called voluntary export restriction agreement—precisely the "gray area" kind of agreement outlawed in the Uruguay Round.

I do not deny that the United States is one of the most open markets in the world, and Brazilians have benefited from that. Yet whenever the United States has a problem in sensitive areas, it, too, deviates from the rules of free trade. Even as US negotiators propose the US liberalization of agriculture, terrible legislation protecting sugar and tobacco, for example, remains on the books.

Secretary Daley spoke eloquently about the US market being penetrated by foreign garments, and that is true. But it is also true that the dismantling of the Multifiber Arrangement is proceeding at a snail's pace. Recent data published by the Textile Exporters Association in Geneva show that although the transition period for dismantling that arrangement is 70 percent complete, only 6 percent of the items in value terms have been liberalized—very little indeed.

Such problems make it difficult for developing countries to believe in the essential fairness of the system. The industrial countries have enjoyed long transition periods in their areas of interest, but this has not been the case for all countries. Let me give two examples.

The first waiver in agriculture was granted to the United States, not to Europe, in the early 1950s. That was the origin of agriculture's exclusion from the system's disciplines. The first waiver in cotton textiles, which later evolved into the Multifiber Arrangement, was also granted to the United States, in the final years of the 1950s. Yet, as we heard from Secretary Daley, the United States nearly a half century later is still not ready to fully liberalize textiles. Similarly, the Europeans are not ready to liberalize agriculture. These are the same nations that deem as too lenient the granting of more than five years for developing countries to adapt to far-reaching changes in intellectual property rights. Is this not imbalance? If not imbalance, then what would you call it?

This is the problem: the system has been shaped according to industrial countries' priorities. The most glaring example of imbalance is the fact that industrial countries to this day can freely, massively subsidize their exports of agricultural products while putting in the nonactionable category, or the "green box" category, their industrial subsidies—for research and development, equipment to reduce pollution, EU regional development—whereas most of the subsidies to which developing countries once resorted have been outlawed. My own country, Brazil, has had difficulty exporting airplanes because of subsidies aimed at equalizing interest rates for export credits. These subsidies were condemned by a WTO panel, whereas the peace clause is protecting European agriculture.

To deserve the name "development round," future negotiations would at a bare minimum have to redress those imbalances. Specifically, they would first have to eliminate the most glaring example of imbalance: the freedom of developed countries to massively subsidize their exports of agricultural products and to place their industrial subsidies in the nonactionable category. Second, they should accelerate the dismantling of the Multifiber Arrangement, under which only 6 percent of the value of restricted items has been liberalized so far. Third, it is time to get rid of tariff peaks and tariff escalation for a large array of products in which developing countries are competitive and to grant bounded free market access to developing-country exports.

There is no alternative to the multilateral trading system, but this does not mean the world must resign itself to the current imbalance. Two decades after the Tokyo and Uruguay Rounds, the vast majority of developing countries have ended up with more trade deficits—3 percent more than in the 1970s—and less economic growth—2 percent less than before. This is in part the result of inadequate domestic policies, although most of those nations have carried out serious adjustment programs and, after the rapid opening of these markets, can no longer be called free riders. There are other reasons: the sluggish growth of these economies and the import demand of advanced countries, the fall in commodity prices, and the consequent deterioration in terms of trade. But a significant cause of this worrisome state is certainly the asymmetries in the balance of mutual rights and obligations, including market access. This must finally be set right.

There are only two options before us. The first is to persist with the mercantilist approach of pressuring developing countries to further open markets that will soon become nonexistent, as those nations will not be able to get the resources they need through exports to pay for their imports. The second is a "lift all boats" strategy that will allow developing economies to export their way out of poverty and underdevelopment, earning them the money to finance their imports of capital goods and technology from industrial countries, without increasing their debt. I hope that we will choose the second road, the only one that can close the "legitimacy gap" and update the old UNCTAD slogan "trade, not aid" with two new formulas: "market access, not speculative capital and debt" and "trade, not hot money."

Let me conclude by asking that you not interpret my statements as aggressive. We at UNCTAD really believe that the system can be improved, and we have to work in that direction from inside the system. Two years ago we launched what we call the "positive agenda." That is, instead of complaining, developing countries should take a proactive attitude. They should put their proposals on the table and negotiate. I am glad to report that, partly as a result of our efforts, of nearly 250 proposals placed on the table in Geneva in preparation for the Seattle ministerial meeting, about 51 percent came from developing countries. This was the first time in history there has been such a result, and I hope it heralds more balanced results in future trade negotiations.

6

Developing Countries' Interests in a "Development Round"

JAYASHREE WATAL

For many decades, developing countries were marginal players in the rounds of multilateral trade negotiations in the General Agreement on Tariffs and Trade (GATT). Instead of aggressively seeking market access in the industrialized world, these countries defensively sought special and differential treatment on commitments to open their markets, and they obtained marginal trade preferences or concessions on a nonreciprocal basis. Not surprisingly, even while they were "free riding" by virtue of the GATT's most favored nation (MFN) principle, they received few concessions of specific interest to them.

The Uruguay Round marked a watershed in the participation of developing countries in the trading system. For the first time, developing-country participants chose to strike bargains on the basis of reciprocity. By and large, they committed themselves to lowered industrial and agricultural tariffs, accepted stringent disciplines in new areas such as intellectual property, and opened up some of their services sectors in return for improved and more secure market access for their exports, particularly for agricultural products and clothing. The new World Trade Organization (WTO) subjected these commitments to a stricter and more effective dispute settlement mechanism, one that developing countries have been increasingly using. Estimates of developing-country gains from these negotiations reveal a mixed picture but overall fairly significant benefits (Martin and Winters 1996).

Jayashree Watal was formerly a director in the Trade Policy Division of the Ministry of Commerce in the government of India and is now a visiting fellow at the Institute for International Economics from the Indian Council for Research in International Economic Relations (ICRIER), New Delhi. Comments from Kimberly Ann Elliott, Atul Kaushik, Aaditya Mattoo, and Jeffrey Schott helped improve earlier versions. Views, interpretations, errors, and omissions remain those of the author.

Yet as the Uruguay Round accords are implemented, developing countries perceive that, in the mercantilist bargaining exercise of trade negotiations, they were losers. This perception arises partly from the fact that implementation of WTO commitments has been more costly than anticipated and partly from the belated realization that they had accepted fairly weak commitments in agriculture and textiles while making substantially stronger ones, especially in new areas such as intellectual property. Moreover, the clauses on special and differential treatment incorporated in these agreements only give time derogations or call for "best endeavor"-type commitments. This is, perhaps, why the heads of the WTO and the World Bank have coined the phrase "Development Round" to emphasize that the new WTO round of trade negotiations must do more to benefit developing countries.

This chapter examines the main interests of developing countries in a new Development Round, in light of the failed third WTO ministerial conference at Seattle at the end of 1999. It concludes that while developing countries have actively participated in the preparations, they may well fritter away costly negotiating capital in making too many demands, some of which may not even be in their own best interests. With some rethinking, agreement on the agenda for a new round is possible and, indeed, is crucial to the success of the WTO and to the interests of developing countries.

Pre-Seattle Initiatives by Developing Countries

Trade experts have often lamented developing countries' lack of preparation in trade negotiations and have recommended that, rather than seeking special concessions, they should become equal partners in such negotiations with a proactive approach to the identification of their own interests (Srinivasan 1998). Developing-country trade negotiators seem to have taken this advice seriously during the preparations for the Seattle meeting. They were willing, and better prepared, to bring to the table their own agenda than they had been during earlier negotiations. They demanded improved market access for their exports to counterbalance proposals made by industrialized countries, particularly the United States and the European Union, on expanding the WTO agenda to include new issues.

Thus preparations for the WTO ministerial meeting at Seattle marked a departure from the past in terms of participation by developing and least-developed members of the WTO. Of the more than 200 written proposals submitted to the WTO General Council in Geneva over the year before the Seattle meeting, about one-half came from developing and least-developed countries. More than 60 percent of the developing-country members of the WTO, including some recognized by the WTO as least developed, submitted one or more written proposals. This was an unprecedented level of participation, particularly for the smaller countries in Africa, Central America, and the Caribbean. Many of these countries grouped together either along the lines of existing regional trading arrangements (RTAs), such as Mercosur or the Andean Community, or regionally, such as the African Group, led by Kenya. Other proposals submitted by developing-country groups cut across continents.

In addition, much greater regional and international coordination of negotiating positions among developing countries took place before Seattle, for example, through the Caribbean Regional Negotiating Machinery and the G-15 meetings (Schott 1999b). This does not mean that developing countries were able to form a common position. Indeed, the interests and priorities of developing countries in the WTO are extremely varied and probably increasingly divergent (Krueger 1999). In some cases, these countries are part of alliances that include developed countries, such as, for example, the Cairns Group of agricultural exporters.

Nevertheless, developing countries do have some common interests, as their proposals for agenda items of a new round have shown. Not surprisingly, many of the developing-country proposals focused on problems arising out of the implementation of the Uruguay Round accords. Developing countries wanted modifications in a wide range of existing agreements to take into account their trade interests or special problems, including the "operationalizing" of special and differential treatment provisions. Some suggestions for this included more time to implement some of the past commitments, while others emphasized more technical and financial assistance. They also introduced new subjects into the WTO such as trade and debt, transfer of technology, protection of traditional knowledge, bioresources, and geographical indications on products originating in their countries.

Unfortunately, there are serious disadvantages in placing such a large number of proposals on the table:

- they spread already scarce negotiating and research expertise thinly over too many areas,

- priorities become blurred and focus is lost as the negotiating agenda is overburdened with unnecessary clutter, and

- they allow other WTO members to pick the easier ones to adopt and then claim that they have come more than halfway.

Even more unfortunately, the content of some of the demands made reveals a lack of adequate reflection. For instance, many of the demands on "operationalizing" special and differential treatment in existing agreements were especially naïve, and it is unclear what developing countries aimed to achieve. So where do the interests of developing countries really lie and what should they do?

Principal Interests on the Seattle Agenda

The proposed agenda for the new round that was to have been launched at Seattle can be placed under four broad categories:

- the built-in agenda—that is, provisions agreed to be revisited under the terms of the Uruguay Round agreements,

- new issues introduced or agreed upon as subjects for further discussion at the first WTO ministerial conference, held in Singapore,

- issues introduced in the preparations for Seattle that arise from implementation of Uruguay Round agreements, and

- other "new" issues proposed for discussion and negotiation in the WTO.

It is likely that these categories will be encompassed within the agenda of any future WTO round.

Built-in Agenda

There are three major sectors in which negotiations mandated by the Uruguay Round began in 1999 or 2000: agriculture, services, and intellectual property. However, substantive negotiations in these sectors will have to be part of a new overall round in order to make any progress. While developing countries have actively pursued their interests in all three areas, the key interests of developing countries lie in the first two, and more particularly in agriculture.

Agriculture

On agriculture, the interests of developing countries are clearly divided into two groups: developing-country exporters of agricultural products and net food importers. The exporters, such as Argentina and Thailand, are part of the Cairns Group, which functioned effectively to demand reduced farm subsidies and increased market access in the Uruguay Round. This group continues to demand further reduction of domestic farm supports, the elimination of export subsidies, and substantial reductions in agricultural tariffs, but it faces opposition from the European Union, Japan, and others that prefer more modest reforms.

This nonetheless represents an area in which a group of developing countries not only have enormous trade interests but also occupy the high moral ground in terms of sound trade policy. Take the example of sugar: with liberalization in this highly protected sector, there would be a global gain of $6.3 billion, with substantial gains to developing countries in Latin America and East Asia (Borell 1999). Although negotiations on agriculture are to begin in Geneva even without a new round, no major movement is expected without it; in any case, a new round could give liberalizing countries the opportunity to make the necessary intersectoral trade-offs.

Net food importers, led by Egypt and Pakistan, while they do not oppose the demands of the Cairns Group, are asking for special exemptions to address their "nontrade concerns," such as food security and rural employment. These countries and their supporters, such as India, fear increased import bills. Besides, they usually have negative measures of support in place, and so they also want to be able to increase non-product-specific support, such as input subsidies, by an equivalent amount. There has been some sympathy for this group since the WTO meeting in April 1994 at Marrakesh, and the recently negotiated Food Aid Convention gives such countries priority in the allocation of food aid (Michalapoulos 1999). It is not clear, however, what these countries want in terms of contractual commitments in the WTO to provide technical and financial assistance. Some argue that removing distortions in the world agricultural markets would itself improve efficiency and welfare even in food-importing countries (Anderson 1999). In the case of India, there are some who recommend that it should negotiate from a position of strength and even join the Cairns Group (Gulati 1999). Certainly, the inclusion of nontrade concerns for this group of countries will have to be carefully circumscribed so as not to allow others to weaken their commitments to liberalize the agricultural sector even further.

Services

On services, developing countries gave little in terms of improved market access during and after the Uruguay Round and in return achieved little in terms of market access for their service providers. Rather than resist liberalization of domestic markets, developing countries need to take a more aggressive stance, demanding liberalization in foreign markets for services while making binding commitments to reform their own service sectors, as there are substantial gains for developing countries in following this strategy (Mattoo 2000). For example, developing countries should push for greater access abroad for their skilled and unskilled personnel who provide a variety of services. In a future round that seeks a "single undertaking"-type of agreement, developing countries can hope to gain more on the movement of natural persons than they had in the sectoral approach followed in the post-Uruguay Round period. The key to success may well lie in designing appropriate rules for domestic regulation of services sectors, on which negotiations have already begun in the WTO (Mattoo 2000).

Intellectual Property

Issues regarding the Agreement on Trade-Related Aspects of Intellectual Property Rights (TRIPs) also are included in the built-in agenda. Review of these began in 1999, and such issues would likely be incorporated in any new round of negotiations. Given developing countries' perception that TRIPs contains serious inequities, they can be expected to make a major attempt to correct these imbalances in future negotiations. There are basically three major proposals: extending the moratorium on "nonviolation" (that is, on making complaints about indirect violations of the agreement), establishing a multilateral system to recognize geographical names of wines and spirits, and including under TRIPs the availability of patents for certain biotechnological inventions, such as plants and animals, that can currently be excluded.

All these issues are likely to await final resolution in a new round, although the extension of the moratorium on nonviolation may take effect by default if no such complaints are brought before the WTO. Of these three issues, the one that raises the most concern for developing countries is that related to biotechnology. Developing countries do not want to go beyond existing TRIPs obligations and, indeed, view the built-in review clause as an opportunity to lower such standards. So far, there has been no demand for higher standards, primarily because of strong domestic interest groups in developed countries that support the developing-country positions. Developing countries have also tried to use this opportunity to raise other issues on the link between the Convention on Biological Diversity and TRIPs, such as the protection of indigenous or traditional knowledge (for example, of native medicinal plants) or access to genetic resources. They have also, as a part of the discussions on geographical names, demanded the extension of the scope of protection to products other than wines and spirits. In this, they are opposed strongly by the United States and others, including some developing countries from Latin America.

There is a need for careful reflection on these demands, as a reopening of TRIPs could mean jeopardizing the considerable leeway that currently exists for excluding certain biotechnological inventions and imposing certain attenuating policy measures such as compulsory licenses. It is not at all evident that examination in the WTO of traditional knowledge issues will actually lead to any agreement to protect it, much less to the "green gold" benefits that developing countries expect to see. Technological developments in combinatorial chemistry and biotechnology have made corporations less dependent on source countries and even on intellectual property protection. Furthermore, it is unclear whether extended protection of geographical indications would yield substantive benefits, considering that no major benefits have yet accrued through the wine and spirits provisions agreed to in the Uruguay Round. Notwithstanding the built-in review clauses, for the moment it is not in the interests of developing countries to spearhead amendments to TRIPs (Watal 2000).

Singapore Issues

The Singapore set of issues includes investment, competition policy, transparency in government procurement, and trade facilitation. At the first WTO ministerial conference at Singapore in December 1996, member countries agreed to include these subjects in WTO discussions, though not necessarily in future negotiations. In this block of issues, developing countries should be the *demandeurs* on competition policy, while engaging positively to incorporate their concerns in the negotiations on the other three subjects. There are clear trade-offs between this set of issues and those in the other three sets, particularly regarding agriculture, antidumping, and peak industrial tariffs.

By agreeing to new negotiations on transparency in government procurement and trade facilitation, developing countries could benefit by improving the efficiency and productivity of their own domestic systems and institutions. It is perhaps for this reason that most developing countries at Seattle supported the limited proposal on transparency in government procurement. India was the only one that did not join this consensus, probably more for strategic reasons, since working around any substantive problems would have been part of the negotiations. Similarly, the inclusion of negotiations on trade facilitation was not inherently controversial. This is one area where the WTO should work out a credible mechanism for providing technical assistance to needy developing and least-developed countries.

By contrast, there was still strong developing-country opposition at Seattle to the European and Japanese proposal to launch negotiations on trade and investment. Most were in favor of continuing the study process begun at Singapore on both this subject and competition policy. Some were willing to agree to launch such negotiations by the fourth ministerial conference. Indeed, inter- and intragroup differences between developed and developing countries are wide but not impossible to bridge (Graham, forthcoming). Moreover, reducing distortions in investment flows, by, for example, restricting locational subsidies and incentives, is in the interests of these countries and can help avoid wasteful competition for foreign investment (Moran 1998), although it is highly unlikely that a WTO agreement can achieve this (Hoekman and Saggi 1999). Finally, strategic engagement on this issue may force the European Union and Japan to be more forthcoming on agriculture (Anderson

1999). The eventual compromise to be made on this subject in setting a new round's agenda cannot completely overlook developing-country concerns about the need to regulate investment inflows, allow countries to define the sectors they want to open up (as in the General Agreement on Trade in Services, or GATS), and incorporate other developmental considerations. However, the more developing countries are prepared to give in this area, the more they can demand and obtain elsewhere.

It is not clear whether negotiations can be launched on competition policy, since the United States and many of the developing countries are opposed to it. Sensibly, negotiations on competition policy should be launched at the same time as those on investment. Although many developing countries are still unsure of the implications, an eventual agreement in the WTO could benefit them by disciplining transfer pricing and other restrictive practices of large multinational companies that so far are outside the purview of WTO rules and beyond the limited bargaining power of even the larger host developing countries. It is for these and other reasons that developing countries should actually be *demandeurs* in this area. Developing countries that are unsure of this strategy should use the time before the launch of a new round to study this subject, although they will have adequate opportunities, even during the negotiations, to study specific issues further and incorporate their interests in the WTO before finally committing to any binding obligations. On the whole, the Singapore set of issues should not cause serious problems for developing countries, provided their other substantive trade concerns are met.

Implementation Issues

The general dissatisfaction among developing countries on implementation of existing WTO agreements has led to a plethora of proposals covering many issues. Most of these seek special concessions or extension of time limits. This section deals with only three of the most important areas of dissatisfaction: textiles and clothing, antidumping, and TRIPs. Again, the efforts of developing countries need to be focused on obtaining substantive benefits from a rewriting of the rules and not on peripheral issues of time derogations or other less meaningful concessions.

The way some developed countries are implementing the Agreement on Textiles and Clothing angers the textile-exporting developing countries (see Rubens Ricupero's chapter in this volume). Therefore, it is natural that in the run-up to Seattle, developing countries aggressively demanded a revision of this agreement to accelerate the liberalization of existing quotas (now due to expire in January 2005) and to agree not to use antidumping measures for at least two years thereafter. Yet at Seattle, there was strong resistance by the United States and others to reopening this issue. All that developed countries were willing to concede was the consideration of problems of small suppliers and least-developed countries. Unfortunately for developing countries, any new round is likely to end only after the textile quotas have been completely phased out. The major textile exporters should therefore refocus their demands on peak tariff reductions, safeguards, and antidumping action in this sector to ensure that Uruguay Round commitments are implemented fully in letter and in spirit. This sector is likely to be one of the focal points for the eventual trade-offs to be made in the next round.

The second area of focus should be reform of existing agreements on antidumping. Antidumping has become the protectionist's "weapon of choice" in many developed and developing countries alike, but for many reasons, developing-country exporters suffer disproportionately from the use of this weapon (Krueger 1999). They are demanding specific modifications based on their experiences, including prohibitions on investigating and penalizing the same product twice. The United States remains one of the countries least willing to renegotiate this agreement. Developing countries should not focus on special rules for developing-country exports but instead submit to common and stringent disciplines applicable to all. India's recent experience in unsuccessfully invoking the special provisions under the balance of payments safeguards of GATT Article XVIII:B should demonstrate conclusively to all developing countries the folly of demanding more such ineffectual clauses. Thus developing countries, while rightly seeking the tightening of provisions on antidumping, should be prepared to subject themselves to the same standards.

The Agreement on Trade-Related Aspects of Intellectual Property Rights (TRIPs) epitomizes what developing countries see as an iniquitous agreement and they want to use the new round to correct the imbalance. In addition to the demands raised in the context of the built-in agenda, they want extensions of transitional periods for a further five years and an agreement to examine the linkage of intellectual property rights to the transfer of technology. They have also raised the issue of access to essential medicines. As noted earlier, to the surprise of many there has been no clear demand on the part of technology-exporting countries to raise the level of intellectual property protection further in a new round. Yet it is clear that developing countries cannot obtain blanket extensions of transition periods. Developing countries may persuade WTO members to examine measures necessary to encourage the transfer of technology and know-how within the framework of TRIPs. But this may not be very useful, as it would only lead to hortatory language of the kind already in TRIPs. The same may be true on the issue of access to essential medicines, as TRIPs already allows a number of policy measures in this regard. A reopening of TRIPs for these hortatory additions would also give developed countries the opportunity to enhance TRIPs standards as a result of the built-in review clauses and new developments elsewhere, notably at the World Intellectual Property Organization (WIPO).

Overall, it is unlikely that developing countries would have net gains in reopening TRIPs (Watal 2000).

Other Proposed "New" Issues

There are some residual but crucial issues that do not fit with those examined above. Of this set, the issue of crucial importance to developing countries is new negotiations on industrial tariffs, with the aim of reducing peak tariffs on products they export. They also need to lock in current openness in electronic commerce, as it presents them with tremendous opportunities. Contrary to conventional wisdom, the dangers of agreeing to discussions on labor and environmental standards may be exaggerated, in light of recent developments in the WTO and the International Labor Organization (ILO). In contrast, the special package of assistance to least-developed countries needs to be evaluated carefully, lest it turn out either to deliver insubstantial benefits or to deliver them at great cost to other poor countries.

Many WTO members, both developed and developing, have demanded industrial tariff negotiations. Developing countries would gain both in terms of increased market access and in terms of reducing their own much higher tariff levels. It is time for the WTO membership to bind such reductions on currently applied tariffs and not on the notional, higher, previously bound rates. However, for the outcome to be beneficial to developing-country exporters, it would have to include the lowering of peak tariffs in industrialized countries. This is a difficult task on account of the resistance from strong protectionist lobbies in those countries (Schott 1999a). Nevertheless, this should be the principal demand of developing countries in this block of issues.

On electronic commerce, the proposal at Seattle was only to continue the moratorium on tariffs, a situation unchanged from the earlier commitment and one that may well be agreed to before any new round, along with other such extensions. Although developing countries are at present insignificant users of electronic commerce, with the right policy measures they could gain in this area. Certainly, the moratorium may be somewhat of a nonissue on products delivered over the Internet if it remains technologically difficult to impose customs duties (see chapter by Catherine L. Mann and Sarah Cleeland Knight). Developing countries may find it more advantageous to obtain commitments on ensuring current openness—for example, binding national treatment and MFN under GATS (Mattoo 2000)—rather than oppose the moratorium issue. Nonetheless, developing countries have demanded that such an extension be linked with an agreement to provide them with technical assistance in this area. It is not clear how such commitments could be defined and monitored in the WTO. This has proved very difficult in another area, TRIPs.

The United States has long desired a WTO agreement on trade and "core" labor standards. In the negotiations at Seattle, a proposal involving a four-organization discussion and a one-time report was actively considered. The differences lay in the procedural detail of this proposal. Nevertheless, it is unclear whether developing countries could agree to it, as it presents some danger of continued work in the WTO on this subject with eventual trade sanctions. However, it is important to remember that this has not happened so far, even with the much stronger mandate, agreed to at Marrakesh in 1994, on trade and environment. It is also unclear whether the United States would accept such a watered-down proposal. In the end, developing countries should keep an open mind on this subject, as much would depend upon the overall deal agreed to in launching the new round. However, whatever the outcome in the WTO, developing countries cannot credibly oppose measures taken in the ILO to strengthen the ability of that organization to promote labor standards agreed to internationally (see chapter by Kimberly A. Elliott).

On trade and environment, the WTO Appellate Body had already satisfied, in part, the US demand to legitimize unilateral trade measures to enforce environmental standards in the famous shrimp-turtle case. The European Union and its supporters may demand some language to incorporate this new trend in any new trade round. Indeed, there may be a case for resolving this issue through negotiations rather than leaving it to decisions by panels and the Appellate Body. However, the resource-constrained developing-country negotiators may find that spreading such discussions over different bodies of the WTO—called "mainstreaming" in WTO jargon—may be disadvantageous for substantive as well as procedural reasons. New negotiations on fisheries subsidies, as proposed by the United States and others, may actually be desirable for developing countries and should not, in any case, pose serious problems.

A very important issue at Seattle for the least-developed-country members was completion of a package of duty-free access, along with financial and technical assistance for these countries as a part of the Integrated Framework for Trade-Related Technical Assistance. This work was initiated in the first WTO conference and involves at least five other international organizations, including the World Bank. Such a package was close to finalization at Seattle, with the European Union signaling its willingness to give duty-free access to essentially all products from these countries by 2005 (Moore 2000). However, the details of this package are not yet clear, and there are likely to be some sectoral carve-outs for agriculture and textiles and clothing. Some have characterized the proposal as unhelpful to the growth of these countries and as amounting to "nothing more than a small bribe" to make these countries accept the link between trade and labor and environmental standards (letter by T. N. Srinivasan to the *Financial Times*, 17 February 2000, p. 16). There is also an element of "robbing Peter to pay Paul," since the benefit to least-developed countries will be at the cost of lost markets for other poor developing countries and not at the cost of the "donors" of such largesse. That said, such a package of measures, if appropriately designed, along with other concessions to developing countries, may be necessary to rebuild the confidence of developing countries in the WTO and to create a positive environment in which to launch a new round.

Conclusion

Overall, developing countries would do well to focus on their major demands in agriculture, services, industrial tariffs, antidumping, and with care, the integrated framework, rather than frittering their efforts on a range of issues related to special and differential treatment or on other illusory benefits. These countries have, perhaps for the first time, established their combined presence with a positive agenda that gives them some stake in the success of a future WTO ministerial conference. They may again go home disappointed if they (and their trading partners) are unwilling to prioritize, negotiate, and make concessions on issues of crucial interest to each other. However, if they succeed in launching a true "development round," there are gains to be made by all.

If WTO members try and fail once again to launch a new round, it will be a major blow to the credibility of the organization. This is in nobody's interest, least of all those developing and least-developed countries that need the WTO to effectively enforce the agreed rules. Those that are not part of any large, working preferential trade arrangement would be the worst off. These countries particularly include those in South Asia and Northeast Asia. Indeed, it is these countries that must ensure that the WTO succeeds, as regionalism would further reduce market access for their exports. Evidently, even the world's largest trading nations have high stakes in an effective multilateral institution, and today they need it more than ever before to arbitrate their trade disputes. Thus, in the final analysis, Seattle failed but the WTO must succeed, and for this to happen, the launch of a "development round" is essential.

References

Anderson, Kym. 1999. Agriculture, Developing Countries, and the WTO's Millennium Round. Paper presented at the Conference on Agriculture and the New Trade Agenda in the WTO 2000 Negotiations, 1-2 October, WTO, Geneva.

Borell, Brent. 1999. Sugar: The Taste Test of Trade Liberalization. Paper presented at the Conference on Agriculture and the New Trade Agenda in the WTO 2000 Negotiations, 1-2 October, WTO, Geneva.

Graham, Edward M. N.d. *Fighting the Wrong Enemy: Antiglobal Activists and Multinational Enterprises*. Washington: Institute for International Economics. Forthcoming.

Gulati, Ashok. 1999. Agriculture and the New Trade Agenda in the WTO 2000 Negotiations: Interests and Options for India. Draft, Institute for Economic Growth, Delhi.

Hoekman, Bernard, and Kamal Saggi. 1999. Multilateral Disciplines for Investment-Related Policies. http://www.worldbank.org/research/trade.

Krueger, Anne O. 1999. *The Developing Countries and the Next Round of Multilateral Trade Negotiations*. World Bank Working Paper. http://www.worldbank.org/research/trade.

Martin, Will, and L. Alan Winters, eds. 1996. *The Uruguay Round and Developing Countries*. Cambridge, UK: Cambridge University Press.

Mattoo, A. 2000. Developing Countries in the New Round of GATS Negotiations: From a Defensive to a Proactive Role. *World Economy*, forthcoming.

Michalapoulos, Constantine. 1999. *Developing-Country Goals and Strategies for the Millennium Round*. World Bank Working Paper. http://www.worldbank.org/research/trade.

Moore, M. 2000. Prospects for the Developing Countries in the Next Round: Address to the Development Committee of the European Parliament, 21 February.

Moran, Theodore, H. 1998. *Foreign Direct Investment and Development*. Washington: Institute for International Economics.

Panagariya, Arvind. 1999. The Millennium Round and Developing Countries: Negotiating Strategies and Areas of Benefit. Draft, University of Maryland-College Park.

Schott, Jeffrey J. 1999a. Prospects for New WTO Trade Negotiations. Draft, Institute for International Economics.

Schott, Jeffrey J. 1999b. Toward the Seattle WTO Ministerial. Draft, Institute for International Economics.

Srinivasan, T. N. 1998. *Developing Countries and the Multilateral Trading System*. Boulder, CO: Westview Press.

Watal, Jayashree. 2000. *Intellectual Property Rights in the World Trade Organization: The Way Forward for Developing Countries*. New Delhi: Oxford University Press; London: Kluwer Law International.

7

Seattle and Beyond:
Developing-Country Perspectives

A. V. GANESAN

Developing countries are fairly conscious of the fact that openness to the outside world in general, and to trade and investment in particular, is critical to their economic development. Their policies are increasingly focusing on how they can best integrate with the global economy and how they can secure access to and compete effectively in world markets. Managing globalization, rather than ignoring or resisting it, is now a central element of their development strategies.

In this context, developing countries have a high stake in the evolving multilateral trading system under the World Trade Organization (WTO). They need a transparent and rules-based trading system and an effective dispute settlement mechanism even more than the developed countries. Their concern is not so much that the WTO is moving toward freer trade or that its agenda is expanding. The policymakers in the developing world well understand both the case for open trade and the need to expand the multilateral trade agenda. But these countries are worried about the direction in which the multilateral trading system seems to be moving.

They have three major concerns, which are interconnected: First, they perceive that the system is becoming less fair and more inequitable as the needs and concerns of the developing countries fail to receive the attention they deserve. Second, the trade agenda is being expanded to incorporate only issues in which developed countries are interested. And third, the multilateral trade rules are increasingly becoming a codification of developed-country policies, laws, and regulations. Consequently, the developing world sees the emerging trade agenda as being shaped

A. V. Ganesan is a former commerce secretary for the government of India.

by the special interest groups of the developed world while their needs and interests are ignored.

This perception must be dispelled if the cause of open trade is to be furthered and a vibrant multilateral trading system is to be established under the WTO. In order for this to happen, the agenda for future negotiations must be balanced and must take into account the interests and concerns of all countries, especially the developing countries. The basic principles of balance and fairness should pervade all areas of the new agenda, be it market access, new issues, or new rules and disciplines.

Specifically, developing countries are most interested in enhancing market access for their goods and services and in increasing flexibility in the implementation of the WTO rules. They are apprehensive, in particular, about incorporating nontrade issues within the WTO.

Market Access

Equal attention must be paid to enhancing market access opportunities for the goods and services that developing countries would like to export to industrialized-country markets. Efforts to introduce zero- or low-tariff regimes are now concentrated on products and sectors that are only of interest to developed countries. Yet across industrial products, agriculture, and services sectors, developing countries continue to encounter trade restrictions in developed-country markets for primarily political reasons. Second, the minimization of nontariff measures that can impede developing-country exports should receive as much attention as lowering tariff barriers. Third, and most important, there must be a holistic evaluation of the market access opportunities provided to the developing countries taking all the four components together: industrial tariffs, agriculture, rules and disciplines pertaining to nontariff measures, and services. They all have a bearing on the market access opportunities available to developing countries. But at present, the four components are viewed and negotiated in isolation, with the focus being on industrial tariffs and services of interest to the developed countries. Liberalization of the trade in agriculture, in which developing countries have considerable interest, is treated on a separate footing for various reasons. Nontariff measures such as antidumping or countervailing duty rules, measures to protect health, safety, and the environment, or even the rules and disciplines relating to intellectual property rights or performance requirements are regarded more as issues falling within the rule-making area, although they have considerable implications for developing-country exports. It is therefore important that, while negotiations may take place by sector or by issue, there be an integrated evaluation at the end to assess how far the negotiations have contributed to or affected the export opportunities for developing countries.

New Issues

The industrialized countries' push to put nontrade issues on the WTO's agenda is a matter of deep concern to developing countries. Core labor standards, workers' rights, and child labor are at the top of the list of these issues. Their importance is not questioned. What is questioned is whether trade sanctions are the right instrument and whether the WTO is the right forum to deal with these issues. The question is also posed regarding the issue of environmental standards: the industrialized countries are seeking to obscure the line of demarcation between what can be legitimately addressed by multilateral trade rules and what is better left to be handled by other instruments or agencies. The fact that these are politically sensitive issues in industrialized countries can hardly be a ground for linking them to WTO rules. Developing countries have good reason to believe that these linkages will prove to be protectionist devices that will erode their competitive advantage.

Again, as regards new issues that are trade-related, there needs to be a proper balance between issues that are of interest to the developed world and those that are of concern to the developing countries. Some of the latter issues may fall under the category of review of existing agreements or implementation of existing agreements. Unless the "new issues" agenda demonstrates such a balance, the credibility of the multilateral trading system may be weakened.

Flexibility in Rules

It is important that developing countries be given sufficient flexibility in WTO rules to enable them to pursue policies that are best suited to their individual needs and conditions. A major deficiency in the existing system is that most of the Uruguay Round agreements allow developing countries a differential treatment only in the form of a longer transition period, while the substantive rules are kept the same for all countries. This "one size fits all" approach ignores not only the differences between developed and developing countries but also the heterogeneity among the developing countries themselves. Where essential, the substantive rules themselves should be different or the rules should allow adequate flexibility for countries to follow their own policies. The need for flexibility is particularly critical in regard to the new issues and new disciplines now being contemplated. Rightly followed, the concept of flexibility could allay the developing countries' apprehensions about the emerging multilateral trading system and may induce them to accept the inclusion of new trade-related issues on the WTO's agenda.

III

THE WTO AGENDA: EXISTING MANDATES

8

Agriculture and the Next WTO Round

TIMOTHY JOSLING

The Uruguay Round Agreement on Agriculture (URAA) mandated further negotiations by the end of 1999. WTO members agreed "that negotiations for continuing the process [of substantial progressive reductions in support and protection] will be initiated one year before the end of the implementation period [2000]" (Article 20, URAA). Agriculture is thus an integral part of the "built-in agenda" that was agreed on in the Uruguay Round and will be a central focus of attention in the post-Seattle WTO negotiations. But the agreement to hold negotiations does not ensure a speedy conclusion to the talks, nor does it restrict the agenda, though it provides a valuable starting point. In fact, the mandate itself offers the prospect of a contentious agenda by qualifying the process of reform with mention of "noontide concerns," thus ensuring that there is plenty of room for disagreement over the extent as well as the pace of market liberalization in agriculture. Japan and the European Union have both indicated that "noontide concerns" should be explicitly factored in to trade rules. For Europe, the concern is that payments tied to environmental and social goals (such as animal welfare) be allowed under trade rules even if they affect trade; for Japan, the basic question is whether self-sufficiency levels and social objectives can be taken into account in deciding on the levels of tariff protection.

The case for another round of agricultural trade talks in the WTO is easy to make, even if it were not mandated in the Uruguay Round agreement. Agricultural markets are protected by tariffs considerably higher than

Timothy Josling is professor and senior fellow at the Institute for International Studies at Stanford University, and author of Agricultural Trade Policy: Completing the Reform *(Washington: Institute for International Economics, 1998).*

those for almost all other goods.[1] These measures effectively tax consumers as well as other sectors of the economy that pay to support high-cost domestic agriculture. Developed countries can perhaps afford this expensive system of rural welfare payments and private-sector subsidies, but developing countries cannot. Moreover, the level of protection is very uneven within the agricultural sector, from relatively open access for tropical raw materials to high protection for many "sensitive" products such as milk, sugar, cotton, and rice, keeping too many of the world's scarce agricultural resources bottled up in markets that are chronically oversupplied. Protection also escalates with the level of processing, particularly in the markets for processed tropical products, preventing the development of value-added activities in developing countries. And finally, protection varies greatly among countries, leading to a much distorted pattern of agricultural trade. Much of the world's high-cost agriculture is located in a few industrial countries, to the detriment of their participation in the trade systems. The extra cost is likely to prove increasingly damaging to those economies as barriers in other sectors are removed.

The next round of agricultural talks should be facilitated both by the greater transparency in the trade system that was a major legacy of the Uruguay Round and by the considerable degree of preparation that countries have already achieved. The level of protection in markets is now much more apparent than it was at the start of the Uruguay Round. Tariffs are much easier to negotiate than nontariff barriers. Export subsidies and domestic support are codified in schedules and thus also straightforward to negotiate. The papers in the informal analysis and information exchange (AIE) process that has been pursued by the WTO Committee on Agriculture in Geneva have tackled many of the other issues, such as the administration of tariff rate quotas and the behavior of state trading enterprises, as well as some "new" topics such as "multifunctionality."[2] Countries know the issues and where their trading partners stand to a much greater extent than at the start of the Uruguay Round.

But although the economic case for pushing ahead with further trade liberalization is clear-cut and the technical aspects of the negotiations are well understood, the political context in which the talks are to take

---

1. Agricultural tariffs average about 40 percent (Josling 1998). Nonagricultural tariffs are below 5 percent for most developed countries and perhaps 15 percent on average for developing countries.

2. Multifunctionality refers to the importance of agriculture as a part of rural society and as a provider of environmental amenities in addition to the production of commodities. This self-evident proposition can sometimes be used as a pretext for arguing for higher protection at the border. In fact it supports the notion of decoupling farm support from the production of commodities and targeting such support to the provision of these other services.

place is becoming more complex. The next stages of agricultural reform will not be successful if there is not a significant opening of the high-cost markets. But this requires broad consensus among industrial countries on the desirability of such an opening. Currently agricultural trade leads to conflict as often as cooperation among industrial countries. Many of the most contentious trade disputes have revolved around agriculture, including the beef hormone and banana disputes that have strained transatlantic relations in recent years. Agreement on the modalities for the reduction of agricultural protection and the clarification of trade rules may be difficult to achieve in such a climate. The next stage in agricultural trade reform could fail to end in agreement as a result of squabbles among countries on issues peripheral to the main agenda.

These political difficulties were also apparent at the time of the Uruguay Round. Fundamental differences between the US and Cairns Group views on agricultural trade and those of the European Union and Japan held up progress in the round for several years. But in the end a framework was agreed on that offered the promise of resolving these differences. Negotiators initiated agricultural trade reform knowing that it would take a few more rounds of negotiations before the conditions of trade were similar to those in other sectors. But the politics of agricultural trade has taken on a new dimension since the Uruguay Round. At least three significant differences can be noted in the politics of agricultural trade, each of which will have an impact on whether further trade reform can be achieved at this time.

The first major difference is the globalization of the food system, which has brought a new set of actors and interests into the picture. The fact that the food system has "gone global" within the past decade extends the agenda beyond the conditions of trade in temperate-zone farm products to include issues such as competition policy, intellectual property, investment rules, and the harmonization of standards. But this has engaged the attention of a group of nongovernmental organizations (NGOs) that have previously taken little interest in agricultural trade issues. They tend to see the liberalization of agricultural markets as being the agenda of multinational corporations and inimical to their own environmental, social, and political objectives. Thus agriculture will be part of the "debate on globalization," both for the NGOs, who see an opportunity for a public show of strength, and for the WTO itself, which is particularly concerned not to lose the argument in the court of public opinion for lack of addressing the issues.

A second major difference is the increased interest of developing countries in the management and functioning of the trade system. In particular, developing countries have begun to take a much more active role in the WTO than they ever took in the GATT. Developing countries have a considerable stake in agricultural trade matters. Many are important exporters of agricultural products and would benefit from better market

access. Even those that import agricultural goods would be able to design their own agricultural development policies in a more predictable
environment if world agricultural markets reflected underlying production costs rather than political influence and government intervention.
But these countries also will face some difficult decisions as agricultural
trade liberalization advances in the WTO. In many cases their own tariffs on imports of agricultural products are high, leading to the prospect
of having to make significant cuts in the next round. Moreover, their
export access is often on concessional terms, implying some reduction in
the degree of preference as most favored nation (MFN) rates decline.
Developing countries undoubtedly have an opportunity to influence the
WTO agenda, and their views on agriculture could carry significant weight.

A third difference is the slackening of the pace of reform in agricultural policies. This is evident in the European Union, where a last-minute
intervention by Jacques Chirac blocked a reform package already agreed
on by the ministers of agriculture in March 1999. The EU Council instituted instead a weaker set of changes that has put the Union in a defensive position once again at the start of a trade round. In the United States,
where policy reform reached a high point with the Federal Agriculture
Improvement and Reform (FAIR) Act of 1996, Congress has not been
able to resist generous handouts for the past two years to farmers in
ways that are only loosely "decoupled" from world prices. So far the
reforms of the past 15 years have not been reversed, but the pace of
reform has slowed notably. It remains to be seen whether the international system of rules can give another boost to policy reform, or whether
we are about to see a period of backsliding toward the commodity-price
policies of earlier decades.[3]

The dominant question is therefore whether the path toward agricultural trade policy reform can be maintained in light of the changed circumstances and the different political constraints on the main participants.
Will a coalition form that can drive through significant liberalization in a
reasonable amount of time? Or will the debate shift to issues other than
trade liberalization and allow those who are not keen on further reform
to avoid significant market opening?

This chapter discusses the agenda items for the next round of agricultural talks. These include further improvements in market access, more
constraints on export subsidies, and the continued disciplines on domestic support as well as the related topic of sanitary and phytosanitary

---

3. There is an ongoing debate as to the influence of trade agreements on domestic agricultural policy decisions. A new book by Orden, Paarlberg, and Roe (1999) on US policy
argues that the FAIR Act was the product of domestic political circumstances and owes
little if anything to international trade rules. Coleman and Tangermann (1997) as well as
Swinbank and Tanner (1996) find strong influences from the Uruguay Round on domestic policy change in Europe.

standards. Since different groups see these agenda items very differently, an attempt will be made in the paper to match the agenda items with the different perspectives of interest groups and countries. In this way one can perhaps anticipate where the main controversies will be and what possible outcomes could emerge from the next three years of negotiations. Some of the different perspectives (i.e., the agendas for particular countries and interest groups) will be examined before turning to the agenda items as defined by the URAA.

Different Perspectives on Agricultural Trade

It is possible to distinguish four main perspectives that countries and nongovernmental interest groups bring to the discussion of agricultural trade. One is that of the need for continued reform of the trade system for agricultural products. From this perspective, the focus of the talks should be on further changes in the trade rules for agricultural products so as to bring these rules into line with those that operate for nonagricultural goods, and on a reduction of the levels of protection for temperate-zone farm products so as to allow an expansion of trade in these goods. The emphasis of the talks would therefore be on market access for cereals, oilseeds, dairy products, sugar, and meat, along with the possible elimination of export subsidies. The major agricultural exporting countries, including the United States and the Cairns Group, take this view. They argue that a further significant improvement in market access is necessary, together with an elimination of export subsidies and a tightening of the rules on domestic support. These countries would prefer to keep the post-Seattle agenda focused on these issues and are wary about "new" items that might divert attention from the task at hand.[4] This perspective is clearly in line with WTO tradition and seemed to be the dominant viewpoint until recently. Even many countries that were unhappy with such an emphasis agreed that that was the agenda. The EU Commission even formulated its proposals for internal agricultural policy and budget reform (Agenda 2000) on the assumption that this would be the probable outcome of the next round.

However, a second perspective on agricultural trade is rapidly emerging to complicate life for trade negotiators and absorb the attention of politicians. This perspective views the WTO as a body that is responsible for a set of issues related to environmental and food safety impacts of modern agriculture. This perspective is in part a consequence of the globalization of agriculture mentioned above, which brings with it the

---

4. These countries have some differences among themselves particularly on whether state trading export monopolies have an unfair advantage in world markets that constitute an export subsidy.

attention of those who see that trend as needing further regulation. Global trade rules offer both an additional opportunity to regulate and an additional challenge to local autonomy. In part it is a reflection of a series of unfortunate food safety incidents that appear to have shaken the faith of consumers in regulators, particularly in Europe. Thus the politics of globalization includes groups that see the WTO as having enviable legal instruments to be used to forge environmental policy and those that believe the organization should be weakened to prevent it from impinging on local decisions. Support for this perspective has been forthcoming from the European Union, in part because it deflects attention from the liberalization of market access as it begins to impinge on sensitive domestic interests, and in part because it faces internal pressures to broaden the agricultural trade agenda in this way. Even the United States is implicitly encouraging the broadening of the agenda by promoting more transparency and inclusiveness in the WTO process. But these governmental positions will be enthusiastically welcomed by NGOs for whom the opening of talks on agriculture present an ideal opportunity to discuss their agenda in a broader public debate.

The issue at the top of the list for these groups is that of the food safety and environmental impact of transgenic crops, and in particular the conditions under which countries can ban the import of genetically modified (GM) foods. The GM foods issue threatens to overshadow the first part of the talks. Conflicts over trade bans arising from health and environmental regulations would normally be dealt with under the Sanitary and Phytosanitary Standards (SPS) Agreement and the Agreement on Technical Barriers to Trade (TBT).[5] But the GM foods issue stretches the interpretation of these agreements and puts excessive strain on the development of international norms that may prove impossible at this early stage of introduction of the technology. Unless a way can be devised to contain the GM foods issue, it could easily derail the process of trade liberalization in agricultural markets.

A third perspective on agricultural trade policy reform is related to its impact on agricultural development in general and the place of developing countries in the trade system in particular. This perspective is gathering importance in part because of the increasing interest of developing countries in the WTO and in part because the future of much trade in "traditional" farm commodities will involve the developing countries

---

5. The SPS agreement deals specifically with regulations that countries impose to protect the health of plants, animals, and people, and requires risk assessments based on scientific evidence. The TBT agreement covers other types of regulation such as labeling and packaging. In both cases, countries are encouraged to enact regulations that disturb trade as little as possible. Banning GM foods on health grounds would fall under the SPS agreement; labeling of GM foods is a TBT issue. Banning GM organisms on environmental grounds would pose more of a problem for the trade rules, as it is not clear on what grounds one could challenge such a policy (see Nelson et al. 1999).

as either importers or exporters. This perspective is shaped by the views expressed by a group of developing countries concerned with the fact that they derived few benefits from the Uruguay Round but face the prospect of having to make yet further changes to their agricultural trade policies in the next round. This group includes large countries such as India and Pakistan that have to balance participation in trade with strong autarkic domestic forces. The emphasis of this group is to request a correction of what they see as an unbalanced Uruguay Round outcome before being required to participate in further liberalization. Developing countries that take this position have yet to articulate an alternative strategy and may never form a coalition strong enough to influence the agenda, but if they were to be joined by China, supported by Japan, or embraced by the globalization opponents, then they could have an impact on the outcome.

A fourth perspective on agricultural trade reform comes from a group of small economies that feel increasingly vulnerable in the global marketplace or that fear the adverse consequences of market disruption if they continue to open up their economies to trade. Many of these economies are also tied to industrial countries through nonreciprocal preference agreements that have already been ruled contrary to the WTO. These countries view the continuation of multilateral agricultural trade reforms is as much a threat as a benefit. They are highly dependent on trade, commonly exporting a small number of commodities, and often have relatively low import barriers. Their concerns are often linked to food security, and include the issues of food aid and of export embargoes, but have more broadly to do with the structure of trade relations. Unless these issues are resolved in the next round, there will be an increasing number of trade frictions among these countries and their industrial benefactors. On the other hand, the influence of these countries alone may be small, and their importance may rest in their support of or opposition to the positions of their industrial trade partners.

The Agenda for the Agricultural Negotiations

As a result of these various expectations, the agenda for the upcoming WTO negotiations on agricultural trade is becoming rather congested. Those interested in the continued reform of the trade rules emphasize the "core" issues, such as the liberalization of market access, the reduction or elimination of export subsidies, and the containment of domestic support that is given in a way that distorts trade. The general presumption is that the Uruguay Round set the rules but did not go far toward reducing protection. The main task of the next round is therefore to make significant progress toward the opening up of agricultural markets. These "core" issues are supplemented by others that have largely appeared as a result of the Uruguay Round Agreement on Agriculture. These include the administration of tariff rate quotas (TRQs) and the activities of state trading enterprises (STEs), both those that control imports and those that are engaged in export activities.[6]

For those governments and interest groups primarily concerned with environmental and food safety issues, by contrast, the "core" issues are of less interest. Instead, a rather different set of agenda items is important. These are closely related to agricultural trade though technically outside the Agreement on Agriculture. These issues include the trade conflicts over sanitary and phytosanitary measures and the potential conflict over GM foods as well as questions of intellectual property rights. For those concerned with developing-country agriculture, there are other issues as important as those in the core, including the question of whether to press for continued "special and differential treatment" in agricultural rules. For those countries concerned about food security, issues such as the need to control the use of export restrictions in times of shortage and the ability of countries to take action against imports that threaten to disrupt markets are important. In addition, the question of the future of trade preferences and the possibility of negotiating compensation for their removal are significant issues that should be on the table.

Market Access

The market access negotiations will be at the heart of the next agricultural round. The talks will not succeed unless substantial steps are taken to reduce the high levels of agricultural tariffs. With varying degrees of enthusiasm, countries have endorsed the objective of improving market access. The United States has called for an "ambitious" target for expansion of market access; the European Union admits that its export interests would be served by an opening of markets but cautions that the process will take time.[7] For the Cairns Group, the negotiations "must result in deep cuts to all tariffs, tariff peaks and tariff escalation."[8] Of the

---

6. Tariff rate quotas were introduced to ensure some minimum access in the cases where conversion of nontariff import measures to tariffs (tariffication) led to very high tariff levels, and also to preserve access under bilaterals and preferential schemes. Many of the nontariff barriers were being administered by state trading import agencies, and the TRQs were designed in many cases to open these markets.

7. The US position is contained in WTO documents WT/GC/W/107, 115, 286, 287, 288, and 290. The EU paper is WT/GC/W/273. The EU paper contains the intriguing statement that it should "pursue an active market access policy with a view to eliminating barriers to entry in certain third country markets."

8. See the Cairns Group "vision" statement, transmitted to the WTO as WT/L/263, and the subsequent communiqué from the Buenos Aires meeting of the Cairns Group, WT/L/312. The Cairns Group members are Argentina, Australia, Brazil, Canada, Chile, Colombia, Fiji, Indonesia, New Zealand, Paraguay, Philippines, South Africa, Thailand, Uruguay.

major players, Japan is naturally the most reticent, contributing only the observation that current tariff levels "reflect particular domestic situations" and that these circumstances should be given due consideration in the negotiations.[9] NGOs are generally less enamored with market access negotiations, associating such liberalization with globalization and the pressure from multinational firms for ever wider markets over which to spread fixed costs. To many of these pressure groups, market access is a part of the problem rather than the solution. Developing countries tend to stress the importance of expanding market access in the products of export interest to themselves.

Modalities for Tariff Reduction

The techniques of negotiating tariff reductions are well established.[10] One can choose between across-the-board tariff cuts or formulas that cut tariff peaks. One can focus on individual sectors (zero-for-zero arrangements) or agree on comprehensive coverage. One can use the "request and offer" method for identifying demands for market access, multilateralizing the results. One can attempt to reduce effective protection by making sure that processed-good tariffs come down at the same rate or faster than those for raw materials.

These methods of market access each have some merit but might not be adequate in themselves. This suggests that negotiators might try a "cocktail" of the various modalities.[11] Imagine agricultural tariffs divided into five categories. Low tariffs—those less than 5 percent—could be reduced to zero, as neither the level of protection nor the revenue collected is likely to be significant. Such nuisance tariffs could be removed with advantage, in agriculture as well as in other areas. Moderate tariffs—those of 5 to 40 percent—could be reduced by a further 36 percent, as in the Uruguay Round, or by the same percentage as other tariffs if the cuts are part of a more general negotiation. Tariffs above 40 percent are probably too high to yield to the same techniques as industrial tariffs; a combination of tariff cuts and TRQ increases might be needed. Thus for tariffs of 40 to 100 percent, the 36 percent cut could be augmented by an expansion of TRQs. For tariffs above 100 percent, some variant of the Swiss formula might be needed along with expansion of TRQs. And for tariffs above 300 percent, it might make more sense to conduct particular "request and offer" negotiations with principal (potential) suppliers.

---

9. The Japanese paper is document WT/GC/W/220.

10. For a discussion of tariff reduction options, see Josling and Rae (1999).

11. See Josling and Rae (1999) for an elaboration of this tariff-cutting technique.

Other Tariff Issues

In addition to the task of tariff level reduction, two other aspects of tariff rules will probably be discussed. One is the common phenomenon of bound rates of tariff that are considerably higher than the rates that are applied.[12] There have been suggestions that these gaps be reduced, for instance by binding the applied rates. But this causes understandable problems for the countries involved, which will argue that the applied rates have not been negotiated in the WTO and that therefore to bind these rates would be unfair to those who have undertaken unilateral liberalization. On the other hand, for those countries with such gaps, reducing the bound rate toward the applied rate is a way of getting "credit" for actions already taken.

The other aspect of tariff policy is the form of the tariff. The URAA mandated a tariff-only regime, but allowed some countries to concoct complex tariffs that involve reference prices and compound rates.[13] Moreover, the Blair House agreement between the United States and the European Union obliged the latter to impose a maximum duty-paid price for cereals that acts very much like the variable levies that were outlawed in the agreement. Many countries also would like to insist on the use of ad valorem tariffs rather than specific duties, which have a somewhat more protective impact when prices are low. The United States is calling for a simplification of complex tariffs; whether any country will take aim at de facto variable levies and specific tariffs is not so clear.

TRQ Expansion

One direct way to tackle the problem of the high levels of tariffs resulting from tariffication is to expand the guaranteed market access that forms a part of the provisions of the Agreement on Agriculture. Some position papers (though not that of the United States) mention the importance of expanding TRQs in the next round. The Cairns Group paper says that "trade volumes under tariff rate quotas must be increased substantially." Other countries suggest further improvements in the TRQ system in addition to the administration of the quotas (discussed below). Canada argues for the elimination of the within-quota tariff whenever the above-quota tariff is prohibitive (presumably to ensure that the quotas are filled, rather than merely increasing quota rents at the expense of government revenue). The same paper suggests the introduction of a TRQ whenever tariffs are higher than a specified level as well as increasing the product specificity of TRQs.

---

12. The US paper specifically mentions the "lowering of bound rates to eliminate the disparity between applied and bound rates."

13. The EU tariff schedule for fruits and vegetables includes tariffs conditional on whether the offer price is below or above a reference price (IATRC 1997).

Administering TRQs

As a number of countries recognize in their position papers, the issue of developing a more uniform system for the administration of the TRQs is one of the most urgent tasks for the new agricultural round. TRQs for agricultural imports have created a new wave of governmental interference with trade through licensing procedures and provided a playground for rent-seeking traders—who will in turn have an incentive to lobby for the continuation of the high above-quota tariffs. The question is how to prevent the TRQs from interfering any more than necessary with the competitive development of trade.

One answer to the question lies in the method of allocation. In some cases allocation is done on a government-to-government basis, usually in accordance with historical market shares. But this perpetuates distortions in trade. To allocate the TRQs to the exporting country government, as is done for instance in the case of US sugar imports, implies a deliberate attempt to influence the pattern of trade in favor of the recipient countries. This has been done in the past to target development aid or to reward political friendship. Such nonmarket allocation schemes may have had their purpose. They do not, however, promote the competitive trade system that is the fundamental goal of the WTO. Efficient producers can make no headway against the assured market shares of the quota holders. Even allocating TRQs by country on the basis of historical market shares does not ensure that the sourcing of supplies for the importer bears any necessary relation to the competitiveness of the supplier.

The simple solution to the efficiency problem is to allow quotas to be auctioned, as has been suggested at various times.[14] This would seem an economically sensible solution to the problem of the capture of rents, and it would counteract the incentives to keep the system in place. But this is also a reason why exporters in particular are likely to resist such a move. If the TRQs were auctioned to the exporter, the impact would be much like a tariff. The exporter would bid up to the height of the tariff concession for the right to sell in the import market. The capture by the government of the rent through the auction process in effect turns the TRQ into a quasi tariff, with the height discovered through the auction process. Where the TRQs replace previous access agreements in which the quota was allocated to the exporter, the result of the auction would be to reduce the return from selling into this market. Thus there could be considerable resistance to the auctioning of TRQs.

---

14. Tangermann (1997) explores the arguments in favor of auctioning the TRQs. The issue of auctioning quotas was addressed some years ago by Bergsten and colleagues (1987) in the context of US import policy. It is an interesting comment on the lack of economic rationality in trade policy—and the attractiveness of rents to trading interests—that such a simple device as auctioning quotas has not so far caught on with politicians and policymakers.

The type of allocation mechanism that causes most problems, however, is that which gives the import rights to domestic concerns. Exporters feel that they are neither getting assured access (as the agency or firm concerned can choose not to import the product, leading to underfill of quotas) or that they are not gaining the benefit of the access (in essence not receiving any of the quota rent). In instances where the TRQs have a deliberate purpose, such as the EU arrangements with the African, Caribbean, and Pacific countries (ACP) and those of the Mediterranean basin, capture of rents by the importing firms negates much of the benefit of the scheme. When competing domestic producers receive the import entitlements (as has happened in a few cases), the market access inherent in the TRQs may be elusive.

Any allocation mechanism is subject to criticism. Using historical shares locks in trade, auctions tax the exporter for what is supposed to be market access, and allocation to import agencies encourages rent seeking. The best solution, in the end, may be to steadily increase the TRQs, as suggested above, or to reduce the rents by cutting above-quota tariffs, until the issue of how to allocate them is rendered moot.

State Trading Importers

The issue of state trading enterprises that have special or exclusive rights in import markets can be thought of as an extension of the problem of market access. Under WTO articles, state trading importers are not supposed to grant more protection than that given by the bound tariff (GATT Article II:4). Countries could, however, go further than just ensuring that state trading importers do not give more protection than the bound tariff. It would be possible, for instance, to link the administration of the TRQs with the import operations of state traders, perhaps converting the TRQ into an obligation to import, rather than an opportunity. This could reduce the suspicion that STEs might be responsible for the underfill of the quotas. At the other extreme, one could mandate that all (or a share) of the TRQ be marketed through private channels, thus providing some competition for the STE and allowing price and markup comparisons to be made.

Curbing Export Subsidies

If the high level of protection sets agriculture apart, the widespread use of export subsidies is perhaps the most disruptive element in the operation of world markets. The practice of subsidizing exports of agricultural products has been constrained by the Uruguay Round, but most of the subsidies are allowed to continue in a reduced form. Countries that import agricultural products have been the gainers in economic terms from the subsidies, but even among these countries the disturbance of the domestic market has often caused problems. In the next round of negotiations, it will be more difficult than ever to persuade countries that export agricultural goods with little or no subsidy to allow countries such as the United States and members of the European Union to continue their market-distorting practices.

Reducing Export Subsidies

A further push to rein in these subsidies is high on the agenda of the Cairns Group, apparently supported by the United States. The Cairns Group paper declares that "there is no justification for maintaining export subsidies." The United States says that members "should agree to pursue an outcome that will result in an elimination of all remaining export subsidies." Canada adds that export subsidies in agriculture should be eliminated "as quickly as possible." Developing countries also are generally in favor of the elimination of export subsidies.[15] Only the European Union would have great difficulty in agreeing to the dismantlement of export subsidies, though it will come under considerable pressure to do so.

The simplest way to continue the process of reducing the incidence of export subsidies would be to extend the schedule of reductions agreed on in the Uruguay Round. As with the market access improvement, this could be done using the same base. This would imply constraining the expenditure on such subsidies by another 36 percent, thus removing 72 percent of the subsidy expenditure that was used in the base period. Continuing the quantity restriction would imply that 40 percent of the volume of subsidized exports would have been removed from the market over the two periods of reform. But since the remaining 60 percent would have to be subsidized with only 29 percent of the expenditure, the disruption that could be caused by such subsidies would be significantly reduced.

The continuation of the process of reduction would be constructive, however elimination of export subsidies altogether would clearly have significant advantages. But the prerequisites for dispensing with export subsidies are a renewed confidence in world markets, with firmer and more stable price levels for the major products, and reduced dependence on intervention buying in domestic policies. The former condition itself depends on the success of the agreement in increasing trade and reducing protection; removing export subsidies may be the only way to create the conditions under which they are not needed. As for domestic programs, it is possible that practice and sentiment in the European Union may have moved further away from the use of market support policies

---

15. Pakistan argues for the immediate elimination of "all kinds of export subsidies by the developed countries."

to other instruments by the end of the negotiations. If these conditions were met, then a new set of negotiations could, say, set a target to phase out export subsidies over a seven-year period.

Disciplines on Export Credits

Besides the question of export subsidies, several problems remain in the area of export competition. In the Uruguay Round, export credits were declared to be a form of export subsidy, but negotiators were unable to agree on constraints. The countries of the Organization for Economic Co-operation and Development have negotiated a code for nonagricultural export credits that puts limits on credit terms and the length of credit extension, but it has not been possible to include agriculture in this agreement. This leaves the topic as one to be dealt with in the next round, though some countries have indicated that they do not wish to "pay twice" for getting rid of such policies. It should be possible to agree on the allowable terms for such credit, and hence to be able to calculate the magnitude of the subsidy that is involved if softer credit terms are offered. The best way to deal with the subsidy equivalent of such concessionary credit is to charge it against the export subsidy constraints in the schedules.

State Trading Exporters

The quantification of export subsidies and their reduction has left more visible the distinction between those countries where exports are privately sold and those where a parastatal agency controls exports. There is widespread concern in those countries where trade is by private firms that the state trading enterprises can obtain cheap credit from their governments, offer better terms to buyers, and generally compete unfairly with the private trade. To the extent that these practices could be labeled as export subsidies, the issue is one of monitoring and transparency. But some commonly used devices such as price pooling (giving the producer an average price over several destinations or time periods) are also seen as giving the producer an unfair advantage. It might therefore be a matter for negotiation as to whether any constraints need be placed upon STEs with regard to their producer pricing policies.

The question of single-desk selling agencies for agricultural products is at the heart of this issue. On this there are some clear conflicts between the exporters. The United States has indicated that it would like to "strengthen rules . . . disciplining activities of state trading enterprises." The Cairns Group (with Canada as a member) is tactfully silent on the issue, but Canada (in its "Initial Position" document) states unequivocally that it wishes to "maintain Canada's ability to choose how to market its products, including through orderly marketing systems such as supply management and the Canadian Wheat Board." It attempts to head off a confrontation with the United States by indicating that it will "not engage in sterile debates over alternative marketing philosophies," though it also indicates a willingness to "discuss any factual concerns" over "alleged trade effects of orderly marketing systems." Demonstrating that the best defense is often a good offense, Canada adds that it will "seek to ensure that any new disciplines proposed to deal with the perceived market power of [single-desk sellers] apply equally to all entities, public or private, with similar market power." What holds for the CWB must hold for Cargill as well![16]

Different marketing practices among exporters are inevitable, and not in themselves undesirable. But international guidance is needed as to which practices of parastatal export agencies are consistent with agreed-on conditions of competition and which distort that competition. Now that the more clear-cut kinds of export subsidy have been identified and included in the country schedules of allowable subsidies, the main task of the negotiations will be to clarify the definition as regards the actions of state trading exporters.[17] This would ensure that such actions as dual pricing and price pooling, if deemed to be hidden subsidies, could be counted against the schedule for that country.

Export Restrictions

In the next round, importers are likely to lead a movement to constrain the ability of exporters to restrict supplies. After all, restraints on exports are no less inconsistent with an open trade system than restraints on imports. Export taxes should be included under the same qualifications as quantitative restrictions. The argument has already surfaced in connection with the Food Security Decision appended to the Uruguay Round agreement (the Ministerial Decision on Measures Concerning the Possible Negative Effects of the Reform Program on Least-Developed and Net Food-Importing Developing Countries). It seems inconsistent to leave in place the possibility of export taxes and quantitative restrictions that have an immediate and harmful impact on developing-country food importers.

The practice of export taxes and export restraints through quantitative controls can conveniently be thought of as an extension of the issue of export competition. Within the GATT, export controls are generally disallowed, though export taxes are deemed innocuous. GATT Article

---

16. Of course one can argue about the interpretation of "similar market power," but it remains true that many Canadian farmers claim that even if they were relieved of the obligation to sell to the CWB, they would have to sell to one of a very few US multinational corporations.

17. In this regard the outcome of the dispute over Canadian dairy exports is useful. The panel report has indicated that the use of special export grades of milk that can be sold at a lower price to processors for export of dairy products constitutes a form of export subsidy under the URAA.

XI prohibits quantitative export restrictions but makes an explicit exception for "export prohibitions or restrictions temporarily applied to prevent or relieve critical shortages of foodstuffs or other products essential to the exporting contracting party." There is a clear conflict between the ability of exporters to withhold supplies to relieve domestic shortages and the reliability of the world market as a source of supplies for importers. The inclusion of stronger disciplines on export taxes and embargoes is likely to be part of the next round of agricultural talks.

Several countries have indicated their views on this matter. Canada indicates that it will seek a ban on "the inclusion of food and feedstuffs in national security embargoes" together with a ban on "export restrictions that would reduce the proportion of the total supply of an agricultural product permitted to be exported compared to the proportion prevailing in a previous representative period." Japan also argues for strengthening the disciplines concerning export taxes and export restrictions, in part to "redress the balance of rights and obligations between exporting and importing countries." Developing countries have so far focused on other aspects of food security, such as putting "teeth" into the Ministerial Decision. The EU paper does not mention export restrictions and taxes; it was the introduction of export levies in 1995 and 1996 to keep cereal prices from rising on the internal EU market that reawakened interest in the issue of export restrictions.

Domestic Support

It is one of the ironies of the Uruguay Round that, although the biggest conceptual breakthrough was the participants' acceptance that domestic policies were a legitimate concern of trade talks, the actual disciplines imposed on those policies through the reduction of the aggregate measure of support (AMS) were rather weak. The key question for the next round is therefore whether to strengthen or abandon the attempt to constrain domestic policies.

The fact that the AMS constraints have not been binding for the large majority of countries does not mean that the constraints on domestic support have been ineffective. The process of reinstrumentation of domestic support programs, away from those that most impede trade, has begun. The institution of the "green box" has in itself been useful in defining this objective. The attractiveness of adopting green box policies is both to guard against challenge from trading partners and to avoid being counted toward the AMS. Thus the AMS constraint is of value even if not particularly onerous.

The slow but fundamental changes that are taking place in the agricultural policies of the major industrial countries need the encouragement and underpinning of international agreements. The changes in these policies have generally been in the direction of improving the climate for agricultural trade, in contrast to the policy changes in the 1960s and 1970s that led to more trade conflicts. The Uruguay Round was able to take advantage of these changes, such as the 1992 Reform of the European Union's Common Agricultural Policy (CAP), and to get firm commitments on future policy directions and support levels. But this process of reform is still at an early stage and needs to continue in order to avoid a swing back toward the costly and ineffective policies of earlier times.

Further Reductions in AMS

Some WTO members put weight on the reduction in domestic support through the aggregate measure of support (AMS). The United States has called for an "ambitious target" to be set for the reduction of support. The Cairns Group points out that the "overall levels of support for agriculture remain far in excess of subsidies available to other industries." But, as with the United States, their target is clearly the trade-distorting ("amber box") policies. Canada, however, indicates that it will seek "an overall limit on the amount of domestic support of all types" (green, blue, and amber). This could prove difficult. The European Union has announced that one of its objectives is to defend the "blue box" (in essence the compensation payments under the MacSharry and Agenda 2000 reforms) so as to avoid challenge to these policies and their scheduled reduction.[18] It missed the chance of changing the nature of these payments to make them compatible with the green box criteria, though this could come at some stage in the negotiations.

The AMS constraints are acknowledged to be the least effective of the Uruguay Round bindings. But this does not mean either that they will not be useful in the future or that a continued reduction would not be appropriate. A continuation from the same base would be a relatively modest move, and yet even that will eventually result in 40 percent of the "coupled" domestic support having been removed or converted into less trade-distorting types of program. But it would be even more effective to "catch up" with the reductions in import barriers and export subsidies. Thus one could envisage an agreed-on reduction of (say) 52 percent in the expenditure on price-related policies.

The Future of the Blue Box

The blue box containing the US and EU direct payments that were granted exemption from challenges under the Blair House agreement was a creature of its time, necessary to get agreement to go ahead with the broader

---

18. As in the case of export subsidies, EU authorities would not be averse to reducing direct payments over time. However, they have not yet found a politically acceptable formula for doing so.

Uruguay Round package. It is, however, still a somewhat awkward bilateral deal not appreciated in other parts of the world. Such an anomaly could possibly be removed in the next round. The policies of the United States and the European Union themselves are changing for internal reasons. The US FAIR Act goes further than ever before to make the payments to farmers decoupled from output and therefore compatible with the green box. The European Union has considered a similar move as a part of the continued reform started in 1992, as a way of making the CAP consistent with enlargement, but for now the idea has been shelved.[19] The task for the new round will be made much easier if the United States and the European Union have both modified their payments such that they meet the conditions laid down in the green box. The blue box could then be emptied and locked.

Redefining the Green Box

The green box currently contains a number of policy instruments that, while probably less trade-distorting than price or income supports, still encourage an expansion of output. Sometimes they are related to such otherwise reasonable programs as crop insurance but incidentally increase the incentive to produce by reducing risk. Other programs may be indirectly linked with production even though the main reason for payment is not output. This might be true of certain environmental payments, which could lead to an increase in output. Exporters fear, however, that to reopen the definition of the green box might allow countries to argue that it be expanded to include food security policies and nondecoupled support schemes designed to keep farming in certain areas.

This issue of the size of the green box appears to be where much of the prenegotiation rhetoric is targeted. The argument is usually shrouded in terms of the "multifunctionality" of agriculture. The concept of multifunctionality is not in itself particularly novel, as agriculture has always played a complex role in rural societies, and rural areas have a vital place in national social and political life. But the European Union has latched onto the concept as a way of both providing cover in the WTO for policies it would like to maintain and providing a rationale for paying farmers in ways that are not tied to commodity output. Exporters are trying to neutralize any impact the idea might have by pointing out that multifunctionality is restricted neither to Europe (though the EU Commission tends to link it to a European farming model, by implication different from the system of farming in competitor countries) nor

---

19. The Agenda 2000 reform of the CAP, agreed upon in 1999, did not change the conditions for the direct payments to cereal farmers. Use of the land in program crops is still required. If new members are admitted under these conditions, it is difficult to see how the European Union could avoid paying the direct payments to their farmers. This would constitute a large part of the budget cost of extending the CAP to new members.

indeed to agriculture. Importers are trying to link it to the "nontrade concerns" mentioned in Article 20 of the URAA as requiring consideration in planning the reform of the trade system.

The basic question remains, what does multifunctionality mean for trade policy? On the one hand, it could merely be a recognition that a variety of programs will be maintained in most societies that target specific aspects of rural life. For the trade system to be seen to rule out such programs would seem to be as risky as seeming to go against concerns of human health and animal welfare. On the other hand, if trade-restricting policies were to become the accepted instrument for maintaining multifunctionality, then that could signal a regression to the time of expensive commodity market distortions. The green box was intended precisely to deal with such rural concerns. It would be better to confirm the criteria for the green box and encourage multifunctional policies to conform rather than opening the green box to be a repository for an assortment of production-related payments.

One change in the constraints on domestic support that will probably be discussed is to make the AMS specific to individual commodities. This was the original intention in the Uruguay Round; it was at the Blair House negotiations between the United States and the European Union that the notion of aggregating the AMS over all commodities was introduced— essentially to weaken its impact. The AMS could thus be made more binding at a stroke by defining commodity-specific amounts of "coupled" price support expenditure that could then be reduced over time.

Health, Safety, and Environmental Issues

Among the most controversial of the issues that will confront negotiators is that of trade measures to support disparate health, safety, and environmental standards. Some of these standards have been around for a long time. Others are new and pose a challenge for the trade system as a result of their novelty. Some reflect increasing sensitivity of consumer and environmental groups to food-related issues. Others arise because firms find that differences in the costs of compliance have an impact on competitiveness.

Conflicts arising from different sanitary and phytosanitary standards have posed problems for the GATT for many years. Under the GATT, sanitary and phytosanitary measures that impinge on trade are covered by Article XX (b), which allows countries to employ trade barriers "necessary to protect human, animal or plant life or health" that would otherwise be illegal so long as "such measures are not applied in a manner which would constitute a means of arbitrary or unjustifiable discrimination between countries where the same conditions prevail, or as a disguised restriction on international trade" (Josling, Tangermann, and Warley

1996). But Article XX was hard to invoke since there was no definition of the criteria by which to judge "necessity." The attempt in the Tokyo Round to improve on this situation through the Agreement on Technical Barriers to Trade (1979), known as the Standards Code, also failed. Though a dispute settlement mechanism was introduced and countries were encouraged to adopt international standards, relatively few countries signed the code, and a number of basic issues were still unresolved.

The SPS Agreement

Intensive negotiations in the Uruguay Round led eventually to a new SPS agreement that tried to repair the faults of existing GATT obligations. This agreement defined new criteria that had to be met when imposing import regulations more onerous than those agreed upon in international standards. These included scientific evidence that the measure was needed; assessment of the risks involved; and recognition of the equivalence of different ways of testing and sampling. In addition, the dispute settlement mechanism was considerably strengthened under the WTO to make it easier to obtain an outcome that could not be avoided by the losing party. The force of the SPS agreement comes in part from the more precise conditions under which standards stricter than international norms can be justified and partly from the strengthened dispute settlement process within the WTO. In this regard, much was expected of the panel report in the beef hormone dispute between the European Union on the one hand and Canada and the United States on the other. This was widely seen as a test case for the new SPS agreement.

The SPS agreement was reviewed in 1999 by the SPS Committee, which found no reason to suggest modifications. The United States and the Cairns Group are not likely to wish to tamper with a hard-won agreement that has "science" at its core. The European Union, however, has let it be known that a few amendments would not be out of place. The desire to build in the reaction to consumer confidence is natural; presumably it could be argued that the beef hormone case would be rendered moot by a well-crafted clause written into a revised SPS agreement. The question of whether the trade system can tolerate regulations that take into account subjective consumer demand shifts is one of the most contentious issues in trade policy between the United States and the European Union.

Handling the Issue of Genetically Modified Organisms

One particularly contentious issue that is directly relevant to the global agrifood system is the extent to which the use of genetically modified organisms (GMOs) is harmful to the environment or indeed to consumer health. Concerns about transgenic crops, such as those with herbicide resistance built into their genetic makeup, have centered on the possibility of unpredictable crosses with wild species and hence the development of herbicide-resistant weeds. Transgenic crops with genetically manipulated insect resistance give rise to concerns about the development of resistant insects and about collateral damage to harmless or beneficial insects. Clearly there needs to be vigilance to avoid the undesirable side effects of otherwise useful technology. Other fears are that consumers who suffer from plant-related allergies may react to the presence of genes from those plants to which they are allergic (IPC 1998). The most commonly recommended remedy for preventing such problems is adequate labeling, but even this creates problems for public policy.

That the GMO issue will come up in the trade talks is inevitable. How it can be resolved, or at least channeled in a way that does not impede other areas of the talks, is less certain. The United States has suggested that "additional approaches that address market access issues for biotechnology products" be pursued. Canada has suggested a working party to look at all aspects of the GMO issue, presumably including labeling and import restrictions, as a way of dealing with the issue directly. The European Union has positioned itself to take the view that existing agreements (such as the SPS and TBT agreements) may need to be revised in light of the challenge of GMOs. The exporters have been trying to coordinate their positions, through the Cairns Group and through bilateral talks. The Asia Pacific Economic Cooperation (APEC) ministers have also been discussing the development of a coordinated plan for the regulation of trade in GMOs. The apparent aim at the moment is to isolate the European Union on this issue rather to engage it in a trade forum.

Animal Welfare

Creeping up behind GMOs as the next controversial issue is that of animal welfare. Few topics engender more public outrage, at least in Northern Europe, and pose more serious problems of international regulation. Farmers in Europe are already having to modify their farming practices to meet new animal welfare standards. They are naturally arguing that it would be unfair to leave them to compete with producers who do not have to meet the same standards. The issue will revolve around whether some degree of protection at the border is allowable to compensate for the extra costs, whether border controls can keep out goods produced under conditions considered unsuitable by the importing country, and whether direct assistance can be given to domestic farmers who are burdened by such regulations without such assistance being considered "amber box" support. In this respect, the animal welfare debate may become part of the discussion on environmental programs, where the same choices apply. But the animal welfare issue could also take on some of the aspects of the GMO controversy, if genetically modified animal products start to be marketed.

Nonagricultural Agenda Items

One aspect of the globalization of the agrifood sector that was emphasized above is that the range of trade rules that impinge on the sector has expanded significantly. Even if the prospect of talks on investment and competition policy is more distant, the review of the Agreement on Trade-Related Aspects of Intellectual Property Rights (TRIPs) will ensure that issues of interest to agriculture will be on the table in other parts of the negotiations.

Intellectual Property and Agriculture

Among the newer aspects of international trade policy is the setting up of rules regarding intellectual property. The Uruguay Round Agreement on Trade-Related Aspects of Intellectual Property Rights brought a degree of harmonization to the disparate treatment of patents, copyrights, and trademarks in various trading countries.

Input Industries and Intellectual Property

One important area of the food and agricultural sector where the rules on intellectual property are significant is in the input industries. The seed sector, in particular, has already made use of such international facilities to try to reclaim some revenue from farmers. The ability to patent plant varieties has been a controversial topic for some years. Now one can patent particular manipulations of genetic material such as is at the root of biotechnology. This would give companies a much greater chance of licensing new varieties to others to plant.[20] This is of concern among some who fear that the highly concentrated seed industry could extract considerable profits from farmers worldwide, as they would have to pay from season to season for planting even their own retained seed.

Geographical Labels

A second linkage between agriculture and intellectual property is in the area of geographical trademarks and indications. It is widely held that such geographical labels help consumers to pick a brand on which they can rely. It is also possible that the same useful information can have the effect of inhibiting competition and earning scarcity rents for the holder

---

20. Though plant breeders' rights have been recognized since the 1930s in the United States, it has proved impossible to patent improvements that come through selection in the field (land race crosses) and not easy to see the justification for doing so. But when the improvement comes in the laboratory, as a result of using particular genetic material in a biotech process, the case for restricting unlicensed use increases.

of the patent. But, regardless of the merits of particular systems of label-ing, some form of brand identification is an important part of the trade system in foods as in other areas. The European Union is particularly keen to see an extension of the protection for geographical indications (it does not wish to consider them as mere trademarks) as a reflection of the commercially important name recognition of many European food specialties. In any package of measures, some further protection of this type could have a useful role as an issue that the European Union can sell to its domestic constituencies.

The Trade Preference Issue

Though not on the formal negotiating agenda, the topic of trade prefer-ences, and more generally the issue of regional trade groups within the trade system, will not be far beneath the surface. Trade preferences have a long history in agriculture. Countries in Europe (particularly France, the United Kingdom, and the Netherlands) have kept close commercial ties with their former colonies based on preferential access to their markets. These ties were assumed by the European Union under successive Lomé Conventions. The European Union has suggested significant changes in the agreement, in part to try to avoid the perpetuation of a dependency relationship based on the export of a small number of commodities with limited market prospects. The Lomé Convention is in any case likely to change markedly in the coming years, as it has been declared to be in contravention of international trade rules.[21] The European Union was granted a waiver until the year 2000 from the obligation to bring the Lomé Con-vention into conformity with the WTO rules. If such a waiver is still required after that year it will have to be renewed annually.[22]

Developing countries face a dilemma in the area of trade preferences. On the one hand, many developing countries benefit from them. On the

---

21. The first banana panel raised the issue of the legality of the Lomé Convention under the GATT. The convention could hardly be justified as a part of a free trade area under Article XXIV of the GATT as it was nonreciprocal. ACP countries did not have to grant duty-free access to the products of Europe. Preferences are also allowed under the "en-abling clause" for giving advantages to developing countries. But the justification of the Lomé Convention as a manifestation of "special and differential treatment" in favor of developing countries, encouraged by the GATT, was rendered doubtful by the fact that many developing countries (in Asia, mostly) did not qualify for ACP assistance and trade benefits.

22. The European Union is not the only body to grant trade preferences. The United States runs regional preferences for Central America and the Caribbean under the Carib-bean Basin Initiative and other schemes. Though these cover more products than the EU protocols, they are also neither WTO-compatible free trade areas nor nondiscriminatory development assistance. They also have required a WTO waiver, and will probably eventually evolve into reciprocal free trade schemes.

other hand, most of them grant preferences at the expense of other developing countries. Exporters who benefit under the schemes gain valuable access and higher prices but get locked into particular markets and products. Those exporters that have not had extensive preferences have in many cases outperformed those that have had such access. Moreover, preferences that are given unilaterally by the importer do not have the same guarantees as trade access under the WTO. Investors may remain wary of the future of some of the commodity preference schemes.

Illustrative of the preference issue is the conflict over trade in bananas. A WTO panel found that several of the mechanisms used to allocate banana imports under the EU regime of quantitative restrictions violated international trade rules. The dispute has put banana-exporting countries at odds with each other and led to the (mistaken) view that the WTO is being used to undermine the economies of the smaller islands that are heavily dependent on the crop for export earnings. The banana issue is the most contentious trade policy issue for the Caribbean and Central American regions.

The European Union has promised a new set of regulations that should prove to be more WTO-consistent. The urgency is that an unresolved banana issue will be a problem for the European Union as it enters into negotiations with its WTO partners. The European Union will, if the beef hormone dispute is not rapidly settled, be saddled with the burden of two adverse panel rulings with which it has not yet complied. But the solution of the banana problem itself could eventually be settled in the negotiations, just as the long-running oilseed dispute was settled in a package (at Blair House) along with the final agreement on agriculture in the Uruguay Round.

Possible Outcomes

From the viewpoint of continuing the process of agricultural trade reform, the next round should be judged a success if it accomplishes the following objectives:

■ A cut in the average level of agricultural tariffs of at least as much as in the Uruguay Round (i.e., 36 percent over six years).

■ A reduction of the higher tariffs by more than the average, either through the use of a formula or by request-and-offer negotiations on tariff peaks.

■ An expansion of TRQs so as to give meaningful access increases where tariffs are still prohibitively high, and their allocation regularized by agreeing on ways to distribute quotas to encourage rather than discourage trade.

- A cut in the level of export subsidies and an agreement reached in principle to phase them out altogether at some future date.

- An agreement that the restrictions on export subsidies should specifically include export credits and subsidies given indirectly by single-desk sellers.

- An extension of WTO disciplines to include export restrictions and embargoes with the objectives of avoiding adverse impacts on developing food importers and increasing trust in the reliability of food supplies.

- Continued reductions in the level of trade-distorting domestic support (amber box), and elimination of the category of payments linked to acreage control (blue box).

- An agreement that acceptable (green box) policies should be encouraged, including those that are related to environmental and similar objectives, and that these should continue to be sheltered from WTO challenge.

Agreement on such a package will not be easy. The first part of the negotiations may well be spent posturing and attempting to redefine the agenda to influence the outcome. Much of the debate could revolve around the nature of noontide concerns and the related concept of multifunctionality. The United States and the Cairns Group will try to avoid diluting the green box with environmental and animal welfare payments, but may in the end have to concede. The European Union will find it difficult to agree to the elimination of export subsidies and may insist on a long phase-out period. The blue box will also be used as a bargaining device, with the European Union insisting that it must be retained. Japan will find it very difficult to agree to deep cuts in megatariffs unless it changes radically its domestic agricultural and food policies.

What may eventually drive countries to an agreement is the prospect of the expiry of the peace clause in 2003, without which farm policies may be subject to widespread challenge under WTO rules.[23] Thereafter, unless the peace clause is renewed, the general WTO rules governing subsidies and dumping will apply to agriculture. This will presumably give a useful boost to negotiations if they are not completed by that date. The promise to renew the peace clause may also be a useful incentive for countries such as the European Union to continue reforms.

Also driving the pace and tenor of the agricultural talks will be the extent to which other sectors are included in the round. It will be much more difficult to reach agreement in the absence of parallel discussions

---

23. The peace clause is an agreement to use "due restraint" in challenging policies that are consistent with the Agreement on Agriculture and the associated schedules.

on trade liberalization in other sectors. In addition, one must not forget the impact of exogenous factors such as the state of world markets. Unless world commodity markets recover from their current depression, it is difficult to see governments opening their markets to trade, though of course this opening up of markets would do much to prevent such weak markets in the future.

Adding to the factors that might delay completion of the round is the increased number of countries that will be taking part. Moreover, China and several other aspirants (though probably not Russia) could also be members either near the start of negotiations or before they conclude. This will bring in important agricultural traders who will have considerable influence on world market conditions, but it may make reaching a solution more difficult.

Does this mean that there will be little incentive to finish the negotiations once they have started? The United States in particular is concerned that the incentives to delay be removed. Hence both the United States and the European Union support a time limit of three years for the talks. With the delay in the launch of the WTO round resulting from Seattle, such a period would conveniently coincide with both the expiry of the peace clause and the end of the current US farm bill, as well as the date that the European Union has set for a review of some of its own farm policy measures and the likely date for the accession of new members.

Perhaps the main determinant of the timing and ambitiousness of the agricultural talks, however, is the decision as to whether they should be a part of a large, multisector negotiation or whether they will be self-contained. Most commentators argue that a negotiation that includes only agriculture will be difficult to conclude satisfactorily. Countries that feel that they stand to lose will have no offsetting gains in other areas. However, no agreement has yet been reached on the scope for the next round, and so it is uncertain what "package" will be possible.

References

Bergsten, C. Fred, Kimberly Ann Elliott, Jeffrey J. Schott, and Wendy E. Takacs. 1987. *Auction Quotas and United States Trade Policy*. POLICY ANALYSES IN INTERNATIONAL ECONOMICS 20. Washington: Institute for International Economics.

Coleman, William, and Stefan Tangermann. 1997. Linked Games, International Mediators, and Agricultural Trade. Paper presented at the International Agricultural Trade Research Consortium Annual Meeting (December).

International Agricultural Trade Research Consortium [IATRC]. 1997. Implementation of the Uruguay Round Agreement on Agriculture and Issues for the Next Round of Agricultural Negotiations. IATRC Commissioned Paper No. 12 (November).

International Policy Council [IPC]. 1998. Plant Biotechnology and Global Food Production: Trade Implications. IPC Position Paper No. 7.

Josling, Timothy. 1998. *Agricultural Trade Policy: Completing the Reform*. POLICY ANALYSES IN INTERNATIONAL ECONOMICS 53. Washington: Institute for International Economics.

Josling, Timothy, and Allan Rae. 1999. Multilateral Market Access Issues for the Next Round of Agricultural Negotiations. Paper for the World Bank Conference on the Next Round of Agricultural Talks, Geneva (October 1-2).

Josling, Timothy, Stefan Tangermann, and Thorald K. Warley. 1996. *Agriculture in the GATT*. London: Macmillan Press.

Nelson, Gerald, et al. 1999. The Economics and Politics of Genetically Modified Organisms in Agriculture. University of Illinois, Urbana-Champaign Experiment Station Bulletin No. 809 (November).

Orden, David, Robert Paarlberg, and Terry Roe. 1999. *Policy Reform in American Agriculture: Analysis and Prognosis*. Chicago: University of Chicago Press.

Swinbank, Alan, and Carolyn Tanner. 1996. *Farm Policy and Trade Conflict: The Uruguay Round and Cap Reform*. Ann Arbor: University of Michigan Press.

Tangermann, Stefan. 1997. A Developed Country Perspective of the Agenda for the Next WTO Round of Agricultural Trade Negotiations. Paper presented at a seminar at the Institute of Graduate Studies, Geneva (March 3).

9

Toward a More Balanced and Comprehensive Services Agreement

BERNARD HOEKMAN

The establishment of a General Agreement on Trade in Services (GATS) was one of the major outcomes of the Uruguay Round. The GATS broke new ground in a number of areas. Not only did it cover measures affecting trade in services—a product group that was mostly not subject to the General Agreement on Tariffs and Trade (GATT)—but also it defined trade in a novel way. Trade under the GATS includes not just cross-border exchange, but also sales by affiliates of foreign companies that have established a long-term commercial presence in a host country, purchases of services made by nonresidents who have moved to the location of their provider, and the sale of services by natural persons made possible by a temporary presence in a host country. The potential reach of the GATS therefore extends beyond that of the GATT, which deals only with cross-border trade in merchandise. One consequence of this broader domain was that governments insisted on being able to maintain national derogations and limitations on the reach of multilateral disciplines. A rather complicated scheduling technology was adopted: each WTO member may list exceptions to the national treatment principle or market access for individual service sectors for any or all of the four modes of supply through which trade can occur. They may also refrain from making any commitment for specific services.

During the Uruguay Round negotiations on services, most attention centered on conceptual and "architectural" issues—how to define trade, what rules and principles should apply to measures affecting this trade, and devising mechanisms to determine the coverage of the agreement.

Bernard Hoekman is senior trade economist at the World Bank. He is grateful to Patrick Messerlin, Jeff Schott, Sherry Stephenson, and Jayashree Watal for helpful comments and discussions. The views expressed in this paper are personal and should not be attributed to the World Bank.

What was created was a framework under which liberalization could be pursued in the future.[1] Article XIX of the GATS calls on members to engage in negotiations to liberalize trade in services five years after the entry into force of the agreement, and periodically thereafter. New negotiations on services therefore are to commence in 2000.

This paper discusses the agenda of the services talks, taking an economic and systemic perspective. Three broad topics are discussed: (1) modalities for expanding the coverage and increasing the relevance of the GATS; (2) achieving reciprocity—attaining a balance of "concessions" made by participants; and (3) improving the multilateral rules of the game that are embodied in the GATS. The premise is that the GATS must become more balanced in terms of the magnitude and distribution of the benefits of the agreement for different groups of countries. This will require a more comprehensive coverage of sectors and modes of supply. Achieving a substantial expansion in the coverage of the GATS is of great importance not only in its own right but also to ensure that multilateral negotiations more generally will be successful. In the run-up to the Seattle ministerial it was clear that many developing countries were of the view that the costs of implementing Uruguay Round agreements in various areas—e.g., the Agreement on Trade-Related Aspects of Intellectual Property Rights (TRIPs), customs valuation—are much greater than was realized when these agreements were signed (Finger and Schuler 2000). Moreover, the benefits from market access agreements in other areas of importance to developing countries were perceived as disappointing because of continued use of highly distorting policies in major markets (agriculture) and/or the back-loaded nature of the liberalization process (textiles and clothing). The services negotiations offer the opportunity for significant market access gains for developing countries, while at the same time improving the regulatory environment for services and the efficiency of domestic industries.

The major challenge confronting negotiators is to create incentives for developing countries to expand their commitments under the GATS. Given ongoing efforts in many countries to adopt a more promarket and procompetitive policy stance, the focus of attention can be expected to center on increasing the extent to which both the status quo and future (autonomous) reforms are scheduled in the GATS. This depends importantly on the value that is placed on such scheduling by reforming economies themselves and by the *demandeur* countries that want governments to lock in reforms in the GATS. Arguments by economists that the WTO can be used as a valuable credibility-bolstering device have proved to be less than compelling to policymakers (see, e.g., Francois 1997). In practice, the mercantilist logic of multilateral negotiations is likely to require that industrialized countries improve export market access opportunities for

---

1. See Hoekman (1996) for a description and assessment of the GATS.

developing countries. Absent such a quid pro quo, it may prove difficult to greatly expand the coverage of the GATS in areas where the economic payoffs are highest—sectors where entry restrictions are most severe or the perceived probability of policy reversal is high.

The Status Quo

The situation that prevails in the GATS is well known.[2] The sectoral coverage of the specific commitments (on national treatment and market access) is limited for many countries. The majority of country schedules list a variety of measures that continue to restrict or limit either market access or national treatment. As of the end of the Uruguay Round, high-income countries had made specific commitments on about half of their services, of which only one-half entailed "free access." Thus, ignoring horizontal restrictions for modes of supply, only 25 percent of all service activities have no limitations on market access or national treatment. In the case of major developing countries, on average "free access" commitments were made for only 15 percent of the services sector; smaller countries generally do not attain even this low level (Hoekman 1996). Subsequent to the Uruguay Round, successful negotiations on basic telecommunications and financial services expanded the coverage of specific commitments.[3] These negotiations were important both for keeping momentum going and for inducing the United States not to invoke a most favored nation (MFN) exception. They were important from an economic perspective because the services involved are vital intermediate inputs.[4]

Not only is the coverage of specific commitments limited for many countries, but also in many cases the commitments are less liberal than the policies that are actually applied—that is, many governments have refrained from binding the status quo. Examples in the financial services area are well documented, with a number of countries scheduling foreign ownership limits that are more restrictive than those currently enforced (Mattoo 1999). One interesting feature that was remarked upon by a number of observers immediately after the Uruguay Round is that more commitments tended to be made with respect to foreign direct investment (FDI) ("mode 3") than cross-border trade ("mode 1") (Hoekman 1996). A

---

2. Feketekuty (1998) and Mattoo (1999b) discuss the status quo and the weaknesses of the GATS, and provide references to the rapidly expanding literature.

3. Cowhey and Klimenko (1999) assess the telecom agreement; Mattoo (1999) analyzes the financial services agreement.

4. These agreements did not lead to a major expansion in the coverage of the GATS relative to my 1996 assessment (Hoekman 1996), as my compilation included commitments made as of 1994 for financial services.

number of countries' commitments also favor infusions of foreign equity into existing firms and limit entry by new firms. Such protection of existing market structure is difficult to rationalize in economic terms, as it can easily result in a transfer of rents to foreign firms rather than a socially desirable increase in competition, lower prices, and higher quality output.[5] Differences in the treatment of modes of supply have the potential to distort incentives to contest or service markets through the most cost-effective means available, and may impede suppliers' ability to sell their services. This can be particularly important for e-commerce (Mann 2000).

Expanding the Coverage of the GATS

In principle, efforts to expand the coverage of the GATS should focus on those sectors and policies in which reforms will have the highest payoff in terms of enhancing efficiency and bolstering economic growth potential. Doing so will be difficult. Available data on barriers and international services transactions remain substantially weaker and less complete than those for merchandise trade. The paucity of data on the restrictiveness of current policies is particularly troublesome. Efforts undertaken during the past decade to improve trade statistics, including data on sales of services by local affiliates of foreign multinationals, have improved our knowledge of the flows involved, especially with respect to "foreign affiliate trade in services"—local sales achieved through establishment (Whichard 1999). Data on trade flows are needed for analytical purposes. But much more important from an economic policy and negotiating perspective are data on the barriers that restrict international competition. Relatively little progress has been achieved in compiling quantitative measures of the barriers restricting trade and investment flows that are comparable across sectors and across countries. Instead, the focus of attention remains largely sectoral, as was the case during the Uruguay Round.[6]

---

5. This is a phenomenon that occurs not infrequently. All other things being equal, many foreign investors are unlikely to be averse to earning rents and limiting competition once established in a market. The pattern of commitments observed in the GATS has also characterized liberalization episodes that predate the GATS. See, e.g., Cho (1988) on the approach Korea used to open access to the insurance market. For discussions of the economics of alternative instruments that are used to restrict access to service markets, see Hindley (1988) and Hoekman and Primo Braga (1997).

6. The launching of the Uruguay Round services negotiations led to a spate of sector-specific research, much of which remains relevant. Examples include a series of monographs prepared for the American Enterprise Institute (see, e.g., Aronson and Cowhey 1988; Kaspar 1988; Walter 1988; and White 1988) and numerous papers commissioned by UNCTAD focusing on developing-country interests (e.g., UNCTAD 1989). Since then the focus has centered in particular on telecommunications and financial services. For recent research output, see www.worldbank.org/trade, www.worldservicescongress.com, and www.cid.harvard.edu/cidtrade.

Some progress is being made in measuring the restrictiveness of services markets across countries and sectors, using frequency indicators of the prevalence of different types of measures, enterprise-level panel data, and US bilateral trade flow data to generate estimates of tariff equivalents.[7] This work suggests that barriers to trade in services are higher than barriers to merchandise trade—although perhaps not as high as some think; that the barriers in major "backbone" services such as transport, financial, and telecommunications services are higher than in business or distribution services; and that barriers are higher in developing countries. A major problem affecting much of this work is that it is based on indirect indicators of openness of sectors or countries and does not rely on direct measures of specific policies. From a national perspective, especially for developing countries, greater efforts are needed to generate information on the level and effects of policies that restrict international competition.

Although the data situation remains far from ideal, seeking a more balanced and comprehensive coverage of services sectors and modes of supply is the most obvious priority for negotiations. There is no a priori reason why national specific commitments should not cover *all* services and *all* modes of supply. Setting targets for expanded coverage to be achieved in the next round would help signal that governments are serious about strengthening the GATS and would provide a focal point for policymakers. Two types of targets or focal points can be envisaged, quantitative and qualitative.

Quantitative indicators that could be considered include: (1) sectoral coverage ratios—the "quantity" of national treatment and market access commitments; (2) the degree of liberalization that has been achieved by WTO members, using some agreed-on characterization of the restrictiveness of applied policies; and/or (3) the extent to which applied policies are bound in the GATS. From an economic and a market access (business) point of view, what matters most is the restrictiveness of applied policy. In GATS negotiations, this has not been the primary focus of attention, however, perhaps in part because there is no simple metric that can be applied to determine the restrictiveness of the set of policy measures that apply to a sector. Instead, efforts have centered on inclusion of sectors in national schedules. This has led to situations where a country may be relatively liberal in terms of applying national treatment or limiting market access, but has not locked this is in, that is, either has not scheduled anything at all, or, if commitments are made, has not bound the status quo in the GATS.

---

7. For recent work in this area, see Findlay and Warren (2000) and Francois and Hoekman (1999). The former use frequency indices to describe the status quo for a number of important sectors in countries for which data are available, and to assess the possible impact of liberalization. The latter use trade and financial data to construct measures of openness across countries and sectors.

In terms of designing possible quantitative focal points for GATS coverage in the next set of negotiations, it is very difficult to focus on the degree of liberalization that countries have attained. Doing so would require a de facto move to a negative list approach to scheduling, something that was rejected during the Uruguay Round, and agreement on a method to determine the level of intervention that is implied by policy (analogous to the aggregate measure of support used in the GATT Agreement on Agriculture). In principle, such measures could be developed, but it is very unlikely that agreement could be obtained from WTO members on the acceptability of any index. More practical focal points are the share of sectors that have been scheduled, and the share of commitments that involve a bound promise not to apply any national treatment of market-access-violating measures. These two indicators are objective in the sense that they do not require any judgment regarding the importance of actual policies that restrict national treatment or market access, whether scheduled or not.

Various qualitative "formula" approaches can also be envisaged. One simple qualitative coverage target would be to prohibit specific commitments for sectors or modes of supply that do not convey information and do not constrain governments: the so-called "unbound" commitments that some WTO members have included (see Hoekman 1996). Another would be to extend the national treatment principle to all instances where a nation decides to make a commitment on mode 3 (commercial presence) for a sector.

One problem with the formula approach to expanding coverage is that sectors that are important inputs into production and sectors where the barriers to trade are currently highest may remain excluded. Inconsistent treatment of interdependent service activities also may result. Consequently, request-offer negotiations cannot and should not be avoided. Priority attention should be given to key "backbone" sectors such as transport, telecommunications, and financial services as well as clusters of interdependent services that are vital to economic development and participation in the world economy (e.g., multimodal transport and express courier services).[8] Increasing the efficiency of such services sectors will have major payoffs for developing countries in terms of lower prices, higher quality, and greater product differentiation.

From a mercantilist perspective, these backbone services are sectors in which enterprises in industrialized countries can be expected to dominate the supply side. In these terms, promoting a reciprocal "balance of

---

8. As illustrated by recent theoretical research—Deardorff (1999) and Markusen, Rutherford, and Tarr (1999)—there are compelling reasons to believe that liberalization of such services deserves priority in the negotiations because they are crucial in terms of both increasing the gains from trade in goods and reducing the costs of international fragmentation of the value chain and production sharing.

concessions" thus requires that services and modes of supply where developing countries have an export interest also be put on the table. Without reciprocal concessions, developing countries are unlikely to want to bind the status quo or to use the GATS as a precommitment device for planned reforms. Even though many countries have been and can be expected to continue undertaking domestic procompetitive reforms in their services sectors, a major challenge for WTO members is to increase the incentives to bind these reforms. Despite the compelling economic arguments that can be made in favor of using international agreements as a vehicle to reduce investor uncertainty—the argument being that making binding commitments can signal a willingness on the part of governments to lock in reforms—in practice, negotiating dynamics often impede the use of agreements for this purpose. The situation that arises is similar to what occurred in the Uruguay Round, during which developing countries sought—rather unsuccessfully—to obtain "negotiating credit" for autonomous liberalization of import barriers that had been implemented in the period leading up to the launch of negotiations, as well as thereafter.

GATS Article XIX:3 requires that negotiations to expand the GATS include guidelines or modalities for the treatment of autonomous liberalization that has occurred in the period after the last multilateral round (in this case since 1994). It is unclear what should be done in this connection, that is, how "credit" should be defined, nor is it obvious that 1994-2000 is the appropriate base period given the discrepancy between applied policies and many country schedules (Fung and Stone 1999). Credit that involves developing countries obtaining the right to "do less" than other countries is unlikely to be in their own interest. It appears more productive to think of credit in terms of the quid pro quo to be put on the table by high-income countries and major middle-income emerging markets in return for a significant increase in bindings by developing countries. Existing market access commitments by OECD countries, while much more comprehensive than those made by developing countries, are not of great export interest to many developing countries. Relevant in this connection is also GATS Article IV:3, which calls for special treatment of the least-developed countries; if taken seriously, this could involve an explicit focus on improving access to markets that are of interest to such countries.

Potential trade-offs within the ambit of the services negotiations can be identified relatively easily. For example, developing countries have an interest in seeking commitments in the area of national social and medical insurance regimes, to allow patients to undergo treatment abroad. Perhaps the most obvious "big" area for trade-offs is liberalization of mode 4—temporary entry of service providers. Although undoubtedly highly sensitive, it is an area where incremental progress can be made, as one of the key instruments used to restrict trade through this mode are quotas (for visas). These can be expanded over time, with within-quota visas not being subject to economic needs tests, and with liberalization facilitated by a mode 4-specific safeguard procedure (see below).[9] It is also an area where opposition among the OECD countries is not monolithic—there are many industries that would benefit from a more liberal temporary access regime, and development of coalitions with such industries could help change the status quo.[10] Of course, a key factor determining the willingness of OECD countries to provide concessions in areas of interest to developing countries is the value that is attached to binding domestic reforms, be it on a sector-by-sector basis, or by mode of supply (e.g., agreeing to national treatment for mode 3).

Strengthening and Simplifying the Rules

The primary disciplines embodied in the GATS are MFN, market access, and national treatment. The latter two apply only on a sector-mode basis and are subject to exceptions: governments may schedule (grandfather) measures that are inconsistent with either principle. The distinction between national treatment and market access is not clear-cut, as some market access exceptions also violate national treatment. Removing such inconsistencies would clarify what a country is committed to (Feketekuty 1998).

The current approach to scheduling distinguishes among the four modes of supply that define trade. As a result, national schedules may distort incentives to use the most efficient mode, while also creating uncertainty about what rules prevail in instances where more than one mode is used to service a market. Such uncertainty also can impede dispute settlement. It creates difficulties in predicting how a panel will interpret the schedules, and thus reduces the perceived benefits from initiating dispute settlement procedures. One way to reduce potential inconsistencies in commitments across modes within a specific sector is to require one-to-one mappings between commitments on modes ("nondiscrimination across modes").[11] Such a technological neutrality principle was embodied in the Agreement on Basic Telecommunications. Modal neutrality is an objective worth pursuing, because, as is often emphasized in the literature, trade and investment have increasingly become complementary. It is also frequently noted that it will become more difficult to maintain a clear distinction between trade in goods and trade in services, as technology may give

---

9. For detailed proposals by developing-country scholars in this area, see Mukherjee (1999) and Chanda (1999).

10. Liberalization of mode 4 is not solely a North-South issue. Hodge (1999) notes that South African firms frequently run into human capital constraints and have an interest in enhancing their ability to rely on temporary services providers.

11. See, e.g., Hoekman (1996), Feketekuty (1998), Mann (2000), and Mattoo (2000).

producers the choice of delivering their products in a tangible or disembodied (digitized) form. A priori, it would appear that any multilateral disciplines should apply equally to international transactions regardless of the mode of supply. The rapid growth in e-commerce illustrates the danger of mode-specific disciplines, as it is unclear whether transactions should be defined under modes 1 or 2 (Barfield and Groombridge 1999; Mann 2000).

There are some fundamental "architectural" issues here. For example, the case can be made that WTO members should consider developing disciplines that distinguish between trade and investment, with trade in goods or services being subject to one set of common rules, and movement of factors of production to another. This, in effect, has been the approach taken in the NAFTA, which includes a separate chapter on investment (in goods or services) that is distinct from the rules relating to cross-border trade (in goods and services). This approach results in much greater consistency and clarity of the applicable rules and disciplines than the current WTO structure. These are longer-run questions that must be addressed at some point. For the time being, within the GATS setting a focus on modal neutrality can be a useful halfway house.

Efforts to attain greater neutrality could be complemented by efforts to expand the ambit of horizontal, procompetitive principles that apply to all sectors. This would help make the GATS both more transparent and more relevant to investors by allowing negotiating efforts to center more on developing disciplines that make sense in terms of long-term growth and economic development. As far as network services are concerned, a start was made in this direction in the Agreement on Basic Telecommunications, which included the development of a "Reference Paper" on regulatory principles in telecommunications. The Reference Paper includes concepts such as "affecting the terms of participation" and "essential facilities" that could usefully be extended to all network services, even those without any background of monopoly or public ownership or control.

Care must be taken to avoid attempts at imposing a one-size-fits-all approach to procompetitive regulatory principles, however, as different services will in general have different requirements and characteristics. Countries also may differ in terms of the weight that is accorded to competition policy (antitrust law) compared to direct regulatory oversight by specialized regulatory agencies. As is the case with competition law, harmonization across countries is unlikely to be first best, and any disciplines, whether sector-specific or horizontal, should be limited to procedural norms that aim at increasing transparency and accountability of regulations and regulators. One dimension that is particularly important in this connection concerns multijurisdictional situations, where central and local governments share responsibility for enforcing regulatory regimes. The "action" often occurs at the state or provincial level, implying that local regulators must be involved in the development and implementation of procedural rules at the WTO level. Improving communications and dialogue between the trade and regulatory policy communities *within* countries and between regulators *across* countries is a precondition for achieving progress in this area.[12]

Similar caution should apply to efforts to "regulate domestic regulation" in sectors where access to a network is not at issue. It has been proposed that one way to address domestic regulation is to adopt a "necessity test"—putting the burden of proof on governments to show that a particular regulation that has detrimental effects on foreign providers is necessary to achieve an objective (Mattoo 2000). Although this has proved to be a powerful procompetitive instrument in the context of the European Union (EU), it is likely to be much more difficult to apply in the WTO, given the much lower integration ambitions that prevail among WTO members and the substantially weaker institutions that will be asked to rule on claims that a regulation is not necessary. Attention could more productively be focused in the next round on expanding the reach of the national treatment and market-access principles.

Another area deserving attention in the next round is the strengthening of the reach of MFN. In the Uruguay Round, countries were permitted to schedule MFN exemptions, in part reflecting a concern on the part of regulators that MFN might impede their ability to intervene, or a desire on the part of governments to discriminate on a sectoral basis (e.g., culture). Existing provisions in the GATS already give regulators the ability to pursue actions that discriminate across firms to achieve regulatory objectives, and provide scope for entering into regional economic integration agreements. Now that some experience has been obtained with the GATS, negotiations should seek to abolish the grandfathering of policies that allow countries to discriminate against certain WTO members. Efforts should also be made to ensure that MFN applies in the area of standards and mutual recognition, with nonrecognition being made easier to contest through dispute settlement. Multilateral cooperation may be required to mitigate the competition-reducing effect of domestic regulations, especially in the area of mandatory standards—for product safety, professional certification, prudential regulation, and so on. All WTO members should be treated equally in terms of having access to the mechanisms that countries create to achieve mutual recognition. Ensuring that initiatives to achieve "deeper integration" among subsets of WTO members do not result in de facto discrimination in areas where this is not inherent in the design of such agreements is an important issue for future rule-making efforts.

---

12. Improved communication and "understanding" between trade and competition authorities was arguably the primary positive result of the working group on trade and competition policy that was created at the 1996 WTO ministerial meeting.

Outstanding Issues: Subsidies, Procurement, and Safeguards

A number of outstanding rule-making issues were left open after the Uruguay Round for further work and discussion: subsidies, procurement, and safeguards. The economic case for GATS-specific disciplines in any of these areas is weak. There is nothing services-specific about procurement: any multilateral disciplines should cover goods and services. Of primary importance for foreign firms is to have access to procurement markets, and frequently this can be achieved only if they have a commercial presence in a country. What matters in terms of economic welfare is therefore not so much policies of discrimination, but the ability of foreign firms to establish. If the sectoral coverage of the GATS is expanded and foreign providers can gain access to markets, the contestability of procurement markets will be enhanced at the same time, independently of whatever discriminatory policies are in place (Evenett and Hoekman 2000).[13]

Multilateral disciplines on subsidies might help avoid mutually destructive policies from the viewpoint of developing countries—for example, seeking to attract FDI via the use of incentives—and eliminate important sources of distortion in OECD markets for some services and modes (e.g., FDI incentives designed to divert investment from developing countries, or operating subsidies for transportation activities). In the services context, any disciplines will have to focus primarily on domestic production or operating subsidies; the distinction between export and production subsidies found in the GATT is much more difficult, if not impossible, to make in practice. It is also much more difficult to envisage emulation of the main GATT discipline—countervailing duties—increasing the need to agree to substantive rules (harmonization). Difficulties will immediately arise in distinguishing between what is "legitimate" and what is not. While there are clearly potential sources of gain for WTO members associated with a set of subsidy disciplines, often subsidies are the most efficient instrument for pursuing noneconomic objectives—to ensure universal service, to promote regional development, to offset income inequalities, and so forth. Cross-subsidies of the types that are often regarded as inefficient and nontransparent mechanisms to achieve an objective sometimes are the best available second-best instruments for developing-country governments.[14]

The GATT/WTO negotiating and implementation history illustrates that agreement on subsidy and related disciplines is difficult to obtain, and that any disciplines may easily be circumvented. Even the EU—which

---

13. It should be noted that this is not the majority view, which focuses more on market access opportunities and not on the welfare effects of procurement policies.

14. See Joskow (1998) and Laffont (1998) for general discussions of these issues from a developing country perspective.

goes much further than the WTO in this area—has encountered recurrent difficulties associated with government policies intended to attract FDI and enforcing its restrictions on the use of state aids. NAFTA does not even try to tackle this issue. Given the rationale for subsidies in many contexts and the revealed preference of many governments to use subsidies, it would appear more effective to seek to extend the reach of the national treatment principle to subsidy policies, especially when the subsidy is aimed at firms that have established a commercial presence (FDI). Given national treatment, there should be less concern about the impact of subsidy policies, allowing the principle of "subsidy freedom" to prevail. As in the procurement case, what matters most is market access and national treatment.[15]

The economic case for safeguards instruments is also weak. Insofar as governments are under pressure to (re)impose protection (discrimination), they already have the opportunity to invoke the renegotiation modalities that are built into the GATS. GATT-type safeguards (emergency protections) are difficult to rationalize in the services context because in many cases they would require taking action against foreign firms that have established a commercial presence (Hoekman 1993). Why a government would want to do this is unclear, as it can have a chilling effect on FDI and would have a negative effect on the national employees of the targeted foreign-owned firms. If safeguards are to be considered, they would therefore most likely exempt mode 3. But then it must be considered that any safeguards instrument that exempts mode 3 can easily act to induce investment, rather than trade (mode 1), thus distorting incentives (leading away from the modal neutrality objective).

There is, however, one potentially compelling argument for seeking to develop a safeguards instrument. The case could be made that the extremely limited nature of liberalization commitments to date on movement of services providers (mode 4) is in part due to the absence of safeguards instruments. As this is a mode of supply that is of major interest to developing countries and one on which almost all countries maintain stringent restrictions, one could envisage a safeguards instrument that is limited to mode 4 liberalization commitments, and is explicitly aimed at providing OECD country governments with an insurance mechanism that can be invoked if liberalization has unexpected detrimental impacts on their societies.

---

15. There are other problems that arise in contemplating subsidy rules in the GATS. Given that much of the action relates to investment incentives and analogous measures, it can again be asked what is services-specific here. Any disciplines that are regarded as beneficial should presumably also apply to investment in manufacturing, mining, or agriculture. It seems inappropriate to pursue multilateral disciplines in the GATS, as opposed to a more general set of investment-related disciplines, if there is a consensus that the issue is important enough to attempt rule making.

Achieving Greater Transparency

It is widely recognized that the "scheduling technology" used in the GATS does not greatly promote transparency. Improving the available information on status quo policies is a fundamental necessity. This will facilitate national reform efforts and help identify where the multilateral process can support such efforts. Unfortunately, there is nothing in the GATS or the WTO that encourages and assists countries in generating comprehensive information on applied policies and evaluating their impact. Some progress was made in the Uruguay Round with the creation of the Trade Policy Review Mechanism, but more can and should be done. Priority should be given to greatly improving statistics and data on trade barriers and entry-cum-operating restrictions in services. Analogous to the role played by the OECD Secretariat in compiling information on agricultural policies in the 1980s, international organizations and multinational business should devote the resources required to document the status quo and to place this information in the public domain.

The importance of strengthening the capacity to collect and analyze information cannot be overemphasized. A common mistake made by governments involved in regulatory reform is to reduce the ability of agencies to compile the information needed to monitor the impact of reforms. Better information on status quo policies, their effects, and the impact of GATS-based liberalization agreements will help governments make policy and provide stakeholders (business, civil society) with the information they need to engage in the domestic policy formation process.[16] The private sector—both the business community and NGOs—must play a prominent role in the collection, dissemination, and analysis of information on applied policies and their effects. The private sector also has a crucial role to play in the enforcement of multilateral obligations. Without active participation by business, WTO dispute settlement will have no relevance as an enforcement device (Hoekman and Mavroidis 2000). Available information and data should be placed in the public domain, including all statistics, databases, and documentation on policy measures collected by the WTO. One option that deserves serious consideration in this connection would be to resurrect an Australian proposal made at the 1996 WTO ministerial meeting to engage in a negative-list *reporting* exercise of prevailing policies in services for transparency purposes. This should be accompanied by adequate technical and financial assistance to help developing countries—and especially the least-developed countries—participate in the transparency exercise.

---

16. Analysis and research by developing-country scholars is very important in this connection, in order to increase ownership and local capacity to develop negotiating positions. Examples of the type of work that is required are emerging—see, e.g., Chadha (1999), Hodge (1998, 1999), Naude (1999), and Tohamy (1999).

Concluding Remarks

Opposition by domestic firms to the prospect of increased competition from foreign firms might not be as strong in services as in goods. The political economy of services liberalization is different from that of goods: the gross negative impact on labor employed in services is likely to be lower (given that foreign entrants will often use mode 3 and employ mostly nationals), the net impact on labor more likely to be perceived as positive (as total employment opportunities can be expected to expand),[17] and support for reform by businesses that would benefit from higher quality and lower-priced services more likely to be stronger.[18] Indeed, the countries that liberalize first might have a strategic advantage—creating further incentives to pursue domestic reforms. Narrow reciprocity—that is, "equivalent" concessions being offered by trading partners—is therefore less of a priority for developing countries than was the case for merchandise trade liberalization by OECD countries (Hoekman and Messerlin 2000). In order to benefit most from GATS talks, the multilateral process should be used to support the implementation of a national reform agenda that has been developed through domestic consultations.

There is widespread recognition among governments and civil society that pursuit of regulatory reforms in services can have very large payoffs. In this respect the political context going into the GATS 2000 talks is quite different from that prevailing in 1986, when the Uruguay Round was launched. Certainly, opposition to liberalization exists in developing countries, and countries differ on the desirable modalities and speed with which to pursue reforms. There are also valid concerns regarding the need to put in place the appropriate regulatory policies and strengthen regulatory institutions before certain types of liberalization are undertaken. But the thrust of policy in the majority of nations is toward a more market-oriented policy stance, as is reflected in widespread privatization of utilities, telecommunications operators, airlines, and so on. The success of the financial and basic telecommunications sectoral talks was largely a reflection of the fact that most of the governments involved were convinced of the need to pursue regulatory reforms in these sectors, including liberalization and elimination of entry barriers. This was a precondition for the agreements to materialize—it was clear that the associated regulatory reforms did not go beyond what had already been accomplished or decided in the national (unilateral) context.

A key factor for the next round will be expanding the extent to which reforms are locked in through the GATS, as this remains quite limited

---

17. And not just for relatively unskilled labor—see Markusen, Rutherford, and Tarr (1999).

18. For recent numerical assessments of the gains from liberalization of trade in services see Chadha (1999), Dee and Hanslow (1999), Brown and Stern (1999), and Robinson, Wang, and Martin (1999).

for many countries. Ideally, the GATS should be regarded as a valuable instrument for anchoring expectations and precommitting to a reform path (Francois 1997). In practice, however, it is not used to this effect. Greater specific commitments and binding of applied policies are unlikely to emerge without a quid pro quo deal. The potential scope for trade-offs in the GATS context is quite large, and there should be no need to rely on cross-issue linkages—although these can certainly be envisaged as well. An obvious linkage strategy *within* services would be a mode 3-mode 4 exchange, with developing countries making bound national treatment and market access commitments on mode 3 across a wide range of sectors, in return for significant expansion of access to high-income markets through mode 4.

Independently of what can be achieved in terms of binding of the status quo, the next round of services negotiations should seek to expand significantly the coverage of national treatment and market access commitments. These constitute the core of the GATS, and there is still an immense scope for expanding coverage. A formula approach might be considered to establish a benchmark or focal point for negotiations. Such a formula could center on the share of commitments that involve full bindings and the share that implies "free trade," defined as the absence of limitations on national treatment or market access. But any formula must be complemented by guidelines ensuring that the key sectors that are vital from an economic development perspective are included—financial services, telecommunications, transport, and the "trade services" sector—the cluster of activities that revolve around trade logistics and facilitation. The latter includes government services such as customs and conformity assessment procedures. While not regarded as "services" and dealt with in GATT forums, these are important activities that have a direct bearing on the ability of countries to participate in the world economy.

References

Aronson, Jonathan, and Peter Cowhey. 1988. *When Nations Talk: International Trade in Telecommunications Services.* Cambridge, MA: Ballinger Press.

Barfield, Claude E., and Mark A. Groombridge. 1999. Breaking Down Barriers in Electronic Commerce. American Enterprise Institute, photocopy.

Brown, Drusilla, and Robert M. Stern. 1999. Measurement and Modeling of the Economic Effects of Trade and Investment Barriers in Services. Photocopy.

Chadha, Rajesh. 1999. GATS and Developing Countries: A Case Study of India. National Center for Advanced Economic Research, New Delhi, photocopy.

Chanda, Rupa. 1999. Movement of Natural Persons and Trade in Services: Liberalizing Temporary Movement of Labour Under the GATS. Indian Council for Research on International Economic Relations, New Delhi, photocopy.

Cho, Yoon-Je. 1988. Some Policy Lessons from the Opening of the Korean Insurance Market. *World Bank Economic Review* 2: 239–54.

Cowhey, Peter, and Mikhail Klimenko. 1999. The WTO Agreement and Telecommunications Policy Reform. World Bank, photocopy.

Deardorff, Alan. 1999. International Provision of Trade Services, Trade, and Fragmentation. University of Michigan, photocopy.

Dee, Philippa, and Kevin Hanslow. 1999. Multilateral Liberalization of Services Trade. Productivity Commission, Australia, photocopy.

Evenett, Simon, and Bernard Hoekman. 2000. Government Procurement of Services: Assessing the Case for Multilateral Disciplines. In Pierre Sauvé and Robert Stern, eds., GATS 2000: New Directions in Services Trade Liberalization. Washington: Brookings Institution.

Feketekuty, Geza. 1998. Setting the Agenda for the Next Round of Negotiations on Trade in Services. In Jeffrey Schott, ed., Launching New Global Trade Talks: An Action Agenda. Washington: Institute for International Economics.

Findlay, Christopher, and Tony Warren, eds. 2000. Impediments to Trade in Services: Measurement and Policy Implications. Sydney: Routledge. Forthcoming.

Finger, J. Michael, and Philip Schuler. 2000. Implementation of Uruguay Round Commitments: The Development Challenge. The World Economy. April. Washington: World Bank.

Francois, Joseph. 1997. External Bindings and the Credibility of Reform. In Regional Partners in Global Markets, ed. A. Galal and B. Hoekman. London: Centre for Economic Policy Research.

Francois, Joseph, and Bernard Hoekman. 1999. Market Access in the Services Sectors. Photocopy.

Fung, Betty, and Michael Stone. 1999. Focus and Priorities of the New Round of Services Negotiations. Prepared for the World Services Congress 99, photocopy.

Hindley, Brian. 1988. Service Sector Protection: Considerations for Developing Countries. World Bank Economic Review 2: 205–24.

Hodge, James. 1998. Developing a Trade and Industrial Policy Agenda for Service Sectors in South Africa. TIPS Working Paper, Johannesburg (September).

Hodge, James. 1999. Examining the Cost of Services Protection in a Developing Country: The Case of South Africa. Prepared for the World Services Congress 99, photocopy.

Hoekman, Bernard. 1993. Safeguard Provisions and International Trade Agreements Involving Services. World Economy 16: 29–49.

Hoekman, Bernard. 1996. Assessing the General Agreement on Trade in Services. In The Uruguay Round and the Developing Countries, ed. Will Martin and L. Alan Winters. Cambridge: Cambridge University Press.

Hoekman, Bernard, and Petros C. Mavroidis. 2000. Enforcing Multilateral Commitments: Dispute Settlement and Developing Countries. World Economy, forthcoming.

Hoekman, Bernard, and Patrick Messerlin. 2000. Liberalizing Trade in Services: Reciprocal Negotiations and Regulatory Reform. In Pierre Sauvé and Robert Stern, eds., GATS 2000: New Directions in Services Trade Liberalization. Washington: Brookings Institution.

Hoekman, Bernard, and Carlos A. Primo Braga. 1997. Protection and Trade in Services: A Survey. Open Economies Review 8 (3): 285–308.

Joskow, Paul. 1998. Regulatory Priorities for Reforming Infrastructure Sectors in Developing Countries. Annual World Bank Conference on Development Economics, World Bank, photocopy.

Kaspar, Daniel. 1988. Deregulation and Globalization: Liberalizing International Trade in Air Services. Cambridge, MA: Ballinger Press.

Laffont, Jean-Jacques. 1998. Competition, Information, and Development. Annual World Bank Conference on Development Economics, photocopy.

Mann, Catherine. 2000. E-commerce, this volume.

Markusen, Jim, Thomas Rutherford, and David Tarr. 1999. Foreign Direct Investment in Services and the Domestic Market for Expertise. World Bank, photocopy.

Mattoo, Aaditya. 1999. Financial Services and the WTO: Liberalization Commitments of the Developing and Transition Economies. Policy Research Working Paper 2184, World Bank (downloadable from www.worldbank.org/trade).

Mattoo, Aaditya. 2000. Developing Countries in the New Round of GATS Negotiations: Towards a Proactive Role. *World Economy*, forthcoming.

Mukherjee, Neela. 1999. Market Access Commitments Under GATS: An Analysis from Developing Countries' Perspective. Prepared for the World Services Congress 99, photocopy.

Naude, W. 1999. Trade in Transport Services: South Africa and the GATS. TIPS Working Paper, Johannesburg (August).

Robinson, Sherman, Zhi Wang, and Will Martin. 1999. Capturing the Implications of Services Trade Liberalization. World Bank, photocopy.

Tohamy, Sahar. 1999. A Case Study of Egypt's Services Liberalization, Services Barriers, and Implementation of the GATS. Egyptian Center for Economic Studies, photocopy (presented at the World Services Congress 99).

UNCTAD. 1989. *Trade in Services: Sectoral Issues.* New York: United Nations.

Walter, Ingo. 1988. *Global Competition in Financial Services: Market Structure, Protection, and Trade Liberalization.* Cambridge, MA: Ballinger Press.

Whichard, Obie. 1999. Measurement, Classification, and Reporting of Services Activities: An International Perspective. World Bank, photocopy (downloadable from www.worldbank.org/trade).

White, Lawrence. 1988. *International Trade in Ocean Shipping Services.* Cambridge, MA: Ballinger Press.

10

Intellectual Property Issues for the New Round

KEITH E. MASKUS

The founding of the World Trade Organization (WTO) ushered in an era of global protection for intellectual property. Each WTO member must establish and enforce policies that meet the minimum standards set out in the Agreement on Trade-Related Intellectual Property Rights (TRIPs). Many developing countries are defining and implementing the laws and regulations under which they will comply with TRIPs. The bulk of the least-developed countries have barely begun this endeavor, for they are not required to be in compliance until 1 January 2006.

Despite the successful negotiations that culminated in TRIPs, significant and contentious issues concerning intellectual property rights (IPRs) remain in the international arena. The TRIPs agreement itself is a work in progress in that a number of unsettled issues remain open for further visitation and renegotiation (Maskus 1998a). In addition, concerns over the effectiveness of the agreement in achieving its goals are mounting on the part of both developed countries and, especially, developing countries. Furthermore, IPR protection bears strong implications for a number of important collateral issues that loom large on the international trade agenda. Among these problems are the use of competition regulations to discipline the anticompetitive effects of IPRs, the potential for patents granted in pharmaceuticals and biotechnology to raise the costs of critical technologies, and the impacts of property rights on the scope for environmental protection.

The fact that TRIPs remains under implementation and is viewed with suspicion in several quarters suggests that it is unlikely to be considerably

---

Keith E. Maskus is professor of economics and director of graduate studies at the University of Colorado at Boulder.

extended in the next round of trade negotiations. If anything, key developing nations may mount an effort to contract its scope, an effort that surely would meet considerable opposition among major developed countries.

Thus, somewhat paradoxically, while IPR protection per se may not be the subject of significant reform in the Millennium Round, the collateral issues it raises could strongly influence discussions over directions in which the trading system could evolve. This possibility would become particularly relevant if the next round is focused on addressing the needs of developing countries in world trade, as is advocated in some quarters (see Stiglitz 1999).

In this paper I argue that, in light of considerable controversy about the international distribution of potential costs and benefits from stronger IPRs, it would be premature, and possibly counterproductive, to substantially revise or extend TRIPs. Such an extension would require widespread confidence that intellectual property protection bears notable and identifiable net benefits in the long run for the bulk of WTO members. This confidence is far from evident, and, if anything, prior enthusiasm about such benefits appears to be waning. An attempt to open TRIPs to further disciplines could encounter offsetting demands to restrict markedly its scope and application.

At the center of this debate lies a critical economic question that bears close examination: What are the short-term and long-term costs and benefits of intellectual property protection for technology-importing countries? This highly complex question for some time has remained largely in the realm of speculation and claims based on case studies. However, sufficient systematic empirical evidence now exists that an assessment may be provided. Thus in the next section I provide summary computations of the possible impacts of TRIPs on short-run rent transfers and long-run flows of foreign direct investment (FDI) and technology transfer. These computations are offered primarily as a basis for discussion rather than as definitive answers. At this time, however, the evidence indicates that many developing countries could gain significant growth benefits from rising technology trade and growing dynamic competition in the long run. However, this effect depends on a number of collateral national policies and economic characteristics. The implication is that as developing countries implement stronger IPRs, they need to work on a broad policy front to achieve these positive impacts.

With this background, in the third section I discuss whether existing provisions of the TRIPs agreement are adequate to support this procompetitive treatment of intellectual property. I argue that the provisions are broadly appropriate to this task but that to use them effectively requires additional commitment on the part of developed countries to diffuse the fruits of technical change within the boundaries of the system. This may be particularly beneficial in the case of pharmaceuticals.

In the fourth section I point out that while TRIPs per se should not be opened to extensive renegotiation, aspects of the agreement invite WTO members to consider whether negotiations are appropriate in competition policy and environmental protection. Detailed treatment of these complex questions is left to other contributors to this volume. My conclusion is that it is appropriate for the WTO to pursue a limited agreement on competition regulation, while environmental agreements should be reached outside the WTO in the main.

International Economic Implications of TRIPs

The TRIPs agreement ushers in extensive obligations for protecting intellectual property through the elaboration and enforcement of minimum standards. An obvious question is the degree to which these policy changes will affect global economic activity. It is difficult to answer such a complex question in a satisfying manner, but recent evidence may be brought to bear. It is useful first to describe briefly the major changes required in TRIPs standards, which have been discussed thoroughly elsewhere (Primo Braga 1996; Watal 2000).

Substantive Provisions of the TRIPs Agreement

For purposes of the present discussion it is sufficient simply to list the most significant changes in required norms of protection. An important general obligation is the introduction of most favored nation (MFN) treatment into IPRs. Patents must be provided for at least 20 years from the filing date. Countries may not exclude any area of technology, such as pharmaceutical goods, from eligibility for patents. There is a reversal of the burden of proof in process patent cases, shifting the burden from the complainant to the defendant, who must now show that his process does not infringe the patent. Patents extend to biotechnological inventions, though exclusions may be permitted for essentially biological methods and higher life organisms. Effective protection of plant breeders' rights is required. Compulsory licenses may be issued in patented technologies only under limited circumstances and must bear adequate compensation. A complicated interim procedure for providing exclusive marketing rights pertains to pharmaceutical products and agricultural chemicals during the ongoing transition to new patent regimes.

Countries must extend protection for well-known trademarks and recognize service marks and collective marks. Compulsory licenses of trademarks are prohibited and circumstances permitting cancellation of registration for nonuse are sharply curtailed. Geographical indications must be protected as well. Each WTO member must develop a system for protecting trade secrets from unfair competition, and commercial data submitted for regulatory purposes must be safeguarded against unfair use and disclosure.

Computer programs and data bases must be protected (at a minimum) as literary devices, thereby requiring copyright coverage for at least 50 years. This protection bars literal copying, and the scope for fair-use decompilation of software remains open to interpretation. Copyright owners are provided rental rights as well.

Countries must develop effective enforcement measures, including scope for awarding damages to rights holders and for issuing criminal penalties against willful infringement. The TRIPs accord also permits the use of competition regulation to discipline the abusive exercise of IPRs. Developing countries have transition periods in which to implement the requirements. Finally, disputes in the intellectual property area are subject to the integrated dispute settlement mechanism.

The Debate over Economic Implications

The advent of this global policy regime invites considerable and heated argument over how it will affect prospects for economic growth. Advocates of intellectual property rights claim that the stronger protection will encourage significant flows of new technology to developing countries. Such flows would emerge from a combination of two impacts. First, there could be a substitution effect, in which tightened IPRs in poor countries would make them more attractive to foreign direct investors relative to developed nations that already have strong systems of protection. Second, there could be a scale effect, in which greater protection would raise the incentives for innovation and expand the supply of new products and technologies. Note that one claim combines these effects: stronger patent rights in developing countries should expand innovation in products of particular interest to their consumers, most prominently treatments for tropical diseases. Advocates of stronger IPRs also claim that innovation within developing countries would flourish as a result of the greater incentives afforded for local market development.

In contrast, skeptics raise concerns about the potential impacts of TRIPs. Stronger IPRs could raise the costs of critical technologies, intermediate inputs, and consumer products and services in technology-importing countries. Particular concerns in this regard are raised about pharmaceuticals, biotechnological inventions, plant varieties, and software. Tightened abilities of rights holders to limit access to their creations could restrict the global diffusion of information, raising further fears about bifurcation between technology haves and have-nots. Stronger IPRs could raise the costs of imitating products and technologies, placing severe pressures on local imitative firms to adjust to new forms of competition. Further, concerns are raised about extending private property rights to areas that many governments consider the domain of public policy, including the provision of medicines, the exploitation of genetic resources, and the preservation of biodiversity.

Economics has much to say about this debate but relatively little to offer in terms of concrete predictions. Intellectual property rights operate inherently in imperfect markets for the creation and dissemination of information. They both create static market power and provide incentives for dynamic competition, meaning that they have impacts that work at cross-currents and vary across countries and over time. Economic theory offers rich descriptions about how IPRs affect these incentives but cannot provide definitive answers as to whether an agreement to strengthen global protection would improve or worsen welfare and growth prospects. Put more starkly, in contrast to the economic dictum that free trade is beneficial for all countries, there is no optimum benchmark for global protection of IPRs. Rather, the questions involved are empirical.

Evidence on Economic Impacts

Attempting to assess the impacts of such complex changes in an empirical framework is difficult for many reasons. Regulatory standards are not readily amenable to measurement, as are tariffs. Intellectual property rights have impacts that vary with economic circumstances in each nation. At their essence, IPRs are aimed at affecting the dynamic conditions of market competition, but data lend themselves more readily to static estimation. Many of the economic activities that IPRs are supposed to influence, such as FDI, technology transfer, and innovation, are poorly measured or not widely reported. Thus empirical estimates of IPRs' impacts should be treated with caution.

Nonetheless, recent studies have made progress in pushing such estimation forward, and it is useful to report the results because they do help shed light on the debate.[1] Results of four such studies, updated to 1995 figures, are listed in table 1 for selected nations.

The first column updates the results of McCalman (1999), who estimated the impacts of stronger patent rights required in TRIPs on the value of patents in place in 1988. Firms own patent portfolios in various countries, the values of which depend on the strength of local protection. McCalman determined the required changes in patent laws, as measured by the index developed by Ginarte and Park (1997), for 29 countries, some of which appear in table 1. His experiment was to apply these changes to 1988 patent portfolios in order to investigate the implied change in rents (profits) had the stronger laws been in place at that time. Thus the analysis holds patenting constant at its pre-TRIPs level and does not

---

1. A full description is provided in Maskus (2000).

Table 1 Estimates of impacts of TRIPs patent changes on international flows of economic activity, for selected countries (millions of 1995 dollars)

Country	Net patent rents	Mfg. imports	High-tech mfg. imports	FDI assets	Unaffiliated royalties and licensing fees
US	5,760	233	−3	n.a.	n.a.
Germany	997	2,304	−18	−1,084	92
Switzerland	28	35	−1	−94	0
Australia	−28	102	−2	−256	2
Ireland	−61	100	−2	−245	13
New Zealand	−68	45	−1	−76	4
Portugal	−110	605	95	89	n.a.
Greece	−149	382	53	47	n.a.
Netherlands	−222	133	−3	−1,380	29
Spain	−436	2,070	319	−313	43
Japan	−555	918	−21	−2,326	719
UK	−684	272	−5	−1,257	26
Canada	−1,294	754	−12	−2,188	63
Panama	0.4	16	n.a.	284	n.a.
Israel	−83	30	5	6	0.6
Colombia	−97	2,927	479	1,093	n.a.
South Africa	−143	154	21	23	10
Rep. of Korea	−326	2,732	588	248	356
Mexico	−562	5,749	1,519	3,182	136
India	−665	1,465	146	128	58
Brazil	−1,172	3,125	627	3,219	114
Argentina	n.a.	1,150	196	662	59
Bangladesh	n.a.	130	14	n.a.	n.a.
Chile	n.a.	2017	276	975	n.a.
China	n.a.	15,379	2,585	631	n.a.
Indonesia	n.a.	6,628	667	1,805	166

n.a. = not available

Sources: Net patent rents from McCalman (1999); manufacturing imports from Maskus and Penubarti (1995); FDI assets from Maskus (1998b); and unaffiliated royalties and licensing fees from Yang and Maskus (1999).

account for any endogenous changes in innovation and applications. It is aimed at understanding how stronger patents would affect net international rent transfers, holding innovation constant. The effects depend on patent stocks in place and the extent of the legal changes required.

I have updated his figures to millions of 1995 dollars through the use of national GDP deflators and exchange rates. While this increases the magnitudes somewhat, it does not affect the central message. Overwhelmingly the United States gains the most income in terms of static rent transfers, with a net inflow of some $5.8 billion per year. This reflects the fact that US-headquartered firms own numerous patents in many countries that must upgrade their intellectual property protection to comply with TRIPs, while US law was subject to virtually no change. Germany receives an additional net income of $997 million on its patent portfolio. Most countries experience a rising net outflow of patent rents, both because of significant changes in their laws and because they tend to be net technology importers. The largest net outward transfer of some $1.3 billion accrues to Canada, in which many US-owned patents would receive stronger protection. Developing countries also end up paying more on the stock of patents, with Brazil experiencing a net outward transfer of around $1.2 billion per year.

These calculations are inherently zero-sum and static in nature. They ask solely what the additional income on existing patents would have been under TRIPs.[2] In that sense, one might characterize TRIPs as an outstanding example of strategic trade policy on behalf of the United States, though it is equally possible to characterize weak IPRs as a mechanism employed by other governments for appropriating rents from American inventors. The figures are interesting because they suggest that TRIPs could have a significant impact on net incomes earned from foreign patents. To put the result in perspective, net royalties and licensing fees earned by US-resident firms amounted to $20.9 billion in 1995 (International Monetary Fund 1997).

However, the figures do not account for any additional activity that TRIPs could create. The next two columns report calculations of predicted changes in imports that could be induced by stronger patent rights, updated from a general equilibrium trade model estimated by Maskus and Penubarti (1995). The authors pointed out that variable IPRs across countries could influence trade flows in a number of ways. The essential trade-off from strengthening patents would be between a contraction of trade because of stronger market power on the part of protected firms and an expansion of trade because such firms would find higher demand for their products. The calculations in column 2 are for total manufacturing imports. They apply elasticities of imports with respect to patent rights, computed from an econometric analysis of bilateral 1984 trade data, to 1995 imports. For this purpose, the patent index used was an instrumented version of that developed by Rapp and Rozek (1990). This index was increased in various amounts for different countries, reflecting their commitments under TRIPs. Thus the attempt is to predict the effect of stronger patents on imports rather than to look at price impacts on fixed trade flows.

The volume impacts depend on patent revisions, market size, and the extent of the imitation threat that TRIPs reduces. Results range from small impacts in the United States and Switzerland, which are not required to undertake much legal revision, to substantial increases in imports in China,

---

2. In principle, the column should sum to zero, but it does not because of the updating and because some countries are excluded.

Thailand, Indonesia, and Mexico, which are so required.[3] In the case of Mexico, it has accelerated the update of its IPR regime in part because of commitments under the North American Free Trade Agreement (NAFTA). The result here suggests that a substantial component of Mexico's increase in manufacturing imports in the 1990s may be attributed, other things being equal, to stronger patent protection. It is instructive that many of the largest predicted impacts are in nations with strong imitation capacities, such as China, Korea, and Brazil. In contrast, Bangladesh experiences relatively weak impacts, though still positive, consistent with its weaker imitation abilities.

The third column reports similar computations for imports of high-technology manufactures, defined as pharmaceuticals, electrical machinery, and professional instruments. Sectoral regression estimates (not reported) implied that stronger IPRs in developed economies would actually reduce such trade in the developed economies because of a market-power effect and a diversion of trade to developing countries, which had strongly positive import elasticities in these goods.

Overall, the trade volume impacts estimated here are significant for developing economies that revise their patent laws extensively. For example, the increase in manufactured imports for Mexico of $5.7 billion amounts to 9.4 percent of its manufactured imports in 1995. But this impact would take years to emerge because the patent obligations are to be phased in over time. In that context, even if the impacts are overestimated the evidence suggests the long-run effects could be substantial.

I also report the results of econometric estimation of a model of FDI and IPRs (Maskus 1998b). The dollar figures in column 4 are derived from coefficients developed in a four-equation simultaneous system, which incorporated the impacts of patent rights on patent applications, affiliate sales, exports, and affiliate assets, estimated with panel data over 1986-94 for the foreign operations of US majority-owned manufacturing affiliates. The assets equation generated a negative coefficient on patent rights, suggesting that, on average and across countries, stronger patents would diminish the local asset stock. However, there was a large positive coefficient on patents interacted with a dummy variable for developing countries that resulted in a positive elasticity. This indicates that at low IPR protection levels difficulties with protecting proprietary technologies encourage maintaining them within the firm through FDI while patent protection gains strength, but that as protection exceeds a particular level there is a substitution effect favoring licensing over investment. In brief, there is a negative elasticity of FDI with respect to patent rights in high-income economies but a strongly positive elasticity among developing economies.

---

3. China has largely met TRIPs requirements in its legislation in anticipation of joining the WTO.

In this context, by applying these elasticities to anticipated changes in patent rights engineered by TRIPs, one can predict the indicated impacts on asset stocks. Reductions in asset stocks are large in absolute terms in Japan and Canada at over $2 billion each, though these impacts are smaller than 1 percent of US-owned 1994 assets. However, FDI assets are predicted to rise significantly in Brazil, Mexico, and Indonesia as a result of stronger patent protection. Indeed, the increase in the Mexican FDI asset stock would be 2.6 percent of 1994 US-owned assets in that country and that in Brazil would be 7.4 percent. On this evidence, it seems that FDI decisions are highly responsive to significant changes in intellectual property rights.

A final issue is whether licensing volumes are sensitive to changes in IPRs. The figures in the fifth column update results from Yang and Maskus (1999), who estimated the impacts of international variations in patent rights on the volume (in 1990 dollars) of unaffiliated royalties and licensing fees (a proxy for arm's-length technology transfer) paid to US firms. They used the Ginarte-Park index in a panel of 26 countries in 1985, 1990, and 1995. In their preferred specification, the patent index had a significant and positive impact on licensing.[4] The elasticity of licensing with respect to patent rights was estimated to be 5.3, suggesting a significant sensitivity of technology trade to IPR protection. Applying this elasticity to anticipated changes in patent rights, using fees existing in 1995, generates the predicted changes in volume reported in the final column. Japan had a large absolute response, reflecting the importance of licensing in the Japanese economy. However, large responses were also discovered in Korea, Mexico, Brazil, and Indonesia. Indeed, the analysis suggests that arm's-length licensing volumes in Mexico and India would double and that in Indonesia it would go up by a factor of nearly five.

The findings reported above are predictions of long-run impacts of TRIPs patent protections on imports, FDI, and market-based technology transfer. Some uncertainty still attaches to these figures, but they are sufficiently robust to allow one to conclude that stronger IPRs could significantly and positively affect transfer of technology to developing countries through each of these channels. This result is especially pertinent in large developing countries with significant imitative capabilities. The results are less striking for the least-developed economies, where the impacts are positive but smaller.[5]

---

4. They also detected a positive impact on licensing of industrial processes and a weaker but positive effect on affiliated royalties and licensing fees. It is impossible to disentangle the extent to which this response entails higher licensing charges on given technologies, higher-quality technologies, or higher contract volumes. However, the response is so elastic there is surely a considerable amount of additional technology being transferred.

5. Smith (1999) finds that bilateral trade volumes are positively and highly elastic to patent rights in middle-income economies but could fall as patents are strengthened in the least-developed countries, other things being equal.

A Growth Benefit?

A question that emerges from this work—one that is at the heart of controversy about IPRs—is whether these results support a finding that TRIPs will boost economic growth by increasing developing countries' access to technology and accelerating its adoption. This question cannot be answered in a straightforward manner because the studies surveyed here did not place their analysis into a growth framework. Nonetheless, it is worth pointing out that other studies support a growing consensus among economists that trade and FDI function as important channels of technology transfer, learning, and competition. In turn, both imports of high-technology goods and inward FDI are associated with higher growth rates.[6] For its part, technology licensing directly transfers technological information into the local production stream. Thus the various econometric results point to a potential growth benefit from the expansion of inward technology flows and their diffusion through the economy via competition and learning effects. To this observation may be added the important finding that international patenting activity strongly supports the spread of technology, at least among OECD countries (Eaton and Kortum 1996).

While it is difficult to translate this impact into a figure on growth enhancement based on current evidence, a result from Gould and Gruben (1996) bears directly on the question. They found no direct impact of patent rights on growth, but there was a significantly positive effect when a patents measure was paired with a measure of openness to trade. Their estimates suggested that growth induced by IPR protection (at moderate levels of protection characteristic of middle-income developing countries) was approximately 0.66 percentage points higher per year in open economies than in closed economies. The argument essentially is that more open economies experience greater competition and higher amounts of competitive FDI (as opposed to tariff-seeking and inefficient FDI), and they acquire advanced technologies for purposes of raising product quality. Moreover, firms in such countries are more likely to shoulder the costs of effective technology transfer and adaptation to local circumstances, which are vital components of innovation in developing economies. However, such innovation will be more in evidence in economies with protection for intellectual property. This growth impact of IPRs in open economies, associated with inward trade, investment, and technology flows, is significant. To illustrate, consider two economies with an initial real income per capita of $5,000. Over a 10-year period, if output in one economy grows 2.0 percent faster than population, its real income per capita will reach $7,430. An identical (but more open) economy growing at 2.66 percent

---

6. On trade and growth, see Frankel and Romer (1999) and Coe, Helpman, and Hoffmaister (1997). On FDI and growth, see Borensztein, De Gregorio, and Lee (1998).

above population would achieve a real income per capita of $8,453. This finding bears the important implication that as countries strengthen their IPRs, accompanying market liberalization provides a more affirmative path to economic growth.

Another relevant study is by Park and Ginarte (1997), who focused on how IPRs affect growth and investment in capital and R&D. They found no direct correlation between patent strength and growth, but there was a strong and positive impact of patents on physical investment and R&D spending, which in turn raised growth performance. This result is consistent with that in Borensztein, De Gregorio, and Lee (1998), who found that FDI has a significantly positive impact on growth, but only in countries that had attained a threshold level of secondary education within their populations. In this sense, IPRs, openness, FDI, and human capital accumulation seem to work jointly in raising productivity and growth.

These findings point out that intellectual property protection becomes more effective in attracting economic activity when it is combined with appropriate collateral national characteristics. Simply strengthening IPRs alone may be of limited utility in promoting FDI, innovation, and technological change in an environment of weak competition and limited skills. Rather, countries in this situation may find that tighter IPRs invite monopoly behavior without much benefit in terms of dynamic competition.

Using TRIPs to Enhance Competition

Within this context, does TRIPs provide an adequate framework for improving global growth prospects yet achieving a balance of interests between technology developers and technology users? In broad terms I believe the answer to this question is yes. Conditions of competition for technology developers will be improved by stronger minimum standards and greater certainty about the degree of protection available in various markets. Creative firms in the copyright industries should benefit from a reduction over time in counterfeiting. Enhanced trademark protection in developing countries should reduce problems with consumer product safety and provide incentives for entrepreneurial business development.[7]

In the short term, developing countries adopting stronger protection could suffer adjustment problems as infringing firms are forced to undertake alternative activities or pay more to acquire licenses for technologies and trademarks. Moreover, costs of implementation, administration, and enforcement are likely to be significant in the intellectual property area. It will also be difficult to overcome entrenched domestic interests favoring continued weak IPRs.

---

7. Maskus (2000) discusses these processes in detail and reports survey evidence supporting them in Lebanon and China.

To make this investment, developing economies need to be convinced that they will see long-term gains from TRIPs. In this context, TRIPs should not be viewed as a rigid device that requires harmonized, strong standards in all countries. Rather, the agreement retains flexibility for choosing standards that pay attention to the development needs of particular economies while meeting TRIPs obligations. Economic development is a dynamic process, and IPRs may be used fruitfully to push it forward. The dynamic shortcoming of weak IPRs is that economies are liable to remain technologically isolated and to lag increasingly behind the information frontier. A strategy of free riding on foreign technologies bears short-run advantages, but those adopting such a strategy suffer from inadequate access to new information and a growing inability to imitate it.

The task in selecting IPR standards is to ensure that they promote dynamic competition, including encouraging transfer of technologies that may be learned and diffused through the economy using fair means. It is evident that countries at different levels of economic development would prefer to set standards of varying degrees of liberality. Least-developed countries might opt for minimal, TRIPs-consistent standards with wide limitations. Middle-income industrializing nations should see the value of more protective standards and the recognition of trade secrets. Countries in which the technology developers predominantly reside would prefer strict standards combined with competition regulation.

Flexibility in TRIPs

In fact, TRIPs provides room for each of these strategies. A brief review of how standards may be varied is instructive. While patents must be applied to all fields of technology, countries may take advantage of allowable exclusions from eligibility for purposes of maintaining public order, national defense, and environmental protection. They may exclude therapeutic, surgical, and diagnostic techniques. Patents need not be extended to discoveries of nature, scientific principles, and algorithms. Patents need not pertain to higher life forms, nor must plant varieties be patented if they are protected by another system. Neither must patents be provided for computer programs, an exclusion that applies in the new patent laws of Brazil, Argentina, and China. Countries also have flexibility in defining the conditions for awarding patent protection. Included here would be the recognition of patent claims with narrow scope of coverage, protection for small inventions through the provision of utility models, and permission for interested parties to oppose the validity of a patent claim before it is granted.[8]

---

8. Maskus and McDaniel (1999) provide econometric evidence that the Japanese patent system, built on these principles in the postwar era, generated notable productivity gains.

Article 30 of TRIPs provides that member states may allow for unauthorized use of patented inventions under certain circumstances, so long as these exceptions do not unreasonably interfere with the exploitation of the patent and do not unreasonably prejudice the legitimate interests of the patent holder. In practice, this allows countries to permit limited use for research and experimental or teaching purposes, for obtaining approval of generic drugs, and for preparation of individual medicines by pharmacies. Such limitations appear in the patent laws of many developed countries. The research and teaching exceptions are particularly important for promoting learning and dynamic competition.

The TRIPs accord places new limits on the use of compulsory licenses but recognizes their potential suitability as competition-enhancing devices or as means of ensuring access to critical technologies. The provisions of Article 31 reflect a compromise between technology developers and users and do not unduly burden policymakers wishing to employ compulsory licenses in specified circumstances. In particular, they may be used to overcome practices that have been demonstrated by authorities to be anticompetitive. Overall, TRIPs amounts to an increase in the cost of acquiring licensed technologies but is not a significant interference with conditions under which licenses may be compelled. For example, the Argentine patent law expressly envisions the use of compulsory licenses, permitting domestic pharmaceutical firms to retain relatively flexible access to foreign-owned patented drugs and chemical processes. This situation is a concern for major international pharmaceutical firms.

Countries are required to afford some form of protection for plant varieties. It is unlikely that many developing countries will adopt patents in this area. Rather, they may provide regimes permitting a breeders' exemption and a farmers' privilege. The latter policy is unpopular among plant variety developers but is widely viewed as an effective antidote to higher seed prices.

Article 39 of TRIPs calls for laws or judicial procedures aimed at preventing unfair acquisition of trade secrets. Left undefined are the acts deemed to be unfair, leaving some flexibility to implementing states. The agreement does not mention reverse engineering, suggesting that this method of learning trade secrets may be considered an appropriate form of competition. From the standpoint of dynamic learning and efficiency, it is sensible for technology followers to recognize a reverse engineering right. This right affords potential rivals the ability to discover and use unpatented information, but only at the cost of undertaking their own potentially costly and time-consuming engineering and design efforts. Overall, a regime of trade secrets protection with liberal treatment of reverse engineering promises one of the greatest potential dynamic benefits for industrializing economies.

Similar comments apply to the specification of fair-use exceptions in copyright protection. It is acceptable to allow limited copying for educational and research purposes. While duplication and slavish copying of computer programs must be prohibited, TRIPs allows for reverse engineering of software by honest means. The ability to decompile software in order to understand the unprotected aspects of the code is partially responsible for the development of applications software in numerous developed and developing economies.

Within this broad milieu, nations have considerable latitude to set IPR standards and to regulate the behavior that those IPRs engender. Governments may be expected to establish standards that, while consistent with minimum TRIPs requirements, could tilt the balance of competition toward technology users. Many choices made during the current implementation period will not be to the liking of intellectual property interests in industrial nations. For example, Brazil passed patent legislation that went into force in 1997. This law extends the term of protection to 20 years from the filing date, recognizes the patentability of pharmaceutical products and agricultural chemicals, and establishes reversal of the burden of proof in process patents. Yet it retains broad procedures for issuing compulsory licenses. For this reason it has been called inadequate by the Pharmaceutical Research and Manufacturers' Association. Similarly, the new South African law on pharmaceutical patents and price regulation is controversial in its liberal treatment of compulsory licenses and parallel imports.

Is TRIPs Working?

That TRIPs is a flexible agreement does not necessarily mean that it operates to everyone's satisfaction. As the examples above suggest, implementation strategies adopted over the near term promise to be contentious. American trade authorities claim that adequate international implementation and enforcement of obligations are US priorities, which should be met before further IPR negotiations are undertaken (interview of Joseph Papovich, assistant US trade representative, *Inside US Trade*, 16 July 1999).

For their part, many developing countries doubt whether TRIPs' intended benefits, in terms of additional technology transfer on reasonable terms, will be forthcoming. Articles 66 and 67 of TRIPs commit industrial nations to identify measures they could take to encourage such transfers in various modes, in particular to the least-developed countries, and to promote mechanisms to build a sound and viable technological base in the recipient countries. To date few efforts have been made in this regard, generating concerns by technology importers that technology exporters do not intend to employ TRIPs equitably. Moreover, authorities in many developing countries express concerns about the medium-term effects of TRIPs on pharmaceutical prices and on the costs of intermediate inputs and critical technologies. In consequence, there is some risk that serious efforts could be mounted in the next round to modify TRIPs in ways that could prove inimical to technology developers, including the negotiation of international principles governing the use of IPRs in technology licensing.

While it may be premature to envision such a modification, the concerns underlying it are real and appear to be mounting. In this connection, negotiators from developed countries ought to devise an active agenda rather than simply defend TRIPs in its current form. That agenda could be based on the proposition that the Millennium Round should be viewed as the Development Round in order to align the interests of developing countries more closely with the international trading system. The treatment of IPRs is a good place to advance this idea, both in terms of the built-in agenda and in collateral measures aimed at regulating rights holders and widening the gains from intellectual property protection.

The Built-in Agenda

The primary issue here is that research-intensive biotechnology firms and plant developers were unsatisfied with the relatively wide exceptions to protection permitted by TRIPs Article 27.3. In order to move TRIPs forward, a compromise was reached wherein members would review the operation of this article in 1999 with a view toward revising it. This review has not been undertaken fully. In light of serious concerns about the implications of tighter protection for users of such technologies in developing (and developed) countries, it seems advisable not to engineer a substantial strengthening of these conditions for the foreseeable future.

The TRIPs agreement is being tested and interpreted through a variety of disputes about the extent of obligations it requires. For example, a recent WTO panel found India to be in violation of TRIPs' requirement to provide effective registration mechanisms and exclusive marketing rights for drugs under foreign protection. This case represented a political failure to meet terms of the agreement, and India has since complied. More difficult are cases in which legal procedures are apparently in compliance with the letter of TRIPs but may violate its basic intention of raising protection for rights holders. The current dispute over South Africa's patent law in pharmaceuticals is a case in point. Further adjudication of disputes will be important in determining the legal boundaries of TRIPs—a task that would seem to take precedence over its significant modification in the next round.

Within the context of TRIPs as it currently stands, developed countries could do much to raise enthusiasm for it by making better efforts to find mechanisms for enhancing technology transfer and to provide additional technical assistance to poor countries. Such programs could be viewed as investments in raising local awareness and support for IPRs, with potentially fruitful payoffs.

Beyond TRIPs

The agreement does much to strengthen intellectual property protection and increase the certainty facing international use of intellectual assets. However, several key issues within the IPR area were not addressed, suggesting that they may become increasingly contentious without some effort to resolve them.

One of these is exhaustion, or the treatment of parallel imports. Parallel imports are goods produced legitimately but imported without the authorization of an IPR owner. Economic theory cannot demonstrate that either a global policy of national exhaustion (banning parallel trade) or of international exhaustion (permitting parallel trade) is uniformly beneficial. Parallel imports could integrate markets but also could interfere with investments in market development and with price regulations taken for purposes of public health and nutrition. Empirical evidence is scarce and currently unpersuasive. At this time there is insufficient information to support an abandonment of the traditional approach of allowing each country to decide its own policy in this area. Pharmaceuticals are a special case, and international negotiations over the scope of parallel trade in this sector may be beneficial.

A second issue regards the relationship of IPRs to environmental protection. It is unclear how TRIPs might affect international environmental use. The impact is likely to be positive in some respects and negative in others. On the one hand, for example, there are concerns that TRIPs will raise incentives to extract genetic materials and develop patentable products from them but that the gains will not be shared with governments or local landowners. The agreement is also criticized for not safeguarding biological diversity while it extends protection to drugs and biotechnological inventions. On the other hand, by extending property rights, incentives for rational conservation efforts could be enhanced. Because of the uncertainty involved, policies at the interface between intellectual property and environmental regulation should address both areas. For example, any attempts to strengthen the TRIPs language on plant varieties and biotechnology could be accompanied by provisions regarding rights in genetic resources. Further, the relationship between TRIPs and the Convention on Biodiversity could be clarified.

Third, it is difficult to overstate the depth of concern emerging in developing countries (and some developed countries) about the potential impacts of pharmaceutical patents on drug prices. The issue is seen largely as one of transferring rents abroad at the cost of higher prices and diminished health status, with little beneficial impact in terms of local pharmaceutical innovation even in the long run. A number of studies question how significant the price impacts will be.[9] Much depends on market structure, the extent of markets that may be subjected to patent protection, alternative products available, and the nature of price regulation. Nonetheless, using reasonable parameters, one could expect sizable price increases. The impact could be particularly burdensome in nations where alternative treatments are scarce.

The problem largely reflects a substantial market and policy failure. Because incomes are low and patent protection is weak in poor countries, research pharmaceutical companies do not devote resources to developing therapies for endemic diseases existing there. For example, the World Health Organization (1996) claims that of the $56 billion spent globally on medical R&D in 1994, only 0.2 percent was on pneumonia, diarrheal maladies, and tuberculosis, which account for 18 percent of global illness and are found overwhelmingly in poor countries. Virtually all of this research was undertaken by public agencies or military authorities. It is conceivable that the stronger patent protection required by TRIPs could expand demand sufficiently to overcome this difficulty and direct adequate resources to finding cures for such diseases. However, this seems quite unlikely over the medium term, as long as disease sufferers in such countries remain impoverished. A review of the available evidence is not persuasive that patent protection in poor countries would make much of a difference in this context.

In this regard, the Sachs proposal for using foreign assistance budgets from wealthy countries to reward R&D in designated diseases presents an intriguing mix of private and public incentives to address the problem.[10] In particular, firms that first develop an effective treatment, such as a malaria vaccine, would be provided a guaranteed payment per unit of output and patent-like production privileges. However, aid resources would be devoted to transferring the dosages at low cost to patients in poor countries. The proposal needs to be fleshed out in detail to examine its feasibility and cost. It is not clear, for example, whether a winner-takes-all approach is the optimal one from a procurement perspective. Moreover, extensive controls on parallel exports of dosages would be required to support the low pricing regimes in recipient nations. Nonetheless, this is an example of a sweeping and positive proposal for addressing a critical need that is only partially addressed by IPRs. A credible determination to go forward with planning such a system could do much to restore confidence in TRIPs among developing countries.

---

9. Maskus (1998c) provides a survey; see also Watal (1999) and Lanjouw (1998).

10. See Helping the World's Poorest, Jeffrey Sachs, *The Economist*, 14 August 1999. Sachs cited a recent study by Wellcome Trust that only perhaps $80 million per year was devoted to malaria research and little of that on developing vaccines.

Impending Issues

The extensive commitments reached in TRIPs are still undergoing implementation, refinement, and interpretation. Indeed, the permissible extent of restrictions on protection remains unclear at this time. It will become clearer only as particular policies come under scrutiny through the dispute settlement mechanism. Moreover, many developing countries remain skeptical about the prospective benefits of heightened intellectual property protection.

In this environment it seems premature to envision a significant alteration of the TRIPs accord itself. Rather, in large part the watchwords should be effective implementation and consolidation of existing commitments. It may be particularly beneficial for the medium-term future of TRIPs for the industrial nations to work harder to effectuate their pledges to increase technical and financial assistance for implementation and enforcement of IPRs. A critical input into this process would be the formation of a working group to study those public mechanisms that could be employed or expanded to encourage technology transfer on reasonable terms.

Some questions emerge regarding the further specification of TRIPs standards. As argued above, it seems inadvisable to consider a significant extension of required patent coverage in biotechnological processes and products. Moreover, a proposal to ensure plant breeders' rights by requiring patent systems to cover them, particularly if they preclude farmers' use of seeds retained from previous seasons, would be questionable economics in its own right and would be widely resisted without some other mechanism for the diffusion of seed technologies.[11]

On a more positive note, there is scope for expanding the range of protection for geographical indications to food products of interest to producers in both developed and developing economies. Many regions in the latter countries are famous for their unique abilities to produce particular foods, such as basmati rice and Darjeeling tea, a situation that additional protection could enhance.

Moreover, negotiations could aim at incorporating into TRIPs the recently concluded Copyright Treaty and the Performances and Phonograms Treaty, negotiated through the World Intellectual Property Organization (WIPO). As I argued in another paper, these treaties should help protect producers and performers whose work is disseminated electronically but also should permit nations to strike an adequate balance between information generation and fair use (Maskus 1998a). The clear importance of

---

11. The recent decision by Monsanto to forgo commercialization of the terminator gene is eloquent testimony to the controversial nature of this issue.

e-commerce in promoting the free international exchange of information services makes the recognition of rights and obligations within this medium a critical issue in the intellectual property area. Again, the medium will serve the global community best if it remains free of trade restrictions on internet transactions.

Whereas negotiators might work toward a limited TRIPs-plus agreement in the next round, involving relatively little in terms of new rule making, the existence of IPRs in the global trading system raises important collateral issues for WTO members. First, TRIPs Article 40 sets out broad language permitting governments to take actions preventing or disciplining the anticompetitive use of IPRs. This is a complex issue that should command attention on the part of many developing nations over the near term (Maskus and Lahouel 2000). The TRIPs language directly introduces competition policy questions into the WTO and might invite further elaboration of rules covering competition maintenance. The first issue that could surface in this area is the possibility of recognized multilateral (or regional, or development-based) guidelines governing impermissible or questionable terms in licensing contracts. If such guidelines were to be negotiated, presumably it would be along the lines of recognized competition principles rather than coercion. However, they could be developed with express recognition of the needs of technology importers.

Second, IPRs are intimately related to issues of agricultural production and technological change. To the extent that stronger protection for plant varieties, biogenetic inventions, and agricultural chemicals shifts competitive advantages, it becomes all the more important for developed economies to provide meaningful market access to developing-country exporters. For one thing, such a promise would encourage efficient global resource allocation as the new technologies come on line. For another, it would ease some of the palpable concerns about the balance of benefits and costs from stronger intellectual property protection in agriculture.

Related questions emerge in the interface between IPRs and environmental regulation. An important question facing the WTO is how to deal with policies that could restrict trade in genetically modified organisms (GMOs), the development of which is directly tied to IPRs. The TRIPs agreement squarely introduces conditions of production into the disciplines of the multilateral trading system. Thus the GMO issue—and others like it—becomes one worth considering at the multilateral level. Similarly, policies regarding the exploitation of genetic resources, which stronger patents would encourage, may need to be visited in the next round. Put simply, whatever the merits of incorporating environmental protection into the WTO, environmental issues arise naturally within the context of IPRs and related agreements, such as that on sanitary and phytosanitary goods.

Concluding Remarks

Like the WTO itself, the TRIPs agreement balances precariously between advocates of its consolidation and reform along more protective lines and skeptics who are concerned about the international distribution of costs and benefits it could generate. The econometric evidence discussed above suggests that such skepticism may be misplaced over the long term, in that stronger IPRs should attract additional technology through a variety of channels to countries with competitive marketplaces and adequate skills. Unfortunately, this evidence also raises questions about the potential impacts on the least-developed economies.

The divide between advocates and skeptics is real and growing wider, suggesting that proposals for extensive revision of TRIPs are premature and could be counterproductive. Rather, efforts could be devoted to ensuring that the new global intellectual property regime will achieve an effective balance between the interests of technology developers and technology users.

The analysis here suggests that the following set of initiatives would work toward this end. First, to increase TRIPs' support in developing nations, developed nations should announce and implement a serious effort to provide technical and financial assistance and to promote mechanisms for effective technology transfer on reasonable terms. Second, developed nations could provide a sympathetic hearing and technical advice to developing countries that propose to extend competition policies to IPRs. Such an approach could extend to multilateral (and nonbinding for the near term) discussions concerning the identification of anticompetitive practices in licensing intellectual property. Third, governments in rich countries should devote more attention to the financing of international public goods related to IPRs. The most significant need in this context is for promotion of research into treatments for diseases endemic in impoverished areas and for disseminating the treatments generated. Fourth, IPRs and the environmental issues they raise can no longer be treated separately on the multilateral agenda.

Ultimately, if TRIPs is to achieve effective compliance in the global economy, developing countries need further convincing that it would generate substantive dynamic gains for them. To a considerable extent, this prospect is in the hands of the developing economies themselves, which would be wise to complement their stronger IPR regimes with further market liberalization, efficient competition rules, investments in human capital, and promotion of adequate technology infrastructures. However, to an important degree the developed economies could raise enthusiasm for the agreement by clearly signaling their intention to provide additional market access in agriculture and labor-intensive manufactures. In this sense, the next round of trade negotiations bears considerable promise for solidifying the potential gains from TRIPs.

References

Borensztein, E., J. De Gregorio, and J.-W. Lee. 1998. How Does Foreign Direct Investment Affect Economic Growth? *Journal of International Economics* 45: 115-35.

Coe, David T., Elhanan Helpman, and Alexander W. Hoffmaister. 1997. North-South R&D Spillovers. *Economic Journal* 107: 134-49.

Eaton, Jonathan, and Samuel J. Kortum. 1996. Trade in Ideas: Patenting and Productivity in the OECD. *Journal of International Economics* 40: 251-78.

Frankel, Jeffrey A., and David Romer. 1999. Does Trade Cause Growth? *American Economic Review* 89: 379-99.

Ginarte, Juan Carlos, and Walter G. Park. 1997. Determinants of Patent Rights: A Cross-National Study. *Research Policy* 26: 283-301.

Gould, David M., and William C. Gruben. 1996. The Role of Intellectual Property Rights in Economic Growth. *Journal of Development Economics* 48: 323-50.

International Monetary Fund. *Balance of Payments Statistics Yearbook: 1997.* Washington.

Lanjouw, Jean O. 1998. The Introduction of Pharmaceutical Product Patents in India: "Heartless Exploitation of the Poor and Suffering?" NBER Working Paper 6366. Cambridge, MA: National Bureau of Economic Research.

Maskus, Keith E. 1998a. Intellectual Property Rights in the World Trade Organization: Progress and Prospects. In Jeffrey J. Schott, ed., *Launching New Global Trade Talks: An Action Agenda.* Washington: Institute for International Economics.

Maskus, Keith E. 1998b. The International Regulation of Intellectual Property. *Weltwirtschaftliches Archiv* 134: 186-208.

Maskus, Keith E. 1998c. Price Effects and Competition Aspects of Intellectual Property Rights in Developing Countries. Background paper for the World Bank. *World Development Report: 1998.* Oxford: Oxford University Press.

Maskus, Keith E. 2000. *Intellectual Property Rights in the Global Economy.* Washington: Institute for International Economics. Forthcoming.

Maskus, Keith E., and Mohamed Lahouel. 2000. Competition Policy and Intellectual Property Rights in Developing Countries: Interests in Unilateral Initiatives and a WTO Agenda. *World Economy,* forthcoming.

Maskus, Keith E., and Christine McDaniel. 1999. Impacts of the Japanese Patent System on Productivity Growth. *Japan and the World Economy* 11: 557-74.

Maskus, Keith E., and Mohan Penubarti. 1995. How Trade-Related Are Intellectual Property Rights? *Journal of International Economics* 39: 227-48.

McCalman, Phillip. 1999. Reaping What You Sow: An Empirical Analysis of International Patent Harmonization. Working Paper in Economics and Econometrics 374. Canberra: Australian National University.

Park, Walter G., and Juan Carlos Ginarte. 1997. Intellectual Property Rights and Economic Growth. *Contemporary Economic Policy* 15: 51-61.

Primo Braga, Carlos A. 1996. Trade-Related Intellectual Property Issues: The Uruguay Round Agreement and Its Economic Implications. In Will Martin and L. Alan Winters, eds., *The Uruguay Round and the Developing Countries.* Cambridge, UK: Cambridge University Press.

Rapp, Richard T., and Richard P. Rozek. 1990. Benefits and Costs of Intellectual Property Protection in Developing Countries. *Journal of World Trade* 24: 75-102.

Smith, Pamela J. 1999. Are Weak Patent Rights a Barrier to US Exports? *Journal of International Economics* 48: 151-77.

Stiglitz, Joseph. 1999. Two Principles for the Next Round, or How to Bring Developing Countries in from the Cold. Speech delivered to World Bank/WTO Conference on Interests of Developing Countries in the Millennium Round, Geneva, 22 September.

Watal, Jayashree. 1999. Pharmaceutical Patents, Prices, and Welfare Losses: A Simulation Study of Policy Options for India under the WTO TRIPs Agreement. Washington: Institute for International Economics. Photocopy.

Watal, Jayashree. 2000. Intellectual Property Rights in the World Trade Organization: The Way Forward for Developing Countries. London: Kluwer Law International. Forthcoming.

World Health Organization. 1996. *Investing in Health Research and Development: Report of the Ad Hoc Committee on Health Research Relating to Future Intervention Options.* Geneva: World Health Organization.

Yang, Guifang, and Keith E. Maskus. 1999. Intellectual Property Rights and Licensing: An Econometric Investigation. University of Colorado working paper. Boulder, CO: University of Colorado.

11

Antidumping and Safeguards

PATRICK A. MESSERLIN

There is almost no possibility that trade remedies—comprising both anti-dumping and "escape clause" measures—will be left out of the coming round of multilateral trade negotiations in the World Trade Organization (WTO). This will remain true even if the WTO round is initially conceived as limited. Remember the Punta del Este declaration, in which antidumping was not listed as an issue for negotiation.

These measures have become such a prominent part of trade negotiations largely because the use of one trade remedy—antidumping—has so much increased and spread among WTO members that it now represents a systemic threat. The average number of countries routinely initiating antidumping cases has more than quadrupled, from five in the late 1980s to more than twenty today. The average annual number of cases has almost doubled, from 113 in 1987-89 to 203 in 1995-97 (figure 11.1). Since 1993, seven new users (Argentina, Brazil, India, Korea, Mexico, South Africa, and Turkey) have initiated as many cases as the five "old" users (Australia, Canada, the European Community (EC), New Zealand, and the United States). Though quite dramatic, these figures underestimate the real evolution: they do not include the many "reviews" of previous or existing cases, which almost systematically extend initial measures for indefinite periods, and they do not take into account the fact that the average number of tariff lines covered by antidumping cases has increased during the 1990s. The evolution of the other trade remedies (safeguards and countervailing duties) is much less dramatic, but this merely reflects the fact that they are less "advantageous" for domestic complainants—

Patrick A. Messerlin is professor at the Institut d'Etudes Politiques de Paris, and director of Groupe d'Economie Mondiale (GEM). He would like to thank J. M. Finger and Jeffrey J. Schott for extremely useful comments and suggestions on a first draft.

Figure 11.1 Antidumping cases notified to the WTO, 1987-97

number of cases

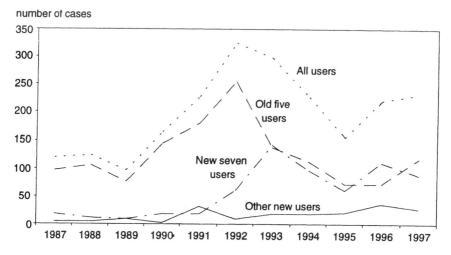

that is, they deliver a lower rate of protection than antidumping procedures.[1]

Not only will trade remedies be a prominent feature, the coming negotiations are doomed to be engulfed in discussions of them. For example, in agriculture, the next round will deal with the first effective reductions of farm tariffs. Now that farm protection has been converted to tariffs, the negotiating process might be more routine, but it will be a daunting task to get the necessary political support in net importing countries. It will be highly surprising if at least a few WTO members do not seek specific trade remedies in order, they will say, to ensure a smooth ride to lower farm tariffs.

Negotiations in services raise a different mix of difficulties. There are no robust techniques for negotiation and little hope of finding them in the coming years. By contrast, political and business support for liberalization is much stronger and wider, across both countries and sectors. However, developed-country negotiators will face a few sectors plagued by pockets of deep hostility to liberalization (such as US maritime trans-

---

1. As indicated by Gauthier, O'Brien, and Spencer (1999), there are many other WTO safeguard provisions. Certain other provisions have a broad intent and scope: general exceptions, such as GATT XX or GATS Article XIV; provisions dealing with changes in commitments, such as GATT XXVIII or GATS Article XXI; and balance-of-payments provisions, such as GATT XII and XVIII or GATS Article XII. Others have a clear focus on sectoral "escapes" (in particular, Article 5 of the Uruguay Agreement on Agriculture and Article 6 of the Agreement on Textiles and Clothing). Moreover, many regional agreements provide similar instruments. This profusion is an obvious source of additional problems—reinforcing the guidelines suggested below to tend progressively toward one safeguard provision.

port or EC audiovisuals), whereas many developing countries fear the apparently overwhelming developed-country comparative advantages in many services and the market power of their large multinationals. In such a context, it would also be surprising if the Uruguay Round's unfinished business on an "emergency safeguard" clause in services did not reemerge.

Lastly, manufacturing is unlikely to be excluded from negotiations. The next round will have to deal with what has been left by the last eight rounds—that is, with the industries that have been skilled and aggressive enough to escape 50 years of liberalization. The ghost of the Uruguay Round Agreement on Textiles and Clothing will float until 2005, and it would not be a total surprise if developed countries tried to extract, at the last minute, additional specific trade remedies as the ultimate price for fulfilling their commitments. Meanwhile, developing countries will be required to decrease their applied *and* bound tariffs, and thus will likely use trade remedies to provide temporary protection for their industries. And since tariff reductions will increasingly involve trade *between* developing countries, the fear of "unfair" competition will spread from industrial countries to developing economies. Last but not least, developing and emerging economies will ask for more disciplines on the use of antidumping measures by developed countries—a demand generated in part by recent attempts to subject oil to US antidumping procedures and textiles to EU antidumping actions.

The Need for a Systemic Approach: Three Guidelines

The systemic threat to the WTO now raised by antidumping regulations is serious enough that a systemic set of guidelines for curing the problem is needed. There is no more hope that ad hoc changes, such as those embodied in the codes of interpretation of the General Agreement on Tariffs and Trade (GATT) Article VI under the Tokyo and Uruguay Rounds, could really work.

Such a systemic approach should begin by abandoning the unhealthy assumption implicitly present in WTO circles: once liberalized, industries will remain open forever. The evidence undermining this assumption can be found *within* each WTO member country: sectors in difficulty are always trying to get remedies from the central government, and they often get them. These remedies entail in "recontracting" previous commitments: for instance, subsidies (a frequent remedy within a country) consist of a change from the national tax burden sharing initially agreed. Now that GATT/WTO is 50 years old (and indeed older than most of its members), WTO members should openly recognize that "recontracting" could also occur between them.

Figure 11.2   GATT renegotiations under Article XXVIII, 1948-93

number of renegotiations

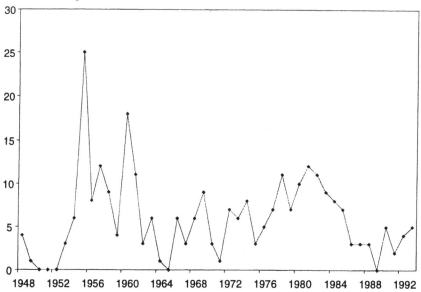

Of course, there is a key difference between the situation in the WTO and the situation within a country. In the WTO, with no central government, the only instrument available for recontracting is the renegotiation of existing commitments (GATT Article XXVIII, and Article XXI of the General Agreement on Trade in Services, or GATS). As a result, the first guideline of a systemic approach to WTO trade remedies should recognize the renegotiation of commitments as the ultimate trade remedy—indeed the only one based on the WTO principle of reciprocity. In fact, as suggested by Finger (1998), renegotiations have been initially used as safeguard actions (and figure 11.2 illustrates this point).

However, a strict application of this first guideline would lead to two major problems: If trade remedies were necessary only for a limited period, renegotiations would be a "disproportionate" instrument. Second, trade remedies should be rapidly available, whereas renegotiations require time. Moreover, a regime of permanent renegotiation might quickly bury the long-term movement toward liberalization under myriad renegotiations, which could be seen as setbacks to trade reform.

In other words, a cost-efficient use of renegotiations requires a safeguard provision—an *emergency* safeguard clause, to use the very appropriate GATS language. However, contrary to what exists today, WTO members would have to recognize that such an emergency safeguard provision may not be used for an indefinite period—it should either be eliminated or lead to renegotiation; this is the second guideline. In other words, a WTO member would not be allowed to escape its commitments forever, and a time would come in which it would be forced either to eliminate its "transitory" reprotection *or* to renegotiate its existing commitments. In this way, renegotiations become a *direct* source of discipline in WTO trade remedies—indeed, the most powerful possible discipline since they are based on reciprocity.[2]

The last guideline is the requirement to have one safeguard clause. There are now several trade remedies (antidumping, safeguards, antisubsidies, and so on). Being substitutable (or fungible), they compete among themselves to provide import relief. The last two decades have amply shown that the provision that guarantees the best deal (antidumping) to complainants—hence the largest damage to existing WTO commitments—supersedes all the others. The bottom line of almost all the empirical economic studies, including those from agencies involved in antidumping procedures (USITC 1995; CBO 1998), is that the vast majority of antidumping cases are driven by the will to protect industries that claim to be in trouble: less than 10 percent of the EU and US antidumping cases would have a chance to escape the accusation of being protectionist, as shown by Morkre and Kelly (1994), Greenaway et al. (1995), Shin (1998), Bourgeois and Messerlin (1998), and Winters, Rubin, and Bond (1998), among others. In other words, 90 percent of antidumping cases are de facto safeguard cases—with the ultimate, highly undesirable result that antidumping regulations are distorted to the extent necessary to provide the desired level of protection.

To sum up, a systemic approach to trade remedies requires simultaneous efforts in three different directions:

- to work on a safeguard procedure that would satisfy both governments under protectionist pressures and a well-functioning open trade system (of course, a lax safeguard could produce an outcome as detrimental to welfare as current antidumping regulations),

- to explicitly tie all existing trade remedies into the renegotiation process by forcing a WTO member (after a given period) either to eliminate its transitory reprotection or to renegotiate its existing commitments, and

- to prepare for a progressive shift from antidumping to safeguard regulations, establishing over time a unique safeguard provision.[3]

---

2. In fact, GATT XIX:3, allowing trading partners to retaliate, mirrors the same preoccupation and constraint.

3. And a shift from antidumping regulations to competition law for the tiny portion (less than 10 percent) of antidumping cases raising competition issues.

This work program already suggests one important proposal in terms of negotiating procedures: during the next round, and contrary to what happened during the Uruguay Round, *one* working group should handle all these interdependent issues. Because the above program likely will be deemed too ambitious for one round, I propose a graduated set of changes—from minimalist reforms in existing GATT/GATS provisions (which may be considered in this round) to maximalist improvements (which might only be part of a future round). The subsequent two sections focus on trade in goods; then I deal with trade in services.

Minimal Medication

When dealing with the three aspects of the work program, a minimal-medication approach should focus on reforms that ensure less contingent protection. This can be achieved by fully connecting the existing Uruguay Round Agreement on Safeguards (URAS) to the renegotiation process; by doing the same thing for antidumping reviews, which represent the strongest systemic threat to the WTO regime because they perpetuate supposedly transitory protection; and by reducing as much as possible the provisions of the Uruguay Round Agreement on Antidumping, which are too biased in favor of finding that dumping has occurred (so much so that these provisions are considered criminal fraud in the legal systems of most WTO members). All the work described below could be initiated in the existing ad hoc WTO committees, before being shifted to a full working group of the coming round, at an appropriate time.

Strengthening the Uruguay Round Agreement on Safeguards

GATT Article XIX is often presented as a failure. Indeed, the few times it has been invoked, it was subjected to efforts to distort its initial spirit (Sampson 1987), leaving the general impression that it was doomed to be useless or to become a back door to protection. However, history suggests that Article XIX has gone unused precisely because it was not a back door to protection, at least not as "efficient" a method as GATT-illegal voluntary export restraints (VERs) used during the 1970s and 1980s or antidumping procedures in place since the 1980s. The reasons for its relative "inefficiency" are well known: it provides strictly nondiscriminatory and transitory measures, provokes a high risk of retaliation by trading partners, and fundamentally recognizes that the protection to be granted flows from the failure of the domestic industry. All these features are in sharp contrast with antidumping measures, which allow almost unlimited discrimination and time-unbound measures, run almost no risk of retaliation (except through "retaliatory" antidumping complaints), are based on the assertion that the protection to be granted is caused by "unfair" foreign behavior, and are not concerned with adjustment policies (all the more so because antidumping cases are concentrated in labor-*non*intensive industries).[4]

The URAS has been a notable effort to revitalize the safeguard instrument while keeping intact its key positive features. The agreement relaxes three existing disciplines on safeguard actions in order to cope with the competition from antidumping. First, Article 2.1 de facto ignores the GATT XIX condition that import surges result from ongoing liberalization. This condition was clearly intended to limit the use of safeguards to the period in which liberalization commitments were implemented, making safeguards a possible competitor to antidumping only for this limited period and hence leaving antidumping as the only trade remedy in the long run. Second, Article 8.3 states that exporters can no longer claim compensation during the first three years of a safeguard measure—a postponement of the quasi-renegotiation process included in GATT XIX:3 through the retaliation process. Third, quotas can be used as safeguard measures in an even more discriminatory manner than before (Article 5.2).

This loosening of safeguard disciplines was believed to be necessary to get three crucial benefits. First, the URAS has eliminated all the existing VERs and other "gray" measures (with the only exception being that of the European Union's VER on Japanese cars, expired in December 1999). Second, safeguard measures were to be imposed for just four years, renewable once (Article 7). Third, safeguard measures in the form of quantitative restrictions were not to reduce the quantity of imports below some defined base levels (Article 5.1). Moreover, the URAS provides several more procedural benefits. For instance, provisional safeguards imposed via tariffs must be refunded in the event that final measures do not appear justified (Article 6), and safeguard protection is to be degressive (Article 7.4).

On balance, the URAS represents progress. But it suffers from four major weaknesses. First, the almost complete disappearance of gray-area measures following the URAS signature in 1994 is probably best explained by their survival as antidumping measures. Second, the limitations on the duration of the measures (two periods of four years) are fragile, being ad hoc and relatively open-ended, leaving open the possibility for the country imposing safeguards to prolong them. Third, the absence of any reference to "unforeseen developments" has excessively increased the ambiguities about this condition (this absence has been interpreted by certain observes, as an obvious upholding of the condition

---

4. Certain domestic versions of GATT Article XIX (such as US section 201) may require adjustment measures by the protected industry, and US enforcement of antidumping over the 30 last years suggests that one look with nostalgia at this escape clause (Finger 1995; Barfield 1999).

and by others as its implicit abandon). Two recent rulings of the WTO Appellate Body have clearly stated that this condition remains, but they are silent about the most important point—how to define "unforeseen conditions." Lastly, benefits from the degressivity of safeguard measures are ambiguous: degressivity could help make the transitory constraint more credible, but it could also make it worse—by amplifying lobbying efforts during the investigation period for getting initially higher levels of protection.

The first weakness cannot be solved through the current URAS: it requires fundamental reforms *in antidumping*. As a result, the coming round could improve the URAS by adopting the following three changes:

- At the end of the second period of enforcing safeguard measures, the country should have only two alternatives: eliminate the measures or renegotiate the tariffs applied to those goods under safeguard measures. In particular, a country should be prohibited from applying an antidumping action (or other trade remedy). All tariff items subject to a safeguard measure should be exempt from all other trade remedies for a substantial period (say, nine years, because that would be a multiple of the three-year period consistent with periodic renegotiations).

- The two periods allowed for enforcing safeguard measures should be reduced to three years to fit with the so-called "periodic" renegotiations scheduled under GATT Article XXVIII:1. The current choice of four years is arbitrary, and such an ad hoc approach is dangerous because it will face pressure for extension. A "systemic" limit to the notion of transitory measures (based on the renegotiating process) is thus essential.

- Because antidumping and safeguard regulations are substitutable and competing, reforming safeguard and antidumping procedures has to be conducted in parallel. This means that all the reforms suggested below for antidumping cases should be introduced in safeguards, when the concerned provisions have a broadly similar content. They could be introduced with the same strength when the two procedures are very similar (such as the definitions of "like product" or of "domestic industry"). Or they could be introduced in a stronger form if the specifics of safeguard required it. In particular, keeping the "unforeseen conditions" could be interpreted as meaning that the de minimis provisions that exempt small suppliers from antidumping actions could be higher in the case of safeguards (in order to mirror the fact that the development has to be unforeseen), and the level of exemption could be raised later on (an illustration of the threshold approach advocated below). However, experience in antidumping leaves little doubt that the misuse of safeguards will be much more seriously curbed from the perspective of a renegotiation process than by defining a concept as volatile and evanescent as "unforeseen developments."

Antidumping Reviews

Focusing on antidumping reviews first rather than on new cases may seem paradoxical at first glance. But it has two justifications. On the one hand, if one sees antidumping as a disguised safeguard clause, focusing on antidumping reviews is a means to ensure that reprotection is as transitory as safeguards.[5] On the other hand, if one believes that antidumping deals with "dumping," reforming antidumping reviews is necessary for enforcing fundamental legal rights and ensuring basic fairness so that defendants are not condemned on the basis of past investigations. Reviews following the imposition of antidumping measures and leading to renewed antidumping measures make sense in only two situations (if one does not assume that alleged dumpers are myopic): when import-competing firms want to perpetuate reprotection, and when a coalition of alleged dumpers and import-competing firms aims at implementing long-term VER-type deals under antidumping regulations. Both situations have little to do with antidumping but much to do with safeguards. Reviews in these circumstances deprive antidumping regulations of the appearance of legitimacy, and they also make a mockery of the sunset clause introduced by the Uruguay Round Agreement on Antidumping (UAA). That being said, there are three alternatives to reforming antidumping reviews.

- The absolute minimum proposal is to systematically introduce for reviews all the reforms that will be adopted for the initial antidumping investigations. This would require, inter alia, closing loopholes, such as the UAA's weaker obligation (for reviews rather than for initial cases) to compare domestic and foreign prices on an average-to-average or transaction-to-transaction basis (a loophole related to the UAA phrase "during the investigation phase," which US antidumping statutes have interpreted as excluding reviews).

- A less minimalist approach would incorporate tough reforms in the review process that WTO members are unlikely to apply to initial antidumping cases during the next round of negotiations. Such an approach would use antidumping reviews to test stricter regulations that could be applied to initial cases, after agreement in subsequent WTO rounds.

- A bolder possibility would be to completely eliminate antidumping reviews and to replace them with safeguard measures (of the second

---

5. Moore's detailed study of US reviews (1999, 16) concludes that "once orders are in place . . . the antidumping process will more closely resemble a type of safeguard rather than necessarily protection against 'unfair' imports." A similar conclusion can be reached for other large users of antidumping regulations.

period) (in turn, this would require limiting the duration of initial anti-dumping to three years). Such an approach supposes that the reforms of the URAS outlined above have been adopted, but it also provides a robust solution to the problem of antidumping measures becoming the trade remedy of choice.

Antidumping Case Initiations

Tinkering with the UAA on case initiations should focus on the determination stage of dumping. There are two reasons for this. First, this stage is potentially the most objective of the three investigation stages (the other two being determinations of injury and causal relationship) in the sense that, compared with the other two, it relies more on facts. Second, reforms at the two subsequent stages will not only be more difficult to design and introduce, but if adopted they will also be more difficult to enforce when the existence of dumping is shown (it is much harder to say "no" to trade measures once a finding of dumping has been made). To sum up, the standard for determining dumping is the best candidate for reform because it is where one can get the largest impact for the smallest amount of reform.

The focus on dumping determination is also justified by the crucial drift that has occurred since the UAA was signed: dumping margins have shown a tendency to increase (CBO 1998; Bourgeois and Messerlin 1998). This evolution underlines the urgent need for improved disciplines. *En passant*, it also mirrors the potentially perverse impact of provisions such as the "lesser-duty" rule, which requires that antidumping duties be limited to offsetting injury rather than the full dumping margin. Such "nice" rules are counterproductive to the extent that they induce complaining firms to magnify dumping margins in order to get the desired level of protection. There are three main reforms to consider in dumping determination:

- Eliminate the exception to the requirement (UAA Article 2.4.2) that price comparisons should be average-to-average or transaction-to-transaction. As is well known, these procedures provide an almost certain recipe for finding dumping.

- Reduce existing biases in the definition of foreign normal value. When there are no (or negligible) domestic sales but when there are export sales, export prices should be considered the mandatory source of information. As foreign firms are very unlikely to "dump" in all their export markets, a firm's average export prices in all export markets could be considered as a minimal standard. A variant would be to use prices charged on the largest export market, which could better mirror

Table 11.1 Do antidumping investigations really look at dumping?

Estimated normal values of exporters based on:	US cases (1995–98)		EU cases (1995–97)	
	Number of cases examined	Average dumping margins	Number of cases examined	Average dumping margins
Prices	5	3.2	8	22.7
A mix of prices and constructed values	33	14.2	33	24.4
Constructed values	20	25.1	12	25.1
Surrogate constructed values (nonmarket economies)	47	40.0	12	45.6
"Best available information"	36	95.6	2	74.5
All cases examined	141	44.7	67	29.6

Sources: Lindsey (1999, 8) for the US cases. Author's computations for the EU cases.

the most competitive situation for foreign firms under scrutiny. When there are no domestic nor export sales on which to base a price comparison, then constructed value remains the only viable option. Article 2.2.2 requires "actual data . . . in the ordinary course of trade." The reference to the ordinary course of trade means that exporters' home-market sales at a loss are excluded from "actual data"—this is, of course, a systematic way to inflate constructed values. This exclusion should be eliminated.

■ Extend the period an investigation covers. This is particularly critical in antidumping cases dealing with cyclical activity (an important source of antidumping activity in developing countries). The thrust of the reform would be to base the investigation on the whole price cycle, not on the usual one-year (or less) basis—a provision that almost guarantees positive dumping findings, since it is just a matter of lodging the complaint at the right time to get the desired protection.[6]

Table 11.1 gives some sense of the potential impact of the first two of these reforms in the US and EU cases. Out of 208 antidumping cases initiated between 1995 and 1998, only 13 were based on a direct price comparison. In addition, 98 cases were based on some kind of constructed value (with an average dumping margin of roughly 21 percent), 59 cases on specific regulations for nonmarket economies (with an average dumping

6. Certain countries' antidumping regulations (for example, Chile's) have indirectly introduced this provision by considering a "price tunnel" based on the preceding three or four years.

margin of roughly 41 percent), and 38 cases on the "best available information" (leading to antidumping measures based on an average dumping margin of roughly 94 percent). Similar evidence could easily be gathered for other users—raising the legitimate and fundamental question of whether antidumping investigations really look at dumping.

Two additional minimal reforms could be introduced concerning injury determination and causal relation. The first involves reducing (preferably eliminating) the cumulation of allegedly dumped imports over countries, provided by UAA Article 3.3. Prusa (1998) has shown how much such cumulation has affected US antidumping outcomes since 1984: it supported the filing of an additional 100 cases during 1984-94, and it also changed the US International Trade Commission's determination in about 60 cases (all other things being constant). Similar results have been found for the European Union (Tharakan, Greenaway, and Tharakan 1998). A weaker variant of a complete ban of cumulation would be to ban cumulation of imports from countries representing less than a given percentage of total imports. A key aspect of using quantitative thresholds is its potential for progressive reduction in subsequent negotiation. For instance, WTO members could agree to start from a low threshold and increase it during the enforcement period of the next round, or they could agree to increase it by increments in future negotiations.[7]

Second, no antidumping cases should be initiated if the allegedly dumped imports are already subject to quantitative restrictions, price surveillance, or any other severe constraints on trade (such as public procurement representing a substantial portion of the market), which could be put on a list to be agreed upon by WTO members. This reform is symmetrical to the ban of shifting from safeguards to antidumping. Further, it is economically sound: the observed dumping (if any) may be the outcome of these other restrictions (such as in the case of public procurement, as shown by the US supercomputer case), and antidumping measures may change the nature of the other restrictions (as shown in the EU cotton bleach case [Hindley 1997]). Again, cumulating trade remedies should be deemed unacceptable—this would be the first step to a unique trade remedy (safeguard).

This minimal medication can only curb the growth of the number of antidumping cases and the magnitude of the antidumping measures imposed. However, sooner or later antidumping complainants will find ways to erode or circumvent these reforms. That is, WTO agreements on antidumping are inherently static, whereas antidumping enforcement is dynamic. This is not new, as best illustrated by the capture of the national interest clause. A few years after its introduction into EC regulations, this

---

7. Other formulas could be to ban the cumulation of imports from countries with no common set of allegedly dumping firms and/or the cumulation of imports from countries where there are operating subsidiaries of complainants.

provision was routinely invoked as the ultimate argument for *imposing* antidumping measures (on the grounds that it was in the country's interest to keep domestic producers, hence to protect them). And recently, the Canadian Tribunal rejected requests by companies to use the national interest clause on the basis that the tribunal was "not convinced that there is a public interest issue that warrants further investigation" (*International Trade Reporter* 16, no. 37 [22 September 1999], 1536).

Substantive Medication

WTO members may be ready to go for more than minimal reforms in the coming round because they face a basic problem underlined by Koulen (1995, 232): "as illustrated by the absence of . . . principles of antidumping action, the Uruguay Round Agreement on Antidumping is an agreement to disagree. Sooner or later, this debate is likely to be resumed in the WTO." The likelihood that the WTO will agree to take the strong medicine needed to fix this problem is briefly examined in the conclusion.

Substantive medication would require that the UAA be rewritten in an economically sound way. Economic issues associated with antidumping include price discrimination, cyclical dumping, and predatory and strategic pricing (Willig 1998). Substantive reforms in antidumping should reflect the economic analysis of these four issues. In a nutshell, the new Agreement on Antidumping should contain provisions making it as difficult as possible to open antidumping cases related to price discrimination and cyclical dumping, whereas it should pave the way for competition authorities to handle (probably in a distant future) the very few predatory and strategic dumping cases within the competition law framework.

Rewriting the UAA in an economically sound way would have a crucial consequence: antidumping regulations could no longer be a harbor for political pressures. Hence reformed antidumping regulations would underscore the necessity for a robust safeguard clause to cope with such pressures. Ultimately, substantive antidumping reform should lead to the elimination of antidumping regulations through a progressive reallocation of antidumping cases into three boxes: "a red box" (no economic or political justification), "an orange box" (no economic justification, but political constraint—hence, application of safeguards), and "a green box" (economic justification requiring the expertise of competition authorities). Of course, the elimination of antidumping regulations is a long way off. It would constitute genuine success merely to initiate this process in the next round.

Specific kinds of reform could ease such a beginning—those in the form of quantitative thresholds (as mentioned above with constraints on cumulation). Such reforms are likely to facilitate the in-depth evolution of antidumping regulations because they have three huge advantages: they are easily negotiable (negotiators can talk in terms of figures or percentages), they give a sense of the magnitude of the concessions granted by both sides, and they can be tightened in future rounds—hence they can deliver the progressive liberalization that WTO members seek. In particular, such a threshold approach can be used in trade-offs on issues other than antidumping or trade remedies. For instance, heavy users of antidumping measures could trade stricter reforms in antidumping in exchange for better market access for trade in goods or services.

Access to Antidumping

Access to antidumping complaints depends upon the definitions of three key terms, whose effects reverberate throughout the procedures and the outcomes: major proportion of the industry, de minimis conditions, and like product. This order of presentation follows a precise logic: reform of the first would have the greatest impact on the number of cases that could be lodged and reform of the last would have the least impact.

Major Proportion of the Domestic Industry

Antidumping cases are lodged by complaining firms that investigating authorities recognize as constituting the major proportion of the domestic industry (Article 4.1). This criterion raises two main issues: How does one define "domestic," and in particular, how does one handle foreign firms established in the country initiating the case? And, how should "major proportion" be defined? There is no unequivocal answer to these questions. For instance, requiring that complaining firms represent a large aggregate market share (25 to 50 percent) may minimize the number of potential complaints, but such a requirement would mean that potential oligopolies or monopolies could complain more easily than the many firms in a competitive environment. Alternatively, protecting a very small firm can be achieved by narrowing the definition of the like product (as happened in the US semiconductor case). As a result, it is much more interesting to simply know the aggregate market share of the complainants *and* defendants (and its breakdown by firm) because this information will better reveal the risks of making the investigated market less competitive by imposing antidumping measures. For instance, complainants and defendants having a combined market share larger than 95 percent represent almost a third of the total number of EU and US cases (Messerlin 1996): this huge share suggests large potential risks of collusion behind antidumping protection and gives ammunition to opponents.

Minimal reform of Article 4.1 would thus consist in adding a requirement that the market shares of all major firms involved in the antidumping proceeding be made public rather than imposing predefined, easily circumvented criteria). A stronger variant would be to require that WTO members agree not to initiate antidumping cases when the aggregate market share of complainants and defendants (or a more sophisticated indicator of concentration, such as the Herfindahl index) is above a given negotiated threshold that could later be tightened up. This would be another example of the "threshold-based" approach.

De Minimis Import Shares

Article 5.8 suggests that antidumping cases exclude "negligible imports," defined on a country basis.[8] However, it makes little sense (particularly in terms of predatory and strategic pricing) to refer to import shares. What counts are market shares in terms of domestic consumption in the importing country.

Reforming Article 5.8 would thus require that de minimis thresholds be expressed as domestic consumption shares held by foreign firms in the importing country. This reform is not as likely to reduce the number of antidumping cases as is reform of the "major proportion of domestic industry" definition. Its effectiveness depends upon the threshold to which the WTO members agree. However, the average share of allegedly dumped imports in terms of domestic consumption is lower than 10 and 18 percent, in the European Union and the United States, respectively. Agreeing on a de minimis threshold of 5 percent during the next round would be progress. More important, WTO members could agree to increase this threshold during the implementation phase of the round (on a predetermined basis) and/or during subsequent rounds.[9]

Like Products

Antidumping investigations start by defining whether domestic and foreign products are like products. The economically sound definition relies on the extent to which domestic and foreign products are substitutes— that is, the magnitude of their cross-price elasticities, which is the basis of a determination of the "relevant" market in competition cases. As noted by Bronckers and McNelis (1999, 75), this market-based definition has already surfaced in a few dispute settlement cases when the like-product definition has been linked to "competition in the marketplace" (for example,

---

8. Namely, 3 percent of total imports, with a collective cap of 7 percent for all allegedly dumping countries.

9. As a comparison, competition cases examining monopolizing behavior or dominant position often use a rule-of-thumb threshold of 25 percent for firm market share. In the case of strategic dumping (requiring "large" sanctuary markets), the threshold could be defined based on extrapolated figures expected for the year after the initiation of the case (in order to capture the dynamic effects).

Japanese Liquor Taxes II and *Korean Liquor Taxes*). An extension of this link to antidumping faces three objections. First, the WTO's loose legal framework does not necessarily mean that what is recognized by the Appellate Body is recognized by antidumping authorities. Second, drawing the contour of the "relevant" market is time-consuming, a feature that does not work well in trade emergencies. Third, the "relevant" market concept will systematically reduce the scope for antidumping actions.

This last objection is not correct, and consequently one cannot rank the reform of the like-product definition very high in its impact on reducing cases (contrary to what is often suggested). In fact, the relevant market definition can be narrower *or* wider than the like-product definition. Moreover, it remains to be seen how many past antidumping complaints have failed because of a definition of like product that is too wide, and what the impact of a narrower definition would be on the level of injury (it could conceivably be higher). As a result, the only sure outcome of reforming the like-product definition is that the relevant market notion would reduce the freedom, or the arbitrariness, of the antidumping authorities. This freedom has proved to be tricky for complaining firms. For instance, defining photocopiers as was done in the 1985 EC copier case (a wide definition) has induced the complaining firm's competitors to enter the only two segments excluded from the investigation—not a good deal for the complainant, which has lost its monopoly position in these segments.

If WTO members are very eager to reform antidumping, one could envisage a transitional reform from a like-product to relevant-market standard that would require greater transparency in the proceedings. The antidumping proceedings should contain not only a detailed physical description of the products included (as is currently required) but also a list of the like products mentioned by the complainants/defendants but excluded by the investigating authorities, with a detailed description of the size of the two sets of markets and of the firms operating in them (to include firms' market shares, connections between firms if any, and so on). Such transparency, which reform of the definition of "major proportion of the industry" would also require, would provide nearly all the information necessary for a preliminary assessment of the relevant market in a typical competition case (and thus would make it easier to adopt the "relevant market" notion at a later stage).

Injury Determination

Minimalist reforms have concentrated on dumping determinations because that is where one can get "the most from the least." Because they deal with economic aspects, substantive reforms should focus instead on injury determination. Ideally, they should aim at making a distinction between competitive trade shocks (healthy because they benefit domestic users, even if they impose adjustment costs on relatively inefficient domestic producers) and competition "distorted" by foreign firms' strategic behavior (based on predation or the existence of a sanctuary market).

Existing antidumping regulations have no clear methodology when estimating injury (nor when establishing a causal relationship between dumping and injury). What counts today at these two levels is less a matter of economic assessment than of political opportunity—for instance, whether there are strong lobbies against imposing antidumping measures; whether a negative outcome in a given case would make the country's overall record on antidumping enforcement more acceptable for the rest of the world. Furthermore, the criteria for injury determination listed in Article 3.4 are potentially redundant (relative price changes can explain market share changes, and vice versa), and they can reflect quite healthy evolutions (a declining market share of a domestic monopoly or dominant firm is the healthy outcome of competition).[10]

There is thus an urgent need to restore the initial Article 3.5 discipline by injecting some economic content. The best compromise between legalities, economic analysis, time constraints, and investigation costs seems to be the use of partial equilibrium models, which permit an estimation of firms' revenue losses related to dumping (and the benefits for users), all other things being constant. The simple criterion of revenue losses could be privileged. Depending on political support in the round, the use of such models could be made mandatory, or they could be merely a systematic source of information. In both cases, the model used and the estimates obtained by the model should be published in the official antidumping proceedings of each case to fulfill the transparency objective, and more important, to give ammunition to the supporters of the "national interest" clause.

If WTO members are eager to push for reforms based on such models, they could introduce thresholds. For instance, they could agree that no measure would be imposed in cases where the level of injury losses is less than a given percentage of the revenues of the initial year, and that percentage could be modified later. In fact, complainants facing losses larger than 5 percent of their initial-year revenues represent only half of the total number of EU and US cases (Messerlin 1996).

---

10. The 1992 panel report on *Salmon from Norway* has added to the ambiguity by suggesting that there was no need for identifying other factors and assessing the specific impact of dumping on injury—hence misconstruing Article 3.5, which states that investigators "shall also examine any known factors other than the dumped imports which at the same time are injuring the domestic industry" and that "the injuries caused by these other factors must not be attributed to the dumped imports" (Palmeter 1996, 53).

Antidumping Measures and the "National Interest Clause"

Antidumping Measures

A substantial proportion of antidumping cases are terminated by measures other than duties (suspension agreements, price or quantity undertakings, and so on), another illustration of the fact that antidumping has a lot in common with safeguards. The key reform in these matters would be to reestablish the preeminence of tariffs, which do not generate the private rents that can fuel long-term protection (as when rents are shared between foreign and domestic firms).

Banning antidumping measures other than duties seems the appropriate reform. However, one may argue that this strong reform runs the risk of triggering private rent-sharing agreements during antidumping investigations—reinforcing the economic forces inducing domestic and foreign firms to strike a deal before the termination of the case (Prusa 1992; Panagariya and Gupta 1998). This risk could be managed by requiring a stricter and more complete notification of the antidumping cases not terminated by antidumping duties (the only measure left) and by having the WTO Safeguard Committee examine these cases after three years to determine whether any gray measure was introduced.

A weaker alternative to a ban would be to continue to accept antidumping investigations that did not end in tariffs (leaving a contradiction between antidumping and the "no private gray measure" discipline of the safeguard provision) but that these investigations would not be subject to antidumping review. Weaker still, they could be prolonged under the same conditions as those imposed during the second period under the safeguard agreement.[11]

The National Interest Clause

The national interest clause allows a WTO member that has demonstrated the existence of dumping and injury to opt not to take protectionist measures on the grounds that such measures would harm other parts of its domestic economy. In other words, this clause opens the door to consideration of domestic consumers' interests, which so far have been excluded from the existing antidumping procedure. However, as mentioned above, this key clause has not worked well: it is invoked too late in the procedure—that is, after dumping, injury, and causal relationship have been demonstrated, at which point it is very difficult for the authorities to say no to the firms that have petitioned for protection.

---

11. In any case, it would be highly counterproductive to adopt a proposal to systematically impose suspensions or price undertakings on allegedly dumped exports from developing countries, and it would be fallacious to assume that such measures would "educate" developing-country exporters in the appropriate pricing of their exports.

Many of the reforms proposed above (in particular, those regarding making information available and transparency) will de facto reinforce the national interest clause. One could add an additional reform with a systemic dimension: each WTO member that has enforced more than a given number of antidumping actions during a given period would be required to provide an economic report on all the cases investigated. These reports could be done every three years. Ideally, they should include an assessment of the estimated costs of the measures adopted during this period, with a focus on the impact of the measures on the domestic (and world) market structure. These reports would constitute the economic basis for a pluriannual review of antidumping practices to be done within the WTO framework—and the basis for future reforms. Moreover, this information on the markets under scrutiny would give domestic interests the necessary ammunition to fight protectionist measures if they wish.

Specific Provisions in the Safeguard Procedure

As already noted, it is essential to make parallel reforms in antidumping and safeguards. In this context, two provisions specific to GATT XIX deserve specific attention: serious injury and nondiscrimination.

GATT XIX refers to serious injury as opposed to the material injury test that arises in antidumping. The specific definition of serious injury could reflect a different threshold for revenue losses than that for material injury. For instance, if material injury is said to occur when domestic firms' losses are greater than 10 percent of their revenues, serious injury could be defined as losses greater than 20 percent—an approach that again offers the possibility of negotiating reforms in quantitative terms (that is, in terms not so different from negotiations on tariffs).

Sticking to the strict GATT XIX requirement to impose nondiscriminatory measures would amount to maintaining forever the primacy of endlessly discriminatory antidumping measures. Some rebalancing must be done. Among the many possibilities, the most logical is to restrict the nondiscriminatory requirement to original negotiators or principal suppliers. The economic logic behind this proposal is to keep the nondiscrimination discipline for the major existing competitors (at the cost of opening the door to discrimination in favor of emerging competitors). The legal logic flows from the fact that renegotiation (one of the two possible ultimate results of a safeguard action) is subject to a provision of the same nature: the right to compensation under GATT XXVIII is essentially reserved for countries having the status of initial negotiators or principal suppliers.[12]

---

12. Lesser rights are reserved for suppliers with a substantial interest in the market. Indeed, a more intensive use of the renegotiation process will require more stable coverage of potential beneficiaries. (The Uruguay Round Understanding on GATT XXVIII has extended this right to products of "great" importance for some supplying countries.)

Trade Remedies in Services

The problems of trade remedies in goods sound an inescapable echo in services. There is no antidumping provision in the GATS, and—following the disastrous experience of antidumping in goods—one can only hope that there never will be.[13] But there is a safeguard clause, namely GATS Article X on "emergency safeguard measures." As of today, GATS Article X merely states that "there shall be multilateral negotiations on the question of emergency safeguard measures." The only substantive point is that the future GATS Article X shall be "based on the principle of nondiscrimination." The empty shell that is GATS Article X raises two questions. Is there some genuine role for GATS Article X? How should GATT XIX reforms and GATS Article X provisions be linked?

A Genuine Role for GATS Article X?

Instruments of protection in services differ from those in goods in several key aspects: they can rarely be fine-tuned (contrary to tariffs), their concessional values are almost impossible to compute (they are rarely available in a quantified form), and their impact is very hard to assess. These features are likely to make liberalization less amenable to incremental implementation and more difficult to control in services than in goods. This in turn makes the demand for a safeguard provision (as insurance) even greater for services liberalization than it is in the case of goods.

In addition to GATS Article X, there are two GATS provisions that could satisfy the demand for safeguards: the renegotiation of commitments under GATS Article XXI and the introduction of specific emergency safeguard provisions in the commitment schedules per se. The second solution is the worst imaginable: it vastly increases the opportunities for trade distortions and the risks of competition between trade remedies. And it is de facto highly discriminatory—that is, countries that export services under strict specific safeguards will be more constrained than countries that export services under lax specific safeguards. As a result, it should be opposed with utmost energy.

Renegotiation of schedules is the ultimate solution for the same reasons that have been invoked for GATT XXVIII in the case of goods. However, an exclusive reliance on renegotiations seems even less appropriate in services than in goods. Renegotiations will be harder in services because the original negotiations proved more difficult and existing schedules of

---

13. However, many domestic regulations (including competition laws) could be used as antidumping instruments in services. For instance, competition regulations on "abnormally low" prices in retail distribution are frequent among WTO members.

commitments have been more difficult to interpret in services than in goods. As a result, renegotiations are likely to require more time, all the more so because initiating the renegotiation procedure is regulated by GATS Article XXI:1(a). All these reasons suggest the same combined solution for services as would be appropriate for goods—namely, the safeguard provision under GATS Article X coupled with the renegotiation procedure under GATS Article XXI.

Links between GATT Article XIX and GATS Article X

GATS Article X could have many provisions similar to those included in GATT Article XIX (such as services, definition of "major proportion of the industry," and so on) without raising specific issues, at least conceptually (enforcement may be more difficult). Other similarities would be the way in which GATS Articles X and XXI could interact. GATS Article X could state that a safeguard measure could lapse only after a limited period and that it could be renewed at the end of this period only once. If at the end of this period the country would like to extend the protection granted to its domestic service providers, it could do so only under the renegotiation procedure (Article XXI). Assuming that renegotiation in services would occur every three years, the lifetime of a safeguard measure (and the renewal period as well) under Article X could be three years.

However, a safeguard clause in services requires two provisions that can be ignored in the case of goods. The first is the "cross-modality" of GATS Article X: Should emergency safeguard measures be defined by mode of delivery or not? Two arguments suggest that Article X should be "cross-modal"—that is, enforced across all modes. First, the four modes of delivery have contributed to making commitment schedules very complicated—to the point that firms' market-access strategies have become distorted. Article X should not exacerbate these existing distortions. Second, as for goods, any "surge" in service imports should be judged on the basis of the domestic consumption of the service in question—independently from the mode of delivery. What counts in a safeguard case is the domestic situation, not the fact that imports, consumers' or producers' movements, or a commercial presence has created "disturbances."

The second question is the type of safeguard measures to be considered. Could such measures take all the possible forms (ad valorem or specific duties, quantitative restrictions, and so on), or should they be limited to certain forms (ideally to ad valorem tariffs, as for goods)? Despite the benefits that could be drawn from the legal similarity between GATT Article XIX and GATS Article X, some caution is necessary. In particular, an instrument deserves a fresh look in the case of trade in services. Quantitative restrictions are likely to have the same dark side in services as in goods (opaqueness, rents creating permanent vested interests, a capacity to isolate the domestic market from world markets). But they have two good sides (relative to other instruments) in the case of services that are not applicable to trade in goods. They can be relaxed in a progressive way: quotas in terms of market share (or in terms of the number of firms allowed to operate) could be enlarged according to a predetermined schedule announced when the measure is adopted. And their use in a nondiscriminatory way may be easy to monitor. For instance, the import-competing country could either impose a global quota on all foreign firms (meaning that the government allows foreign firms to make their own arrangements for market sharing and possibly collusion within the framework of this global quota), or it could impose a quota by firm in a nondiscriminatory way (for instance, by taking into account the past performances of the firms involved—that is, their historical market shares).

It seems wise to impose a mandatory review of the final GATS Article X within a reasonable period in order to change provisions that have proved inadequate. In this perspective, it might be wise not to lay down very detailed provisions in Article X itself but rather to write a brief, general Article X and to complement it right away with an agreement on its interpretation so that upon review there will be the maximum degree of freedom for changing or fine-tuning provisions.

Concluding Remarks

This chapter has discussed reforms in trade remedies under two crucial constraints: it has taken into account the existence of antidumping and its powerful capacities for protection, and it has suggested reforms that could be expanded incrementally in the future by using quantitative thresholds that are easier to negotiate because they are measurable.

The first constraint has imposed a very pragmatic tone here. It should thus be made clear that from the economists' perspective the best proposals are the most radical—or, alternatively, that there is a price to be paid for any departure from the maximalist proposals, either in domestic and world inefficiencies, in conflicts, or both. The economists' stance flows from careful study of the existing cases, even though it is always possible to find some cases, at least in theory, (in which antidumping does not have an adverse effect on welfare (for a review of the literature, see Messerlin and Tharakan 1999).

The second constraint is particularly important for the next round, which is likely to be the most difficult ever undertaken. This is true for several reasons: It will face problems that previous rounds have avoided (for example, liberalization of agriculture and manufacturing, which have resisted reform for 50 years). It will deal with effective services liberalization. It will be in the media spotlight to a greater extent than previous rounds. And it will need support from a public that does not understand the benefits it could bring—partly because the Uruguay Round has been greatly oversold. A coalition for reform will depend on the growth in the number of those using antidumping protection and whether the major antidumping users are themselves frequent targets of antidumping measures. The number of cases notified to the WTO during the last decade presents a worrisome picture: antidumping users are more numerous, and the "balance of cases" is positive among the major (old and new) antidumping users, Korea being the only exception (Miranda, Torres, and Ruiz 1998). Much will depend on the stance of China and Taiwan, which have a large negative balance of cases.

The paper has left aside two issues. First, nothing has been said about subsidies. This is for two reasons. Many of the proposals suggested above could be extended to countervailing actions quite straightforwardly. More important, it is not certain that subsidies will be an across-the-board key issue during the next round. They will certainly be a central issue in agriculture, but the challenge there is to put the farm sector on par with existing disciplines in manufacturing. Subsidies will also be an important topic in services. But they will still remain more as a "conceptual" issue, to the extent that effective liberalization has not yet begun in almost all services sectors. As a result, it may be important to think about possible distinctions between, for instance, "industrial" and "cultural" subsidies in audiovisuals (a distinction that could benefit from the "traffic light approach" in agriculture), but making these notions operational would first require some initial progress in liberalization.

Second, the paper has suggested a few—and only indirect—links between trade remedies and competition law, again for two reasons. First, as mentioned above, the overlap of competition issues (predatory and discriminatory dumping) in trade remedy cases is so small that the costs of not using competition law in these cases is likely to be negligible in the short or medium run. Second and more important, linking these two topics runs the risk of wrecking competition policy on the very sharp rocks of protectionist interests (Messerlin 1996). The European Union, which is the most vocal supporter of linking trade and competition policies, gives an interesting illustration of the difficulties ahead in this domain. In a recent merger case, two firms committed themselves to renouncing all their antidumping activities in the products covered by the proposed merger. The merger, however, was not accepted, leaving a European market without a merger but with antidumping measures intact—not particularly a staunch endorsement of a strong linkage between trade and competition policies. In such a context, it seems much better that trade remedies, having raised serious trade problems, be reformed within the framework of trade policy.

References

Barfield, C. 1999. Steel: Use Safeguards Clause. *Journal of Commerce* (March 4).

Bourgeois, J. H., F. Berrod, and E. G. Fouvnier, eds. 1995. Negoiating History. In *The Uruguay Round Results: A European Lawyer's Perspective*. Brussels: European Interuniversity Press.

Bourgeois, J. H. J., and P. A. Messerlin. 1998. The European Community Experience. *Brookings Trade Forum*. Washington: Brookings Institution.

Bronckers, M., and N. McNelis. 1999. Rethinking the "Like-Product" Definition in the WTO Antidumping Law. *Journal of World Trade* 33 (3): 73-92.

Congressional Budget Office (CBO). 1998. *Antidumping Action in the US and around the World: An Analysis of International Data* (June). Washington.

Finger, J. M. 1995. Legalized Backsliding: Safeguard Provisions in the GATT. In W. Martin and L. A. Winters, eds., *The Uruguay Round and the Developing Countries*. Washington: World Bank.

Finger, J. M. 1998. GATT Experience with Safeguards: Making Economic and Political Sense of the Possibilities That the GATT Allows to Restrict Imports. Policy Research Working Paper 2000. Washington: World Bank, Development Research Group.

Gauthier, G., E. O'Brien, and S. Spencer. 1999. Safeguards and Subsidy Disciplines in Services Trade: Déjà Vu or New Beginning? Washington: World Services Congress. Photocopy.

Greenaway, D., T. A. Lloyd, C. R. Milner, W. O. Morrissey, G. V. Reed, and G. Hutton. 1995. *The European Union's Antidumping Policy and Non-Tariff Barriers to Trade*. CREDIT, University of Nottingham. Photocopy.

Hindley, B. 1997. EC Antidumping: Has the Problem Gone Away? In O. Memedovic, A. Kuyvenhoven, and W. T. M. Molle, eds., *Multilateralism and Regionalism in the Post-Uruguay Round Era: What Role for the EU?* Dordrecht: Kluwer Academic Publishers.

Koulen, M. 1995. The New Antidumping Code Through Its Negoitating History. In J. H. J. Bourgeois, F. Berrod, and E. G. Fouvnier, eds., *The Uruguay Round Results: A European Lawyer's Perspective*. Brussels: European Interuniversity Press.

Lindsey, Brink. 1999. The US Antidumping Law: Rhetoric versus Reality. Center for Trade Policy Studies, no. 7. Washington: Cato Institute.

Messerlin, P. A. 1996. Competition Policy and Antidumping Reform. In J. J. Schott, ed., *The World Trading System: Challenges Ahead*. Washington: Institute for International Economics.

Messerlin, P. A., and M. Tharakan. 1999. The Question of Contingent Protection. *World Economy* 22, no. 9 (December): 1251-70.

Miranda, J., R. A. Torres, and M. Ruiz. 1998. The International Use of Antidumping: 1987-1997. *Journal of World Trade* 32, no. 5: 5-71.

Moore, M. 1999. Antidumping Reform in the United States—A Faded Sunset. *Journal of World Trade* 33, no. 4: 1-19.

Morkre, M., and K. H. Kelly. 1994. *Effects of Unfair Imports on Domestic Industries: US Antidumping and Countervailing Duty Cases, 1980-1988*. Washington: Federal Trade Commission, Bureau of Economics.

Palmeter, David. 1996. A Commentary on the WTO Antidumping Code. *Journal of World Trade* 30, no. 4: 43-69.

Panagariya, A., and P. Gupta. 1998. Antidumping Duty versus Price Negotiations. *World Economy* 21, no. 8: 1003-19.

Prusa, T. J., 1992. Why Are So Many Antidumping Petitions Withdrawn? *Journal of International Economics* 33: 1-20.

Prusa, T. J. 1998. Cumulation and Antidumping: A Challenge to Competition. *World Economy* 21, no. 8: 1021-33.

Sampson, G. 1987. Safeguards. In J. M. Finger and A. Olechowski, eds., *The Uruguay Round: A Handbook on the Multilateral Trade Negotiations*. Washington: World Bank.

Shin, Hyun Ja. 1998. Possible Instances of Predatory Pricing in Recent US Antidumping Cases. *Brookings Trade Forum*. Washington: Brookings Institution.

Tharakan, P. K. M., D. Greenaway, and J. Tharakan. 1998. Cumulation and Injury Determination of the European Community in Antidumping Cases. *Weltwirtschaflitsches Archiv* 20, no. 10: 320-39.

US International Trade Commission. 1995. *The Economic Effects of Antidumping and Countervailing Duty Orders and Suspension Agreements*. Publication 2900. Washington.

Willig, R. D. 1998. Economic Effects of Antidumping Policy. *Brookings Trade Forum*. Washington: Brookings Institution.

Winters, L. A., M. Rubin, and A. R. Bond. 1998. Antidumping Action on American Imports from Russia. *Post-Soviet Geography and Economics* 39, no. 4: 183-224.

IV

THE WTO AGENDA: NEW ISSUES

12

Getting beyond No. . . !
Promoting Worker Rights *and* Trade

KIMBERLY ANN ELLIOTT

The protesters in the streets of Seattle last November had myriad concerns, but among the most prominent was the demand that trade negotiations address workers' rights and the environment. Inside the World Trade Organization (WTO) meeting, however, some trade ministers from developing countries threatened to walk out if a US proposal to have the WTO analyze trade-related labor issues was not taken off the table. The worker rights issue never came to a head at the WTO ministerial in Seattle because conventional issues—agriculture, dumping, textile and apparel restrictions, and investment—blocked consensus on the broader negotiating agenda. But the issue will not disappear.

While unions have been in the forefront demanding a trade-labor linkage, surveys show that large majorities of Americans believe trade agreements should address labor (and environmental) issues (Kull 1999). This suggests that reconstructing a broad-based consensus in the United States in support of a liberal trade policy requires that the WTO address these issues in some fashion. Thus far, however, opponents have blocked even a discussion of labor issues in the WTO. Given the strong union backing for the American proposal, the opponents of a trade-labor linkage believe the primary motivation for raising the issue is to provide a rationale for new restrictions on developing-country exports. They argue that there is no direct link between trade and labor standards and that the International Labor Organization (ILO) is the appropriate arena in which to deal with labor issues.

Kimberly Ann Elliott is a research fellow at the Institute for International Economics, Washington. She would like to thank the Ford Foundation for financial support and Anthony Freeman, director of the Washington Branch Office of the ILO, for helpful comments on ILO rules and procedures. She is particularly grateful to Mary Covington of that office, who was extraordinarily helpful and generous with her time. Any remaining errors are the author's.

Taken at face value, the Clinton administration's proposal before the WTO was quite modest. It called for creation of a working group to examine the relationship between trade and investment and such issues as employment and social protections, core labor standards, and the use of positive trade policy incentives to encourage respect for core labor standards. In the most controversial section, it proposed examining

- "the extent of forced or exploitative child labor in industries engaged in international trade" and

- "the effects of derogation from national labor standards (including in export processing zones) on international trade, investment and economic development."

Opponents point to these two items and claim that this "selective" focus on problems most likely to be found in developing countries is evidence that the proposal is really aimed at restricting low-wage imports. This view was buttressed by comments President Clinton made to a Seattle newspaper that core labor standards should be a part of trade agreements "and ultimately I would favor a system in which sanctions would come for violating any provision of a trade agreement" (*Seattle Post-Intelligencer*, 1 December 1999, p. 1). It is difficult to know what the president really intended with this comment, especially since other members of the administration had so carefully avoided that topic. But he explicitly rejected protectionism, and less nefarious interpretations of the administration's proposal are certainly possible. One is that the administration was not purposely selecting priority areas that would target developing countries but that it wanted to focus on areas that are clearly beyond the pale, in the case of forced labor, and are directly trade related, in the case of derogation from national standards to promote exports or attract foreign investment.

However modest the actual text of the administration's proposal appears, the politics of the issue has become so divisive that there is still staunch opposition to any discussion, *within* the WTO, of labor issues. The European Union tried an alternative proposal calling for "a joint ILO/WTO Standing Working Forum on trade, globalization, and labour issues" to examine these issues while "explicitly exclud[ing] any issue related to trade sanctions." To reassure developing countries that their interests would be protected, the proposal was later amended to include participation by the World Bank and UN Conference on Trade and Development (UNCTAD). The European Union also offered to host, "no later than the year 2001, a ministerial-level meeting which would examine the work done in the joint standing working forum." Even the EU proposal apparently proved too strong. Documents obtained by *Inside U.S. Trade* show that by late afternoon on the last day of the WTO ministerial, the proposal had been watered down to call for a dialogue among all interested parties, with no organizational or steering role for the WTO (or anyone else), no clear mandate, and no deadline for coming to conclusions or issuing a report. This version is likely to have been too weak to serve as even a fig leaf for US negotiators.

In looking for a way to shift the terms of the dialogue and to nudge the process forward, this chapter makes three points:

- The opponents of a WTO role are right to point to the ILO as the most "competent" organization to deal with labor standards issues. As discussed below, it has extensive experience and elaborate supervisory mechanisms already in place, and it can be as strong and effective an institution as its members want it to be.

- The WTO has neither the expertise nor the desire to be the enforcer for the ILO, but the areas of potential trade-labor linkage will grow as the trade agenda expands, and these areas cannot be ignored. For political as well as economic welfare reasons, the WTO should address violations of worker rights that are directly related to trade or investment competition.

- "Slippery slope" arguments against trade-labor linkages should not be used to block all dialogue on the issue. They are not unfounded, but they are exaggerated.

When the parties are ready to seriously negotiate the launch of a new round of trade negotiations, both developing countries and the United States will need to move beyond a simple no on the issues raised in Seattle.[1] Relatively poorer, weaker developing countries are justified in their skepticism of new rules on worker rights that would likely be used more often against them than against developed countries, no matter how elaborate the protections against abuse. But they also benefit the most from a trading system based on rules rather than power, and support for that system will continue to wane if it is not perceived as responding to people's legitimate concerns. In turn, the United States will also have to move beyond no on issues of interest to developing countries. When US negotiators are ready to launch a new round, they will have to be more forthcoming on implementation issues and the need for capacity building in developing countries, they may have to give something on the use of antidumping procedures, which frequently target emerging market exports, and they will have to put remaining US tariff peaks on the table (see chapter by Jayashree Watal in this volume).

Moving beyond no on labor issues in the WTO does not necessarily mean going far, and it still places a heavy burden of expectation on the

---

1. The European Union and Japan will also have to move in areas where they have been recalcitrant, particularly in agriculture.

ILO to play a more prominent role. Whether those expectations can be met depends on the depth of the commitment by its members to making the ILO more effective, a commitment that will be tested in 2000. The first reports were just released in the spring of 2000 under the ILO's 1998 "Declaration on Fundamental Principles and Rights at Work," which provides a consensus definition and strengthens the monitoring of respect for core principles. In addition, the International Labor Conference (ILC) must decide in June whether to take historically unprecedented action against Myanmar for continued violations of the forced labor conventions. Unfortunately, efforts by some developing countries to weaken the resolution against Myanmar, and opposition by others to parts of the follow-up mechanism for implementing the declaration, raise questions about how committed some members are to an ILO that supervises and enforces labor standards more forcefully.

Testing the ILO Track

The key difference between the ILO and the WTO is not the number of "teeth" each has but the degree to which their members view them as serving their interests. The United States responded to judgments against it in several recent WTO disputes, not because it feared trade retaliation from Venezuela, Thailand, or India, but because it believes a rules-based system is broadly in its interest and that blatantly violating its obligations would undermine that system. The commitment by most members to the ILO has traditionally been far more shallow, and the consequences of embracing its standards more in rhetoric than reality were not viewed as serious. Thus the important question is whether members will find it more in their interest today than previously to bolster the ILO's capacity to deal with increasing concerns about the effects of globalization on workers and their families.

The issue is one of commitment rather than legal authority because the ILO is not inherently weak and toothless. Until 1946, Article 33 of the ILO Constitution provided that members could take "measures of an economic character" against another member for refusing to come into compliance with a convention, as recommended by an independent commission of inquiry (International Labor Office 1946). A constitutional review undertaken after World War II broadened Article 33 to "leave the Governing Body discretion to adapt its action to the circumstances of the particular case," but the amended language does not explicitly exclude the possibility of economic or any other sanctions (International Labor Office 1946; see also International Labor Office 1999).[2]

---

2. There is disagreement on this point, with some members arguing that a reference to the UN Security Council in the 1946 report implies that only that body has the authority to impose economic sanctions.

The constitutional review was undertaken as part of the adaptation of the ILO to the new UN system and the anticipated expansion of its membership to include former colonies and other nonindustrial economies. In this context, the report accompanying the recommendations for amendment of the constitution recognized both the limitations of sanctions and the importance of a genuine commitment to change on the part of key domestic actors. The report argues

> that the problem is primarily one of national standards of law enforcement and that international action should therefore be directed towards promoting the progressive development of more effective national administrative machinery. (p. 56)

This is a reality now confronting those who pushed aggressively to move protection of intellectual property rights (IPR) from the World Intellectual Property Organization to the WTO because the WTO has teeth. Countries have largely complied with the letter of the new rules, but effective enforcement of domestic IPR laws has lagged and is likely to remain a problem as long as the will and capacity to enforce them are lacking. Studies of international financial institutions' efforts to condition their loans on far-reaching internal reforms also support the conclusion that such conditionality is seldom effective unless the country is receptive to reforms and is seeking external assistance to implement them. Arm-twisting simply has limited utility in such situations. Thus experience in other areas suggests that the ILO is right to focus on positive efforts to work with countries to improve enforcement of labor standards. But it also has the authority to respond to egregious violations when necessary.

As the only League of Nations institution to survive World War II, the ILO has over 80 years of experience in the development and implementation of labor standards. It also has a unique tripartite governing structure and is the only international organization that extends voting rights to groups other than government delegates (see box 12.1). Its membership now includes government, worker, and employer representatives from 175 countries. As of 1999, the annual ILC had approved 182 conventions creating international standards for various aspects of work and employment—some regarding fundamental rights, most more technical in nature. While the ILO's role in developing and promoting labor standards is relatively well known, the mechanisms for monitoring implementation and responding to noncompliance are less well known. It has both a routine reporting and review process and ad hoc procedures for handling complaints by worker or employer groups or governments that a member is not satisfactorily implementing a convention that it has ratified (box).

Although there have been efforts over the years to streamline reporting requirements, the system still suffers from both too much information and

Box 12.1 The ILO: Institutional structure and supervisory mechanisms

I. Institutional Structure

The International Labor Organization, founded in 1919, is a tripartite organization composed of representatives of workers and employers as well as governments from 175 countries. Each country delegation comprises two government representatives, one representing employers and one for workers, for a current total of 700 voting delegates. The worker and employer delegates vote independently and are not bound by their government's position. Delegates gather annually as the International Labor Conference (ILC), where new conventions may be adopted and implementation of existing conventions is reviewed.

The Governing Body (GB) is the ILO's executive, with responsibility for developing policy, overseeing the work program, and responding to complaints about inadequate implementation of conventions. The GB has 28 government members, 10 of which are permanent (United States, United Kingdom, France, Germany, Italy, Japan, Russia, Brazil, China, and India), 14 employer members, and 14 worker members.

The International Labor Office, headed by the director general, is the secretariat of the organization, with headquarters in Geneva and branch offices around the world. The office provides advisory services—for example, on how to create or reform laws for social protection; carries out research projects; and, under a separate budget, conducts technical cooperation programs.

II. Routine Supervisory Mechanisms

The Committee of Experts on the Application of Conventions and Recommendations (CEACR) comprises 20 independent members, and it reviews all the routine reports on the application of conventions and recommendations that members are required to submit every two to five years, depending on the convention. The CEACR in turn prepares a report to the ILC in which it reviews developments during the previous year (for example, conventions adopted, ratified, or denounced) and makes general observations about the status of conventions across countries or of several conventions within a country. In the most detailed section of the report, it makes "individual observations" about potential problems with the application of particular conventions in particular countries. It may also request that a member state provide additional information, beyond that submitted in its report to the committee.

(continued next page)

not enough. On the one hand, as more countries have joined and more conventions have been adopted, the number of routine reports required of member states has risen from an annual average of just over 600 in the 1930s to 2,036 in 1998, and the proportion submitted in timely fashion has fallen from 85 percent or so to only 71 percent in 1998. On the other hand, until this year, only countries that ratified conventions were required to report *routinely* on implementation. Other countries were asked to report periodically on the reasons they had not ratified a particular convention

Box 12.1 (continued)

The Conference Committee on the Application of Conventions and Recommendations (CACR) is a tripartite body formed at each ILC. It reviews the CEACR report and then prepares its own report to the full conference. This report includes a section on "compliance with specific obligations," highlighting areas of both progress and inadequate compliance. This section reviews countries' performance with respect to ratifying conventions on a timely basis and submitting reports as required, as well as failure to implement ratified conventions. If needed, the CACR may include a separate subsection listing cases where there is a "continued failure to implement." The conference committee report also makes "individual observations," drawing on the observations in the CEACR report to highlight particularly serious or urgent cases.

III. Ad Hoc Supervisory Mechanisms

Article 24 representations can be made by any employer or worker organization (not just those serving as ILO delegates) alleging inadequate implementation by a member state of any convention that the member has ratified, or of protection of freedom of association, regardless of ratification status. If not otherwise resolved, representations may be submitted to a tripartite committee of three members of the GB.

Article 26 complaints, originally intended for state-to-state disputes, may be made by any conference delegate. Government representatives may only bring complaints regarding implementation of conventions that their country has also ratified. If not otherwise resolved, the GB may appoint an independent, ad hoc commission of inquiry to investigate the complaint. The commission then submits a report to the GB with its findings and recommendations for rectifying the problem, if applicable. Within three months of the report, the member state must decide whether to accept the recommendations or appeal the case to the International Court of Justice. If the defendant country does not implement the recommendations of the commission (or of the court if appealed) within the applicable period, the GB may recommend to the conference that it take "such action as it may deem wise and expedient to secure compliance therewith."

The Committee on Freedom of Association receives complaints or representations by worker or employer organizations (usually the former) alleging violations by a member state of this fundamental right. Because it is regarded as a constitutional obligation of membership, freedom of association complaints can be brought against any member state, regardless of whether it has ratified Convention no. 87.

and to describe what they were doing under their national laws to achieve the goals of the convention.

In 1998, in response to the 1995 World Social Summit communiqué, which identified core labor standards that should serve as the "social pillar" of the global economy, and to a WTO ministerial communiqué a year later committing its members to observe them, the ILC approved a "Declaration on Fundamental Principles and Rights at Work." Part of the motivation for the "follow-up mechanism" appended to the declaration was to focus attention and systematize the reporting on the four internationally recognized core principles:

- freedom of association and the "effective recognition of the right to collective bargaining,"
- freedom from forced labor,
- the "effective abolition of child labor," and
- nondiscrimination in employment.

Thus the follow-up mechanism requires *all* member countries that have not ratified one or more of the eight conventions associated with these rights to report annually on what they are doing to promote them (though not the more detailed obligations in the conventions).[3] Employer and worker groups are invited to provide comments on the submissions, and a group of independent "expert-advisers" then examines the reports and writes an introduction to the compilation of national reports. In addition, the director general will prepare an annual global report focusing on each of the principles in turn to highlight overall trends in their application. The first global report, which focuses on freedom of association, was released in May 2000.

These new reporting mechanisms will only be useful if member countries and their worker and employer representatives cooperate and if the experts and the director general are willing to present a clear summary of trends and to highlight specific cases of progress and failure in clear, transparent language. The first compilation of country reports with the experts' introduction was released as this chapter was being written, and the initial results appear mixed. The experts' report was clearly written and frank in identifying weaknesses in the reporting process, and it provided useful suggestions for improving it. But only a little over 50 percent of the required reports were received in time to be reviewed (the laggards are clearly identified by the experts in a table), and the experts noted that many of the reports are inadequate to provide a baseline against which progress can be measured. The expert-advisers also lamented the fact that so few employer and worker groups chose to comment on the reports. Overall, it is difficult to piece together a picture of how well the core standards are being enforced around the world.[4]

Thus while a more integrated and focused assessment would appear to be just what is needed to make the vast amount of information generated

---

3. The relevant conventions are numbers 29 and 105 on forced labor; 87 and 98 on freedom of association and collective bargaining; 138 and, when it enters into force later this year, 182 on child labor; and 100 and 111 on nondiscrimination.

4. The experts' report and the compilation of country reports are available on the ILO Web site at http://www.ilo.org.

by ILO supervision accessible and compelling to a broader audience, the members' cooperation with the process has so far been disappointing. During the debate on the 1998 declaration, some important developing countries opposed the very suggestion that the director general prepare a global report. Even after extensive negotiations on the language, several developing-country government delegates abstained from the vote, and though there was no vote against the declaration, it garnered only nine more than the minimum needed to gain approval.[5] It should be noted, however, that all but two of the governments whose delegates abstained provided reports in compliance with the declaration. (Another report, Pakistan's, was submitted too late to be reviewed by the independent advisers.)

In addition to this new mechanism and the routine reporting and review of compliance by independent experts and conference delegates, the ILO also provides multiple avenues for worker, employer, and government representatives to raise issues of alleged noncompliance (see box 12.1). While any worker or employer organization can make a "representation" under Article 24 of the ILO Constitution, Article 26 may be invoked only by one of the official delegates to the ILO and is generally reserved for the most serious cases. In this context, the US government is constrained: a government can only bring a complaint against another member if it has also ratified the relevant convention, and the United States has ratified just 13 conventions and only two of the core conventions—no. 105 on the abolition of forced labor and the new convention on the worst forms of child labor, no. 182.[6] There are also special procedures for freedom of association, however, because it is regarded as a fundamental obligation of membership, and a member need not have ratified the relevant conventions for a complaint against them to be brought before the Committee on Freedom of Association.

The procedures governing Article 26 complaints echo some of the social clause ideas proposed for the WTO (Elliott 1998a). After a complaint is made, the Governing Body will usually seek the member's permission to send a "direct contacts mission," representing the director general, to explore the problem. If that does not produce a resolution, a commission of inquiry may be appointed to formally investigate the charges. The commission then submits a report presenting its findings and, if appropriate, recommending ways in which the member can conform its laws

---

5. According to Article 17 of the ILO Constitution, unless otherwise specified, a vote is not valid unless the total number of votes cast is at least half the number of delegates attending the conference. Since 526 delegates attended in 1998, at least 264 votes were needed (*ILO Focus* 11, no. 2 [Summer/Fall 1998], Washington Branch Office of the ILO, p. 1).

6. The US Council for International Business, representing US employers, or the AFL-CIO, representing American labor, could bring a complaint even though the United States has not ratified a particular convention.

and practices to the relevant convention. The target of the complaint is given the opportunity to appeal to the International Court of Justice. But if the commission's findings are not appealed or are upheld, the country will be asked to report to the CEACR on what it has done to implement the commission's recommendations. If satisfactory compliance is still not forthcoming, Article 33 provides that "the Governing Body may recommend to the Conference such action as it may deem wise and expedient to secure compliance therewith" (International Labor Office 1999).

In 1919, when the ILO was created, the Commission on International Labor Legislation observed that the complaint procedures had "been carefully devised in order to avoid the imposition of penalties, except in the last resort, when a State has flagrantly and persistently refused to carry out its obligations under a Convention. It can hardly be doubted that it will seldom, if ever, be necessary to bring these powers into operation" (quoted in International Labor Office 1999, 4). Indeed, between 1919 and 1960, there was only one Article 26 complaint. In the following four decades, there was a steady average of six complaints per decade, and in all only six commissions of inquiry were appointed.[7] None of these commission reports were appealed to the International Court of Justice, and although implementation of the commissions' recommendations appears to have been variable, the application of Article 33 was never raised—until this year.[8]

Without invoking Article 33, the 1999 ILC approved a resolution condemning Myanmar for its refusal to comply with a commission's recommendations to change its laws and practices with respect to forced labor. The resolution also prohibited technical assistance to Myanmar, except as might be requested to implement the recommendations, and banned it from most meetings—the first such action in ILO history. Even this modest penalty attracted opposition from some member governments.[9]

---

7. All but three of the complaints since 1960 addressed alleged violations of one of the four fundamental rights, usually freedom of association or forced labor (*International Labor Standards: How Are They Enforced?* http://www.ilo.org/public/english/standards/norm/enforced/complnt/a26_use.htm_[accessed 24 April 2000]).

8. One assessment finds that most governments have accepted the findings of commission reports. Poland, however, refused to cooperate with the commission of inquiry appointed to investigate a freedom of association complaint raised in the early 1980s when the government was trying to break the Solidarity union movement. Germany also rejected a commission finding that it unfairly discriminated against public employees for political reasons. In other cases, governments nominally accepted the conclusions of a commission, but remedial actions have been inadequate (Romano 1996). The Washington office of the ILO has also commissioned a report to examine cases of progress on worker rights, due at least in part to ILO pressure.

9. At the time of the resolution, Myanmar was not receiving any technical assistance, and the total value of such assistance from the ILO was only $1.5 million from 1991 to 1996. The ban on meetings is also more symbol than substance since no member can be barred from constitutionally authorized Governing Body and ILC meetings.

Cuba, seconded by Mexico, Colombia, and Venezuela, offered a motion to separate the part of the resolution condemning Myanmar's noncompliance from the portion imposing penalties. The motion was defeated by voice vote when representatives of the employer and worker groups, joined by the government members from the United States and United Kingdom, indicated their opposition, thereby ensuring that the motion would not receive the necessary two-thirds approval (*ILO Focus*, 12, no. 2 [Summer/Fall 1999]: 1).

In March 2000, the Governing Body invoked Article 33 for the first time and recommended that the June 2000 ILC take further action against Myanmar because of its continued intransigence. The decision, approved without a vote, suggests a variety of actions that the ILC might take, including calling on member states "to review their relationship with the Government of Myanmar (Burma) and to take appropriate measures to ensure that Myanmar 'cannot take advantage of such relations to perpetuate or extend the system of forced or compulsory labour. . . .'" Possible actions also include calling on other international organizations to consider whether any of their activities "could have the effect of directly or indirectly abetting the practice of forced or compulsory labour."

The US government members and representatives of the employer group, including the US Council for International Business, have been working hard to increase the profile of the ILO and make it a more effective organization. Unfortunately, the apparent ambivalence regarding action against Myanmar, joined with opposition from some key developing countries to certain parts of the Declaration on Fundamental Rights, imply that developing countries may be more committed in principle than in practice to making the ILO more effective. But if the ILO is not able to move toward more effective enforcement, as well as promotion, of core labor standards, demands to give the WTO a role are likely to continue.

Examining the WTO Track

Even if the view of the ILO as weak and ineffective is not overstated, the WTO cannot and should not be expected to act as the arbiter for all manner of international rules and agreements simply because it is seen as having the strongest enforcement mechanisms.[10] In addition, theoretical studies suggest there is no systematic relationship between core labor standards and comparative advantage, while empirical studies suggest any effect is probably small in magnitude (OECD 1996; Maskus 1997; Martin and Maskus 1999). Union rights, for example, could either lower or raise unit labor costs, thereby affecting comparative advantage

---

10. The issues in this section are discussed in further detail in Elliott (1998a).

positively or negatively, depending on the economic and institutional context. Discrimination would, under most circumstances, be expected to lead to a less efficient allocation of resources and thereby reduce competitiveness. Forced labor and exploitative child labor, on the other hand, could be expected to lower unit labor costs and provide an illegitimate competitive advantage.

While this suggests that a broad social clause in trade agreements is inappropriate, the WTO can and should address trade-related violations of fundamental worker rights. As noted above, the most obvious, though also probably the least common, is the use of forced labor in export activities. There is already an exception in Article XX(e) of the General Agreement on Tariffs and Trade allowing countries to ban imports of goods produced using prison labor, and it would be analytically illogical, as well as politically awkward, to prevent the extension of that provision to other forms of forced labor, including child labor that is coerced. Thus if WTO members agree, Article XX(e) might be reinterpreted or amended to make clear that it allows countries to ban imports of goods produced with forced labor.[11] Under this limited exception, however, import restrictions could not be extended to other products and could not be used to sanction the use of forced labor elsewhere in the economy.

Another area of potential trade-labor linkage that should at least be examined is the alleged suppression of labor rights to attract foreign investment in some export processing zones (EPZs). Explicit derogation from labor laws in order to attract foreign investment does not appear to be common, but it is not unknown. According to an ILO study, Bangladesh and Pakistan explicitly exclude EPZs from coverage under labor and industrial relations laws, and Malaysia, Panama, and a few other countries restrict the application of labor laws, particularly with regard to freedom of association (International Labor Office 1998; see also US Department of Labor 1989-90).[12] In response to an observation by the CEACR in 1994, Pakistan conceded that its exemption of EPZs from certain labor laws was the result of a "deal with foreign investors who have invested in this zone on the basis of certain exemptions provided to them."[13] This example also suggests that the WTO should consider

---

11. A 1985 "wise men's" report setting the stage for the Uruguay Round suggested that it was clear in the GATT that countries could not be forced to import products made with slave labor. But that interpretation is not binding, and it is not known whether a dispute settlement panel would allow a country to take action against forced labor products under this exception.

12. The ILO report also indicated there were concerns about Zimbabwe's treatment of EPZs, but according to ILO sources the law in question has been amended. Perhaps this is an example of the effectiveness of ILO supervision.

13. In an associated complaint, the investor in question was identified as Daewoo (see the ILO database, ILOLEX, http://www.ilo.org).

rules to prevent foreign investors from demanding or benefiting from such agreements.

While such blatant restrictions on worker rights to attract foreign investment are rare, the ILO study notes several examples where unionization rates in EPZs are much lower than in the rest of the economy. The authors note that this could be because wages and conditions are better in the zones than elsewhere, but they also point to several cases where that hypothesis is contradicted by evidence of growing worker unrest in EPZs. If the WTO agenda expands to encompass broader rules for foreign investment, this derogation issue will be increasingly difficult to avoid.

Another issue that could be raised in the future is the expansion of the General Agreement on Trade in Services to cover the cross-border provision of "worker agency services." The idea is that worker associations provide a variety of services that are market supportive: they alleviate market failures associated with collective action problems, workplace public goods, and imperfect information, and they discipline practices that border on coercion and create market power to countervail anticompetitive market power of firms. These services encompass not just bargaining over compensation, but also workplace safety monitoring, grievance and dispute settlement, training and education, and management of other services, such as child care, pensions, and health insurance (Richardson 2000; Stiglitz 2000; Freeman and Medoff 1987). It would be consistent with the WTO's mission to encourage the liberalization of "trade" in such market-supportive services.

Finding Traction on the Slippery Slope

Developing countries have repeatedly affirmed their support for core labor standards—in 1995 at the World Social Summit, in 1996 at the WTO ministerial in Singapore, and in the 1998 ILO Declaration on Fundamental Principles and Rights at Work. If there are also potential trade-labor linkages, as argued above, then the fundamental argument against asking the WTO to address such linkages boils down to a fear of increased protection against developing-country exports. The argument against even discussing labor issues in the WTO is that it starts the organization down the slippery slope toward protectionist abuse of otherwise acceptable standards.

A slippery slope scenario is possible, but the question is whether a well-constructed pair of boots could prevent an inevitable slide to the bottom. For example, no one who has looked at the details of the social clause proposed by the International Confederation of Free Trade Unions (ICFTU) could conclude that the objective is increased protectionism; the procedural safeguards are simply too elaborate (Elliott 1998a). To take another example, developing countries have similar concerns about linking trade and environmental issues and only reluctantly acquiesced in the creation of the Committee on Trade and Environment (CTE) in 1995. Contrary to developing-country fears, the CTE has proved useful in clarifying key differences among members and has not led to negotiations to include more environmental issues in the WTO or to expand the use of trade sanctions. Some opponents also point to the intellectual property rights agreement as an example of the inappropriate use of unilateral trade threats and sanctions to force new rules down the throats of developing countries. But again, recent experience suggests that the negotiating environment has changed in significant ways and that developing-country fears of coercion and protectionist abuse are less well founded today than before the Uruguay Round.

First, developing countries learned much from the Uruguay Round experience and are far more formidable negotiating partners now than before. At the same time, American leverage is weaker because the WTO Dispute Settlement Understanding (DSU) means that trade threats can no longer be used as a tool of "aggressive unilateralism," as they were on intellectual property, for example, to force countries to change their policies or to agree to negotiate new multilateral rules. Second, recent experience suggests that protectionist abuse of the rules can be contained as long as any trade measures related to labor issues are subject to multilateral review and discipline under the DSU. Indeed, the system has demonstrated that it can protect smaller, poorer countries from "unjustified" or "arbitrary" discrimination against their exports. For example, developing countries have challenged several US trade measures related to the environment and have prevailed in the WTO, leading the United States to modify its policies.[14]

Two other exaggerated claims are made to support the argument that linking worker rights to trade is protectionism in disguise. One is that the American proposal focuses on labor practices, such as child labor, that primarily occur in poorer countries and ignores areas where the United States falls short, such as union rights and exploitation of migrant labor. But the Clinton administration proposal, like that of the ICFTU, refers to internationally recognized labor standards, which have now been clearly defined and broadly accepted under the ILO's Declaration on Fundamental Principles and Rights at Work. In addition, experience with the North American Free Trade Agreement's side agreement on labor, whatever its weaknesses, does not support the contention that the United States resists scrutiny of its own labor practices. The side agreement covers treatment of migrant agricultural workers, for example,

---

14. The United States has modified its application of the law that led to the shrimp-turtle dispute but is still struggling to find a solution that satisfies both the demands of its trading partners and the requirements of the law.

and the United States has been forced recently to respond to a Mexican complaint about the practices of the Washington State apple industry.

Another allegation is that the emphasis on sticks relative to carrots reveals a protectionist bias in US efforts, especially since only large countries can effectively use sanctions. The evidence, again, belies the charge that the United States is seeking sanctions *instead of* pursuing more effective positive strategies. The Clinton administration has not been notably more aggressive than its predecessors in withdrawing trade preferences from countries for insufficient protection of worker rights (as required under the Generalized System of Preferences program). It has rejected a little more than half the labor conditionality petitions received (7 of 13), compared with 49 percent for the Bush administration (17 of 35) and 32 percent for President Reagan (11 of 34), and it has suspended the eligibility of beneficiary countries in 15 percent of cases, compared with 6 percent for Bush and 24 percent for Reagan (Elliott 1998b).

Moreover, the administration has substantially increased the use of carrots. It increased its contribution to the ILO's International Program for the Elimination of Child Labor tenfold in 1999 and proposed increasing it another 50 percent for fiscal 2001, to $45 million. The administration also proposes providing the ILO with $20 million for a program of technical assistance for countries improving enforcement of the core labor standards, as well as $20 million to the Department of Labor for bilateral assistance to help countries improve the administration of labor laws and social safety net programs (*ILO Focus* 13, no. 1 [Spring 2000]: 7). In addition, American delegates to the ILO worked hard to gain approval of both the Declaration on Fundamental Principles and the new convention calling for immediate action to eliminate the worst forms of child labor. During the Seattle WTO ministerial meeting, President Clinton signed that convention, which he had worked with Senator Jesse Helms and the US Senate to get approved as quickly as possible.

In terms of any future negotiation on trade-labor linkages, what developing countries should oppose absolutely is any proposal that mentions "social dumping" as a basis for remedial action. The current antidumping laws in the United States and elsewhere have demonstrated all too well how such mechanisms can be distorted for protectionist purposes. What anyone should be willing to explore with an open mind is how to deal—multilaterally—with egregious violations of core labor standards that everyone claims to support. Where there is no direct link to trade or foreign investment, the issue should be resolved in the ILO. If, however, the violation is linked to an effort to gain competitive advantage—however misguided—the WTO must find a way to respond. Otherwise, it will find itself under attack from ever more people who deplore the apparent indifference to such practices, and the WTO will find that its support is dangerously thin.

Recommendations

In sum, the ILO should do more to promote and enforce international labor standards, particularly the fundamental rights identified in the 1998 declaration, and the WTO should address distortions in trade and investment flows that are linked to violations of worker rights. If this division of labor is to be maintained, however, countries and groups that have opposed a social clause in the WTO need to be fully supportive of the efforts to strengthen the supervisory mechanisms of the ILO and to take concrete, tangible action against egregious violations such as the widespread use of forced labor in Myanmar. At the same time, the ILO needs to further streamline reporting requirements and continue efforts to make their presentation less opaque. Governments and business groups that argue that carrots are more effective than sticks need to put their money where their mouth is, as the United States and others have begun to do, and ensure that the ILO's technical assistance and advisory functions are adequately funded.

The WTO's role should be to address direct trade-labor linkages in order to ensure that markets work as well as possible and that the international trading system attracts enough political support to move forward. In the short run, the effort should be limited to identifying potential market distortions and analyzing how to address them. One such distortion is clear, however, and WTO members should consider affirming, perhaps in a ministerial communiqué, that forced labor, especially affecting children, is morally unacceptable as well as violative of fundamental market principles. Though it has never been done, members might consider using the language of the communiqué to direct future panels to treat all forms of forced labor, not just prison labor, as covered under the provisions of Article XX(e) (subject to DSU review). To guard against protectionist abuse, panelists should look to the ILO supervisory process for evidence that a problem exists. This would not necessarily involve formal collaboration but could be similar to the Appellate Body's reference to the Convention on International Trade in Endangered Species (CITES) classification of sea turtles as endangered when it ruled that a US shrimp ban targeted a legitimate environmental problem. (The Appellate Body nevertheless ruled against the United States because the shrimp ban was implemented in arbitrary and discriminatory fashion.)

Further, labor issues will be harder to avoid as the WTO agenda on foreign investment expands. Therefore, members should ask the existing working group on investment to examine the application of labor standards to foreign investment projects, particularly in EPZs and perhaps in cooperation with the team that prepared the recent ILO report. Developing countries should welcome such a study because, while there is little evidence to suggest that trade between developed and developing countries has significant impact on the developed-country standards, developing countries competing for foreign investment could find themselves in a "race to the bottom" on labor standards. Finally, WTO members should consider establishing a joint working group with the ILO to consider how the General Agreement on Trade in Services might be adapted to encourage the provision of "worker agency" services, as described above.

To reiterate the major point, the WTO has no experience, no expertise, and no desire to enforce international core labor standards. To foist that responsibility onto it would weaken the ILO as well as the WTO and undercut efforts to promote stronger worker rights, in addition to impeding efforts to liberalize trade.

To say there should be a division of labor among international institutions, however, is not to say they should not cooperate more systematically, as recommended repeatedly by ILO Director General Juan Somavia.[15] There are overlapping effects from the policies promoted by the international financial institutions, the ILO, the WTO, and various UN agencies, and there is a growing need to ensure not only that the various policy recommendations are not contradictory but that they reinforce one another in pursuit of the common goal of shared growth and sustainable development. A multi-institutional forum, such as proposed by the European Union as an alternative to the US proposal for a WTO working group, would be a useful starting point for a broad discussion of globalization's impact on workers and their families.

References

Elliott, Kimberly Ann. 1998a. International Labor Standards and Trade: What Should Be Done? In Jeffrey J. Schott, ed., *Launching New Global Trade Talks: An Action Agenda*. Special Report 12. Washington: Institute for International Economics.

Elliott, Kimberly Ann. 1998b. Preferences for Workers? Worker Rights and the US Generalized System of Preferences. Unpublished paper, Institute for International Economics.

Freeman, Richard, and James Medoff. 1987. *What Do Unions Do?* New York: Basic Books.

International Labor Office. 1946. *Reports I and II and Constitutional Questions*, 29th session of the International Labor Conference. Geneva.

International Labor Office. 1998. *Labour and Social Issues Relating to Export Processing Zones*. Report for discussion at the Tripartite Meeting of Export Processing Zones-Operating Countries, TMEPZ/1998, Geneva.

International Labor Office. 1999. *Measures, including action under Article 33 of the Constitution . . . to secure compliance by the Government of Myanmar*. GB.276/6, 276th session of the governing body, Geneva, November.

Kull, Steven. 1999. *Americans on Globalization: A Study of Public Attitudes*. Opinion poll, Program on International Policy Attitudes, University of Maryland, College Park, 16 November.

---

15. Recent speeches by Somavia to UNCTAD and the World Bank, as well as his submission to the WTO ministerial in Seattle, are available on the ILO Web site, http://www.ilo.org.

Martin, Will, and Keith E. Maskus. 1999. Core Labor Standards and Competitiveness: Implications for Global Trade Policy. Unpublished paper, World Bank.

Maskus, Keith E. 1997. *Should Core Labor Standards Be Imposed through International Trade Policy?* Policy Research Working Paper 1817. Washington: World Bank.

Organization for Economic Cooperation and Development (OECD). 1996. *Trade, Employment, and Labour Standards: A Study of Core Workers' Rights and International Trade.* Paris.

Richardson, J. David. 2000. The WTO and Market-Supportive Regulation: A Way Forward on New Competition, Technological, and Labor Issues. *Federal Reserve of St. Louis Quarterly Review* 82, no. 4 (July/August).

Romano, Cesare P. R. 1996. *The ILO System of Supervision and Compliance Control: A Review and Lessons for Multilateral Environmental Agreements.* E-96-1. Laxenburg, Austria: International Institute for Applied Systems Analysis.

Stiglitz, Joseph. 2000. Democratic Developments as the Fruits of Labor. Keynote address to the Industrial Relations Research Association, Boston, January.

US Department of Labor, Bureau of International Labor Affairs. 1989-90. *Foreign Labor Trends: Worker Rights in Export Processing Zones.* FLT 90-32. Washington.

13

Trade, Competition, and the WTO Agenda

EDWARD M. GRAHAM

As a tool of domestic economic policy, competition policy has been in existence in the United States for more than a century, and in Canada for even longer.[1] And, since the late 1950s, competition policy has also been an integral element of the law and institutions of the European Common Market, now the European Union. More recently, about 70 countries have adopted some form of competition law or are actively contemplating doing so.

While the goals of competition policy and liberal trade policy are largely the same (as discussed in the next section), the two are not formally integrated in the sense that there are no multilateral agreements or institutions to ensure that private business practices do not create welfare-reducing barriers to international trade flows. There have been several failed efforts to do so, including the stillborn Havana Treaty to create the International Trade Organization of 1947. During the late 1990s, however, there have been calls from several quarters, including prominent former US trade officials, for a new effort to negotiate multilateral rules to link competition policy with trade policy.[2] These rules could reside under the aegis of the WTO but might possibly exist in some other context.

In fact, some WTO members actively support the notion that such a negotiation be included in a future round of multilateral trade negotiations. These proponents constitute a diverse lot, including the European Union, Japan, and South Africa. However, the United States opposes such

---

Edward M. Graham is senior fellow at the Institute for International Economics.

1. "Competition policy," a term of European origin, encompasses both antimonopolies (antitrust) and regulation of state aids (i.e., subsidies and subsidy-like measures).

2. See, e.g., Fox and Ordover (1995) and Sauvé and Zampetti (2000).

a negotiation, as do many developing nations that resist a broadening of the WTO agenda.

Even if the European view were to prevail, however, it is unlikely that the WTO would emerge as the repository of a "global antitrust act" under which the WTO would serve as a supranational antitrust enforcement agency. At most what might ensue is that the WTO, or WTO dispute settlement panels, be given some limited powers in the competition area—perhaps the right to request of member governments that antitrust investigations be initiated by domestic authorities and/or that the results of such investigations, along with any proposed remedies that might emerge, be reported to the WTO and be subject to scrutiny for compliance with WTO obligations.[3]

In the meantime, the US government has pursued with some success the negotiation of bilateral international cooperation agreements (ICAs) on antitrust pursuant to the International Antitrust Enforcement Assistance Act of 1994. To date, only one full-blown agreement—with Australia—has been concluded under this act.[4] Another is expected to be concluded in 2000, with Canada. In addition, two as-of-yet not "full-blown" agreements—these amount to exploratory agreements—have been struck with the European Union and Japan.[5] Other bilateral ICAs not involving the United States, including between Japan and the European Union, are under consideration. A network of bilateral ICAs thus could be an alternative route by which competition policy is effectively multilateralized.[6] It should be noted, however, that bilateral ICAs do not explicitly link competition policy issues to trade policy issues. Rather, they are largely meant to establish procedures by which competition policy authorities from different countries can cooperate internationally on specific cases of possible infringement of competition laws where these cases cross national boundaries.

This chapter explores whether or not there is an argument to be made for competition policy linked to trade policy via the multilateral trading

---

3. A number of proposals along these lines are discussed in Graham and Richardson (1997, chapter 17). A somewhat different set of proposals is offered by Fox (1997a). See also Scherer (1994) and Lawrence, Bressand, and Ito (1996).

4. The Australia-US agreement is "full-blown" in the sense that it allows for exchange of otherwise confidential information necessary for relevant officials to determine whether there has been a violation of competition law, and, if so, what harm it has done.

5. These "exploratory" agreements call for some measure of cooperation even now, but this falls short of exchange of confidential information. Graham and Richardson (1999) discuss the potential for greater cooperation between the United States and the European Union. On this, see also Fox (1997b).

6. A parallel situation exists in international investment, where a growing number of bilateral investment treaties collectively serve the function that might be served by multilateral trade and investment rules.

rules, and examines the alternative route of creating multilateral competition policy via a network of ICAs. As a first step, the next section explores whether or not the objectives of competition policy and trade policy are consistent. (I conclude that they largely are.) In the following section, the issue of whether or not some formal linkage between competition policy and the multilateral trade rules might be needed is examined. The countercase is that most nations of the world have or are putting into place unilateral domestic competition policies, and these in combination with a series of bilateral ICAs could arguably achieve the same end as competition policy integrated with the multilateral trade rules. My overall conclusion is nonetheless that the case in principle for such an integration remains strong. But even if all WTO members were to reach a consensus to begin negotiating on competition policy as a WTO issue, the actual negotiation and implementation of new and effective rules will be difficult. The final section provides some recommendations as to what might be done.

Are Competition Policy and Trade Policy Serving the Same (or Consistent) Substantive Objectives?

What I argue here is that liberal trade policy and competition policy largely serve the same ends in terms of economic objectives. Indeed, most concrete steps taken to liberalize trade policy are bound to increase competition in the affected markets. For example, whenever the removal of an entry barrier in a specific sector is achieved in the continuing General Agreement on Trade in Services (GATS) negotiations, this also serves to increase the amount of competition in this sector, thus furthering the objectives of competition policy. Likewise, actions taken by competition policy officials that reduce entry barriers to a market also serve the interests of liberal trade policy. Conversely, however, a measure taken by trade policy officials that increases barriers to market entry ill serves the objectives of competition policy and vice versa. Indeed, the tension between the two largely arises because of inconsistencies in exceptions.

Reduced to its essence, the goal of competition policy is to help ensure that the value of output is maximized given input resource constraints or, put differently, that efficiency of output is maximized in accordance with societal preferences. One general means of ensuring this is to have markets that are, to as great an extent as possible, competitive.[7] Competitive

---

7. The relationship between competitive markets and achievement of efficiency is discussed in some detail in Graham and Richardson (1997). The conclusion there is that both static (allocative) efficiency and dynamic efficiency (having mostly to do with the rate of technological progress) are enhanced by competitive markets notwithstanding some exceptions mentioned in the text below. This is by no means a new idea. It is at the essence of economic thinking, dating back to Adam Smith.

markets function such that the price consumers pay for a good or service is equal to the value of the resources required to produce the good or service, a prerequisite for optimal use of available resources. A competitive market requires above all else that sellers and potential sellers be as free as possible to enter and leave a market as they see fit—or, in other words, that markets be contestable.

However, this does not imply that each and every potential seller must succeed in its efforts. A would-be seller that attempts to sell an inferior product or a product at a higher price than an equivalent product offered by a rival seller, or a seller that is unable to provide needed after-market services (e.g., repair and maintenance services) might not succeed in establishing itself in the market. Rather, the goal of competition policy is to ensure that a potential seller is not blocked from market entry by practices of incumbent sellers that act to foreclose such entry, or is not forced out of the market by practices designed to force such exit, where these practices are undertaken only for the purpose of foreclosure of entry or forcing of exit and the practices generate no offsetting benefit.[8] Thus, such practices as improving the product or reducing the costs at which it is delivered would not normally be seen as objectionable, even if the ultimate effect is to force less efficient or innovative sellers out of the market.

Indeed, there is a consensus among both legal and economic scholars that the goal of competition policy definitely should not be to protect incumbent sellers from their own ineptitude or the superior performance of competitors.[9] Here, too, the goal is not to ensure that every attempted market entry is successful. A conundrum often arises in cases where a firm fails to gain entry into a market: Was the failure because the would-be entrant lacked some characteristic needed to gain acceptance in the market, or was it because the entrant was stymied by some practice by competitors clearly intended only to foreclose the entry? Often the evidence might not clearly point in one direction or the other.

Such conundrums in fact lie behind one of the reasons why there is disagreement as to whether competition policy should be on the WTO

---

8. Alas, as a practical matter, it is not often easy for authorities or courts to determine whether a seller undertakes a practice with the intent of driving rivals out of business or blocking entry into a market. Thus, the regulator or judge often is left with the task of balancing harmful effects (but effects that bestow benefit upon the seller that instigates the practice) with positive ones in trying to determine whether a particular practice is to be judged as improper or not. Competition law enforcement thus encompasses a doctrine of "rule of reason," whereby the particular circumstances of a given case can be instrumental in determining whether a practice is deemed objectionable or not.

9. To be sure, some portions of competition law in the United States in particular were originally drafted with protection of small competitors from large ones in mind. The Robinson-Patman Act, for example, originally was intended in part to protect small retailers from large retailing chains; even this law, however, allows for at least some exemptions for practices of the larger firms when these serve to enhance efficiency.

agenda. Some proponents of competition policy as a WTO issue have argued, in effect, that the failure of certain sellers to gain access to a nation's markets in which they are not incumbent (even though they might be major sellers in some other nations' markets) is prima facie evidence of "unfair" private practices (or state intervention) that should be addressed by new competition rules in the WTO. Indeed, some trade specialists believe that private practices constitute "the largest remaining distortion of world trade" (Wolff 1998). However, as Evenett and Suslow (1999) have shown, although a firm's failure to gain market access might indicate the existence of private practices that create market foreclosure, by itself it does not positively demonstrate that such practices exist. Drawing on Graham and Richardson (1997), Evenett and Suslow argue that there are at least four other partially overlapping reasons why such a failure might occur even in a market that is contestable. These can be summarized as follows:

> *Reputational effects:* The quality of most services, and of some goods, especially when bundled with services, might not be observable. Thus, customers might stick with incumbent sellers in a particular market even if a new entrant provides a product that is equivalent or superior to that of the incumbent in terms of price and quality.

> *History and experience:* Incumbent firms might have detailed knowledge of the customs and tastes of local consumers that a new entrant lacks, such that this knowledge gives the incumbent strong advantages.

> *Nontradability:* Some products and many services are not tradable for a variety of reasons, including transport costs, requirements for local facilities (e.g., it is difficult to sell temporary lodging, a service, if the seller does not own local hotels or other modes of lodging). This obstacle can often be overcome via foreign direct investment, however, and this suggests that one element of an effective competition policy can be to ease or eliminate restrictions on foreign direct investment (as discussed later in this chapter).

> *Noncompetitivity:* A new entrant, especially one trying to enter a foreign market, might simply not be cost-competitive for a variety of reasons, including the classic reason—differing relative factor input costs.

It is also possible that a market simply is not contestable. A noncontestable market can exist if the fixed costs of entry are sufficiently high that, given the potential demand, only one producer can efficiently supply the market.[10] In such a case, a natural monopoly exists, and the main job of public policy is not to try to achieve more contestability but rather to ensure that the monopoly position is not abused. Such regulation is,

---

10. It is not necessary, however, that these costs be sunk, that is, that they are not recoverable if the seller decides to exit the market. In fact, one means to achieve higher levels of efficiency if the highest possible level is not achieved by the incumbent would be to permit and even encourage the acquisition of the fixed assets by another investor who might utilize them more efficiently.

alas, subject to "capture" by the incumbent, which sometimes results in regulatory measures that make the market even less contestable than need be, for example, by forbidding acquisition of the incumbent seller by new investors who might increase efficiency.

None of this indicates that private practices are not a major distorting factor in international trade—they might well be. What it indicates is that the job of identifying the extent to which these practices do distort trade is far from finished.

In some sectors where technological progress requires that sellers commit large amounts of resources to research and development (which is a sunk cost in most instances) and where the commercial products resulting from the R&D can be replicated at a cost much lower than that of the original development, a case can be made for actually reducing market contestability. This is because, if faced with competitors who can replicate the results of R&D relatively cheaply, innovating firms might reason that they cannot recover sunk costs of R&D and, consequently, will not perform the R&D. If this were to occur, innovation would stop, to the overall detriment of society. This possibility is reflected in the existence of intellectual property laws that act as a sanctioned exemption to most competition law and allow innovators to hold limited monopoly rights over intellectual property that they create. International strengthening and expansion of intellectual property laws have been accomplished by means of the WTO Agreement on Trade-Related Aspects of Intellectual Property Rights (TRIPs).

Even so, there is also a case to be made that there can be excessive intellectual property protection, such that increasing this protection will retard rather than promote technological advancement. This is because much technological progress is driven by a dynamic process by which sellers in a market constantly try to reduce costs, improve products, or introduce new products in the expectation that their rivals are doing likewise. Part of this dynamic entails imitation—for example, one seller replicates the product of another and then attempts to make improvements on it. If intellectual property protection is so strong that this imitation ceases altogether, the dynamic might stop, especially if a firm holding a currently dominant technology believes that it no longer has to fear the introduction of competitive technologies by rival sellers. One problem from an analytical perspective is that it is very difficult to determine what is the optimal amount of intellectual property protection. Indeed, it is far from certain that current laws are optimal in terms of the incentives for innovation they create or the distribution of benefits that result from these innovations.[11]

---

11. It is very likely that the optimal level of intellectual property protection differs substantially from market to market. For example, it is generally believed that the "right" amount of such protection for pharmaceuticals is likely higher than for computer processor chips. For an extended discussion, see Scherer (1992) and Maskus (2000).

As I suggested earlier, some scholars would argue that competition policy should be concerned with government practices as well as private practices that inhibit market contestability. Such government practices might include, for example, regulatory measures that have the effect, possibly unintended, of discriminating against new entry in favor of an incumbent seller. In practice, however, in most jurisdictions competition policy officials have little power over state actions. (One major exception is in the European Union, where the European Commission wields substantial powers to annul state aids to industry that have the effect of reducing competition.) Indeed, some argue that the main goal of any future linkage of competition policy to the multilateral trade rules should be to create a means of reducing "behind the border" regulatory measures that unduly restrict market entry by nondomestic firms into a domestic market (Feketekuty 1998).

In this regard, it is notable that the rules of the multilateral trade system themselves are largely designed to reduce or eliminate measures taken by governments at the point of entry of imports of goods or services where the measures have the effect of excluding such imports or making them more costly. Also, the "national treatment" provisions of the GATT and the GATS are meant to eliminate regulatory measures whose effect is to discriminate against imported goods and services relative to like goods and services supplied by domestic sellers.[12] Thus, the effect of multilateral trade rules is to make markets more contestable by eliminating or reducing governmental measures that deter entry by foreign sellers. To be sure, these rules are subject to numerous sanctioned exceptions. But, in the end, these rules, and especially the core articles of the GATT (Article I's most favored nation provisions, Article II's tariff bindings and the process by which they have been lowered, and Article III's national treatment provisions) and their somewhat more limited counterparts in the GATS, unquestionably work in the direction of increasing market contestability.

At one time, most economic analysts would have argued that liberal trade policy served a goal somewhat different from, albeit complementary to, that of competition policy. The goal of open trade was seen as enabling countries to realize maximum allocative efficiency by specializing in the production of goods and services in which they held comparative advantage, itself determined by relative factor prices ultimately determined by relative factor abundance. But models of comparative advantage generally assumed that all underlying markets (both for end products and for factors of production) were competitive, and hence the efficiency gains from specialization came on top of those achieved by competition. More and more, however, trade economists have come to realize that in most nations, domestic markets for many goods and

---

12. However, not all services are covered by national treatment provisions under the GATS.

services are not highly competitive and hence that much of the gain from open trade policy results from making these markets more competitive. Thus, in addition to achieving the gains from specialization, the goal of open trade has increasingly come to be seen also as the enhancing of competition.[13]

It is clear, then, that the goals of liberal trade policy and competition policy are substantially the same. Indeed, the case is strong that liberal trade policy should be considered essentially a subset of competition policy. However, the underlying laws and the bureaucratic processes by which the two sets of policies are administered in individual nations are, for the most part, separate, and it is because of this separation that, in the practical world of trade negotiations, trade and competition policies are considered to be separate domains. Should these two sets of policies be formally linked at the multilateral level? The following section deals with this issue.

Is There a Case for Multilateralization of Competition Policy? If So, How Should It Be Implemented?

The simplest and perhaps the strongest argument for multilateralization of competition rules is that private or regulatory barriers to market entry do exist "behind the border," and they act to offset the gains that governments seek from further liberalization of the world trading system. This would never be a problem, of course, if competition agencies everywhere were to take action to remove these behind-the-border barriers. But, or so it is alleged, in many nations this simply does not happen, even where such action is called for and effective remedies potentially could be implemented. In some nations, this failure occurs simply because neither competition law nor agencies to enforce such law yet exist. Thus, it has been suggested that the creation and enforcement of competition law might be made an obligation of WTO membership, and countries currently not meeting this obligation be given a transition period to create such a law and a means of enforcing it.

However, in certain nations where competition law is in place and an enforcement agency exists, it is alleged that the agency has insufficient power (or insufficient will) to open domestic markets to competition from abroad or, in some cases, even to new domestic entry. Also, even in nations where an effective competition law and a strong enforcement agency both exist, other agencies have powers to override competition agencies in certain instances. Furthermore, these other agencies often act,

---

13. This does not imply that comparative advantage no longer figures in this goal. In fact, competitive markets in nations will drive sellers to seek to specialize in activities in which they have relative advantage.

wittingly or unwittingly, to protect incumbents against foreign entry (or, for that matter, domestic entry). For example, in many nations, governments restrict entry into many service sectors, including typically banking, telecommunications, electric power generation and transmission, and other services typically classified as "public utilities."

It is clear that such regulatory foreclosure is not the direct consequence of private practices so much as public policy choices by governments themselves, although these choices can reflect capture of public policy by incumbent sellers who benefit from the status quo. It is also clear that formal competition policy might not be the best possible remedy for the harm, if any, that is done by this foreclosure. If regulatory measures do unnecessarily protect incumbent interests, regulatory reform rather than competition policy would seem to be the first best remedy. However, if the regulatory process itself is "captured" by the service providers, reform of this process from within is unlikely, and some sort of agent outside of the regulatory process might be necessary to achieve the reform. In fact, in many cases where procompetitive regulatory reform has been successfully implemented, it has resulted from change in policy originating at the highest political levels (e.g., by Presidents Carter and Reagan in the United States in the late 1970s and early 1980s, and by Prime Minister Thatcher in the United Kingdom about the same time). However, competition agencies potentially could serve as agents of reform; indeed, in some places—Australia, for example—they have played this role.[14]

It is also possible that in some instances foreclosure is created by some combination of regulatory practice and private practice where the latter is not necessary to ensure the fulfillment of the objectives of the former. In such instances, it is possible that application of competition policy (or, at least, competition principles) could increase the contestability of the market for the relevant good or service even if the regulation remained in place. A problem in this regard is that the fulfillment of this objective—to make the market as contestable as possible—might require close cooperation of the two relevant agencies, that is, regulatory authorities and competition authorities. In most governments, no tradition of such cooperation exists.[15]

This results from the fact that in virtually every government, trade policy, competition policy, and regulatory authority have been organized

---

14. See Thomson (1997). Also, in Canada there has been some effort to have the Bureau of Competition vet certain regulatory actions for competitive effect. See Goldman, Bodrug, and Warner (1997).

15. Indeed, in instances where governments have succeeded in introducing new competition into regulated markets, this has resulted more often from the relevant regulatory agency internally adopting a more competition-oriented philosophy than from competition agencies working with the regulatory agencies.

under different organizational entities. (The responsibility for regulatory authority can, of course, be under many different agencies.) Communication and coordination among these entities is often lacking. In some instances, they do not even share the same objectives and hence may work against one another. And, in most governmental contexts, it is not always clear, if the objectives of two of these sets of actors conflict, whose objectives are overriding.

Indeed, this last point figures importantly in one of the main *objections* to the multilateralization of competition policy at the WTO, which has to do with who would be in control. Operational authority for participation in the WTO in virtually every government (and in the European Commission) is vested in trade policy officials. One reason why competition officials in virtually every WTO country then are chary of competition policy as a WTO issue is that if the WTO were to be granted competence in this domain, these officials would likely be forced to cede part of their "turf" to trade policy officials. In many instances, competition officials are reluctant to do so, not simply because they would lose control but also because they are not certain that competition principles would be adequately upheld by trade policy officials.

Competition policy officials tend to be wary of the very process by which WTO rules are negotiated. This process is one that might best be termed "channeled mercantilism." Even if, from an economic perspective, the main goal of these rules is market opening so as to achieve welfare-enhancing efficiency gains, as a matter of pragmatic politics, few nations are willing unilaterally to open their markets to competition from foreigners in the absence of reciprocal market opening. Thus, the WTO, and the predecessor GATT, have largely worked by pitting producer interests seeking international market access against one another, with the outcome that governments grant as "concessions" access to their own markets in exchange for access for their domestic producers to other nations' markets. Some prominent economists have lampooned the "cart before the horse" nature of this process of trading "concessions,"[16] but it has generally worked reasonably well in creating a more open international economy, that is, more contestable markets. Why, then, are competition policy officials generally wary of the process?

The main reason is tied to the principle, as noted in the previous section, that competition policy is not about protecting the interests of competitors but about protecting and promoting the process of competition itself. Thus, from the point of view of competition officials, judged against this principle, the trade negotiation process is corrupt. Even if it ultimately succeeds in creating more contestable markets worldwide, the process of opening markets is based on governments serving as advocates for the interests of specific domestic producers. Competition officials thus worry

---

16. Beginning, I think, with Krugman (1987).

that, if put into the trade policy venue, competition policy itself could be corrupted, at least in the sense that the principle that competition policy should never be used to protect the interests of specific firms would be routinely violated.[17]

One consequence of this mistrust of trade policy is that competition officials from a number of nations, prompted by US officials and recognizing that many of the issues with which they deal have an increasingly international dimension, have begun discussions among themselves about the international aspects of competition policy.[18] Also, as noted earlier, the US government, under authority created by the International Antitrust Enforcement Assistance Act of 1994, is seeking to enter into bilateral agreements with a number of nations to cooperate with competition enforcement officials in these nations to better enforce existing competition laws.

Are bilateral ICAs an effective alternative to negotiations to include elements of competition policy in the multilateral trade rules as a means of internationalizing competition policy? There are a number of arguments in favor of bilateral ICAs. These include, first and foremost, that they are agreements undertaken by competition officials themselves. Thus, the problem of "who is in control" of multilateral competition policy is largely avoided. Also, the worry of competition policy officials that their domain would become corrupted by trade policy is eliminated. Presumably these officials, if worried about this possibility, simply would not allow it to happen. And, most important, at the level of substance, cooperation among competition authorities of different nations via such agreements might ultimately solve the "competition policy stops at the border" problem cited at the beginning of this section, where barriers to market integration enabled by further border opening might be stymied by private practice.

But there are problems with the bilateral ICA approach. For example, it is legitimate to ask whether bilateral ICAs would be effective in addressing or remedying market access problems that are caused by

---

17. In this matter, US officials note that the ultimate venue for deciding competition cases is the US court system, in which a high standard of impartiality is maintained. In contrast, these officials see the process by which trade policy is determined in the United States as highly politicized, such that the "squeaky wheel gets the grease" irrespective of the merits of the case. However, this line of argument is to some extent undermined by the fact that the ultimate venue for deciding trade disputes is the WTO Dispute Settlement Body, which itself is building some substantial credibility for impartiality. (See the chapter by John H. Jackson in this volume.) Even so, competition authorities worry that evidentiary standards at the WTO are not as high as those required in US legal proceedings.

18. The main venue for these meetings has been the Organization for Economic Cooperation and Development (OECD). A number of non-OECD member nations that have competition laws in place send representatives to these meetings who, although they are not formally delegates to the OECD Competition Committee, nonetheless participate on an informal basis.

combinations of government regulations and private practices rather than by private practices alone. As suggested earlier, competition policy agencies even at the domestic level have not proved to be very effective in dealing with this type of problem. In contrast, the WTO, especially in the domain of services, has begun to tackle the very big issue of how to deal with market access in sectors where regulatory barriers pose the greatest obstacle to market contestability. To be sure, the WTO work in this area is nascent, and relatively little progress has been made in opening markets where these barriers loom large, such as telecommunications and financial services. But it is a beginning.

Also, if cooperation among competition policy officials as enabled by bilateral ICAs is to prove effective in combating "behind the border" private practices that offset "at the border" market-opening measures, this would require that competition agencies actually be inclined to cooperate to remedy such practices where they can be shown to exist and to create harmful effects. However, in some countries enforcement agencies do not seem to be inclined to do so—and it is not clear what good a cooperation agreement will do if one of the parties to the agreement chooses not to cooperate. In the WTO, by contrast, if a party fails to abide by an obligation and fails to remedy its noncomplying measures, dispute settlement procedures can be invoked against that party and sanctions applied.

Furthermore, a proliferation of bilateral ICAs would not necessarily address effectively the problem of compartmentalization of competition, trade, and regulatory policy. Indeed, the problem could even be exacerbated, given that the compartmentalization would be extended from national governments into the international arena.

Are these problems likely to be predominant, such that bilateral ICAs would not likely prove to be particularly useful? Or, alternatively, in spite of these problems that can be identified even before bilateral ICAs come into force, will ICAs prove to be effective means by which global competition concerns can be addressed? The answer to both questions is, very simply, that no one knows. Again, the only full-blown bilateral ICA that currently exists is that between the United States and Australia, and precious little experience has accumulated to date under this agreement. In short, bilateral ICAs are an untested instrument.

The effectiveness of bilateral ICAs as a means of resolving competition-related trade disputes may prove to depend on the nature of the entry barriers provoking the disputes. If, for example, cross-border anticompetitive private practices proliferate, a network of bilateral ICAs might indeed prove to be a fruitful means of coping with them. But if the dominant barrier to cross-border market contestability proves to be government regulation that imparts advantages to market incumbency, the WTO is likely to be more effective at resolving them (and, as noted, the WTO and its predecessor already have a substantial track record in this arena in both at-the-border government measures and certain behind-the-border measures).

Thus, the main alternative to bilateral ICAs as a vehicle for multilateralization of competition policy is the WTO. Although some maintain that the WTO is also untested in this area, this is not entirely true, since the WTO already has limited competence in the domain of competition policy. Examples are contained in other chapters in this volume that detail specific WTO agreements containing provisions that deal directly with competition policy issues.[19]

However, the issue at hand is not whether the WTO is already involved in competition policy but whether there should be a negotiation that might formally create an extension of WTO competence in this area. Indeed, given the nature of the problems that the WTO is best suited to handle—that is, government measures that inhibit cross-border market contestability—it might be that the optimal path is for the WTO to tackle these problems by deepening existing agreements (especially the GATS) rather than by striking a new agreement encompassing "trade and competition policy." The case for this "deepen existing agreements" route would be strengthened if measures to be addressed prove to be sui generis to specific service sectors. In this case, provisions agreed upon to achieve market opening in one sector might not be relevant to market opening in some other sector. However, there might also be a case for at least some WTO competition rules that cut across all of the existing agreements, if it were to become clear that certain barriers to market contestability appear common to many sectors.

One fact that must be taken into account in this matter, however, is that the WTO works on the basis of a consensus among the member nations, and the positions of these nations (and certainly of the most influential among them) are driven in large measure by the interests of major domestic constituencies. It is difficult to discern major constituencies in any of these nations that are enthusiastic backers of granting the WTO additional broad competence in competition policy. In no nation would the business community, for example, unanimously support such a move, for understandable reasons: competition policy can at times be (and is) used to end specific business practices that are deemed to hurt competition but that might nonetheless be quite profitable to particular firms. Business enterprises are at best ambivalent about competition rules. Some firms might benefit from an end to these practices, but others would lose. Hence the business community widely and rightly views competition policy as a two-edged sword.

However, some business constituencies might nonetheless favor competition principles in the WTO writ narrow. Such constituencies would

---

19. For example, see the chapters on the TRIPs agreement by Maskus, the GATS agreement by Hoekman, and GATT jurisprudence by Jackson.

be those whose interests are hurt by specific measures that benefit rivals. For example, US telecommunications services providers are certainly in favor of the ending of government policies that grant monopoly rights in the provision of telecommunications services to local providers. Such rights have long been insurmountable barriers to market access. Although many nations are now in the process of ending or substantially modifying state-sanctioned telecommunications monopolies, these markets nevertheless will remain highly regulated and probably not very contestable. Further market opening measures by the WTO in this domain are welcomed by providers that stand to gain market access.

Other constituencies in favor of competition policy at the WTO are difficult to find. The logical constituency in favor of competition policy in general would be consumers, simply because effective competition serves, more than anything else, to enhance the welfare of consumers. However, this constituency is not well organized in any nation, and, indeed, organized groups claiming to represent consumers often prove to be advocates for special causes. (For example, in Japan there are groups claiming to be consumer interest groups that are in fact advocates of banning the importation of rice on the somewhat dubious theory that home-grown rice is somehow better for the public there than imported rice. In the United States, the largest consumer group, Public Citizen, is vocally anti-WTO for reasons that leave this author befuddled.) Thus, there is no consumer-advocacy constituency visibly pressing for inclusion of competition policy in the WTO.

Rather, most of the advocacy for (and, indeed, against) competition policy in the WTO comes from government bureaucracies or from persons closely associated with them. It has already been noted that the major proponent of including competition policy as a WTO negotiating issue has been the European Union, and the main advocacy within the EU has originated in the bureaucracy of the European Commission itself. This advocacy was initiated by former EU Commissioner Sir Leon Brittan, who first proposed that competition rules be created within the context of WTO when he was in charge of competition policy, and he continued to advocate it when his portfolio changed to external relations (i.e., international trade). Both the current trade and competition commissioners as well as the bureaucracies under them continue to hold to this position, even though the competition policy directorate itself (the Directorate General IV, DGIV) simultaneously seeks to develop direct formal working relationships with their counterparts in other nations.

Apart from the European Union, the major WTO member government in favor of going forward with competition policy has been Japan. Until recently, the major Japanese interest was to advance competition policy as a substitute for the current WTO antidumping regime. However, in the face of substantial opposition to any linkage of competition policy with antidumping, the Japanese government has backed away from insisting on such linkage (opponents included the European Union, otherwise an ally of Japan on competition policy).

In the United States, by contrast, there is relatively little enthusiasm in the executive branch for any enlargement of WTO competence in competition policy. The Antitrust Division (ATD) of the Department of Justice has been largely opposed to such an extension. However, the head of ATD has created an outside advisory group, the International Competition Policy Advisory Committee (ICPAC, pronounced "icepack") to advise the Department of Justice on this matter. As of January 2000, the group had not issued a recommendation. The second US enforcement agency, the Federal Trade Commission (FTC), does not appear to be quite as opposed as the ATD but has not been an advocate. The Department of Commerce has been steadfastly opposed to any work on competition policy being included in the WTO largely on the grounds that this might be linked to antidumping reform. However, this position has been rendered somewhat moot because, as noted above, the major advocate of such a linkage, Japan, has indicated that it would support the trade and competition agenda at the WTO without this linkage.

One argument against a role for the WTO in the domain of competition policy that has been advanced by US competition authorities is the fear that competition policy might be captured by special interests if allowed to escape from the control of these authorities. This fear is not easily dismissed, given that the interests of export-oriented firms dominate the politics of trade. US competition officials have raised two more objections. The first is that evidentiary standards at WTO are not as high as those in US courts, including when these courts must judge on competition issues. The second is that, unlike the US judiciary, the panelists who serve as judges in WTO cases simply do not have the technical expertise needed to decide on complex competition issues.

The first of these is a genuine problem, occasioned in large part by the fact that the WTO does not have the broad powers to compel "discovery" that US courts have (or, for that matter, courts in many nations). US and other nations' courts can compel the disclosure of relevant information and can penalize parties that knowingly withhold information or present misleading or erroneous information; the WTO simply does not possess this type of power. However, it is a long jump from there to the second criticism, that WTO panelists lack the expertise needed to make the complex judgments required in cases involving competition issues. To begin with, WTO panelists already are being called upon to make judgments in areas as difficult and complex as competition and the environment (e.g., whether genetically modified organisms pose a threat to human or ecological safety and health). Where judgments must be made on complex technical issues, WTO panelists can (and do) turn to expert advisers, just as do judges in domestic courts. Furthermore, if potential panelists for WTO cases lack the technical qualifications to make the needed technically complex decisions, other potential panelists who do have the requisite qualifications can be added to the roster.

In short, the argument that the WTO should not venture into competition policy because it is an area too complex for this organization should be seen as a shibboleth. I mention it here because it seems to be given special credence in the debate on whether there should be any negotiation on trade and competition policy at the WTO.

What Should Be the WTO Agenda with Regard to Competition Policy?

Let us summarize the main arguments made thus far:

- In their ultimate objectives, competition policy and liberal trade policy are quite similar. Both aim to enhance economic welfare by making markets more contestable. Indeed, reflecting this, the WTO already has substantial competence in the domain of competition policy.

- However, in countries in which competition law and enforcement agencies exist, the bureaucratic dynamics and politics of competition policy and trade policy tend to be quite different.

- There is no consensus among major nations on whether there should be a broad extension of the competence of the WTO in the domain of competition policy. Without such a consensus, it is unrealistic to expect a WTO negotiation on "trade and competition" to begin in the near future. Even so, the WTO is likely to gain additional competence in competition policy via the enlargement and deepening of existing agreements, especially the GATS.

- There is a route other than via the WTO to the multilateralization of competition policy, namely, the extension of the nascent network of bilateral ICAs. However, ICAs are largely untested. They are likely to be effective if private anticompetitive practices on a global scale prove to be a major problem associated with globally integrated markets. They are not likely to be effective at removal of government measures that inhibit cross-border market contestability by conferring advantage on incumbent sellers.

Given this, what should be done? The main thing that I would advocate would be to "let a thousand flowers bloom"—or, more prosaically, let at least two flowers bloom.

The first flower is expansion of the existing bilateral ICAs. Even though bilateral competition agreements between nations are in their untested infancy, they might prove to be a very useful vehicle for ensuring that private practices that result in restriction of competition do not mar the efficient functioning of emerging globally integrated markets. It is not clear whether or not such practices constitute a significant problem, but there is at least some evidence to suggest they might (Evenett and Suslow 1999). Thus, competition agencies should continue to negotiate these pacts and to try to make them work to address those disputes among nations that can be identified as arising from objectionable private practices.

But this does not mean that the issue of "trade and competition" at the WTO should be allowed to wither. Lack of consensus on whether or not to include a broad mandate for negotiation of competition rules in the next multilateral round of trade negotiations suggests that there will not soon be a WTO "Agreement on Trade and Competition." However, it would be desirable to continue the work of the present Working Group on Trade and Competition and to require that the group report to the next WTO ministerial meeting a set of recommendations as to where to go from that point.

To avoid the risk that bureaucratic inertia will cause key governments simply to stick to their present positions, ministers should not only renew the mandate for the Trade and Competition Working Group, but they should charge it with commissioning an impartial, independent, nongovernmental group of international experts to convene, to study the issues at hand, and to prepare a recommendatory report to the working group. The study should focus on the following:

- What are the natures of and causes for failures of markets to be contestable internationally? What harm is caused by such failures? Does the harm result primarily from private practices, from government regulation, or from some combination of these?

- Can these failures be effectively addressed by international cooperation among competition enforcement agencies? By the existing WTO rules and processes? By the WTO, but with additional competence?

- If the latter, should the new competence be in the form of some sort of agreement on competition rules, or enlargement and deepening of existing agreements such as the GATS?

The experts in this group should be chosen both for their stature and for their expertise. The group should include persons with both trade and competition backgrounds, and persons with both legal and economic training.

The working group would not, of course, be bound by the experts' recommendations. However, with luck, their recommendations would be both pragmatic and normatively desirable, and hence difficult to dismiss.

References

Evenett, Simon, and Valerie Suslow. 1999. The Empirics of Private Restraints. Unpublished paper.

Feketekuty, Geza. 1998. An American Trade Strategy for the 21st Century. In *Trade Strategies for a New Era*, ed. Geza Feketekuty and Bruce Stokes. New York: Council on Foreign Relations.

Fox, Eleanor M. 1997a. Toward World Antitrust and Market Access. *American Journal of International Law* 91, 1 (January): 1-25.

Fox, Eleanor M. 1997b. US and EU Competition Law: A Comparison. In Edward M. Graham and J. David Richardson, eds., *Global Competition Policies*. Washington: Institute for International Economics.

Fox, Eleanor M., and Janusz A. Ordover. 1995. The Harmonization of Competition and Trade Law: The Case for Modest Linkages of Law and Limits to Parochial State Action. *World Competition* 19 (December): 5-34.

Goldman, Calvin S., John D. Bodrug, and Mark A. A. Warner. 1997. Canada. In Edward M. Graham and J. David Richardson, eds., *Global Competition Policies*. Washington: Institute for International Economics.

Graham, Edward M., and J. David Richardson. 1997. *Competition Policies for a Global Economy*. POLICY ANALYSES IN INTERNATIONAL ECONOMICS 51. Washington: Institute for International Economics.

Graham, Edward M., and J. David Richardson. 1999. A US-EU Road toward Multilateralism in International Competition Policy. *Economic Perspectives* 4, 1 (February), at http://www.usia.gov/journals/ites/0299/ijee/iie.htm.

Krugman, Paul R. 1987. Is Free Trade Passé? *Journal of Economic Perspectives* 1, 2 (Fall): 131-44.

Lawrence, Robert Z., Albert Bressand, and Takatoshi Ito. 1996. *A Vision for the World Economy: Openness, Diversion, and Cohesion*. Washington: Brookings Institution.

Maskus, Keith E. 2000. *Intellectual Property Rights in the Global Economy*. Washington: Institute for International Economics. Forthcoming.

Sauvé, Pierre, and Americo Beviglia Zampetti. 2000. Subsidiarity Perspectives on the New Trade Agenda. *Journal of International Economic Law* 3, 1 (January).

Scherer, F. M. 1994. *Competition Policies for an Integrated World Market*. Washington: Brookings Institution.

Scherer, F. M. 1992. *International High Technology Competition*. Cambridge, MA: Harvard University Press.

Thomson, Graeme. 1997. Australia and New Zealand. In Edward M. Graham and J. David Richardson, eds., *Global Competition Policies*. Washington: Institute for International Economics.

Wolff, Alan William. 1998. Goals and Challenges for US Trade Policy. In Geza Feketekuty and Bruce Stokes, eds., *Trade Strategies for a New Era*. New York: Council on Foreign Relations.

14

Investment Issues

THEODORE H. MORAN

The central accomplishment of the Uruguay Round regarding investment issues was the Agreement on Trade-Related Investment Measures (TRIMs), a modest effort that proscribed domestic-content requirements and certain kinds of export performance requirements placed on foreign investors. Developed countries were given two years to phase out their use of these measures, developing countries five years, and least-developed countries seven years. Developing and least-developed countries were allowed to petition for an extension of the phaseout period.

Many developing countries still impose domestic-content and export performance requirements on foreign investors and want either to continue to use them or to have more time to eliminate them under Article 5.3 of the TRIMs agreement. Most developed countries object to such requirements and have shown no inclination to grant extensions of the phaseout period. So there is a worrisome possibility of some backsliding, both in terms of reopening the debate about developing countries' current obligations and in terms of extending the period for meeting those obligations.

At the same time, however, the TRIMs agreement provides for a self-review (Article 9), beginning no later than five years after the entry into force of the World Trade Organization (WTO), in early 2000, and it stipulates that this review consider whether the agreement should be "complemented" with other investment-related trade and competition policy measures. Since the TRIMs negotiations first began in the 1980s, the use of investment-diverting and investment-distorting measures not covered in the current agreement has vastly increased. Consequently, this review opens the door to much broader consideration of the instruments that are being deployed in the struggle to influence the location of international

Theodore H. Moran is director and professor at the Karl F. Landegger Program in International Business Diplomacy at the School of Foreign Service, Georgetown University.

investment.[1] Consideration of petitions for extension of the phaseout period under Article 5.3 and the self-review under Article 9 are due to take place independent of a new round of trade negotiations.

Quite apart from the fate of the Multilateral Agreement on Investment (MAI) conducted under the auspices of the Organization for Economic Cooperation and Development (OECD) or the agenda for a new round of WTO negotiations, there is an agenda built into the Uruguay Round that provides a setting for discussion and negotiation of investment issues that affect developed as well as developing countries. The review of the TRIMs agreement under Article 9 could offer an opportunity, in fact, to take important steps toward constructing a truly level playing field in which comparative advantage is the sole determinant of international direct investment patterns, an outcome in which both developed and developing countries have a great stake.

What are the interests of the developing countries in the review of the TRIMs agreement? What are the interests of the developed countries? And how might the contentious issues that are certain to arise be woven together to begin to bring the most serious investment-diverting and investment-distorting measures under multilateral discipline?

The TRIMs Review and the Developing Countries

The nearly two decades since the TRIMs negotiations were launched have produced a much clearer understanding of the impact that performance requirements have on foreign direct investors' operations. This experience can provide valuable policy guidance for host countries that want to use foreign direct investment (FDI) to enhance their own prospects for development and can offer a fresh perspective on what approaches might best advance developing-country interests in the TRIMs review.

The Most Beneficial FDI Projects

The first discovery is that full-scale foreign plants, integrated into the global sourcing network of the parent companies, provide benefits to the economies where they are located considerably beyond the capital, management, and marketing conventionally expected. These plants are almost always wholly owned and unencumbered by domestic-content or technology-transfer mandates.

The operations of investors using the developing-country locale as a site from which to strengthen their larger competitive position in international markets do bring higher-than-average wages and benefits, advanced technology, and sophisticated managerial and marketing techniques. Re-

---

1. This analysis draws on Moran (1998).

inforcing these inputs, the evidence also shows a dynamic "integration effect," which carries more rapid technological upgrading, tighter quality control, more intensive human resource development, and closer placement along the frontier of best management practices and highest industry standards than any other avenue through which the host economy might acquire such benefits.[2]

The interaction between the home corporation and the local subsidiary in these tightly integrated relationships is much more potent than the conventional term "outsourcing" might imply. The foreign investor is not merely shopping around for cheap components. Instead, the home corporation has an interest in providing persistent parental supervision so as to raise the performance of the local subsidiary to major league standards as part of its own "team," so to speak, and keep it there.

Moreover, rather than engaging only in low value-added "screwdriver" tasks—a charge frequently leveled against wholly owned subsidiaries— there are many industries in which important responsibilities for design and system integration are assigned to the overseas affiliates and the value added of the output is quite large. The economic benefits from these production systems integrated across borders extend well beyond the workers and operations at the foreign-owned plants. The backward linkages from the foreign operations are frequently both extensive and dynamic, with indications of abundant spillovers and externalities to local firms in the industry.

Foreign investment in the automotive and computer/electronics industries in Latin America and Southeast Asia provides a good illustration of these dynamic integration effects.[3] Having grown up as suppliers to foreign investors, these local companies often begin to export to other affiliates of those investors in other countries, then to independent buyers in the international marketplace. Within five years after the Mexican automotive sector reoriented its operations from purely internal toward external markets, some 110 Mexican suppliers generated sales of more than $1 million per year. Many started to sell abroad as well as domestically, with six of the ten largest auto parts exporters in the first decade of global sourcing from Mexico being entirely locally owned (Perez Nuñez 1990).[4]

2. The most extensive evidence comes from automobiles/auto parts and computers/electronics among industrial sectors and from processed foods in the agribusiness sector.

3. For an examination of the self-interest of parent firms in investing in the business practices and quality control procedures of the suppliers upon which their competitive position depends, see Caves (1999).

4. More broadly, Aitken and Harrison (1997) have found that international manufacturing investors have acted, in general, as export catalysts for domestic firms in Mexico. They report that the probability of a Mexican-owned plant engaging in exports is positively correlated with its proximity to foreign plants but uncorrelated with the concentration of other exporters.

Similarly, in the semiconductor industry in Malaysia, an indigenous machine tool industry grew from supplying the totality of its rather elemental output to foreigners, to providing successively more sophisticated generations of high-precision computer-numeric tools and factory automation equipment for international as well as domestic markets (Rasiah 1994, 1995; see also Lim and Fong 1982). Their initial exports went to the regional counterparts of the foreign firms they supplied locally. With this experience behind them, they began to export more than one-third of their output to independent buyers abroad, beating out mature competitors from Japan, Taiwan, and Germany in the process.

Contrary to contemporary perceptions about the speed and ease of globalization, however, the history of those industries in which the spread of foreign investment has been most extensive (automotive, petrochemical, and computer/electronics) shows that international market pressures alone have been quite sluggish in reallocating the global and regional sourcing networks of the major international corporations along lines that have proved to be least-cost and most efficient.

Instead, to position themselves within the regional and global sourcing networks described above, host governments in Latin America and Southeast Asia have had to take assertive steps with carrots and sticks—including export subsidies and export performance requirements—to push a leader in each industry to be the first to abandon the established structure of international production. Once this was accomplished, however, the effort triggered a burst of moves and matching moves among the principal players within each industry, leading to subsequent streams of globally competitive exports running in the billions of dollars annually. The public support that has accompanied the export performance requirements can be rigorously justified as a transitory method to "lock into" the parents' externality-filled family network (a strategic approach quite different from simply subsidizing all exporters).

As developing countries embark on a review of TRIMs, the findings cited above provide a baseline of cases of wholly owned subsidiaries without domestic-content or technology-sharing requirements against which to measure foreign investment projects that do have joint venture, domestic-content, and technology-sharing mandates imposed upon them. These findings should reassure host authorities who are willing to liberalize their investment regimes that the outcome will enhance their prospects for development. But these findings also leave developing countries with complicated calculations about what stance to take toward export performance requirements.

The Least Beneficial or Most Harmful FDI

Equally important for the developing countries' calculations regarding the TRIMs review and subsequent policy formation has been a new understanding of those circumstances in which FDI is likely to be least beneficial or most harmful—sometimes actually damaging—to the growth and welfare of the host country.

There is a common assumption that if international companies conduct their activities with the same "good citizenship" standards abroad that they do at home their contribution to the host economy can only be positive. But this reasoning hinges, implicitly, on the presence of highly competitive conditions surrounding the international companies from sources internal and external to the economies where they operate. When these competitive conditions are absent, the assumption becomes highly problematic. There are indeed important undesirable activities—such as creating pollution, carrying out operations with inadequate health and safety standards, or tolerating the behavior of abusive subcontractors— that could be righted by common "good citizenship" standards for behavior at home and abroad. However, the possibility that foreign investment might lead to fundamental economic distortion and pervasive damage to the development prospects of the country is ever present and is not at all mitigated by "good citizenship" standards of behavior.

The most frequently used intervention on the part of host authorities in the developing countries and economies in transition is their insistence that foreign investors meet high domestic-content requirements in tightly protected markets. This intervention stifles rather than enhances competition and harms host-country development. The imposition of domestic-content requirements leads to effective rates of protection ranging from 50 percent to more than 600 percent and prices 200 to 300 percent higher than the cost for comparable products outside the host economy. Furthermore, intensity of use of those products is reduced to less than half of what international standards should lead one to expect—an impact sufficiently negative that the host society would often be better off not receiving the foreign investment at all.

Not only are the resulting operations highly inefficient, the infant industry rationale of trying to demonstrate the underlying appeal of a given host to multinational corporations is ineffective. Except in the largest countries, economies of scale are seldom realized, and there are weak incentives for the foreign firms to upgrade technology, to maintain the highest standards of quality control, or to improve human resources. Conventional expectations notwithstanding, backward linkages to domestic suppliers are less sophisticated and exhibit fewer indications of training, assisting, or providing technological and marketing externalities than foreign operations with fewer restrictions (Borrus 1994; Ernst 1999).

The imposition of high domestic-content requirements in protected markets tends moreover to generate a perverse political economy in which foreign investors themselves frequently join domestic forces in opposing further liberalization of trade and investment. A case in point is IBM's proposal for an outward-oriented production facility in Mexico in return for wholly owned status and much greater freedom over sourcing of inputs—a proposal that marked a turning point in Mexico's approach to foreign investment. Heavily protected Hewlett-Packard and Apple helped wage the fight within the higher echelons of the Mexican political establishment, in vain, against the IBM initiative and the policy shift it represented (Harvard Business School 1990). There is similar evidence from contemporary Eastern Europe, where Suzuki (in Hungary) and Fiat (in Poland) have successfully lobbied for continued or even increased trade restrictions to safeguard their small domestic assembly operations, allying with local workers and suppliers to slow the prospects for accession into the European Union. Automotive companies that profess to want an end to domestic-content requirements worldwide have nevertheless urged that they be maintained in India.[5]

For both economic and political reasons, therefore, protecting foreign investors in return for high domestic-content levels generates a drag on economic growth and on the creation of higher standards of living.

While imposing domestic-content requirements on foreign investors may produce the most damaging consequences for developing countries and economies in transition, two of the other most popular approaches in the treatment of foreign firms—joint venture mandates and technology transfer mandates—also have negative impacts and are highly questionable as policy tools.

For many kinds of operations, the joint venture relationship offers benefits to all parties. When the partnership is required rather than spontaneous, however, rates of dissatisfaction are intense, with the likelihood of dissolution within a few years high. US and European parent firms shun joint venture arrangements where international sourcing, quality control, rapid technological change, product differentiation, and integration with external markets rather than purely domestic sales dictate corporate strategy. Japanese firms may now be exhibiting the same tendency (Beamish and Delios 1997).

Many host governments argue that joint ventures might lead to greater technology transfer, greater access to external markets, and greater backward linkages into the local economy than that experienced by wholly owned foreign operations. But the data show otherwise (Mansfield and Romeo 1980; Ramachandran 1993; Kokko and Blomstrom 1995).

Technology transferred to joint ventures is older (almost one-third older) while the pace of upgrading is slower than in the case of wholly owned subsidiaries. Export performance is less strong. Backward linkages lose in quality what they may (or may not) gain in quantity: there is less of the coaching and training of suppliers that comes from the intimate rela-

---

5. Comments of A. V. Ganesan, former commerce secretary of India, at the conference on "The World Trading System: Seattle and Beyond," sponsored by the Institute for International Economics, Seattle, 30 November 1999.

tionship with a parent that is basing its competitive position in international markets on the performance of local producers.

As for technology-licensing requirements as a substitute for foreign direct investment (the "Japan-Korea" model), host governments that try to fortify domestic companies via mandatory technology sharing agreements have found that the resulting operations exhibit the same kind of economic disadvantages as joint ventures: technology and management practices that are far from the cutting edge in the industry, poor performance in penetrating international markets, and weak contributions to the development of internal suppliers.

The adoption of a strategy to build national champions via mandatory technology licensing (to the exclusion of foreign investment and foreign acquisitions) inevitably opens the door to the core "industrial policy" problem of special pleading and special preferences on the part of powerful rent-seeking constituencies who may well be unable to distinguish their own self-interest from their interpretation of the national interest.

Based on the experience of the Asian financial crisis of 1997-98, there is reason to doubt that a system of import restraint and export promotion that focuses on chosen sectors and preferred national firms, powered by state-dictated technology-licensing arrangements, can ever escape the political-economic corruption and "crony capitalism" that have figured so prominently in the history of many Asian economies.

These findings provide a valuable perspective from which to judge whether it is in the developing countries' interest to try to extend the phaseout period for the use of domestic-content requirements or, conversely, to comply as promptly as possible with the TRIMs agreement. They also suggest the intriguing possibility that the developing countries might want to consider expanding the list of proscribed TRIMs to include joint venture and technology-sharing/technology-licensing requirements, with the aim both of enhancing their own development prospects and of gaining leverage to enlarge the range of multilateral disciplines over the investment-shifting and investment-distorting actions of others.

Although domestic-content, joint venture, and technology-licensing requirements are ill-advised methods to capture the benefits from FDI, it would be mistaken to suppose that, in their absence, host authorities in the less-developed world are best advised to merely sit back, improve the "fundamentals" in their own economies, and wait for international markets to deliver appropriate amounts of foreign investment to their countries. Instead, policy strategists in these countries who are seeking to optimize FDI's utility for stimulating growth and mulling their approach to the TRIMs review will want to scrutinize the larger array of investment-diverting and investment-distorting practices that the home countries of international corporations are deploying with particular effect.

The TRIMs Review and the Developed Countries

While the developed countries have led the way in reducing the use of tariffs over the past two decades, they have simultaneously been expanding the use of other measures that not only protect internal industries but have a substantial impact in redirecting or diverting investment flows. Moving in the opposite direction from win-win trade liberalization, these efforts have been leading to zero-sum struggles over the location of international investment. Both developed and developing countries have a growing interest in bringing these "trade-related investment measures" under common control. The three principal measures of concern for the TRIMs review are high domestic-content rules of origin, escalating locational incentives, and discriminatory antidumping regulations.

High Domestic-Content Rules of Origin

While the direct imposition of domestic-content requirements on foreign investors has been circumscribed within the TRIMs agreement, the use of domestic-content requirements on the part of developed countries and their partners in regional trading agreements has been greatly expanded through the use of specially crafted rules of origin.

Rules of origin provide criteria for determining which products receive the benefits of a preferential trade agreement. They prevent outsiders from enjoying access to the regional market unless they grant reciprocal access to their own internal economies. Rules of origin can also be used as protectionist devices, however, by muting competition from external sources. Finally, they may serve as investment-forcing measures by requiring companies that want access to the preferential trade area to engage in local production to qualify.

The method of determining origin with the least economic distortion is a "change of tariff heading" rule, which allows goods with local processing sufficient to move them from one standard industrial trade classification (SITC) code to another to receive the status of an internal product. The further rules of origin depart from this standard, by requiring greater amounts of local content for a product to qualify as domestic, the more protectionist the impact and the greater the diversion of investment needed to meet the requirement.

The United States and the European Union have outdone each other in designing rules of origin to protect local industries and to shift foreign investment into member states (Jensen-Moran 1995, 1996; Skud 1996). A complicated mix of protectionism and investment shifting was evident in the US effort in the North American Free Trade Agreement (NAFTA) to prevent assembly operations from being set up within the borders of Canada, the United States, and Mexico that could use low-cost inputs from outside. NAFTA rules of origin that mandate a high level of domestic content include textiles, tobacco products, fabricated metals, furniture, household appliances, machine tools, forklift trucks, automobiles, telecommunications, and electronic products such as printers, copiers, television tubes, and automobiles. European, Japanese, Korean, and US companies have, by their own testimony, had to shift investment from lower-cost or better-positioned sites elsewhere to North America to comply with the rules.

The European Union has adopted high domestic-content rules of origin in semiconductors, automobiles, textiles, printed circuit boards, and telecom switching equipment, with similar investment-shifting impact. In response to the requirement that semiconductor "diffusion" (wafer fabrication) be carried out within Europe to avoid a 14 percent tariff, Intel built a $400 million fabrication and assembly plant in Ireland. Over the course of the 1990s, seven of the largest ten US producers have located fabrication facilities in Europe. Most recently US investors have been lining up new production sites in a variety of industries around the periphery of Europe to meet the EU rules.

The result is a beggar-thy-neighbor dynamic in which both developed and developing countries are attempting to pull investment into their regional blocs, with multinational investors caught in the middle. The latest battlegrounds stretch from the Mercosur countries in Latin America to those Eastern European countries that are completing accession agreements with the European Union, in which competing origin regimes prevent international companies from sourcing from the least-cost sites for the assembly of their final products (Yeats 1997).

Escalating Locational Incentives

While trade- and financial-balancing export performance requirements have been banned in the TRIMs agreement (and all kinds of export performance requirements have been banned in NAFTA), the use of locational incentive packages, which have the same impact in attracting and holding world-scale production facilities, has escalated.

There are learned disputes about whether the "lagging regions" of Europe, the provinces of Canada, or individual US states lead in this incentive competition (Thomas 1999). In 1986 concern that the escalation of investment incentives carried "trade- and competition-distorting side-effects" led the OECD to collect statistics on the provision of grants, subsidies, tax breaks, and other assistance to lure new investment or induce existing investment to remain in place.

In the first self-study, Ireland reported in 1994 that the country's special incentive packages had attracted more than 1,000 foreign firms to the country, employing nearly 100,000 workers and contributing more than half of the nation's industrial output and three-quarters of its manufactured exports (OECD 1994). These special incentive packages included unrestricted grants up to 60 percent of fixed assets, training assistance up to 100 percent of all training costs, free building sites and rent subsidies in industrial parks, with tax rates one-third of the OECD average, and "special incentives for very large projects." This approach to investment promotion has come to be known as the "Irish model."

Reports from other EU members on the parts of their countries that did not qualify as "lagging regions" showed less generous, although still substantial, investment incentive packages throughout Europe. Overall there are indications that German grants for investment in the former East Germany may have "far exceeded levels previously set by EU states" (*Financial Times*, 8 October 1996).

The United States uses tax expenditures, in particular at the state and municipal levels, more than grants and subsidies. While more difficult to calculate precisely, the OECD nonetheless has reported that incentive packages in the range of $50 million to $70 million per project have become "typical." While US locational arrangements are typically not at all transparent, detailed surveys in the automotive sector show state and local subsidies have grown from $27,000 per job in 1985, to $65,000 per job in 1992, to $200,000 per job in 1996.

While the competition among developed countries and between developed and developing countries for some kinds of projects is limited, the evidence from case studies and from econometric measurements portrays a struggle of increasing intensity among alternative sites, especially within given regions.

Microstudies from individual business cases suggest that strategists in international companies insist that alternative sites be selected on the basis of equivalent prospects for "long-term viability." Site negotiators are then sent to generate rivalry among the finalists, producing incentive packages that are used as "tiebreakers," in the words of General Motors, to determine the placement of individual plants (Harvard Business School 1993).

Econometric analysis of aggregate data shows that changes in the treatment afforded international investors that had the equivalent of raising or lowering their relative tax burden by 1 percent led to a corresponding change in the location of investment of 1 percent in the early 1980s, 3 percent in the mid-1990s, and 5 percent in 1997 (Hines 1996; Grubert and Mutti 1996; Hufbauer 1997; Wei 1997; Altschuler, Grubert, and Newlon 1998). The latter study measured the relationship between changes in the treatment of investors or direct investment flows from 14 home countries to 34 host countries. These measurements suggest that during the past two decades there has been a marked increase in international firms' responsiveness to incentives.

Overall, the evidence indicates that the contours of international economic geography are being shaped in the midst of a subsidy contest in which developed countries are providing locational packages worth tens of thousands of dollars per job created, sometimes more, with increasing impact on the outcome.

Developing countries are not absent from this bidding war, but they seldom have the resources to match the investment promotion efforts of the OECD members (Shah 1995). To make up the difference, they have been turning to the credits they can mobilize from multilateral lending agencies and to trade rents they can create from offering market protection to the target investors.

Both developed and developing countries have been moving along a path, in consequence, that leaves them all losers, by common acknowledgment. The only way out of entrapment in this prisoners' dilemma is to agree to a common self-binding effort to bring about a cease-fire and to roll back the use of investment incentives.

Discriminatory Antidumping Regulations

Finally, over the same period antidumping regulations have been transformed from a legitimate shield against unfair practices to a distortionary intervention in the marketplace with both protectionist and investment-diverting consequences.

The rationale for antidumping measures has traditionally been based on preventing international price discrimination. Selling in foreign markets at a price lower than in the domestic economy is unfair because it is indicative of trade barriers in the home market; otherwise arbitrage and the reimportation of domestic goods would eliminate the price differential. Trade barriers in the home market, in turn, generate rents that can be used to reinforce the predatory impact of lower external prices, forcing producers in overseas markets out of business and leaving the dumping firm in a monopoly position.

In the past decade and a half, however, the United States and the European Union have added selling below "the fair cost of production" to price discrimination as the legal test for dumping and have established a definition of "fairness" as average total cost plus a markup for overhead and profit.

Since competitive conditions drive all firms to price their output near marginal cost, the specification of average cost to characterize "fairness" is highly inefficient. More important, however, it constitutes a legal discrimination against foreign-based producers: firms producing within the domestic market are free to respond to competitive conditions by selling at marginal cost, but firms producing outside cannot match this behavior without finding themselves guilty of dumping. Under the average-cost standard, two firms (one operating inside the market and the second operating outside the market) can engage in precisely the same actions, pricing their output at precisely the same level, with opposite results: the internal firm proceeding freely, the external firm penalized for dumping.

Although the cases brought against imports—increasingly produced by international companies in the developing countries and economies in transition—are filled with rhetoric about foreign firms' "unfair behavior," an OECD review of antidumping cases in the European Union, the United States, Australia, and Canada showed that 90 percent of the import sales found to be "unfair" were completely legal according to domestic competition standards—that is, they would qualify as perfectly "fair" if an internal firm made the same sale (Finger 1997).

Antidumping regulations lead to investment diversion in two ways: First, they inhibit international firms from investing in otherwise viable export operations outside the market protected by the average-cost standard. Second, they encourage international firms to position their operations under the cover of domestic competition law, producing where they want to sell their output rather than exporting from lower-cost external sites.

In the period 1988-96, the developed countries initiated 1,138 antidumping investigations, winning 70 to 80 percent of the subsequent cases. The biggest losers have been the petrochemical producers and electronics exporters in the developing countries. Exports from the economies in transition have been particularly vulnerable, with the European Community prevailing more than 75 percent of the time against East European exporters and the United States achieving a perfect score of victory in every case brought against the states of the former Soviet Union.

When the United States and the European Union joined forces to get the average-cost-plus-markup test adopted in the Uruguay Round and consequently enshrined as the international standard in the WTO, this seemed like a way to strengthen the position of US and EU firms in international markets. Instead, however, there has been an explosion of cases against American and European firms, with the fastest growth in cases coming from the developing countries. US companies are now the number two recipient of antidumping actions, second only to China.

Only fundamental antidumping reform, returning to international price discrimination as the sole test for unfair behavior, can restore a sound economic basis to the multinational corporate calculus of where to invest and produce.

Taken together, these three measures—high domestic-content rules of origin, escalating locational incentives, and discriminatory antidumping regulations—are not simply being used as mechanisms of protection but more broadly as tools to reshape the geography of international economic activity in patterns that do not reflect comparative advantage. In the process, trade wars are being replaced to a considerable extent by investment wars, with adverse consequences for developed and developing countries alike.

Investment Issues in the Next Round

The review of the TRIMs agreement is thus likely to open the door to consideration of broader trade-related investment-diverting and investment-distorting measures that affect the developed countries even more than they do the developing countries. Neither side should resist broadening the agenda. Both sides have an interest in reaching out to reformers in the other camp to explore ways in which to lower the barriers and diversions of investment throughout the global economy. The real question is, how might initiatives that reflect the self-interests of both developing and developed countries be combined in the TRIMs review to produce an outcome in which all benefit?

Domestic-Content Requirements

As indicated earlier, the TRIMs agreement targeted domestic-content requirements for elimination. Developed countries had two years to accomplish this. Developing countries have a five-year phaseout period. Least-developed countries have a seven-year phaseout period.

On the basis of the evidence introduced above, the assessment of what is most advantageous for the growth and welfare of the developing countries is quite straightforward. The imposition of domestic-content requirements on foreign direct investors misallocates local resources, generates high-cost local production, penalizes the more competitive users, and lays a burden on consumers. Foreign investors subjected to domestic-content requirements employ less advanced technology, less quality control, and introduce fewer state-of-the-art management practices than they do when they are not burdened with domestic-content requirements, and they upgrade their inputs less frequently. Backward linkages into the local economy do not exhibit those externalities or spillovers that are most beneficial for local business development. Meeting the TRIMs requirement for the elimination of domestic-content requirements is in the developing countries' self-interest. How rapidly should the developing countries want to comply?

As mentioned earlier, Article 5.3 of the TRIMs agreement allows developing countries to request an extension of the phaseout period for the use of domestic-content measures. One possible rationale for extending the phaseout could derive from infant industry considerations—namely, that the firms in countries employing these measures could use the extra time to gain experience and knowledge that would make them more competitive. But the evidence shows that rather than dynamic learning and the accumulation of competitive experience, local subsidiaries with domestic-content restrictions find themselves saddled with relatively older technology and less-advanced business practices, in plants that often do not capture full economies of scale. This is a recipe for prolonged infancy without much prospect of catching up to the performance of more energetic leaders in the industry.

A second possible rationale for extending the phaseout period might be based on the need for time to adjust. The abrupt termination of domestic-content protection for many foreign investor operations will invariably lead to economic dislocation for the firms and workers involved. In other Uruguay Round agreements where a substantial amount of economic dislocation was anticipated, such as the Multi-Fiber Agreement, a phaseout period of 10 years was awarded, suggesting that domestic-content requirements receive a second five-year period for elimination.

However, this justification is weakened by the fact that such lengthy interim periods have seldom been used for adjustment in the past. Quite the contrary, the extension of domestic-content requirements has led workers and managers to fight to maintain their uncompetitive positions indefinitely rather than easing them out of the industry. Signals become mixed. In developing and least-developed countries, the longer the domestic-content requirements are maintained, the more effectively the industry participants and their political supporters use what clout they can mobilize to prevent adjustment from beginning. There is no evidence that prolonging the phaseout would aid the transition or ease the burden of adjustment when it finally comes.

The interests of the developing countries (including the least-developed countries) would be best served therefore by a requirement that petitions for extension under Article 5.3 be accompanied by an explicit schedule for drawing down the domestic-content requirements and for reducing associated protection over the period of the extension. This would send the appropriate signals to firms and workers and ensure that the purpose of the extension is achieved.

With regard to complementing TRIMs commitments on domestic content with other trade and competition policy measures, TRIMs Article 9 raises questions of consistency and fairness: what if TRIMs rules regarding domestic-content requirements are vigorously prosecuted while high domestic-content rules of origin in preferential trade agreements are left alone?

The use of high domestic-content rules of origin finds technical defense under Article XXIV of the General Agreement on Tariffs and Trade (GATT), which allows preferential trade agreements as long as those agreements do not raise external barriers against outsiders. But this defense has come under increasingly critical scrutiny. The economic equivalence of a TRIMs requirement and of a rule-of-origin requirement is clear when, in each case, investors that agree to produce a given amount of content receive access to a given market, and those that do not, do not. Japan and the EU companies have complained, for example, that the US-Canada auto pact violates the TRIMs agreement by establishing a ratio of value added in

Canada to sales that companies must meet to avoid tariffs on finished autos and auto parts (*AmericasTrade* 5, no. 18, 3 September 1998, and vol. 6, no. 21, 21 October 1999). US trade negotiators are torn between wanting to object to Mercosur's 60 percent local-content requirement for autos under the TRIMs agreement, for example, and not wanting to undermine NAFTA's own high domestic-content requirement for many products under the umbrella of Article XXIV.

The TRIMs review offers the opportunity to enlarge the scope of the attack on domestic-content requirements by bringing high domestic-content rules of origin under multilateral discipline. This can be accomplished by transforming the WTO's work program on harmonization of nonpreferential rules of origin into an exercise on harmonization (and reduction) of preferential rules of origin.

This outcome would allow both developed and developing countries to broaden and deepen their regional trading agreements without, in the process, engaging in beggar-thy-neighbor struggles to shift production arbitrarily from one bloc to another, as is now the case. The multinational corporate community would then be able to rationalize their regional and global sourcing strategies on the basis of productivity, quality, and cost considerations in place of the political dictates that now disrupt their operations.

Export Performance Requirements

Export performance requirements that take the form of trade-balancing or foreign exchange-balancing mandates are also subject to elimination under the TRIMs agreement. This issue raises complex strategic considerations for the developing countries. Not only might elimination of these requirements cause some economic dislocation for foreign investor export operations that were not economically viable, but their abolition might deprive the developing countries of a tool for generating foreign investor export operations that are quite viable on their own.

As shown earlier, developing countries have sometimes used these requirements to trigger multinational investors to reorient their global and regional sourcing strategies (although it has not always worked). At the same time, the use of export performance requirements has helped fuel the bidding war for large investment facilities among the developing countries and between themselves and developed countries.

An extension of the period for eliminating trade- and financial-balancing measures for adjustment purposes (under Article 5.3) might therefore be profitably used to pursue a cease-fire in this bidding war more generally. It is not logical to focus exclusively on subsidy competitions for export-oriented plants and to ignore the award of locational incentives (including subsidies and tax breaks from national and subnational authorities), which perform the same function for all kinds of world-scale production facilities.

The "Irish model" of using grants and fiscal incentives to entice foreign investors to use the country as an export platform for Europe, for example, has been similar in impact to the export TRIMs that launched Mexico and Brazil into international auto parts markets (although simpler in design). More generally, it is disingenuous to claim that locational incentives offered by Alabama or South Carolina have no effect on trade patterns while the export performance requirements of the developing world do.

Once again, in the review of the TRIMs agreement under Article 9, the efforts to restrain investment-shifting measures used predominantly by developing countries are likely to lead once again to consideration of comparable measures serving the same purpose that are used predominantly by developed countries. The logical outcome would be to bring not just export performance requirements but all locational incentives under multilateral discipline. This would provide relief to domestic authorities, North and South, from a lose-lose competition—the race to the bottom in giving away subsidies and giving up fiscal revenues that currently plagues countries trying to attract and hold corporate activities within their borders.

A Greater Vision: Toward a Broad Agreement on Investment-Related Issues

Given the contentious battle over the MAI, it may be difficult to imagine how renewed efforts to negotiate a broad agreement on investment-related issues could be successful. But the analysis here suggests that there are more elements in place for a mutually positive outcome than is commonly understood.

The starting point for consideration is the use of joint-venture and technology-sharing mandates by the developing countries. These are not included in the illustrative list of the TRIMs agreement. But the newly documented drawbacks that joint venture and technology-sharing requirements impose on host countries, in comparison to countries that do not impose such requirements, opens a new vista for developed- and developing-country negotiations.

The promises of foreign firms to choose local partners or to share technology have been the predominant elements (along with pledges to create local content or to export) in host-country determinations of whether to award right of establishment in certain cases or to deny national treatment in others. But as more countries come to see the detrimental impact of joint venture and technology-sharing requirements, along with domestic-content and (possibly) export requirements, the rationale for awarding national treatment to some foreign firms and denying right of establishment to others will fade.

Many developing countries are beginning to abandon the use of joint venture and technology-sharing mandates unilaterally, building technology parks and export zones where international companies are free to structure their operations as best suits the competitive needs of their particular industries. At the same time, as part of the General Agreement on Trade in Services (GATS) several developing countries are agreeing to allow service providers a legal presence within their countries (right of establishment) and granting them nondiscriminatory treatment (national treatment), at least for those sectors listed in the country's schedule of commitments.

Rather than reluctantly acceding to this trend, it would be better to combine disciplines on the entire range of investment-diverting and investment-distorting measures in a broad agreement that serves developing-country interests much more dramatically than the previous versions of a general agreement on investment that the developed countries have introduced.

The objective of such an agreement would be to let comparative advantage be the predominant determinant of how FDI is deployed. And as developing countries consider putting national treatment and right of establishment on the negotiating table in order to accomplish this, the world community ought to complete the list of proscribed investment-shifting and investment-distorting measures. This would mean adding not only disciplines on high domestic-content rules of origin and locational incentives to the negotiations, but antidumping reform as well.

Antidumping reform fits under many categories in the agenda for WTO negotiations. To accomplish the goal of eliminating distortion in investment behavior, antidumping reform would have to include limiting what constitutes unfair practice to international price discrimination, ending the protectionist and discriminatory use of average cost plus markup in determining guilt. This reform would remove a major barrier to developing countries' ability to penetrate international markets via indigenous as well as multinational investment. It would remove the multinational corporate community as the target of punitive action and protect it from multiple new angles of attack for doing no more than engaging in normal business pricing strategies. And it would provide a dramatic step forward as developed countries attempt to harmonize their trade and competitiveness policies.

Achieving the changes and reforms in the most objectionable investment-related policies of all parties, North and South alike, will doubtless be a long, hard, uphill battle, with the outcome highly dependent upon the ability of visionaries in developed and developing countries to galvanize the international business community on the side of multilateral reform. But at least it is possible to see more clearly now what kinds of trade-offs are essential, within the WTO framework, and what kind of outcome would be most beneficial to all parties.

References

Aitken, Brian, Gordon H. Hanson, and Ann Harrison. 1997. Spillovers, Foreign Investment, and Export Behavior. *Journal of International Economics* 43, no. 1-2 (August): 103-32.

Altschuler, Rosanne, Harry Grubert, and T. Scott Newlon. 1998. *Has U.S. Investment Abroad Become More Sensitive to Tax Rates?* Working Paper 6383. Cambridge, MA: National Bureau of Economic Research.

Beamish, Paul W., and Andres Delios. 1997. Incidence and Propensity of Alliance Formation by U.S., Japanese, and European MNEs. In P. W. Beamish and J. P. Killing, eds., *Cooperative Strategies: Asian-Pacific Perspectives*. San Francisco: New Lexington Press.

Borrus, Michael. 1994. Left for Dead: Asian Production Networks and the Revival of U.S. Electronics. In Eileen M. Doherty, ed., *Japanese Investment in Asia: International Production Strategies in a Rapidly Changing World*. San Francisco: The Asia Foundation and Berkeley Roundtable on International Economics.

Caves, Richard E. 1999. Spillovers from Multinationals in Developing Countries: The Mechanisms at Work. Draft, Department of Economics, Harvard University.

Ernst, Dieter. 1999. Convergence and Diversity: The Asian Production Networks of Japanese Electronics Firms. In Michael Borrus, Dieter Ernst, and Stephan Haggard, eds., *Rivalry or Riches: International Production Networks in Asia*. Cornell, NY: Cornell University Press.

Finger, J. Michael. 1997. GATT Experience with Safeguards: Making Economic and Political Sense of the Possibilities That GATT Allows to Restrict Imports. Washington: World Bank. Photocopy.

Grubert, Harry, and John Mutti. 1996. Do Taxes Influence Where U.S. Corporations Invest? Paper prepared for the Conference on Trans-Atlantic Public Economics Seminar, Amsterdam, Netherlands, 29-31 May 1996. Photocopy.

Harvard Business School. 1990. *Mexico and the Microcomputers*. Case 9-390-093. Cambridge, MA: Harvard Business School.

Harvard Business School. 1993. *Adam Opel AG*. Case 9-392-100, 101, 127. Cambridge, MA: Harvard Business School.

Hines, James R. 1996. *Tax Policy and the Activities of Multinational Corporations*. Working Paper 5589. Cambridge, MA: National Bureau of Economic Research.

Hufbauer, Gary. 1997. Directions for International Tax Reform. In J. M. Poterba, ed., *Borderline Case: International Tax Policy, Corporate Research and Development, and Investment*. Washington: National Academy Press for the National Research Council.

Jensen-Moran, Jeri. 1995. Trade Battles as Investment Wars: The Coming Rules of Origin Debate. *Washington Quarterly* 19, no. 1: 239-53.

Jensen-Moran, Jeri. 1996. Choice at the Crossroads: Regionalism and Rules of Origin. *Law and Policy in International Business* 27, no. 4: 981-89.

Kokko, Ari, and Magnus Blomstrom. 1995. Policies to Encourage Inflows of Technology through Foreign Multinationals. *World Development* 23, no. 3: 459-68.

Lim, Linda Y. C., and Pang Eng Fong. 1982. Vertical Linkages and Multinational Enterprises in Developing Countries. *World Development* 10, no. 7: 585-95.

Mansfield, E., and A. Romeo. 1980. Technology Transfer to Overseas Subsidiaries by US-based Firms. *Quarterly Journal of Economics* 95, no. 4: 737-50.

Moran, Theodore H. 1998. *Foreign Direct Investment and Development*. Washington: Institute for International Economics.

Organization for Economic Cooperation and Development (OECD). 1994. *OECD Reviews of Foreign Direct Investment: Ireland.* Paris.

Peres Nuñez, Wilson. 1990. *Foreign Direct Investment and Industrial Development in Mexico.* Paris: Organization for Economic Cooperation and Development.

Ramachandran, Vijaya. 1993. Technology Transfer, Firm Ownership, and Investment in Human Capital. *Review of Economics and Statistics* 75 (November): 664-70.

Rasiah, Rajah. 1994. Flexible Production Systems and Local Machine-Tool Subcontracting: Electronics Components Transnationals in Malaysia. *Cambridge Journal of Economics* 18, no. 3 (June): 279-98.

Rasiah, Rajah. 1995. *Foreign Capital and Industrialization in Malaysia.* New York: St. Martin's Press.

Shah, Anwar, ed. 1995. *Fiscal Incentives for Investment and Innovation.* New York: Oxford University Press for the World Bank.

Skud, Timothy. 1996. Customs Regimes as Barriers to Trade. *Law and Policy in International Business* 27, no. 4: 969-79.

Thomas, Kenneth P. 1999. *Competing for Capital: European and North American Responses.* Washington: Georgetown University Press.

Wei, Shang-Jin. 1997. How Taxing Is Corruption on International Behavior? Cambridge, MA: Kennedy School of Government, Harvard University. Photocopy.

Yeats, Alexander. 1997. *Does Mercosur's Trade Performance Raise Concerns about the Effects of Regional Trade Arrangements?* Policy Research Working Paper 1729. Washington: World Bank, International Economics Department, International Trade Division.

15

Environment and the Trading System: Picking up the Post-Seattle Pieces

DANIEL C. ESTY

Seattle represents a watershed for the international trading system. The high-profile protests against globalization in general and the work of the World Trade Organization (WTO) in particular mark the end of the days in which trade negotiations can be conducted by a close-knit group of trade cognoscenti out of sight of the rest of the world. Trade policymaking is now a very high-profile business (Esty 2000). This fact transforms how future trade negotiations can and will be conducted. It also means that the substantive interaction between trade rules and procedures and other policy realms will have to be refined. Nowhere is this more true than with regard to the linkage between trade and the environment.

The public increasingly understands the central role that the WTO plays as part of the emerging structure of global governance (Schott 1996; Jackson 1996, 1997). The misleading suggestion advanced by some trade experts that the WTO is nothing more than an intergovernmental body that provides a forum for trade negotiations can no longer be sustained (Dunoff 1997). The rules and procedures of the trading system are now understood to be critical elements of the world community's efforts to manage economic interdependence.

Traditional trade community logic has argued that more liberalization can be accomplished if the public does not know what is going on than would be achieved through open debate in the light of day. This argument recognizes the "public choice" difficulties inherent in trade liberalization: the benefits are diffused across a great number of people who cannot

Daniel C. Esty is associate dean of the Yale School of Forestry and Environmental Studies; he also teaches at Yale Law School. He is former deputy chief of staff and deputy assistant administrator for policy at the US Environmental Protection Agency, where he served as EPA's chief NAFTA negotiator. He co-chairs the US Trade Representative's Trade and Environment Public Advisory Committee.

easily be mobilized for political support of open markets while there are a few "losers" who will fight hard to prevent increased competition from imports. In an open political process, the received wisdom has it, special interests manipulate outcomes in a welfare-reducing manner. But this view fails to take seriously the corrosive effects of the perception that trade policymaking is undemocratic and systematically biased toward the needs of multinational corporations. Whether the proposition favoring a cover-of-darkness approach to trade liberalization was ever correct is now moot. The WTO will never again be able to operate beneath the public's radar. Moreover, the demands at Seattle for a new WTO culture of openness came not just from environmentalists and civil society more broadly but also from officials from many developing countries who felt marginalized by the complex and arcane negotiating process.

To overcome the Seattle-fueled hostility toward globalization and to restore market-opening momentum will require a sweeping and convincing WTO commitment to transparency. In the months ahead, the WTO will have to redouble its efforts to hear and take seriously views from the South and simultaneously to institutionalize its outreach to civil society and to the many nongovernmental organizations (NGOs) that have been excluded from past trade policymaking.

Shifting to a "sunshine" strategy will not be easy. Almost all of the WTO officials and the national representatives who participate in WTO activities in Geneva are steeped in the traditional "diplomatic" approach to trade policymaking, involving complex horse trading in which confidentiality is essential and indirection is prized (Jackson 1992; Esty 1994b). Ironically, many of the delegations from the developing world that were most outraged about their perceived exclusion from the *real* negotiations in the restricted-access "green rooms" in Seattle remain skeptical about greater NGO participation in global-scale trade policymaking.

Both the United States and the European Union recognize the necessity and inevitability of a more transparent trading system, and each advanced ideas in Seattle to open up the WTO in general and the dispute settlement process in particular. As the trading system is transformed from a system based on tit-for-tat tariff reductions to one that is rules-based, greater transparency is increasingly important. Simply put, the style of operation that served the trade community in the past will not serve it well in the future. The prevailing ethos of the WTO must shift from closed-door negotiating mode to process-conscious administrative law.

Why Link Trade and Environment Policies?

Though some continue to question the need to address environmental concerns in the context of trade liberalization, sophisticated political leaders and trade officials increasingly recognize that, because of the centrality of the trade regime in a highly interdependent world, the WTO cannot avoid rubbing up against other policy realms, such as the environment (e.g., Summers 2000; Clinton 2000; Blair 2000). Indeed, the trade-environment link is not really a choice but a matter of fact. Beyond descriptive reality, the trade-environment link should be recognized as having normative value as well.

Trade policy, and particularly trade liberalization, inescapably affect the natural environment. And where environmental resources are mispriced, trade may magnify the harms. The WTO itself acknowledges this reality (Nordstrom and Vaughan 1999). Simultaneously, environmental policy affects trade. The presence of regulatory requirements—health standards, emissions limits, disposal requirements, labeling rules, and so on—channels (and may confine) trade flows, creating a potential for trade-environment clashes. As economic interdependence grows, the number of points of intersection expands and concomitantly so does the potential for conflict (Dua and Esty 1997). The range of recent tensions—including the Venezuelan challenge to the reformulated gasoline regulations promulgated under the 1990 US Clean Air Act, the ongoing US-EU beef hormone dispute, and the WTO case arising from Thai shrimping practices that killed endangered sea turtles—supports this proposition.

Fundamentally, trade and environmental policy interactions are inevitable in a world of economic integration (Esty 1999; Charnovitz 1998). International commerce needs to be governed by rules and procedures that bound behavior; some of these requirements will relate to environmental matters. Setting boundaries creates the potential for differences of opinion and therefore dispute. As we push for further trade liberalization, the number of realms where environmental questions may be raised will grow. The question of how biotechnology will be regulated and to what degree genetically modified organisms will be permitted in food represents one high-profile example of the difficulties that lie ahead. Serious attempts to control greenhouse gases, which may radically alter the prices of fossil fuels and therefore affect the value of hundreds of billions of dollars in industrial assets and existing energy investments, could have significant competitiveness effects and create further trade-environment tensions. Similarly, efforts to take more seriously the need to protect biodiversity or to expand the linkage between the trade regime and the Convention on International Trade and Endangered Species (CITES) might also lead to future conflict.

Beyond these economic interactions, trade and environmental policy become entangled as a function of ecological realities. A number of environmental challenges are global in scale. From the depleted fisheries in many of the world's oceans, to the need to protect the ozone layer, to the buildup of greenhouse gas emissions that may produce climate change, a number of problems cannot be dealt with on a national basis because of their scale. Indeed, any country that sets out unilaterally to address a transboundary problem will find that its own efforts cannot resolve the issue. International cooperation is essential. From the perspective of sound economics, there must be some mechanism in place to discipline "free riders," those who decline to bear a fair share of the burden of addressing global challenges. Whether countries are "doing their share" has to be understood as a question that has important economic consequences and implications—and therefore a tight link to trade policy.

The failure to address environmental harms that spill across national boundaries represents an uninternalized externality that, if left unaddressed, leads to market failure (Baumol and Oates 1988). Pollution spillovers and mismanagement of shared natural resources make a degree of trade-environment linkage not just inescapable but advisable (Hudec 1996). The efficiency and integrity of the international economic system depends on the presence of procedures to address transboundary environmental externalities. While leadership in establishing the policies and mechanisms to ensure that these challenges are taken seriously must come from environmental authorities, the trading system must support, and not undermine, these efforts (Esty 1994a). Where environmental policies have been agreed upon at the international level, the trading system should reinforce the obligations that have been spelled out. Trade measures should not be the only tool available for enforcement of multilateral environmental agreements (Jacobson and Brown Weiss 1997). But lacking other effective mechanisms and recognizing the inexorable link between global-scale environmental harms and the efficiency as well as integrity of the international economic system, the WTO should provide a degree of discipline on those who might "free ride" on the efforts of others or otherwise shirk their responsibilities.

A third reason to take the trade-environment linkage seriously derives from the political economy of trade policymaking. In the United States, in particular, successful efforts at trade liberalization in recent years have always been accompanied by express strategies to address related environmental questions. Most observers do not believe the North American Free Trade Agreement (NAFTA) would have cleared the US Congress but for the environmental provisions written into the agreement and the substantial environmental side agreement that was negotiated in parallel. Many Congress watchers attribute the failure of the Clinton administration's 1997-98 fast-track proposal to the lack of a comparable environmental commitment.

More broadly, one of the key lessons from the WTO fiasco in Seattle is that deeper economic integration depends on a sense of political community—and a belief that there are shared values that justify a commitment to open markets (Lawrence et al., 1996; Dua and Esty 1997). If trade policymakers fail to appreciate the need to address this political dimension of liberalization, their efforts to promote a new round of multilateral negotiations will falter.

Perhaps more important, the long-term legitimacy and durability of the international trading system will be enhanced to the extent that international economic policy evolves in ways that intersect constructively with other policymaking realms such as the environment (Esty 1998). WTO decisions will not win the degree of popular acceptance that they must have to keep the trade system functioning smoothly unless the organization develops procedures to enhance the authoritativeness, procedural and substantive fairness, and representativeness of its policy choices and directions. At a very basic level, the world community needs a deeper and richer WTO "politics." To facilitate more vigorous debate, the WTO must develop more open procedures and a broader outreach to civil society as well as *all* member governments.

To a significant degree, of course, the problems of international environmental policy cannot be laid at the doorstep of the trade community. The deeply flawed global environmental regime must bear most of the responsibility. In this regard, a number of opinion leaders have recently called for the creation of a global environmental organization, or GEO (Ruggiero 1999; Chirac 1999; *The Economist*, "Why Greens Should Love Trade: The Environment Does Need to Be Protected but Not from Trade," 9 October 1999, 18). A more robust global environmental governance structure, constructed out of some of the pieces of the existing system, including the United Nations Environment Program (UNEP), might facilitate a more systematic international response to challenges of pollution control and natural resources management (Esty 1994b). A GEO might also provide support for better international environmental policymaking as well as facilitate information exchanges on cutting-edge policy approaches and technologies. Most important, a functioning global environmental regime would take pressure off the WTO, sparing it from the burden of acting as an adjudicator of environmental disputes that go beyond the realm of its well-established trade expertise (Dunoff 1997).

Trade and environmental policies cannot be kept on separate tracks. The points of intersection are too frequent and too significant to prevent these policy realms from becoming intertwined. Thus the question is not, do we want trade and environmental policy linkage? It must be, how will we integrate trade and environmental policymaking in ways that both promote open markets and environmental protection?

The policy focus must be on how to fold environmental sensitivity into the trading system. Integration of environmental considerations in the trade domain could be accomplished through responses to "trade and environment" crises and through dispute resolution cases. But such a haphazard approach to policymaking is unlikely to yield good long-term results. A much better alternative would be to expressly, deliberately, and thoughtfully negotiate how trade and environmental policies will intersect. The trade-environment agenda cannot be an environmentalist's wish list but rather should be a carefully defined, theoretically grounded, and narrow set of procedural and substantive advances that promotes the peaceful coexistence of these two important policy realms. Building an environmental dimension into the international trading system will require both procedural WTO reforms and substantive changes in the WTO rules.

Procedural Advances

The WTO's day-to-day procedures could be opened up to ensure greater environmental sensitivity. With regard to the WTO's "executive" operations, it would make sense to invite NGO (and media) observers to watch the General Council meetings, during which the 130 member states work through basic policies and administrative matters. Secrets cannot be kept in a meeting of this size, so the presence of NGOs will not chill candor nor otherwise change the tenor of these sessions. Opening these meetings would go a good distance toward demystifying the WTO and providing a window on what issues are discussed, what points of view are raised, what assumptions drive decision making, and what arguments are deemed persuasive. It should also be possible to provide NGOs with a limited period in which they would be allowed to ask questions or offer comments on the issues under debate.

A number of ideas have been advanced for building greater transparency into the WTO's quasi-judicial dispute settlement procedures to ensure that environmental issues are raised and addressed carefully and systematically. First, dispute panels should conduct their hearings in public. The taking of evidence in open court is a fundamental element of sound judicial process in almost every country in the world. The existence of "secret tribunals" links the WTO in the minds of too many to dictatorships and other undemocratic governance systems. Likewise, as part of an effort to ensure that the public is aware of the arguments that are driving dispute settlement outcomes, it would be useful to have all briefs or position statements made public. In addition, NGOs should be permitted to share with dispute panels their views on any issue in question. Such a procedure, akin to the *amicus curiae* briefs permitted in US courts, would provide WTO dispute settlement decision makers with access to the broadest range of relevant information. To complete the commitment to transparency, the WTO should release dispute panel decisions as soon as they are rendered.

It might also be advantageous to have a more clearly defined mechanism for incorporating by reference the judgments of other bodies, notably environmental entities, into the WTO dispute settlement process. For example, if a question were raised about a country's compliance with a multilateral environmental agreement, it would be very helpful to have the judgment of the parties to that agreement on whether a violation has occurred. Such procedures already exist with regard to WTO advice from the International Monetary Fund (IMF).

Future trade negotiations might also be conducted somewhat more openly, leading to significant credibility and legitimacy benefits for the WTO. Obviously, at a certain point, there are trade-offs that must be made in negotiations, and national negotiators will have to keep secret some issues, particularly those relating to their willingness to compromise on certain points. Nevertheless, many opportunities exist to inform the public about the issues under discussion. In this spirit of openness, it would make sense for the WTO to invest in an easily accessed interactive Web site and conduct regular briefings for NGOs about the progress of all ongoing negotiations.

Demystifying the international trade regime stands out as a critical job for the WTO in the weeks and months ahead. The organization's credibility and future viability are threatened by public perceptions of it as undemocratic and biased toward multinational corporations and other special interests.

To ensure that critical environmental questions are not overlooked during negotiations, environmental reviews should be undertaken at the outset. The US government and a number of other countries have already committed to such reviews. It would be useful if the WTO, perhaps with help from UNEP or other UN bodies with environmental expertise, were to provide support to developing countries that would be interested in pursuing this sort of analysis.

The WTO's Committee on Trade and Environment (CTE) might also be called upon to instill environmental sensitivity into negotiations. In particular, the CTE might be empowered to serve as an environmental advisory board to each negotiating group so that whenever the negotiations touched upon pollution or resources management, a degree of expertise would be available and a sense of coherence over how to address environmental questions might emerge across the whole effort.

Opportunities for Substantive Progress

In Seattle's wake, finding a way forward on the substance of the trade-environment conflict will be difficult. The environmental community feels empowered by the "success" of the street protests. But, in fact, the Seattle outcome represents a major tactical failure from the environmental point of view. Developing-country officials now seem more convinced than ever that the proposed "trade and environment" agenda constitutes nothing more than a new guise for protectionism. The sight of hundreds of environmental protesters walking arm in arm with unabashedly protection-ist union members provided all the corroboration that most developing-country officials needed to lump the environmentalists in with others who are irretrievably hostile to freer trade.

The easiest place to begin in creating a viable trade-environment agenda is with "win-win" opportunities such as the elimination of subsidies. Ending agricultural price supports, as well as energy, water, timber, and fisheries subsidies, would help remove an important trade distortion, stop environ-mental harms, reduce the fiscal pressure on budget-burdened govern-ments, and create opportunities for developing countries to export their products. Subsidy reduction stands out therefore as a "win-win-win-win" possibility.

A second potential "win-win" item might be "super-liberalization" of environmental goods and services. A bold goal, such as zero worldwide tariffs on all environmental goods and a real commitment to reducing nontariff barriers for environmental services, might galvanize broad-based support. Liberalizing trade in environmental goods and services would represent an important initiative to promote environmental technology transfer to the developing world. The recipient nations obtain access to better environmental results at lower costs. The exporting countries get expanded markets for their eco-goods and services. Everyone wins. Only countries that are profoundly confused could oppose super-liberaliza-tion in pursuit of environmental progress.

Refining the WTO's approach to circumstances where trade and envi-ronmental rules clash represents a particularly difficult set of issues, but one critical to reduced trade-environment tension. In this regard, the WTO might seek ways to ensure that the trading system reinforces, rather than undermines, existing multilateral environmental agreements. It would also be useful if the WTO were to bless the use of eco-labels, perhaps in exchange for a negotiated set of disciplines that would constrain the use of such labels. Codifying the results of recent GATT trade-environment jurisprudence, in particular the logic of the Appellate Body's decision in the recent shrimp-turtle case—endorsing the GATT-consistency of legiti-mate environmental policies—would also represent a significant advance on prior trading system thinking.

If the rules of international trade are clear—and if they are perceived to be supportive of important environmental values—then their legitimacy will be much greater. Over the long term, public support for the WTO depends on a perception that it is balanced and fair (Esty 1998). Efforts to address the issues identified above could greatly enhance the WTO's repu-tation. Competing trade and environmental principles could best be bal-anced through creation of an interpretive statement that focuses on how the "exceptions" spelled out in Article XX would be implemented, rather than through full-blown renegotiation of the environmental elements of the trading system.

Conclusion

The world trading system is undergoing a major transformation. It is evolving from a forum for negotiation where the dominant mode is horse trading into a rules-based system where disputes are settled in a peaceful fashion that facilitates trade, reflects broad public values, and provides predictability about what is acceptable in the realm of international commerce. Such a system is essential to the successful management of economic interdependence. A rules-based regime is also very much in the interest of the smaller countries, whose hope for getting a fair deal rises if there are broadly accepted disciplines and procedures that every nation, even the most powerful, is obliged to accept and follow.

Finding ways to address the environmental issues that inescapably arise in the context of deeper economic integration must be seen as an important trade policy priority, as a matter of WTO commitment to undergirding the trade regime with sound economic theory, and as a matter of political necessity. Building a trading system that is more sensitive to pollution control and natural resources management issues is mandated by the growing degree to which these realms intersect with trade and economic policy. Systematic and thoughtful efforts to make trade and environmental policies mutually reinforcing are also advisable to the extent that the presence of trade rules that internalize externalities will prove to be more economically efficient over time. Institutionalizing the links from the trade regime to environmental actors and other elements of civil society will also pay dividends. A culture of openness within the WTO is likely to generate policies that the public accepts and that therefore become more useful and durable.

References

Baumol, William J., and Wallace E. Oates. 1988. *The Theory of Environmental Policy*, 2d ed. Cambridge, UK: Cambridge University Press.

Bhagwati, Jagdish. 1996. Trade and Environment: Does Environmental Diversity Detract from the Case for Free Trade? In Jagdish Bhagwati and Robert Hudec, eds., *Fair Trade and Harmonization: Prerequisites for Free Trade?* Cambridge, MA: MIT Press.

Blair, Tony. 2000. Speech at the World Economic Forum Annual Meeting, Davos, Switzerland, 28 January.

Charnovitz, Steve. 1997. Two Centuries of Participation: NGOs and International Governance. *Michigan Journal of International Law* 18, no. 2 (Winter): 183.

Charnovitz, Steve. 1998. The World Trade Organization and the Environment. *Yearbook of International Environmental Law* 8:98.

Chirac, Jacques. 1999. Speech before the IUCN (World Conservation Union), Fontainebleau, France, 3 November.

Clinton, Bill. 2000. Speech at the World Economic Forum Annual Meeting, Davos, Switzerland, 29 January.

Dua, André, and Daniel C. Esty. 1997. *Sustaining the Asia Pacific Miracle: Environmental Protection and Economic Integration.* Washington: Institute for International Economics.

Dunoff, Jeffrey L. 1997. Trade and Recent Developments in Trade Policy and Scholarship—And Their Surprising Political Implications. *Northwestern Journal of International Law and Business* 17, no. 2/3: 759.

Esty, Daniel C. 1994a. *Greening the GATT: Trade, Environment, and the Future.* Washington: Institute for International Economics.

Esty, Daniel C. 1994b. The Case for a Global Environmental Organization. In Peter B. Kenen, ed., *Managing the World Economy: Fifty Years after Bretton Woods.* Washington: Institute for International Economics.

Esty, Daniel C. 1996. Greening World Trade. In Jeffrey Schott, ed., *The World Trading System: Challenges Ahead.* Washington: Institute for International Economics.

Esty, Daniel C. 1998. NGOs at the World Trade Organization: Cooperation, Competition, or Exclusion. *Journal of International Economic Law* 1, no. 1: 123.

Esty, Daniel C. 1999. Economic Integration and the Environment. In Norman J. Vig and Regina Axelrod, eds., *The Global Environment: Institutions, Law, and Policy.* Washington: CQ Press.

Esty, Daniel C. 2000. An Environmental Perspective on Seattle. *Journal of International Economic Law* 3, no. 1: 10.

Esty, Daniel C., and Damien Geradin. 1998. Environmental Protection and International Competitiveness: A Conceptual Framework. *Journal of World Trade* 32, no. 3: 5.

Hudec, Robert E. 1996. GATT Legal Restraints on the Use of Trade Measures against Foreign Environmental Practices. In Jagdish Bhagwati and Robert Hudec, eds., *Fair Trade and Harmonization: Prerequisites for Free Trade?* Cambridge, MA: MIT Press.

Jackson, John H. 1992. World Trade Rules and Environmental Policies: Congruence or Conflict? *Washington and Lee Law Review* 49 (Fall): 1227.

Jackson, John H. 1996. Reflections on Constitutional Changes to the Global Trading System. *Chicago-Kent Law Review* 72: 511.

Jackson, John H. 1997. *The World Trading System.* Cambridge, MA: MIT Press.

Jacobson, Harold K., and Edith Brown Weiss. 1997. *Engaging Countries: Strengthening Compliance with International Environmental Accords.* Cambridge, MA: MIT Press.

Lawrence, Robert, et al. 1996. *A Vision for the World Economy.* Washington: Brookings Institution.

Nordstrom, Hakan, and Scott Vaughan. 1999. *WTO Special Report 4: Trade and the Environment.* Geneva: World Trade Organization.

Ruggiero, Renato. 1999. Speech to the World Trade Organization Symposium on Trade and the Environment, 15 March, Geneva.

Schott, Jeffrey J. 1996. *Challenges Facing the World Trade Organization.* In Jeffrey J. Schott, ed., *The World Trading System: Challenges Ahead.* Washington: Institute for International Economics.

Summers, Lawrence. 2000. Speech to the Confederation of Indian Industry, 18 January, Bombay.

16

Electronic Commerce in the WTO

CATHERINE L. MANN and SARAH CLEELAND KNIGHT

"Electronic commerce" is a shorthand term that embraces a complex amalgam of technologies, infrastructures, processes, and products. It brings together whole industries and narrow applications, producers and users, information exchange and economic activity into a global marketplace called the Internet. There is no universal definition of electronic commerce because the Internet marketplace and its participants are so numerous and their intricate relationships are evolving so rapidly.[1] Nonetheless, one of the best ways of understanding electronic commerce is to consider the elements of its infrastructure, its impact on the traditional marketplace, and the continuum of ways in which electronic commerce is manifested. This approach demonstrates clearly why electronic commerce should be addressed in the World Trade Organization (WTO).

Electronic commerce as it has evolved thus far requires three types of infrastructure:

■ *Technological infrastructure to create an Internet marketplace.* Electronic commerce relies on a variety of technologies, which are developing at breakneck speed (e.g., interconnectivity among telecommunications, cable, satellite, or other Internet "backbone" components; Internet service providers (ISPs) to connect market participants to that backbone; and end-user devices such as personal computers, televisions, or mobile telephones).

Catherine L. Mann is senior fellow at the Institute for International Economics and Sarah Cleeland Knight was a research assistant at the Institute. Our thanks are due to Sue Eckert, who contributed importantly to earlier drafts.

1. For more elaborate discussion of definitions, see www.oecd.org/dsti/sti/it/ec/act/sacher.htm and OECD (1999, box 1.1).

- *Process infrastructure to connect the Internet marketplace to the traditional marketplace.* This infrastructure makes payment over the Internet possible (through credit, debit, or Smart cards, or through on-line currencies like Flooz). It also makes possible the distribution and delivery (whether on-line or physical) of products purchased over the Internet to the consumer.

- *"Infrastructure" of governing protocols, laws, and regulations.* This infrastructure affects the conduct of businesses engaging in and affected by electronic commerce, as well as the relationships among businesses, consumers, and government. Examples include technical communications standards; the legality of digital signatures and certification; encryption and interconnectivity standards; and disclosure, privacy, and content regulations.

Together, these infrastructures enable electronic commerce to innovate the traditional marketplace in three ways:

- *Process innovations:* Electronic commerce simplifies, makes more efficient, reduces costs of, or otherwise alters the process by which an existing transaction takes place. Take, for example, Cisco Systems, which replaced its telephone and fax ordering process with an on-line ordering process, thereby saving more than one-half billion dollars and reducing error rates from 25 percent to 2 percent (OECD 1999, 60-61); or Boeing, which used computer-aided design and electronic communication to coordinate 238 design teams in the globalized production of the model 777 aircraft, a process never before attempted in this way, and which cut error rates by 50 percent and reduced both costs and time to market.[2]

- *Product innovations:* Electronic commerce creates or facilitates new industries and products not previously available. The MP3 music format and player, for example, which allows consumers to play music downloaded from a computer, constitutes a new medium for producing, marketing, and distributing music. Companies such as WebMD repackage existing health information in an easy-to-use, on-line format, offer opportunities to "chat" with people with similar health concerns, and provide real-time answers to health questions.

- *Market innovations:* Electronic commerce also creates new markets in time, space, and information that previously did not exist because transaction and coordination costs were prohibitively high. Take, for example, the on-line bank Wingspan, which offers 24-hour bill payment

---

2. See http://www.boeing.com/news/releases/1995/news.release.950614-a.html.

features; or PeopleLink, which advertises globally via the Internet for artisans in remote parts of Latin America and Africa; or reverse auctions through Priceline, which inform businesses of the exact prices consumers are willing to pay for their products.

In reviewing the infrastructures that make electronic commerce possible, as well as the impact electronic commerce has on the traditional marketplace, we can see why electronic commerce belongs in negotiations taking place in the WTO:

■ *Electronic commerce is global from the very start.* While traditional borders still matter in the world of international trade, electronic commerce diminishes their importance. No longer do customers need to be physically present to see or hear what they are buying. As a result, companies with a presence on the Internet instantly become international: Amazon was selling books to customers in over 40 countries during its first *month* of existence; the company now sells a variety of products to customers in over 160 countries. The WTO, as the world's multilateral trading body, is thus the appropriate venue to address issues concerning this new marketplace.

■ *Electronic commerce is free from trade barriers.* The electronic marketplace is currently free from explicit trade barriers. The absence of international tariffs or other barriers on electronic commerce encourages more people to try and to continue using the new Internet marketplace, creating a greater level of efficiency and economic benefit for its participants. The WTO can play a leading role in safeguarding the pristine state of electronic commerce.

■ *Electronic commerce is integral to existing WTO commitments.* While there are currently no explicit trade barriers on electronic commerce, the infrastructural elements that make electronic commerce possible are still burdened by a myriad of trade and investment barriers. The growth of electronic commerce depends on continued liberalization of these elements, many of which are already part of WTO commitments. Most important are computers and other information technology products (covered by the Information Technology Agreement completed in April 1997, or ITA I, and under consideration for ITA II), telecommunications (covered by the Basic Telecommunications Agreement), financial services (addressed in the Financial Services Agreement), distribution (relevant under the Agreement on Trade-Related Investment Measures [TRIMs]), and delivery services (under consideration for the General Agreement on Trade in Services [GATS] 2000), among others. Electronic commerce depends on the synergies among these service-sector industries for its maximum economic benefit.

Given the rapid and accelerating growth of electronic commerce, no time is better than the present for WTO members to address this new way of trading internationally. Respected sources such as Forrester Research expect worldwide electronic commerce revenues to surpass US$300 billion by 2002. Currently an overwhelming (close to 85 percent) share of electronic commerce is concentrated in the United States, but that concentration is expected to diffuse quickly into Europe and Asia and then into Latin America and Africa. Even in developing countries, Internet use is now growing exponentially. In India, for example, the number of Internet users is estimated to have nearly doubled in 1998 to 270,000, and it could rise to over 2 million by the end of 2000.[3] In Africa, Somalia recently added its first ISP, becoming one of the last remaining unwired countries to come on-line; and in South Africa, electronic commerce is expected to generate US$1.1 billion in revenues in 1999.[4]

Clearly, developing countries will need to address a number of socioeconomic and regulatory barriers before their rates of electronic commerce use match those of the United States, Europe, or Japan. High Internet connection rates, low penetration of electronic means of payment (such as credit, debit, or Smart cards), and cumbersome delivery systems are some of the primary obstacles to the growth of electronic commerce in these countries. Governments around the world are increasingly becoming aware of and trying to address these barriers through legislation and private-public partnerships, and their efforts are being assisted by development agencies like the World Bank. While the international digital divide most likely will persist for some time, electronic commerce nonetheless increasingly is the preferred mode for doing international business—even in traditional industries like textiles and apparel—and it has significant growth potential for the future. The timing is right, therefore, to address electronic commerce in the WTO, so that both the industrial and the developing world can grasp the many benefits that it has to offer.

What Is the Current State of Play?

The WTO has done a substantial amount of work with regard to electronic commerce, but the cross-cutting and rapidly evolving environment of electronic commerce poses a true challenge both to the organizing structure of the WTO (the General Agreement on Tariffs and Trade, or GATT, the GATS, and the role of subcommittees) and to the operational method of its members (request-offer negotiations and negative versus positive commitments).

---

3. See http://www.emarketer.com/estats/102599_india.html.

4. See http://www.nua.ie/surveys.

The initial approach taken at the 1998 Geneva ministerial conference distinguished between the physical and the electronic delivery of products purchased via the Internet. But the rapid evolution of the Internet marketplace, particularly in the greater use of digitized information, soon blurred the traditional distinction between goods and services. On the one hand, products purchased electronically but delivered physically (such as vitamins from Drugstore.com that reach their destination via DHL) would appear to be subject to existing WTO rules on trade in goods. On the other hand, an architectural blueprint delivered electronically would likely be a kind of service. But consider, for example, music that is downloaded from the Internet (and that does not exist on a hard medium such as a CD). Is this a good or a service? Should these products fall under the purview of GATS, GATT, or neither? In order to allow further time to examine the issue, WTO members agreed at their second ministerial conference in Geneva in May 1998 not to impose customs duties on products delivered over the Internet until the third ministerial conference, at which time members could vote on an extended moratorium.[5]

To help clarify these issues, the Geneva ministerial declaration mandated that the WTO General Council implement a comprehensive work program on all trade-related aspects of electronic commerce. The General Council assigned the work program in parts to the Goods Council, the Services Council, the Council for Trade-Related Aspects of Intellectual Property Rights (TRIPs), and the Trade and Development Committee (to consider how electronic commerce affects developing countries). In addition to examining the treatment of products delivered via the Internet, the work program more generally considered how the WTO should approach electronic commerce relative to the scope of work of other organizations like the World Intellectual Property Organization (WIPO), the Organization for Economic Coordination and Development (OECD), and regional trading groups.

Far from achieving definite conclusions, however, the General Council's work program on electronic commerce highlighted a number of issues that warranted further review. Several of these issues were brought to the negotiating table at the Seattle ministerial. Given the failure of WTO members to produce a declaration from the ministerial, these issues still need to be resolved.

Should the Moratorium on Customs Duties for Digitized Products Be Extended? If So, for How Long?

WTO negotiators came to Seattle with a remarkably broad consensus on extending the current moratorium on customs duties for digitized

---

5. WTO, "Geneva Ministerial Declaration on Global Electronic Commerce," 20 May 1998, http://www.wto.org/wto/ecom/e_mindec1.htm.

products, but with less consensus on how long that extension should last. The consensus on extension per se reflected the view of many countries (spearheaded by the United States) that electronic commerce is a revolutionizing force for the way information is exchanged and for how companies do business, and therefore it should be kept free of trade barriers. Moreover, most WTO members agreed that they should refrain from imposing new barriers—in part because the overarching principles of the WTO command this view, and in part because such barriers would have to be negotiated away in the future. Finally, extending the moratorium would acknowledge that implementing customs duties on digitized products is, for the time being, technologically difficult.

How long the moratorium should stay in place was a topic for negotiation in Seattle. Despite indications that the US negotiating team would strive for a *permanent* extension of the moratorium, the United States followed Australia's lead in pushing for an *indefinite* moratorium. This wording prompted objections by the European Union, Canada, Japan, and most developing countries. They argued that "indefinite" could mean "permanent," or it could mean that members could back out of the moratorium at any time. These countries pushed for a moratorium with a more specific timeline, with consideration of a permanent moratorium to take place in the future.

Three days into the Seattle ministerial, US Secretary of Commerce William Daley announced that WTO ministers were in broad agreement on extending the moratorium for 18 to 24 months.[6] Whether that agreement holds will depend in part on the outcome of the procedural debate that has followed the inconclusive disbanding of the ministerial. The United States argues that the ministerial was suspended and can be revived at any time under US chairmanship; therefore, the moratorium is still in effect. Other countries, however, argue that the ministerial ended, and therefore the moratorium has expired.[7] As this debate continues, it appears that the original consensus on extending the moratorium may be unraveling, with the European Union and some developing countries indicating that any extension is still a matter for debate.[8]

Should Electronic Commerce Be Classified under GATT, GATS, Both, or Neither?

Another issue—and one that could have an even greater impact on the development of electronic commerce—involves the classification of

---

6. "WTO Agreed on Short-Term Net Tax Ban," *CNET News*, 2 December 1999.

7. "WTO Grapples with Next Steps After Failed Ministerial Meeting," *Inside U.S. Trade*, 10 December 1999, 1.

8. "Developing, Industrialized Countries to Clash over WTO Extensions," *Inside U.S. Trade*, 17 December 1999, 1.

digitized products as goods, as services, or as some kind of new hybrid product. The European Union strongly asserts that "all electronic transmissions consist of services," and that therefore these products should fall under the purview of GATS. Most countries, including the United States, agree that services delivered over the Internet are covered by GATS, but other products are more like a good or are a hybrid between a good and a service (electronic books are a popular example). Thus the United States is arguing that more time is needed to monitor the development of electronic commerce before any final classification takes place. Deputy US Trade Representative Susan Esserman has pointed out that classifying these products under GATS could make their treatment under the WTO less liberal, because market access in GATS exists only in sectors where members have made specific commitments (software downloaded from the Internet is not covered by GATS, for example). Moreover, whether existing GATS commitments include electronic transmissions as a mode of delivery is itself under contention.[9]

A possible compromise between the European Union and the United States on this issue would be to classify digitized products as services, but to make all such products subject to most favored nation and national treatment provisions. A different compromise, and one that would be more liberalizing, sidesteps the classification issue and requires that WTO members follow the course of most liberal treatment of these products, under either GATT or GATS, particularly when a specific product does not fit neatly within a negotiated service-sector commitment.

One manifestation of the classification issue is whether country delegations will begin emphasizing the "horizontal" approach to negotiations on electronic commerce. The initial US proposal on services in mid-summer 1999 argued for the "use of all appropriate negotiating modalities, including request-offer, horizontal, and sectoral approaches."[10] In the horizontal approach, negotiators seek to apply liberalizing measures, such as transparency and good governance in regulations as well as consistency of ownership across sectors, to a broad range of services all at one go. For example, negotiators would seek to eliminate any discrimination across a particular mode of delivery, such as electronic commerce, or in rights of establishment across a range of services, rather than negotiate piecemeal using the request-offer approach—for instance, by liberalizing economic transactions for financial services in return for extending protections on ownership of small-package delivery firms.[11]

9. WTO, "Communication from the European Communities and Their Member States on the WTO Work Programme on Electronic Commerce," 9 August 1999.

10. Preparations for the 1999 ministerial conference; communication from the United States, "Further Negotiations as Mandated by the General Agreement on Trade in Services (GATS)," as replicated in *Inside U.S. Trade*, 30 July 1999.

11. Susan Esserman, "Approaching the New Round: American Goals in Services Trade," testimony before the Senate Finance Subcommittee on Trade, 21 October 1999.

Should the WTO Work Program on Electronic Commerce Be Extended?

The different country positions on how—or whether—to continue the WTO's work program on electronic commerce mirror the classification conflict. The European Union asserts that because all electronic deliveries are services, the work program must proceed under the auspices of the Services Council. The developing countries, while not assuming rigid positions on the GATT vs. GATS classification issue, are having a difficult time staffing all the meetings taking place in the various councils and would prefer to see electronic commerce addressed only in the General Council. The United States is proposing that a "nonnegotiating working group" be set up in the WTO's General Council. This proposal would satisfy the needs of the developing countries for fewer meeting venues, but as a nonnegotiating group, it would not presuppose the outcome of the classification issue.

Another point of difference between the United States and the European Union is what issues the work program should consider. The European Union wants the work program to have a more extensive coverage of the trade-related aspects of electronic commerce, including authentication, contracts, privacy, consumer protection, and content. The United States, on the other hand, asserts that these issues are already being addressed through other international groups such as the Global Business Dialogue on E-Commerce, the United Nations Commission on International Trade Law (UNCITRAL), the OECD, and the WIPO.[12]

Should Electronic Commerce Commitments under the WTO Address the Particular Needs of Developing Countries?

Several developing countries are concerned about how electronic commerce commitments under the WTO will affect them. These concerns include infrastructure development, equitable access, and technological and human capacity for electronic commerce growth. A few of these countries, including the Southern African nations, have gone so far as to propose that an extension of the moratorium be tied to "technical assistance for the building of telecommunication infrastructure" for developing countries.[13] The United States, while indicating a willingness to

---

12. US Undersecretary of Commerce for International Trade David Aaron, speech on the US objectives for the Seattle ministerial, Institute for International Economics, 26 October 1999.

13. "SADC Ministers' Agreed Negotiating Objectives for the Third WTO Ministerial Conference," WTO preministerial communication from the Southern African Development Community, 1 October 1999.

"assure that developing countries benefit from the expansion of electronic commerce,"[14] has not yet agreed to any linkage between the moratorium and technical assistance.

What Should Future Negotiations Accomplish?

Because of the economic and social importance and the global reach of electronic commerce, it is essential that WTO members commit themselves to obtaining the deepest level of liberalization of electronic commerce, including an extension of the moratorium on customs duties for digital transmissions. WTO members should also agree to continue the electronic commerce work program in their mandate for new negotiations. Doing so could pave the way for a liberal, comprehensive treatment of electronic commerce—as well as its prerequisite infrastructures—that would encourage its growth and secure its benefits for all WTO members.

Accordingly, future trade negotiations should seek broad consensus on the following points: existing WTO principles apply to e-commerce, the moratorium should be extended, and the classification of e-commerce as a good or service should remain flexible. In addition, future US negotiation strategy should emphasize the horizontal approach within the services sector while acknowledging that the request-offer approach of e-commerce liberalization by developing countries in return for greater liberalization of key industrial markets might be appropriate. Finally, negotiations should ensure that the WTO continue its program of education on e-commerce in a nonnegotiating forum.

Reaffirm That Existing WTO Principles and Disciplines Apply to Electronic Commerce

While the electronic world poses certain challenges to the current trade policy framework, traditional WTO principles of nondiscrimination, transparency, neutrality, and market openness remain valid and should be applied to electronic commerce. New rules are not necessary if liberalizing commitments embodied in GATT, GATS, TRIPs, and other WTO agreements are honored.

Where there is confusion on the application of these agreements to electronic commerce, the most liberalizing approach should prevail. In

---

14. US Undersecretary of Commerce for International Trade David Aaron, speech on the US objectives for the Seattle ministerial, Institute for International Economics, 26 October 1999.

some cases, this could mean that electronic delivery of goods and services would be treated more favorably than other forms of delivery. For example, insurance products could be sold over the Internet even though the physical presence of a foreign insurance firm had not yet been scheduled for liberalization under GATS. The liberalization bias thus engendered by electronic commerce can act as a positive force, stimulating further the development of electronic commerce as well as encouraging deeper liberalization and deregulation throughout the economy.

On the other hand, governments do have a legitimate concern that their standards and regulations (e.g., pharmaceutical prescriptions, gambling restrictions, and the prudential regulations of banks) might be undermined by the more favorable treatment afforded to electronic commerce. This is a good time, therefore, for governments to review how electronic commerce places existing standards and regulations under stress, and to decide what combination of private-sector response and public legislation will secure for their citizens the greatest benefits from electronic commerce. Given the global nature of electronic commerce, governments should make every effort to coordinate (which need not mean harmonize) new regulations with other countries, on both a bilateral and a multilateral basis.

Extend the Moratorium on Duty-Free Treatment of Electronic Transmissions

Ideally, WTO members will make permanent and binding the practice of not imposing customs duties on digitized products. The longer countries keep electronic commerce duty-free, the more these activities will take hold and flourish and make apparent the benefits of a more liberal domestic and international trade environment. If WTO members allow the moratorium to expire, they will encourage the development of an environment fragmented by different international tax/tariff types and rates, leading to wasteful "forum-shopping" by businesses, and discouraging technological growth in countries where seamless global markets are most important.

Maintain Flexibility Regarding the Classification of Electronic Commerce

With electronic commerce still in its infancy, it is too early to determine whether digitized products delivered over the Internet should be classified into a traditional goods or services category. A premature decision on classification could have a profound impact on the growth of electronic commerce, given the differences in how GATT and GATS approach liberalizing commitments. How digitized products can be classified in the existing WTO structure in a way that encourages the growth of electronic commerce is an important topic for the WTO work program (discussed more below).

Emphasize Horizontal Negotiations Going Forward

Horizontal negotiations recognize that services sectors are interconnected and that liberalization must proceed on several fronts at once to get the maximum economic benefits. Otherwise the benefits from liberalizing one sector (say, lower telecommunications costs) are simply absorbed into a protected sector (such as higher air cargo costs). The horizontal approach to liberalization is particularly valuable for electronic commerce, where the synergies among services sectors are especially apparent.

Extend the Electronic Commerce Work Program

It is essential that WTO members foster an environment that allows debate as well as consideration of how electronic commerce issues are unique yet are also part of the existing WTO mandate for liberalization. This can most easily be accomplished through the continuation of a work program on electronic commerce. The current work program has just begun to scratch the surface of understanding how electronic commerce is changing the global economy. Questions that a nonnegotiating body could address include the following: Should the Agreement on Basic Telecommunications Services be expanded to include issues of broadband infrastructure and services? Should information technology products related to the Internet be included for tariff reduction under ITA II? Should the issues of interoperability, standards, and universal access be addressed in the WTO as well as in other negotiating bodies? Such questions could be explored through the WTO work program, with special attention given to developing-country concerns.

A future WTO work program on electronic commerce should have the following features:

- The work program should be reconstituted under the General Council rather than fragmented throughout the WTO. While input from the different councils and committees is important, the cross-cutting nature of electronic commerce means that leadership from the General Council is a critical factor. Moreover, close coordination of the work program under the General Council would help developing countries, which have smaller negotiating staffs, to participate more fully.

- Private-sector participation has been the hallmark of all the regional trade forums' discussions of electronic commerce (including those proceeding under the Asia Pacific Economic Cooperation [APEC] forum and the Free Trade Area of the Americas [FTAA] process). The private sector is leading the way in setting global technological standards for electronic commerce; it can also help resolve policymaking concerns such as tax administration and privacy protection. The contribution the private sector can make to the WTO work program is therefore vital.

Be Prepared to Negotiate with Developing Countries across Industrial Sectors

US businesses and workers, especially in the high-tech and services sectors, stand to benefit from the liberalization of electronic commerce and its infrastructure. Other countries also stand to benefit, through the new opportunities created by electronic commerce as well as through the increased efficiencies electronic commerce is making to traditional sectors. This is a clear win-win proposition for the United States and its trading partners. The overall benefits could be reduced, however, if markets are not open for the goods and services countries will come to produce more efficiently than they do now. Developing countries, for example, face US barriers in textiles and apparel and some elements of data processing, communications, and software programming—precisely the areas in which electronic commerce can enhance the competitiveness of developing-country producers.

Trade negotiations often involve political as well as economic considerations. If US negotiators fail to acknowledge the need to lower trade barriers, developing countries may limit their commitments to liberalize key areas of electronic commerce (such as an extension of the moratorium on customs duties), which would reduce the benefits for everyone. While it might be politically difficult for the United States, trading reduced barriers in other sectors for an extension of the moratorium could be the most liberalizing and most beneficial outcome for future negotiations.

While WTO negotiators should be prepared to negotiate across industrial sectors, they need to be wary of developing-country demands that extending the moratorium be paired with technical assistance or Internet access requirements. The WTO does not have the human capacity or the funds to meet such requirements. Other organizations, such as UNCTAD and the International Telecommunications Union, are better suited for providing technical training to developing countries, and the World Bank and the regional development banks can offer much-needed funding for infrastructure investment. These organizations can help to ensure that the benefits from electronic commerce accrue equitably among countries of different development levels.

Conclusion

WTO members face an important task: to establish a predictable environment in which electronic commerce can thrive, allowing the benefits of this new form of international trade to be realized by all consumers in all countries. In accomplishing these objectives, the WTO can work to ensure that electronic commerce remains free from international trade barriers and continues to drive domestic and global growth.

The stakes are enormous. In the United States, where electronic commerce has its strongest hold, the information technology sector contributes to approximately 8 percent of the economy. The remarkable growth in information technology-related industries, especially those directly linked to electronic commerce, has helped to create the longest period of peacetime economic growth (with low inflation) in US history. In fact, over the past four years the output of information technology-related industries has contributed to more than one-third of the growth of real output for the US economy.[15]

Such gains are available to all countries, not just first users like the United States and Europe; liberalization via electronic commerce is not a zero-sum game. In fact, electronic commerce offers particular promise to developing countries. Market innovations and improved market efficiencies gained through electronic commerce and its prerequisite infrastructural elements will have the greatest impact in those sectors and countries where coordination and transactions costs are highest. The services sectors in many developing countries often are inefficient, undermining the competitiveness of related industries. For example, apparel firms in Sri Lanka cannot move to higher-profit "up-market" styles because they cannot participate in fast-paced on-line design, order fulfillment, or electronic finance; nor are there airfreight systems to transport textile products quickly and efficiently to retail outlets abroad. Service-sector liberalization will go a long way toward improving these circumstances.

For all countries, a failure to acknowledge the way electronic commerce fully integrates both services and goods sectors, to treat it as a separate sector, or to tax it as a service would undermine the WTO objective of liberalization and would hinder the exploration of new processes, products, and markets. As the preceding examples showed, the successful uptake of electronic commerce both depends on and facilitates liberalization in many traditional sectors. Key synergies exist among the telecommunications, financial infrastructure, distribution and delivery, and governance sectors. Liberalization of only one of these sectors would not be sufficient to promote electronic commerce. If WTO

---

15. See the Department of Commerce's "The Emerging Digital Economy II" (June 1999) at http://www.ecommerce.gov/ede for a comprehensive study of the impact of information technologies on the US economy.

members fail to use electronic commerce to make domestic markets more open to global trade, they will squander the opportunity to leap forward to the next stage of economic development, where value is created not just by resource endowments or manufacturing might, but also by knowledge, information, and the use of technology.

Reference

Organization for Economic Cooperation and Development. 1999. *The Economic and Social Impact of Electronic Commerce.* Geneva.

V

THE WTO AGENDA: INSTITUTIONAL ISSUES

17

Dispute Settlement and a New Round

JOHN H. JACKSON

On 1 January 1995 the new international economic organization called the World Trade Organization (WTO) came into being as the result of the complex Uruguay Round negotiation. A very important part of this organization (some say the central part) is the new dispute settlement procedures, particularly embodied in a document entitled the Dispute Settlement Understanding (DSU), which is annex 2 to the WTO "charter." Many officials and nongovernmental observers believe this new dispute settlement system has been very successful in its beginning years. Of course, it is not without faults, and it would be surprising if its many innovative features all worked as originally intended. After five years of experience with the process, it is appropriate to pause and reflect on its operation and effects. Indeed, the decisions at the final Uruguay Round conference at Marrakesh, Morocco, in mid-April 1994 called for a review of the WTO dispute settlement procedures within four years after they came into force. Particularly during the last few years, there has been considerable discussion about perceived problems as well as the merits of WTO dispute settlement. A number of governments have developed position papers, sometimes labeled "nonpapers," with a variety of suggestions for reforming the process. In addition, nongovernmental personnel, private practitioners engaged in representing disputants, and others have suggested potential reforms (*Journal of International Economic Law* 1, no. 2 [1998] and vol. 2, no. 2 [1999]).

John H. Jackson is a professor at the Georgetown University Law Center, Washington. Portions of this article build upon an article published by the author in 1998 in Journal of International Economic Law 1: 329-51. In turn, that article was a revision and extension of a manuscript first presented at the WTO academic conference in Geneva on 30 April 1998, commemorating the 50th anniversary of the General Agreement on Tariffs and Trade (GATT).

The inventory of suggestions gleaned from commentaries and papers probably well exceeds 100. This chapter will outline only some of them, sometimes addressing a group of suggestions under a general topic and focusing to some extent on the more controversial reform proposals.

The chapter first reviews the historical and basic policy ideas underlying dispute settlement procedures and notes some of the characteristics and statistics of the first five years' experience as well as the reactions of policy leaders to the procedures and their impact. Next, the chapter takes up specific reform suggestions. Finally, I make a few remarks about the new procedures in the context of the WTO's broader "constitutional" problems.

History and Policy Assumptions

When the GATT was created at the end of 1947 in Geneva (and came into effect 1 January 1948), it was not supposed to be an organization. The GATT was designed to depend on an International Trade Organization (ITO), which never came into being. In addition, the GATT was applied provisionally, under a Protocol of Provisional Application, pending the establishment of an ITO. But in the absence of the ITO, the GATT continued under the protocol throughout its initial history. Although the WTO has been created as an institution to replace the GATT, the GATT *obligations* have been incorporated in the new WTO in annex IA to the WTO charter.

GATT dispute settlement was based on some very meager clauses in that treaty instrument, and consequently the practice as it developed over the decades was the most significant creator of the specific attributes of the GATT dispute settlement procedure. The basic role of the GATT dispute settlement system has always been a matter of dispute. To oversimplify, some have believed, based on the very meager language in the GATT concerning dispute settlement, that the purpose of GATT dispute settlement was simply to facilitate the settlement by government contracting parties to the GATT of disputes between them regarding GATT matters. Others thought that the dispute settlement procedure played a much more significant role in providing an impartial third-party judgment on vital legal questions about implementation of GATT obligations. In that process, therefore, the reports of panel proceedings would effectively develop a "jurisprudence" and a record of practice under the GATT agreement on which governments could in part base their interpretations of the GATT. In this role, the procedures would thus facilitate greater precision, predictability, and stability of the GATT rules.

During the more than four decades of the GATT, the dispute settlement system evolved toward the latter view, sometimes called the "rule orientation approach." The procedures became quite sophisticated, particularly in the 1980s. They also attracted attention from other countries and interest groups that admired the procedures enough to want to become participants. Thus many nations acceded to the GATT agreement, possibly in part because of the perceived value in the dispute settlement procedures. In addition, parties interested in new subjects for the GATT, such as intellectual property and trade in services, felt there was value in these procedures.

However, despite the merit perceived in the procedures, there were serious faults in dispute settlement, partly due to the "birth defects" of the GATT. A Uruguay Round negotiating group was charged with looking at these faults and coming up with new procedures, which it did. Thus there are now in the WTO new procedures that prevent a "blocking" of the results of the panel and also provide for a new "appellate" process quite unique in international law. The overall result of these reforms, however, is to provide a measure of rigor and more automatic implementation of the results of the panel proceedings, and in some cases this has made sovereign nations uncomfortable.

As mentioned previously, there have been two schools of thought on the role of dispute settlement, a dichotomy that has persisted despite the continuing trend toward rule orientation. This dichotomy is manifest in the WTO procedures. For example, one clause in the DSU (Article 3.2) calls the procedures the "central element in providing security and predictability to the multilateral trading system" while another clause refers to "prompt settlement of situations" as being "essential to the effective functioning of the WTO" (Article 3.3).

In the context of a major international economic agreement, it has been argued that a chief value of a dispute settlement system is enhancing the predictability and stability of the obligation norms of the system. This better enables millions of entrepreneurs to make decisions regarding international investment, market penetration, market access, and so on. In turn, it is suggested that such a system reduces the risk involved in these cross-border transactions. Economists often call this reducing the "risk premium," which might be reflected in a higher rate of return on capital than would otherwise be the case. Thus the dispute settlement system could be seen as reducing this risk premium and thereby enhancing world welfare through better allocation of investment flows and better business decisions. Appreciation of these core policies, or some of these core policy disputes, is an important part of the setting in which the WTO must determine what changes should be effected in dispute settlement.

The First Five Years

The WTO Secretariat issues an extremely interesting and useful document, regularly revised, that describes cases brought before the Dispute Settlement Body and outlines statistics about them. This document,

"Overview of the State-of-Play of WTO Disputes," is available on the WTO's Web site.[1] At the end of 1999, it tallied cumulative data for the DSU's first five years: 185 consultation requests, 144 distinct matters (where a single panel examines multiple complaints), 32 active cases, 26 completed cases, and 39 settled or inactive cases.

In general, governments and diplomats seem reasonably satisfied with the overall performance of the dispute settlement process. Often this process is described as the jewel in the WTO institutional structure. Clearly, governments have been using the system very extensively, and there are also indications that the tenor and nature of diplomacy in the WTO context is changing because of the emphasis on dispute settlement and rule orientation. In many respects, these are attractive developments that are beneficial to the essential goals of the trading system—namely, providing a better world both in economic and lifestyle terms.

Although 1998 and 1999 were supposed to be the time of overall review of the dispute settlement system, governments have not been very diligent in conducting that review. As demonstrated in Seattle, governments are unlikely to press for fundamental reforms in the DSU. There is a certain amount of fine-tuning that would be advisable, and some near-term problems need to be fixed. In addition, for the longer term there are important issues that must be faced.

Improving the WTO Dispute Settlement System

As indicated earlier, there have been many proposals for improving the WTO dispute settlement system, some of them detailed and precise—which might be called fine-tuning. Others are more general, and some of these are controversial. The following discussion touches on some of both types of proposals.

Efficiency of the Panel Process

Now that the dispute settlement process has been launched and is perhaps drawing to the end of its "shakedown cruise," it becomes apparent that improvements could be made in the process's efficiency (measured by time and cost) and in its fairness and credibility in the eyes of the public. Some of these proposed changes involve time limits. For example, it has been suggested that plaintiffs or complainants have a great advantage, since they have the time to prepare extensively, whereas once the complainants actually start a procedure by submitting the necessary documents, the respondents have an extremely limited time to address to the allegations.

---

1. See http://www.wto.org/wto/dispute/bulletin.htm (26 November 1999).

There are a number of other suggestions, some regarding the "consultation period" required at the beginning of the procedure. One of the questions raised concerns whether third parties who believe they have a stake in what results from a given case should be able to participate in the consultations or otherwise have access to some of the information regarding a particular case. Although the DSU has formal provisions for certain third parties, who have somewhat more limited access to information and inputs than do the disputants themselves, these provisions have been criticized and suggestions for reforming them have been made. Another problem noted is that the system lacks a smooth way to achieve "preliminary rulings," which may help determine whether a case can or should be brought at all. Just about the only credible, definitive way to do this is to create a panel before such rulings can be achieved. Some have suggested that this would be relatively wasteful if a preliminary ruling were to determine that no panel is authorized. It has also been suggested that the timing of the adoption of a report—whether at the end of the first-level panel process or at the issuance of the report of the Appellate Body after an appeal has been made—could be altered to give somewhat more flexibility to the disputants. Another problem is the lack of interim relief measures, which might be particularly desirable for cases of some urgency, such as those that might affect pending near-term major business or governmental decisions or involve such things as perishable goods or dangers to the environment. Without interim relief, the process must play out completely before any relief is available, which could take several years.

One of the background problems that impinges on all these suggestions is the lack of a definitive set of rules of procedure for the first-level panel processes. The procedures are sometimes baffling to the participants, such as governments (particularly those that might be relatively new to the procedure) and the counsel that governments retain to represent them or assist their representation. These procedures can be guided to some extent by practice, but it has been suggested that a definitive set of procedural rules could be formulated under the supervision of the Dispute Settlement Body (DSB). This body must make decisions by "consensus," which sometimes makes it difficult to achieve needed reforms.

Convening a First-Level Panel

The process of convening the first-level panel has been worrisome to a number of observers, partly because it depends on ad hoc participation of voluntary panelists and it gives the disputing parties a large measure of autonomy to determine who the panel will be. If they fail to come to an agreement, however, the director general is authorized to step in and impose a panel (and has done so). There have been many suggestions for improving the first-level panel personnel and convening process, possibly by establishing a permanent roster analogous to that of the Appellate Body.

Various proposals have been put forward, for example, to create a more or less permanent roster of people who agree to serve as needed for certain terms (such as four years). Assuming that such a roster might have 20 or 30 names, there might be a way to rotate the roster that would make selection more efficient and less heavily influenced by disputants' predictions of a particular panelist's choice rather than his ability to make impartial decisions. A system could be devised to go outside the permanent roster for panelists in certain circumstances.

A related aspect is the worry that the current procedures do not provide for the Appellate Body to "remand a case" to the first-level panel. Some argue that a remand is not permitted; others argue that a remand would in any case be inefficient since it would lengthen the time for completion of the case and raise questions about to whom a remand could be sent. If there were a relatively stable roster of first-level panelists, presumably such panelists could, when they are called into the membership of a particular panel, also be ready to receive remands. As it now stands, the first-level panel is generally discharged after it issues its report, although sometimes the members have been willing to reconvene for later ancillary questions.

Choice of Counsel

For some time, there has been controversy about whether governments should be entitled to choose and hire private counsel to represent them or assist them in their dispute settlement cases. Private counsel could always be hired to assist a government, but there have been instances under the GATT and in early WTO cases when private counsel have not been permitted to be present at a hearing or to speak or to represent their client governments. This issue now seems to be resolved in favor of protecting a sovereign member disputant's choice to hire private counsel. In that case, however, questions about ethical or appropriate conduct rules may arise. Ideas about these "rules" could be approached in different ways, including voluntary codes or commentary from authors that could influence how governments relate to their private counsel. More attention may be needed to this question. In addition, the WTO should develop methods to reduce the cost burden on developing countries of participation (as either complainant or respondent) in the dispute proceeding.

Problems of Factual Evidence and Evaluating Scientific Opinions

There is a perception that the WTO dispute settlement process is woefully inadequate when it comes to evaluating detailed and complex sets of facts. There has also been some concern about how panels, particularly first-level panels, evaluate some very difficult and complex scientific evidence underlying a case (for instance, in the *Beef Hormones* case or the *Shrimp Turtle* case). Certainly, there are limited resources devoted to these evaluations, and the dispute settlement rules do not give much guidance. Clearly, more attention is needed, although it is very difficult to know what specific rules or principles to suggest. Perhaps a "commission of legal experts" could be convened to study the problem and provide some thoughts about reform.

Implementing Panel Results

One of the most difficult areas has been implementing the results of a panel ruling, whether at the first-level panel report, unappealed, or after an Appellate Body report has been adopted. The *Banana* case, for example, was a prominent case that encountered some of these implementation problems. Problems in the implementation process have led to considerable discussion in the WTO Councils and the DSB, quite a bit of diplomatic interchange, and many proposals. These problems include questions of what is a "reasonable" time for implementing the recommendations and rulings of the DSB, whether compensation is an acceptable substitute for performance, how to determine the adequacy of performance, and how to determine adequate compensation, or the level of suspension of concessions if the recommendations and rulings are not implemented within a reasonable period.

Reasonable Period for Implementing a Panel Report

DSU Article 21.3 provides for binding arbitration on the question of a reasonable period. There have been several such arbitrations that have been successful in resolving some of the problems, but there is often a rather strong presumption in favor of a 15-month period. Some observers have argued that this is either too short or too long, but in any event the period should be adapted more to particular circumstances, such as whether legislation is required in a particular member's constitution. Special attention could be given to the problems and costs of these questions for developing countries.

Compensation in Lieu of Performance

There has been some controversy concerning "compensation." When an Appellate Body or adopted panel report mandates that a government change its activities, can the government choose to accept or provide "compensatory measures" instead of making the change? Although the DSU is not free from ambiguity on this point, I believe the general thrust of the DSU, and what a panel is likely to accept if it is confronted with this question, is that compensation is only a fallback in the event of non-performance and that compensation does not relieve the respondent from an obligation to change its behavior (Jackson 1997).

Determining Adequacy of Performance

A particularly difficult problem is the relationship between DSU Articles 21.5, 22.2, and 22.6. This problem has led to extremely sharp disagreements in the *Banana* case and thus has provoked a variety of proposals for resolving them. It does seem to many that there must be a multilateral dispute settlement-type determination (perhaps analogous to the binding arbitration for "a reasonable period of time") to make some of the determinations called for in Articles 21.5 and 22.2.

Suspension of Concessions

There are important questions about the level of suspension of concessions and how that should be measured. Here, too, the DSU calls for an arbitration, although this would present some practical difficulties and potentially create more ambiguity.

A fairly serious revision of the DSU text in Articles 21 and 22 is advisable to alleviate the problem created by ambiguities, gaps, and the lack of consistency in the clauses.

In general, it appears implementation has been quite good, including the responses of some of the most powerful members of the organization, even in the face of panel determinations in favor of complainant members who are not as powerful.

Transparency and Participation

There are some extremely important issues, with long-term systemic and fundamental implications, regarding the operation of the dispute settlement process and its credibility in the eyes of both member-state governments and nongovernment observers, including those that come under the rubric "civil society." These issues can be lumped into two categories: transparency and participation.

With respect to transparency, there is a concern about the amount of secrecy and confidentiality involved in WTO dispute settlement. Many have strongly recommended, for example, that panel hearings be open to include not only member government observers but also nongovernment observers, including possibly the press. These recommendations do not seek participation or the right to speak in the dispute settlement proceedings, so it would seem that opening hearings to public view could add to the credibility of the procedures as well as solve the problem that members themselves have with access to information about ongoing cases.

Some governments strongly resist this idea, and it requires more careful thought and discussion. For example, opening hearings does have resource implications, such as the costs of providing access.

With respect to participation, the issues are somewhat more difficult. There is not much inclination among the members to give a right of participation in dispute settlement panels to those outside the government, with the possible exception of *amicus curiae* advocacy papers (or briefs). The Appellate Body has ruled that the broad language of the DSU permits a first-level panel to receive and examine *amicus* briefs from nongovernmental organizations. This ruling, however, does not obligate a first-level panel to receive or look at such communications. Because of this possibility, however, the nongovernmental organizations or civil-society participants will likely want to present viewpoints they think are essential to the increasingly important procedures of the WTO. Thus the WTO will find itself under considerable pressure to make such opportunities available in one form or another. Again, this has considerable resource implications.

One possibility would be to formulate "regulations" as to when, why, and how nongovernment communications could or should be received. These regulations could be deemed to be adopted by any first-level panel in formulating procedures for a particular case unless otherwise explicitly indicated with reasons. Likewise, it is important to ensure that all parties to a dispute have easy access to any communications a panel accepts. Web publication is one way to make access relatively inexpensive. How a panel processes and assimilates the arguments in nongovernment communications is an issue that would also have to be addressed. Obviously, staff help is likely to be used extensively in this situation, and maybe there would need to be page limits or other limitations. Some international organizations have rosters of NGOs that have certain rights to send communications or otherwise receive information, and the WTO could consider comparable measures.

Emerging Problems

Every institution has to evolve and change in the face of conditions and circumstances not originally considered when the institution was set up. This is most certainly true of the original GATT and now of the WTO. With the fast-paced change of a globalizing economy, the WTO will have to cope with new factors, new policies, and new subject matters. If it fails to do that, it will sooner or later be marginalized. This could be very detrimental to the broader multilateral approach to international economic relations, pushing nations to solve their problems through regional arrangements, bilateral arrangements, and even unilateral actions. Although these forms can have an appropriate role and also can be constructive innovators for the world trading system, they also run considerable risks of ignoring key components and the diversity of societies and societal policies around the world, thereby generating significant disputes and rancor among nations and undermining multilateral cooperation.

Another problem is the gaps and ambiguity present in the Uruguay Round and WTO treaty—perhaps this also is an inevitable feature of institutions, and particularly treaties involving so many participants. How can these many issues be considered and dealt with in the current WTO framework? First of all, it must be recognized that there is a delicate interplay between the dispute settlement process and the prospects for negotiating new treaty texts or making decisions already authorized by the Uruguay Round treaty text.

What are the possibilities for negotiating new text or making decisions pursuant to the explicit authority of the WTO charter? Clearly they are quite constrained. In the last months of the Uruguay Round negotiations, the diplomatic representatives present there felt it was important to build "checks and balances" into the WTO charter to constrain decision making that might be too "intrusive on sovereignty." Thus the decision-making clauses of Article IX and the amending clauses of Article X established a number of limitations on what the WTO membership can do.

Apart from formal amendments, one can look at the powers concerning decisions, waivers, and formal interpretations. But in each of these cases, there are very substantial constraints. Decision making (at least as a fallback from attempts to achieve consensus) is generally ruled by a majority-vote system, but there is language in the WTO charter (Article IX:3), as well as a practice under the GATT, that suggests that any decisions made cannot impose new obligations on members.[2] Waivers were sometimes used in the GATT to innovate and adjust to new circumstances, but that process fell into disrepute and led the negotiators to include language in the Uruguay Round texts constraining the use of waivers, in particular limiting their duration and specifying the authority under which they could be revoked. The GATT had no formal provision regarding "interpretations," and thus the GATT panels probably had a bit more scope for setting forth interpretations that would ultimately become embedded in the GATT practice and even subsequent negotiated treaty language. However, the WTO addresses this issue of formal interpretations directly, imposing a very stringent voting requirement of three-fourths of the total membership. Since many people observe that often a quarter of the WTO membership is not present at key meetings, one can see that a formal interpretation is not easy to achieve. Some observers note, how-

---

2. Final Act Embodying the Results of the Uruguay Round of Multilateral Trade Negotiations, opened for signature April 15, 1994, Marrakesh, Morocco, 33 I.L.M. 1140-272 (1994), Articles IX:2, X:3, X:4, and annex 2, Dispute Settlement Understanding Article 3.2.

ever, that in some contexts the technical requirements of consensus (not unanimity)[3] may not always be so difficult to fulfill.

Given these various constraints, it would be understandable if member countries or other observers were tempted to look to the dispute settlement process and the general conclusions of panel and appellate reports to provide interpretation of many of the ambiguous treaty clauses or to bridge gaps in them. However, the Dispute Settlement Understanding itself (Article 3.2) warns against proceeding too far in this direction: "Recommendations and rulings of the DSB cannot add to or diminish the rights and obligations provided in the covered agreements." The Appellate Body reports tend to defer to national government decision making. The Appellate Body appears to be pursuing "judicial restraint," along the lines suggested in DSU Article 3.2 and sought by those who fear the WTO will intrude on national sovereignty. The power, explicit in the WTO charter, of "formal interpretation" with a supermajority requirement also arguably constrains how far the dispute settlement system can claim that its report rulings and recommendations are "definitive." In short, the dispute settlement system cannot and should not be in the business of formulating new rules, either by filling gaps in the existing agreements or by setting norms that carry the organization into totally new territory, such as competition policy or labor standards.

In addition, as noted above, there are many procedural questions. Part of the genius of the GATT was its ability to evolve partly through trial and error and practice. Indeed, GATT dispute settlement evolved over four decades quite dramatically—with such concepts as "prima facie nullification," or the use of "panels" instead of "working parties," becoming gradually embedded in the process—and under the Tokyo Round Dispute Settlement Understanding (DSU) became "definitive" by consensus action of the GATT Contracting Parties.

But the language of the DSU (as well as that of the WTO charter) curtails such an approach. DSU Article 2.4 reads as follows: "Where the rules and procedures of this understanding provide for the DSB to take a decision, it shall do so by consensus." The definition of consensus is then supplied in a footnote, and, although not identical with "unanimity," it allows an objecting member to block consensus. Likewise, the WTO charter itself provides a consensus requirement for amendments to annexes 2 and 3 of the WTO—annex 2 being the DSU and the dispute settlement procedures. Thus the opportunity to evolve by experiment and practice seems more constrained under the WTO than was the case under the very loose and ambiguous language of the GATT, with its

---

3. WTO Agreement Article IX, footnote 1, defines consensus as follows: "The body concerned shall be deemed to have decided by consensus on a matter submitted for consideration, if no member, present at the meeting when the decision is taken, formally objects to the proposed decision."

minimalist institutional language. As a result, there is potential for dead-lock and for participants to be without the means to cope with some of the problems that will face or already face the WTO.

Perhaps the WTO can develop somewhat better opportunities for explicit amendment by using the two-thirds (and three-fourths in substance cases) power of amendment in the WTO charter. Also, perhaps the WTO membership at its ministerial meeting or various council meetings can "creep up on" some of the issues by making incremental decisions that pave the way for reform. These decisions would become part of the "practice under the agreement" referred to in the Vienna Convention on the Law of Treaties. What are some other possibilities? With respect to the dispute settlement details and potential changes in procedures, it may be possible to work within the "consensus rule" to make some changes in the DSU. It at least appears that this rule does not require national government member approvals of treaty text amendments and thus avoids some of the elaborate procedures of national government ratification of treaties, for example. The question of consensus arises in at least two kinds of decisions: changes in the text of the DSU and decisions by the DSB, which could involve incidental or interstitial and ancillary procedural rules, assuming that such rules are not inconsistent with DSU treaty provisions. Again, of course, the consensus rule apparently applies. There may be a few situations where small and relatively unimportant decisions can be made dealing with the administration of the dispute settlement system, such as how to interpret time deadlines, or the form in which complaints should be filed, or the development of a relatively uniform set of procedural rules about activities of panels and panel members, translations, documentation, and so forth. Even then, there is at least some likelihood that an objecting member could force an issue to go to the DSB and that member could dare to block consensus.

It might be feasible to develop certain practices about reaching consensus that would lead member nations to restrain themselves from blocking a consensus in certain circumstances. In other words, the General Council or the DSB (the General Council acting with different hats) might develop criteria about consensus concerning certain kinds of decisions that would strongly suggest to member states that if the criteria are fulfilled they should refrain from blocking consensus. Perhaps this could develop a bit like the practice in the European Community history and jurisprudence of the "Luxembourg Compromise," where it has been understood that governments would refrain from exercising their potential veto against a measure in certain circumstances unless the measure involves something of "vital interest" to the member nation involved. While not pursuing the analogy too far, one might see something similar develop in the WTO. A "vital national interest" declaration could be a condition for blocking consensus, but a practice could develop to subject such declarations to inquiry, debate, and criticism.

It is possible that such an approach to reaching consensus could avert the risk of stalemate and paralysis in the face of new problems in the global economy. These criteria could be developed through resolutions of the General Council or the DSB in the form of "recommendations to members" and might provide the relatively informal practice that nevertheless could be effective over time.

Implementing Reforms

As indicated above, the constraints on the decision-making and amending powers of the WTO are substantial, and this raises the question of how one could actually go about introducing some of the reforms that have been mentioned above. A full exposition of this question would take many pages, but a brief review follows, more in the nature of an inventory of possibilities. These possibilities could vary by subject matter. For example, the reform measure chosen, even though it is supposed to involve dispute settlement, could vary between an agricultural measure and an intellectual property measure. In each case, an evaluation would have to include whether the reform desired could be achieved without actually altering the specific treaty language in either the Uruguay Round text more generally or in the DSU itself. These are some of the possibilities:

- ■ Informal practice, perhaps initiated by Secretariat advice to a panel or the Appellate Body, could be adopted. This might work for various fine-tuning interstitial decisions, such as whether a deadline falling on Saturday would be deemed to be in force only on Monday.

- ■ The panel and Appellate Body decisions themselves have addressed certain procedural elements, and we can anticipate a certain amount of evolution in dispute settlement procedure through these processes.

- ■ The Dispute Settlement Body (DSB) could appoint a subordinate advisory group, which could give advice on certain changes and reforms to the DSB for DSB action, or possibly even be delegated certain interstitial and "ministerial" powers.

- ■ The DSB can, of course, take action itself. However, any decision of the DSB must be by "full consensus" under the DSU. Thus such decisions would be subject to blocking by any member of the WTO. Nevertheless, following some of the guidelines mentioned above, it might be feasible for the DSB to take some initiative and work on some proposals.

- ■ The WTO charter provides (Article IX:2) that a definitive interpretation can be made by three-fourths vote of all WTO members. Insofar as the interpretation is not a substitute for amending the treaty text, this could be a route for certain kinds of reform.

■ WTO members acting through the council or the ministerial conference can make some decisions, subject, of course, to the constitutional restraints discussed earlier. Thus a waiver might temporarily resolve a particular problem and thereby introduce a reform on a temporary basis that could later be solidified in a treaty text or other decision. Likewise, the WTO bodies could provide resolutions or recommendations.

■ Annex 4 of the WTO is for "plurilateral agreements," which are not necessarily binding on every member of the WTO. It might in some cases be feasible to add a plurilateral agreement to annex 4, which would recognize and create certain reforms insofar as they would apply only to the signatories of that agreement. If the number and composition of members who accept the plurilateral agreement were sufficiently great and if the agreement fully encompassed the subject matter (sometimes called a "critical mass"), some reforms could be feasible.

■ Additions to the schedules, either goods schedules or services schedules, can be a way to create reform. This has been ingeniously used in the case of the telecom agreement and the agreement on financial services.

■ Amendment is always a possibility, though perhaps the most difficult to achieve, partly because it would often require members to go through constitutional and parliamentary approval processes, which could not only take a considerable amount of time but quite a bit of political effort.

■ Finally, but not to be recommended, there is always the possibility of using the Uruguay Round approach, which brought members from the GATT to the WTO—namely, to exit entirely from the old treaty, thereby rendering it useless or void, and to enter into a completely new treaty. Some commentators have observed that this probably could only be done once a generation, if that.

Reference

Jackson, John. Editorial Comment: The WTO Dispute Settlement Understanding—Misunderstandings on the Nature of Legal Obligation. *American Journal of International Law* 91 (1997): 60-64.

18

Decision Making in the WTO

JEFFREY J. SCHOTT and JAYASHREE WATAL

Seattle will be remembered as the city where street demonstrations stopped global trade talks cold. But the Seattle protesters don't deserve such notoriety. The meeting actually fell victim to serious substantive disagreements among the member countries of the World Trade Organization (WTO) over the prospective agenda for new trade talks. These policy differences probably could have been bridged if the WTO's decision-making process had not broken down. Much of the damage to the WTO was self-inflicted.

Efforts to relaunch new trade negotiations will likely face similar difficulties until member countries agree to rationalize decision making within the WTO.[1] We analyze the WTO's main problems in this area and propose management reforms to ensure that all WTO members are fully represented at the bargaining table.

Why the WTO Doesn't Work Like the GATT

Throughout the postwar era, governments worked together in eight rounds of multilateral trade negotiations in the General Agreement on

Jeffrey J. Schott is a senior fellow at the Institute. Jayashree Watal was formerly a director in the Trade Policy Division of the Ministry of Commerce in the government of India, and is now a visiting fellow at the Institute for International Economics from the Indian Council for Research in International Economic Relations (ICRIER), New Delhi.

1. By decision making we mean the process by which member governments resolve issues concerning the conduct of trade negotiations and the management of the trading system. We do not include rulings by dispute panels, which are not intergovernmental decisions, although changes to the WTO's Dispute Settlement Understanding (DSU) under which those panels operate would be relevant. The broader issue of the transparency of WTO decision making to the general public is beyond the scope of this chapter.

Tariffs and Trade (GATT) to produce concrete benefits for all participants. GATT agreements substantially opened industrial-country markets (although high barriers remain in agriculture and apparel) and contributed importantly to economic growth in developing countries, particularly in Asia and Latin America.

Countries came to the GATT to "do business" and largely left their political rhetoric to the talkathons of the United Nations and its agencies. The system worked by consensus: no votes on senseless resolutions, no decisions by majority rule.[2] The consensus rule was not abused. Developed countries, particularly the United States and the European Community, drove the GATT agenda and negotiations but did not insist on full participation by all countries. In turn, developing countries did not block progress in trade talks—both because the accords posed few demands on them and because they made huge gains from the commitments of the developed countries extended to them on a most favored nation basis. Moreover, as the weaker partners in the GATT, they benefited significantly from the well-functioning multilateral rules-based system.

The WTO still operates by consensus, but the process of "consensus building" has broken down. This problem emerged long before the WTO ministerial in Seattle; indeed, it was evident at the birth of the WTO itself (Schott 1994, 138-40). It has two main causes:

First, WTO membership has greatly expanded, encompassing many developing countries that previously were outsiders or inactive players in trade negotiations. The GATT had 23 signatories when it came into effect in January 1948 and 84 signatories by the end of the Tokyo Round in 1979. More than 110 countries signed the Uruguay Round accords in Marrakesh in April 1994 (including several countries with observer status in the GATT). As of January 2000, the WTO had 135 members, with an additional 31 in the process of accession. As a result of domestic economic reforms, including trade liberalization undertaken unilaterally and pursuant to GATT negotiations, developing countries now have a greater stake in the world trading system and a greater claim on participation in the WTO's decision-making process.

Second, WTO members can no longer "free ride" on negotiated agreements. Starting with the Uruguay Round accords, countries have had to participate in all of the negotiated agreements as part of a "single undertaking." This requirement means that developing countries have to commit to substantially greater reforms of their trade barriers and trade practices than they did in the past. Consequently, they need to be better informed about issues under negotiation. In the Uruguay Round, many countries had to accept obligations developed without their participation,

---

2. Consensus is achieved if no member present disagrees with a decision. Votes can be held if a decision cannot be arrived at by consensus but rarely occur.

and which required the implementation and enforcement of regulatory policies that they have had great difficulty in fulfilling.

In sum, GATT decision making worked in the past because there were fewer countries actively engaged and there was no compulsion for all countries to adhere to the results. Decisions could be taken by the "committee of the whole" because only a few countries were significantly affected by the results. Consensus building engaged a small group of countries; the rest were relatively passive. This process has fallen victim to the GATT's success in integrating developing countries more fully into the trading system and requiring them to be full partners in new trade agreements.

More active participants, representing more diverse interests and objectives, have complicated WTO decision making. China's prospective accession will amplify this problem by adding another politically powerful player that will demand a strong voice in the WTO. In addition, WTO decision making has become more complicated as member countries face increasingly complex issues (for example, intellectual property rights) on the WTO negotiating agenda.

The traditional "green room" process, in which a relatively small number of self-selected developed and developing countries get together to decide on divisive issues, excluded too many newly active players in WTO negotiations and thus had problems building consensus. In the course of preparations for the Seattle ministerial, developing countries put on the table about half of the proposals made for the WTO agenda. The Geneva decision-making machinery could not accommodate the diversity of views.

While it is unfair to characterize the green room process as "medieval," it does need to be modernized. At present, participation in the green room varies by issue and has increased over time. For instance, in the Tokyo Round, these talks normally involved less than 8 delegations, while today it is not uncommon to have up to 25 to 30 participants in a "full" green room. There is no objective basis for participation in these meetings, but generally only the most active countries in the negotiations participate. As it has evolved, green room consultations typically include the Quad (that is, the United States, European Union, Canada, and Japan), Australia, New Zealand, Switzerland, Norway, possibly one or two transition economy countries, and a number of developing countries. Developing countries that often participate in the green room include Argentina, Brazil, Chile, Colombia, Egypt, Hong Kong, China, India, South Korea, Mexico, Pakistan, South Africa, and at least one country from the Association of Southeast Asian Nations (ASEAN); most smaller developing countries stay out for lack of adequate resources or capabilities.[3] For instance, 18 of the WTO members from Africa have no representation in Geneva.

---

3. Thus even today about half to two-thirds of any "full" green room process would comprise developing-country participants.

Decisions made in the green room are conveyed to the larger membership for final decision. Before Seattle, the larger membership rarely differed with proposals developed by the small group. But the system broke down in preparations for and deliberations in Seattle.[4]

In sum, the current system provides input into the decision-making process by a number of large developing countries but excludes representation of the interests of the majority of WTO members. Ironically, these largely developing countries are the ones being asked to undertake more substantial liberalization of their trade barriers and reform of their trade practices than are their industrialized partners; they deserve more of a voice in the WTO's decision-making process.

Making Decisions More Inclusive and Efficient

The WTO has outgrown its increasingly unrepresentative system of decision making. A new, permanent management or steering group needs to be established to make WTO procedures more equitable and efficient.

At first blush, reforming the green room process seems easy; in fact, the task has long been opposed by the very countries it would have benefited. Previous attempts to establish a smaller steering group or executive board (akin to those in the World Bank and the International Monetary Fund) to represent the broader membership in the negotiation of trade accords have failed because of strong resistance from the majority of developing countries. These WTO members, especially the small and least-developed countries, have objected to smaller groups in which they have no input. Accordingly, they did not want to institutionalize a system of proportional representation and thus formally undercut the myth of majority rule in the GATT/WTO if issues were taken to a vote on a one-country, one-vote basis. Ironically, they opted by default for decision making dominated by the Quad countries.

As the preparations for and talks in Seattle demonstrated, the current ad hoc arrangement for green room debates has become unwieldy. The number of participants continues to grow; the process threatens to become so inefficient that it may eventually break down.

What needs to be done? Simply put, the WTO needs to establish a small, informal steering committee (20 or so in number) that can be delegated responsibility for developing consensus on trade issues among the member countries. Such a group would not undercut existing WTO rights and obligations nor the rule of decision making by consensus; we

---

4. Adding insult to injury, many developing countries actively engaged for the first time in WTO preparations for a new round and were angered at their exclusion from the decision-making process in Seattle.

Table 18.1   Value of trade, 1996 (billions of dollars)

1. European Union[a] (extra-EU)		2,065*	14. Brazil[a]	116
2. United States[a]		1,805	15. Norway[a]	113
3. Japan[a]		914	16. Indonesia[a]	104
4. Canada[a]		446	17. India[a]	97
5. Hong Kong, China[a]		369	18. Turkey	94
6. Republic of Korea[a]		331	19. Poland[a]	78
7. People's Republic of China[b]		326	20. Israel	67
8. Singapore[a]		299	21. South Africa[a]	66
9. Switzerland[a]		231	22. Czech Republic[a]	63
10. Mexico[a]		207	23. The Philippines[a]	60
11. Malaysia[a]		170	24. Argentina[a]	55
12. Australia[a]		158	25. Venezuela	40
13. Thailand[a]		155		

*Taken and adapted from the *WTO Annual Report*, 1997, tables 1.6 and 1.7.
a. At present, likely participant in green room. Other likely current participants not shown include Chile ($39 billion), New Zealand ($37 billion), Hungary ($35 billion), Egypt ($34 billion), Colombia ($32 billion), and Pakistan ($25 billion).
b. PRC is not yet a member of the WTO but is included as its accession is imminent.

Source: Compiled from World Bank, *World Development Report 1998/99*, table 15: Balance of Payments Current Account and International Reserves.

are not advocating proportional or weighted voting. Each member would maintain the ultimate decision to accept or reject such pacts.

Participation should be representative of the broader membership and based on clear, simple, objective criteria:

- absolute value of foreign trade (exports and imports of goods and services), ranked by country or common customs region, and

- global geographic representation, with at least two participants from all major regions.

Table 18.1 shows the top 25 countries based on the value of their trade in 1996, a pre-Asian crisis year.[5] The European Union is taken together, in terms of its extra-EU trade, as it speaks with one voice in the WTO, having its own internal rules and procedures for arriving at intra-EU consensus. Under the world trade share criterion, a large number of the current green room participants would continue, including important Asian and Latin American developing countries. However, some of the regions, notably Sub-Saharan Africa, the Andean Community, the Caribbean, and Central America would not be represented. That is why the second criterion is needed to ensure global geographic representation.

---

5. This exercise can also be done using three- or five-year averages.

As proposed above, the green room would have 20 seats, with a certain number reserved for representatives from previously underrepresented regions in Latin America and the Caribbean, Africa, and Asia. Of course, there will be competition for the slots. Some countries will qualify simply because of their dominant trade share; most others, however, will have to coordinate with other trading partners to ensure that their cumulative trade passes the bar.

Groups of countries, based on existing regional arrangements or formed on an ad hoc basis, would be encouraged to pool resources and share representation (just as the Nordic countries did for many years during GATT negotiations). In fact, several groups of developing countries have already done so in preparing for the new round (for example, the Mercosur and the Caribbean Regional Negotiating Machinery). The formation of groups would be voluntary; each group would then select its representative for a particular meeting from among its membership based on the interests of its members and the expertise of their WTO delegates.

Such arrangements would not impede, and may encourage, issue-based alliances among different groups in the green room. For example, the Cairns Group on agriculture might find support among a sizable share of green room delegates.

To be sure, many countries, especially those whose representatives normally attend the green room talks, oppose reforms, fearing that their influence would be diluted if participation were limited or contingent on group representation. But these countries would be even worse off if the green room process were marginalized—which is the most likely alternative to green room reform.

The idea of a group of countries represented in an international organization by only one of them is not new. Presently, both the World Bank and the IMF have country groupings represented by a single director on their boards. The current country groupings in the IMF executive board are given in table 18.2. The list is only illustrative of the point that country groupings are possible and does not in any way suggest similar groupings in the WTO. Indeed, since the European Union speaks with one voice in the WTO and many countries in table 18.2 are not members of the WTO, the IMF groupings are not relevant for the WTO.

The formation of groups of countries would serve two important functions. First, it would significantly increase the number of WTO members represented in the green room process. Second, it would provide a forum for information sharing and consultation among group members and a channel for the provision of technical assistance on WTO matters. Small countries in particular would benefit from such pooling of resources.

An illustration of how the green room could be reconstituted is given in table 18.3. The new, previously unrepresented regions/countries could include the following:

- the Central American and Caribbean countries, with extraregional trade of $38 billion,

- the Francophone African group, the last group listed in table 18.2, with a trade volume of over $40 billion,

- the other African group that includes Angola in table 18.2, with a volume of trade of over $60 billion, even excluding South Africa,[6]

- Bolivia, Colombia, Ecuador, and Peru through the Andean Community, with an extraregional trade of about $75 billion (in place of Venezuela alone),

- the current WTO members of North Africa and the Middle East, which when linked with Egypt have a trade volume of $148 billion,

- Uruguay and Paraguay, which would share representation with Argentina and Brazil through Mercosur, with an extraregional trade of about $129 billion,

- The Central European Free Trade Agreement (CEFTA), with an extraregional trade of about $190 billion, and

- Brunei Darussalam and Vietnam through ASEAN, which has an extraregional trade of about $570 billion.

Clearly, table 18.3 illustrates only one way in which country groupings could afford broader representation in the WTO decision-making process. Some countries may fault our proposal because many WTO members can only be represented if they volunteer to participate as part of a group. For instance, Sub-Saharan African members or even North African and Middle Eastern members will only be represented if they form groups. Smaller developed and developing countries may lose their current individual participation but normally would be represented if they aligned themselves to their regional partners. But, in return, they would benefit from the more efficient and equitable operation of the green room process, involving a workable number of participants representing all major geographical regions.

The proposal made here presents one approach for resolving problems with the WTO decision-making processes, so clearly evidenced in Seattle. There can surely be other ways of representing WTO members in the green room process, including by allocating a fixed number of seats on a regional basis. However, we believe that the more objective the basis for selection, the more acceptable it would be to the entire membership of

---

6. This grouping could also be that of the Southern African Development Cooperation (SADC) region. In this case it would include South Africa but would exclude Burundi, Gambia, Kenya, Nigeria, Sierra Leone, and Uganda.

Table 18.2   Country groupings in the Executive Board of the IMF
(listed in order of importance by voting power)

1. United States

2. Germany

3. Japan (same total votes as Germany)

4. France

5. United Kingdom

6. Belgium (Austria, Belarus,* Czech Republic, Hungary, Kazakhstan,* Luxembourg, Slovak Republic, Slovenia, Turkey)

7. Netherlands (Armenia,* Bosnia and Herzegovina,* Bulgaria, Croatia,* Cyprus, Georgia,* Israel, Macedonia,* Moldova,* Romania, Ukraine*)

8. Mexico (Costa Rica, El Salvador, Guatemala, Honduras, Nicaragua, Spain, Venezuela)

9. Italy (Albania,* Greece, Malta, Portugal, San Marino*)

10. Canada (Antigua and Barbuda,* The Bahamas,* Barbados, Belize, Dominica, Grenada, Ireland, Jamaica, St. Kitts and Nevis, St. Lucia, St. Vincent and the Grenadines)

11. Denmark (Estonia, Finland, Iceland, Latvia, Lithuania,* Norway, Sweden)

12. Saudi Arabia*

13. Angola (Botswana, Burundi, Eritrea,* Ethiopia,* Gambia, Kenya, Lesotho, Liberia,* Malawi,* Mozambique, Namibia, Nigeria, Sierra Leone, South Africa, Swaziland, Tanzania, Uganda, Zambia, Zimbabwe)

14. Australia (Kiribati,* Korea, Marshall Islands,* Micronesia,* Mongolia, New Zealand, Palau,* Papua New Guinea, Philippines, Samoa,* Seychelles,* Solomon Islands, Vanuatu*)

15. Egypt (Bahrain, Iraq,* Jordan,* Kuwait, Lebanon,* Libya,* Maldives, Oman,* Qatar, Syrian Arab Republic,* United Arab Emirates, Yemen*)

16. Thailand (Brunei Darussalam, Cambodia,* Fiji, Indonesia, Lao People's Democratic Republic,* Malaysia, Myanmar, Nepal,* Singapore, Tonga,* Vietnam*)

17. Russia*

18. Switzerland (Azerbaijan,* Kyrgyz Republic, Poland, Tajikistan,* Turkmenistan,* Uzbekistan*)

19. Brazil (Colombia, Dominican Republic, Ecuador, Guyana, Haiti, Panama, Suriname, Trinidad and Tobago)

20. India (Bangladesh, Bhutan,* Sri Lanka)

21. Iran* (Algeria,* Ghana, Morocco, Pakistan, Tunisia)

22. China*

23. Chile (Argentina, Bolivia, Paraguay, Peru, Uruguay)

24. Gabon (Benin, Burkina Faso, Cameroon, Cape Verde,* Central African Republic, Chad, Comoros,* Congo, Cote d'Ivoire, Djibouti, Equatorial Guinea,* Guinea, Guinea Bissau, Madagascar, Mali, Mauritania, Mauritius, Niger, Rwanda, Sao Tome and Principe,* Senegal, Togo)

*Not members of the World Trade Organization.

Source: http://www.imf.org/external/np/sec/memdir/eds.htm

Table 18.3 Value of trade, 1996, with country groupings
(billions of dollars)

1. European Union (extra-EU)	2,065
2. United States	1,805
3. Japan	914
4. People's Republic of China and Hong Kong, China	700
5. ASEAN[a] (extraregion)	570
6. Canada	446
7. EFTA[b] (extraregion) and Turkey	334
8. Republic of Korea	331
9. Mexico	207
10. Australia and New Zealand	195
11. CEFTA[c] (extraregion)	190
12. North Africa and the Middle East (Egypt, Bahrain, Kuwait, Morocco, Qatar, Tunisia, UAE)	148
13. South Asia (India, Bangladesh, Sri Lanka, and Pakistan)	143
14. Mercosur[d] (extraregion)	129
15. Andean Community[e] (extraregion)	75
16. Israel	67
17. South Africa	66
18. Africa 1 (see table 18.2, Angola et al.)	60
19. Africa 2 (see table 18.2, Gabon et al.)	40
20. CACM[f] and Caricom[g]	38

a. ASEAN: Singapore, Malaysia, Indonesia, Thailand, Philippines, Brunei Darussalam, and Vietnam.
b. EFTA: Iceland, Liechtenstein, Norway, and Switzerland.
c. CEFTA: the Czech Republic, Hungary, Poland, Slovenia, and the Slovak Republic.
d. Mercosur: Argentina, Brazil, Paraguay, and Uruguay.
e. Andean Community: Bolivia, Colombia, Ecuador, Peru, and Venezuela.
f. CACM: Costa Rica, El Salvador, Guatemala, Honduras, and Nicaragua.
g. Caricom: Antigua and Barbuda, The Bahamas, Barbados, Belize, Dominica, Grenada, Guyana, Haiti, Jamaica, St. Kitts and Nevis, St. Lucia, St. Vincent and the Grenadines, Suriname, Trinidad and Tobago, and the dependent territory of Montserrat.

Source: Compiled from World Bank, *World Development Report 1998/99,* table 15: Balance of Payments Current Account and International Reserves; *WTO Annual Report,* 1997, tables 1.6, 1.7, 1.8, and 1.9; and Inter-American Development Bank, *Periodic Note,* October 1999, annexes A and B.

the WTO. The merit of our proposal lies in the twin criteria chosen: the value of trade and global geographic representation. This is both objective and relevant to decision making in the WTO and causes the least disruption to existing green room players, while bringing in others previously excluded.

Reference

Schott, Jeffrey J. 1994. *The Uruguay Round: An Assessment*. Washington: Institute for International Economics.

Other Publications from the Institute for International Economics

* = out of print

31 **The Economic Opening of Eastern Europe*** John Williamson
May 1991 ISBN 0-88132-186-9

32 **Eastern Europe and the Soviet Union in the World Economy*** Susan M. Collins and Dani Rodrik
May 1991 ISBN 0-88132-157-5

33 **African Economic Reform: The External Dimension*** Carol Lancaster
June 1991 ISBN 0-88132-096-X

34 **Has the Adjustment Process Worked?*** Paul R. Krugman
October 1991 ISBN 0-88132-116-8

35 **From Soviet disUnion to Eastern Economic Community?*** Oleh Havrylyshyn and John Williamson
October 1991 ISBN 0-88132-192-3

36 **Global Warming: The Economic Stakes*** William R. Cline
May 1992 ISBN 0-88132-172-9

37 **Trade and Payments After Soviet Disintegration*** John Williamson
June 1992 ISBN 0-88132-173-7

38 **Trade and Migration: NAFTA and Agriculture** Philip L. Martin
October 1993 ISBN 0-88132-201-6

39 **The Exchange Rate System and the IMF: A Modest Agenda** Morris Goldstein
June 1995 ISBN 0-88132-219-9

40 **What Role for Currency Boards?** John Williamson
September 1995 ISBN 0-88132-222-9

41 **Predicting External Imbalances for the United States and Japan*** William R. Cline
September 1995 ISBN 0-88132-220-2

42 **Standards and APEC: An Action Agenda** John S. Wilson
October 1995 ISBN 0-88132-223-7

43 **Fundamental Tax Reform and Border Tax Adjustments** Gary Clyde Hufbauer
January 1996 ISBN 0-88132-225-3

44 **Global Telecom Talks: A Trillion Dollar Deal** Ben A. Petrazzini
June 1996 ISBN 0-88132-230-X

45 **WTO 2000: Setting the Course for World Trade** Jeffrey J. Schott
September 1996 ISBN 0-88132-234-2

46 **The National Economic Council: A Work in Progress** I. M. Destler
November 1996 ISBN 0-88132-239-3

47 **The Case for an International Banking Standard** Morris Goldstein
April 1997 ISBN 0-88132-244-X

48 **Transatlantic Trade: A Strategic Agenda** Ellen L. Frost
May 1997 ISBN 0-88132-228-8

49 **Cooperating with Europe's Monetary Union** C. Randall Henning
May 1997 ISBN 0-88132-245-8

50 **Renewing Fast-Track Legislation** I.M.Destler
September 1997 ISBN 0-88132-252-0

51 **Competition Policies for the Global Economy** Edward M. Graham and J. David Richardson
November 1997 ISBN 0-88132-249-0

52 **Improving Trade Policy Reviews in the World Trade Organization** Donald Keesing
April 1998 ISBN 0-88132-251-2

53 **Agricultural Trade Policy: Completing the Reform** Timothy Josling
April 1998 ISBN 0-88132-256-3

54 **Real Exchange Rates for the Year 2000** Simon Wren-Lewis and Rebecca Driver
April 1998 ISBN 0-88132-253-9

55 **The Asian Financial Crisis: Causes, Cures, and Systemic Implications** Morris Goldstein
June 1998 ISBN 0-88132-261-X

56 **Global Economic Effects of the Asian Currency Devaluations** Marcus Noland, Li-Gang Liu, Sherman Robinson, and Zhi Wang
July 1998 ISBN 0-88132-260-1

57 **The Exchange Stabilization Fund: Slush Money or War Chest?** C. Randall Henning
May 1999 ISBN 0-88132-271-7

58 **The New Politics of American Trade: Trade, Labor, and the Environment** I. M. Destler and Peter J. Balint
October 1999 ISBN 0-88132-269-5

59 **Congressional Trade Votes: From Nafta Approval to Fast-Track Defeat** Robert E. Baldwin and Christopher S. Magee
February 2000 ISBN 0-88132-267-9

BOOKS

IMF Conditionality* John Williamson, editor
1983 ISBN 0-88132-006-4

Trade Policy in the 1980s* William R. Cline, editor
1983 ISBN 0-88132-031-5

Subsidies in International Trade* Gary Clyde Hufbauer and Joanna Shelton Erb
1984 ISBN 0-88132-004-8

International Debt: Systemic Risk and Policy Response* William R. Cline
1984 ISBN 0-88132-015-3

Trade Protection in the United States: 31 Case Studies* Gary Clyde Hufbauer, Diane E. Berliner, and Kimberly Ann Elliott
1986 ISBN 0-88132-040-4

Global Competition Policy
Edward M. Graham and J. David Richardson
December 1997   ISBN 0-88132-166-4
Unfinished Business: Telecommunications after
the Uruguay Round
Gary Clyde Hufbauer and Erika Wada
December 1997   ISBN 0-88132-257-1
Financial Services Liberalization in the WTO
Wendy Dobson and Pierre Jacquet
June 1998   ISBN 0-88132-254-7
Restoring Japan's Economic Growth
Adam S. Posen
September 1998   ISBN 0-88132-262-8
Measuring the Costs of Protection in China
Zhang Shuguang, Zhang Yansheng, and Wan
Zhongxin
November 1998   ISBN 0-88132-247-4
Foreign Direct Investment and Development: The
New Policy Agenda for Developing Countries
and Economies in Transition
Theodore H. Moran
December 1998   ISBN 0-88132-258-X
Behind the Open Door: Foreign Enterprises in the
Chinese Marketplace   Daniel H. Rosen
January 1999   **ISBN 0-88132-263-6**
Toward A New International Financial
Architecture: A Practical Post-Asia Agenda
Barry Eichengreen
February 1999   ISBN 0-88132-270-9
Is the U.S. Trade Deficit Sustainable?
Catherine L. Mann / *September 1999*
ISBN 0-88132-265-2
Safeguarding Prosperity in a Global Financial
System: The Future International Financial
Architecture, Independent Task Force Report
Sponsored by the Council on Foreign Relations
Morris Goldstein, Project Director
October 1999   ISBN 0-88132-287-3
Avoiding the Apocalypse: The Future of the Two
Koreas   Marcus Noland
June 2000   ISBN 0-88132-278-4
Assessing Financial Vulnerability: An Early
Warning System for Emerging Markets
Morris Goldstein, Graciela Kaminsky, and Carmen
Reinhart
June 2000   ISBN 0-88132-237-7
Global Electronic Commerce: A Policy Primer
Catherine L.. Mann, Sue E. Eckert, and Sarah
Cleeland Knight
July 2000   ISBN 0-88132-274-1
The WTO after Seattle
Jeffrey J. Schott, editor
July 2000   ISBN 0-88132-290-3

SPECIAL REPORTS

1   Promoting World Recovery: A Statement on
Global Economic Strategy*
by Twenty-six Economists from Fourteen
Countries
December 1982   ISBN 0-88132-013-7

2   Prospects for Adjustment in Argentina,
Brazil, and Mexico: Responding to the Debt
Crisis*   John Williamson, editor
June 1983   ISBN 0-88132-016-1

3   Inflation and Indexation: Argentina, Brazil,
and Israel*   John Williamson, editor
March 1985   ISBN 0-88132-037-4

4   Global Economic Imbalances*
C. Fred Bergsten, editor
March 1986   ISBN 0-88132-042-0

5   African Debt and Financing*
Carol Lancaster and John Williamson, editors
May 1986   ISBN 0-88132-044-7

6   Resolving the Global Economic Crisis: After
Wall Street*
Thirty-three Economists from Thirteen
Countries
December 1987   ISBN 0-88132-070-6

7   World Economic Problems
Kimberly Ann Elliott and John Williamson,
editors
April 1988   ISBN 0-88132-055-2
Reforming World Agricultural Trade*
Twenty-nine Professionals from Seventeen
Countries
1988   ISBN 0-88132-088-9

8   Economic Relations Between the United
States and Korea: Conflict or Cooperation?*
Thomas O. Bayard and Soo-Gil Young, editors
January 1989   ISBN 0-88132-068-4

9   Whither APEC? The Progress to Date and
Agenda for the Future
C. Fred Bergsten, editor
October 1997   ISBN 0-88132-248-2

10   Economic Integration of the Korean
Peninsula   Marcus Noland, editor
January 1998   ISBN 0-88132-255-5

11   Restarting Fast Track   Jeffrey J. Schott, editor
April 1998   ISBN 0-88132-259-8

12   Launching New Global Trade Talks:
An Action Agenda   Jeffrey J. Schott, editor
September 1998   ISBN 0-88132-266-0

WORKS IN PROGRESS

The Impact of Increased Trade on Organized Labor in the United States
Robert E. Baldwin

New Regional Arrangements and the World Economy
C. Fred Bergsten

The Globalization Backlash in Europe and the United States
C. Fred Bergsten, Pierre Jacquet, and Karl Kaiser

The U.S.-Japan Economic Relationship
C. Fred Bergsten, Marcus Noland, and Takatoshi Ito

China's Entry to the World Economy
Richard N. Cooper

The ILO in the World Economy
Kimberly Ann Elliott

Reforming Economic Sanctions
Kimberly Ann Elliott, Gary C. Hufbauer, and Jeffrey J. Schott

Free Trade in Labor Agency Services
Kimberly Ann Elliott and J. David Richardson

The *Chaebol* and Structural Problems in Korea
Edward M. Graham

Fighting the Wrong Enemy: Antiglobal Activists and Multinational Enterprises
Edward M. Graham

The Political Economy of the Asian Financial Crisis
Stephan Haggard

Ex-Im Bank in the 21st Century
Gary Clyde Hufbauer and Rita Rodriquez, eds.

NAFTA: A Seven Year Appraisal of the Trade, Environment, and Labor Agreements
Gary Clyde Hufbauer and Jeffrey J. Schott

Prospects for Western Hemisphere Free Trade
Gary Clyde Hufbauer and Jeffrey J. Schott

Price Integration in the World Economy
Gary Clyde Hufbauer, Erika Wada and Tony Warren

Reforming the IMF
Peter Kenen

Imports, Exports, and American Industrial Workers since 1979
Lori G. Kletzer

Reemployment Experiences of Trade-Displaced Americans
Lori G. Kletzer

Transforming Foreign Aid: United States Assistance in the 21st Century
Carol Lancaster

Globalization and Creative Destruction in the US Textile and Apparel Industry
James Levinsohn

Intellectual Property Rights in the Global Economy
Keith Maskus

Measuring the Costs of Protection in Europe
Patrick Messerlin

Dollarization, Currency Blocs, and U.S. Policy
Adams S. Posen

Germany in the World Economy after the EMU
Adam S. Posen

Japan's Financial Crisis and Its Parallels to U.S. Experience
Adam S. Posen and Ryoichi Mikitani, eds.

Sizing Up Globalization: The Globalization Balance Sheet Capstone Volume
J. David Richardson

Why Global Integration Matters Most!
J. David Richardson and Howard Lewis

Worker Perceptions and Pressures in the Global Economy
Matthew J. Slaughter

India in the World Economy
T. N. Srinivasan and Suresh D. Tendulka

Exchange-Rate Regimes for East Asia: Reviving the Intermediate Option
John Williamson

Australia, New Zealand, and Papua New Guinea
D.A. INFORMATION SERVICES
648 Whitehorse Road
Mitcham, Victoria 3132, Australia
tel: 61-3-9210-7777
fax: 61-3-9210-7788
e-mail: service@dadirect.com.au
http://www.dadirect.com.au

Caribbean
SYSTEMATICS STUDIES LIMITED
St. Augustine Shopping Centre
Eastern Main Road, St. Augustine
Trinidad and Tobago, West Indies
tel: 868-645-8466
fax: 868-645-8467
e-mail: tobe@trinidad.net

United Kingdom and Europe (including Russia and Turkey)
The Eurospan Group
3 Henrietta Street, Covent Garden
London WC2E 8LU England
tel: 44-20-7240-0856
fax: 44-20-7379-0609
http://www.eurospan.co.uk

Northern Africa and the Middle East (Egypt, Algeria, Bahrain, Palestine, Jordan, Kuwait, Lebanon, Libya, Morocco, Oman, Qatar, Saudi Arabia, Syria, Tunisia, Yemen, and United Arab Emirates)
Middle East Readers Information Center (MERIC)
2 bahgat Aly Street
El-Masry Towers, Tower #D, Apt. #24, First Floor
Zamalek, Cairo EGYPT
tel: 202-341-3824/340 3818;
fax 202-341-9355
http://www.meric-co.com

Taiwan
Unifacmanu Trading Co., Ltd.
4F, No. 91, Ho-Ping East Rd, Sect. 1
Taipei 10609, Taiwan
tel: 886-2-23419646
fax: 886-2-23943103
e-mail: winjoin@ms12.hinet.net

Argentina
World Publications SA.
Av. Cordoba 1877
1120 Buenos Aires, Argentina
tel/fax: (54 11) 4815 8156
e-mail:
http://wpbooks@infovia.com.ar

People's Republic of China (including Hong Kong) **and Taiwan** (sales representatives):
Tom Cassidy
Cassidy & Associates
70 Battery Place, Ste 220
New York, NY 10280
tel: 212-706-2200   fax: 212-706-2254
e-mail: CHINACAS@Prodigy.net

India, Bangladesh, Nepal, and Sri Lanka
Viva Books Pvt.
Mr. Vinod Vasishtha
4325/3, Ansari Rd.
Daryaganj, New Delhi-110002
INDIA
tel: 91-11-327-9280
fax: 91-11-326-7224 ,
e-mail: vinod.viva@gndel.globalnet.
ems.vsnl.net.in

South Africa
Pat Bennink
Dryad Books
PO Box 11684
Vorna Valley 1686
South Africa
tel: +27 14 576 1332
fax: +27 82 899 9156
e-mail: dryad@hixnet.co.za

Thailand
Asia Books 5 Sukhumvit Rd. Soi 61
Bangkok 10110 Thailand
(phone 662-714-0740-2 Ext: 221, 222, 223
fax: (662) 391-2277)
e-mail: purchase@asiabooks.co.th
http://www.asiabooksonline.com

Canada
RENOUF BOOKSTORE
5369 Canotek Road, Unit 1,
Ottawa, Ontario K1J 9J3, Canada
tel: 613-745-2665
fax: 613-745-7660
http://www.renoufbooks.com

Colombia, Ecuador, and Peru
Infoenlace Ltda
Attn: Octavio Rojas
Calle 72 No. 13-23 Piso 3
Edificio Nueva Granada, Bogota, D.C.
Colombia
tel: (571) 255 8783 or 255 7969
fax: (571) 248 0808 or 217 6435

Japan and the Republic of Korea
United Publishers Services, Ltd.
Kenkyu-Sha Bldg.
9, Kanda Surugadai 2-Chome
Chiyoda-Ku, Tokyo 101
JAPAN
tel: 81-3-3291-4541;
fax: 81-3-3292-8610
e-mail: saito@ups.co.jp
**For trade accounts only.
Individuals will find IIE books in leading Tokyo bookstores.**

South America
Julio E. Emod
Publishers Marketing & Research Associates, c/o HARBRA
Rua Joaquim Tavora, 629
04015-001 Sao Paulo, Brasil
tel: (55) 11-571-1122;
fax: (55) 11-575-6876
e-mail: emod@harbra.com.br

**Visit our Web site at:
http://www.iie.com
E-mail orders to:
orders@iie.com**